THE INVESTMENT DECISIONS OF FIRMS

THE CAMBRIDGE ECONOMIC HANDBOOKS

General Editors

THE INVESTMENT
DECISIONS
OF FIRMS

By

S. J. NICKELL

READER IN ECONOMICS IN THE UNIVERSITY OF LONDON
AT THE LONDON SCHOOL OF ECONOMICS

JAMES NISBET & CO. LTD
Digswell Place, Welwyn

CAMBRIDGE UNIVERSITY PRESS

First published 1978
by James Nisbet and Company Limited
Digswell Place, Welwyn, Herts.
and the Cambridge University Press

SBN 0 7202 0311 2 Board
SBN 0 7202 0310 4 Paperback

Printed in Great Britain at the University Press, Oxford

PREFACE

This volume is the first to be published in the Cambridge Economic Handbook series for some considerable time. It differs markedly from its distinguished predecessors in that it has been written for the reader who is not only economically literate but has a sound grasp of elementary calculus. This is not to say that students of economics whose grasp of elementary calculus is less than sound would be incapable of reading it. They could, by omitting the appendices and by judiciously skipping pages from time to time, go through the book and extract most of the meat. A number of theoretical niceties would, however, pass them by. On the other hand, no more than a sound grasp of elementary calculus is required to understand everything in the book. The somewhat magical formulae of the calculus of variations or the maximum principle are never referred to, all relevant results being simply derived from the standard principle that the costs and benefits of any change must be equal at the margin, otherwise it is always possible to do better.

As the title suggests, the book is concerned with explaining the level of expenditure on fixed capital goods by individual firms. It does not, therefore, deal either with the question of how firms *should* manage their expenditures on fixed capital or with the determination of the *aggregate* level of fixed capital investment. In the first few chapters, the discussion focuses on why and how the future affects the present when firms make investment decisions. This leads naturally to a consideration of the role of uncertainty in a temporal model where the discussion is firmly grounded in the real as opposed to the financial decisions of the firm. Any consideration of the relationship between these two types of decision is thus postponed until later in the book and, since this is a slightly unnatural ordering from a theoretical viewpoint, the underlying rationale should perhaps be explained. First the reason why it is odd is that the objective of the firm in an uncertain world is inextricably linked with its financial environment. For example, it may well depend on whether or not it operates in an economy with a well developed stock market. So when the impact of uncertainty is first discussed without reference to the financial environment, somewhat *ad hoc*, although plausible, objectives for the firm are, of necessity, assumed. In spite of this, however, I feel that the impact of uncertainty is initially easier to grasp in the context of straightforward real investment decisions and, for this reason, the unnatural ordering is retained. What is more, the problem of the correct objectives for the firm in a world of uncertainty has only been solved under very restrictive assumptions and so the use of plausible *ad hoc* criteria is hardly a serious drawback.

Following the basic theory of the early part of the book, in the middle section we consider a number of particular theoretical issues in the general area of finance, taxation and government policy. Finally the last few chapters use the extensive theory set out earlier to analyse and review the empirical work in this field. As before, the emphasis is on the *firm's* investment decisions and empirical work is only considered in this context rather than the context of the determination and prediction of aggregate investment.

The majority of the first draft of the book was written during a very enjoyable stay in Paris in 1974–75 visiting the École Nationale de la Statistique et de l'Administration Économique. I am most grateful to my hosts, in particular Jean-Claude Milleron, for providing the perfect environment for writing. Since that time the book has been extensively revised in the light of a large number of comments on the first draft and innumerable discussions on the subject matter. The book in its final state owes a lot to Kate Davies, Kate Esdaile, John Flemming, Lucien Foldes, Charles Goodhart, Frank Hahn, Oliver Hart, Dale Jorgenson, Mervyn King, Guy Laroque, Marcus Miller and Sue Pegden. In many cases I took their advice and incorporated their ideas into the text. In some cases I did not and the reader must judge whether I was wise in these matters or not.

Stephen Nickell
London School of Economics
October 1977

CONTENTS

CHAPTER 1

INTRODUCTION

The act of investment involves the acquisition of a good which is destined not to be consumed or entirely used up in the current period. It is thereby a means by which individuals or groups can attempt to influence their future wellbeing by the sacrifice of current consumption. At the individual level such decisions are usually taken in order to improve future consumption prospects and also because the act of investment involves an increase in wealth which may be desirable in itself, wealth being one of the well-springs of personal power. Investment by individuals may take the form of the direct purchase of capital assets which are either intangible, such as education, or tangible, such as houses. Alternatively, individuals may purchase financial assets which are essentially claims to some pattern of future payments, such assets typically being sold by other individuals, firms or governments. In the case where individuals or firms sell financial assets it is clear that in order to be in a position to make the requisite future payments, they themselves must either purchase further financial assets or invest in real capital. In the case of firms this latter can take myriad forms. They may invest in certain types of training for their employees, in 'goodwill' via advertising expenditure, in 'knowledge' via research and development activities, in stocks of finished goods or raw materials or work in progress and finally in fixed capital stock such as plant or machinery, office blocks or vehicles.

It is the decisions by firms to invest in this last category of goods with which this book is chiefly concerned. The importance of these decisions cannot be doubted. Individually they are crucial to the firms which make them and in aggregate they are crucial to the short- and long-term economic future of the country in which the firm operates.[1] As far as the long-term economic development of a country is concerned investment in fixed capital is clearly vital. Denison (1967) has estimated that in the post-war period the increase in the stock of non-residential structures and equipment has

1

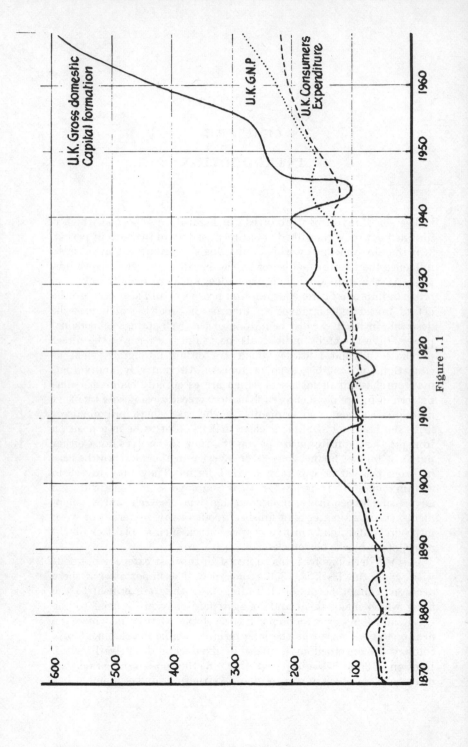

Figure 1.1

contributed about 14% to the economic growth of North-west Europe and the United States.[2] Furthermore, fixed capital investment is one of the driving forces behind short-run economic fluctuations in capitalist economies, varying far more than consumption or income, as is illustrated in Figure 1.1.

It is most important to understand these fluctuations in fixed capital investment and, as far as the private sector is concerned, they are clearly based on the vagaries of the investment decision process at the level of the firm. The decision by the firm to undertake an investment project is a matter of serious import, in part because, once taken, it is often difficult to undo. Since the firm will be encumbered with the consequences of its decision for anything up to fifty years, it must attempt to discern the pattern of those future events which are relevant to the success or failure of the project. It is this aspect of the decision to acquire fixed capital—the fact that it is so crucially influenced by expectations about events a long way in the future[3]—which distinguishes it from most other purchasing decisions.

As a consequence of this, the role of expectations and uncertainty looms large in this book. Indeed the whole of the strictly theoretical part of our discussion, which occupies the next eight chapters, is dominated by the problem of how to gain some insight into the way in which judgements about the future affect current decisions. We shall, of course, consider other aspects of the investment decision but we shall find ourselves returning again and again to one or other facet of this basic problem. Then in the final two chapters we shall be discussing ways in which it is possible to discriminate between some of the competing theories of investment decisions and what practical progress along these lines has been achieved as a consequence of the enormous volume of empirical research which has already been undertaken in this area. We begin, however, with the theories and it is the simplest of these which is the subject of the next chapter.

Footnotes

[1] It is no accident that in reality the individuals who are typically concerned with such decisions more or less make up the ruling class, whatever the socio-economic structure of the society concerned.

[2] See Denison (1967), Tables 21.1–21.18.

[3] Indeed it is often hypothesized that it is the volatility of these expectations which is the main cause of the high degree of variability in fixed capital investment.

CHAPTER 2

A SIMPLE MODEL OF INVESTMENT DECISIONS

1. Perfect Capital Markets and Present Values

In order to initiate the discussion of the forces underlying the investment decisions of firms, it is useful to construct a very simple, abstract model of both the firm and the environment in which it is placed. The first important simplifying assumption concerning the environment is the following:

Assumption 1. There exists a perfect capital market.

This assumption implies that all economic agents, including firms, are in a position to borrow or lend, at each and every point in time, as much as they wish at the going rate of interest; that is, all the agents behave as price takers in the market for funds.

The most important implication of this assumption is that it enables a money flow to be compared both with other money flows and with stocks of money at different points in time. Consider a flow of money in the form of a stream of money income. This income stream may be designated in formal notation by $\{x(t)\}_{T_0}^{T_1}$ where $x(t)$ is measured in money per unit time, $x(t)\,dt$ is the quantity of income forthcoming between time t and time $t+dt$, and T_0 and T_1 are the two points in time at which the income stream commences and ceases. So if the stream commences at time zero and never ceases it is designated by $\{x(t)\}_0^\infty$. The reason why assumption 1 enables the ready comparison of different income streams is that it provides an answer to the question; what is the value at time zero of the income stream $\{x(t)\}_0^\infty$? Consider first that portion of the income stream that arrives between time t and $t+dt$, namely $x(t)\,dt$. Its value at time zero, v say, will be that sum of money which, if invested at time zero at the going rate of interest, will grow to the sum $x(t)\,dt$ after t units of time. *If the rate of interest is constant at r* a sum of money v will, if invested, grow to a sum $v \exp{(rt)}$.[1] So the sum of money v must satisfy

$$v \exp{(rt)} - x(t)\,dt,$$

5

and hence

$$v = \exp\left(-\imath t\right) x(t) \, dt.$$

The total value of the income stream at time zero will be the sum of the v's corresponding to all portions of the income stream. This sum is referred to as the *present value* of the income stream, which is denoted by V, and is given by the formula

2.1
$$V = \int_0^\infty \exp\left(-rt\right) x(t) \, dt.$$

So the present value of an income stream is that sum of money which can be made to yield that particular income stream by using a suitable investment plan. The owner of a sum of money is therefore able, by means of differing investment plans, to turn it into any of the income streams which have a present value equal to that sum. Alternatively the owner of the right to an income stream can, at time zero, borrow an amount equal to its present value, safe in the knowledge that his income stream will be just enough to cover the loan repayments plus interest.

Now suppose we have two income streams which have the same present value. The owner of the right to the first of these can borrow its present value at time zero, using the stream that he owns to cover the gross repayments. Furthermore he can then use the money which he has borrowed to yield the second stream, since this has the same present value as the first. Thus the existence of a perfect capital market enables any individual, by using appropriate borrowing and lending policies, to convert one income stream into *any* other income stream with the same present value.

Two further points should be noted at this stage. First the formula 2.1 refers only to those situations where r is fixed; if r varies over time then the formula must be adjusted to read

2.2
$$V = \int_0^\infty \exp\left(-R(t)\right) x(t) \, dt$$

where $R(t) = \int_0^t r(s) \, ds$.

Second the simplicity of the perfect capital market world breaks down completely if individuals are uncertain about, or have different expectations concerning, the future values of the interest rate. For the moment this problem will be somewhat crudely sidestepped by making the following assumption.

Assumption 2. The world is one of perfect certainty concerning the future (or equivalently all individuals hold the same certain expectations about the future).

2. The Firm's Objective Function

The two assumptions made in the previous section enable us to derive the objective of firms from the utility maximizing behaviour of individuals. A firm is actively engaged in the production of goods and services using other goods and services as inputs. Since it buys and sells the goods and services in the market, it produces a net income stream which is the difference between its revenue and its costs at each point in time. The owners of the firm are those individuals who have claims over this income stream, each owner having the right to some fixed proportion of the stream. Now suppose for simplicity that there is one composite consumption good and that its price may be taken as unity implying that all other goods are valued in terms of it. The income stream produced by the firm is then measured in consumption units and the owners of the firm can convert their portions of this income stream into *any* consumption stream of the same present value, although the particular consumption streams chosen will, of course, depend on individual tastes. All the owners are, however, agreed on one thing, they want the income stream produced by the firm to have the largest possible present value. Anything less would mean that the resulting consumption streams they choose would have lower present values than others open to them. Among these last would be ones that yield a uniformly higher consumption stream, i.e. more consumption in every period. Assuming the owners are not satiated, these would certainly yield a higher utility so the lower present value streams could never be chosen.[2]

We may therefore conclude that in a world of certainty and with a perfect capital market, maximization of the present value of the income stream produced by a firm is the objective consistent with individuals maximizing the utility of consumption. Assumptions 1 and 2 thus allow us to ignore the preferences of the firm's owners when considering the firm's decisions.

3. A Model of the Firm

The firm invests in fixed capital stock in order to provide itself with capital services. The firm's investment decision is thus clearly related to its demand for capital services and it is this demand which we now analyse in the context of a simple model of the firm. All the assumptions connected with this model are first stated and then their relevance and importance are discussed.

Assumption 3. The firm employs only two factors of production, capital and labour, which it uses to produce but a single output. Efficient production techniques can be summarized in the form of a twice differentiable production function and there are strictly diminishing returns to scale everywhere.

Assumption 4. Capital has the same productive characteristics whatever its age or birthdate; however, as it ages, it evaporates at an exponential rate.

Assumption 5. The firm acts as a price taker in all markets. In particular capital can be bought and sold in any quantity and becomes productive immediately upon purchase.

Assumption 6. There are no costs involved either in the sale and purchase of capital goods or in the productive implementation of new capital.

Assumption 7. There are no taxes of any description.

Assumption 3 describes the firm's technology. The simplicity of this technology, implied by the existence of only two factors and one output, is assumed purely for expositional convenience. Assumption 4 is of crucial importance; it enables capital of different ages to be aggregated, since capital is the same stuff whatever its age. The exponential decay assumption gives rise to further simplification since it implies that the amount of depreciation in any period depends solely on the amount of capital that is depreciating and not upon its age structure. This also relates to assumption 5, for here it is assumed that the firm can buy or *sell* capital at the going rate. Given that capital of any age is a homogeneous substance this is not an unreasonable assumption; new capital goods are indistinguishable from old ones and there is simply one market for capital goods with one price.

These latter two assumptions when combined with assumption 6 portray a world in which capital goods are like evaporating jelly which can be costlessly and instantaneously purchased and put to work and, furthermore, what remains of it after evaporation can be equally costlessly sold at some later date. Some considerable portion of this book is devoted to an analysis of the results of relaxing these somewhat unappealing assumptions which form a good starting point, however, since they reduce the investment decision to a simple static problem in the theory of the firm. The reasons for this are straightforward. If the firm can always buy or sell capital stock freely and instantaneously at the going price then it need never worry about the future. It can simply adjust its capital stock each day to the needs of the moment and let tomorrow look after itself. Thus a restaurateur from this particular world who had more customers on weekends as opposed to weekdays would be observed to buy a small restaurant for weekdays but would sell it on Friday nights and purchase a large restaurant for the weekend, reselling it on Monday mornings.

To provide a formal analysis of this model and in particular to shed more light on the result which has just been discussed, we must first introduce some notation. So we let

$K(t)$ be the capital stock employed by the firm at time t.
$L(t)$ be the labour input employed by the firm at time t.
$I(t)$ be the investment in new capital stock by the firm at time t.
$p(t)$ be the price of output at time t.
$q(t)$ be the price of capital goods at time t.
$w(t)$ be the wage rate at time t.
$r(t)$ be the rate of interest at time t.
δ be the exponential rate of decay of capital stock.
$F\{K(t), L(t)\}$ be the maximum output which can be produced by the firm at time t, given $K(t)$, $L(t)$ units of capital stock and labour services respectively.[3]

The net income produced for the owners of the firm at time t is given by

2.3 $\qquad x(t) = p(t)F\{K(t), L(t)\} - w(t)L(t) - q(t)I(t),$

which is the difference between the cash inflow and the cash outflow at this time.

From equation 2.2 the present value of the firm at time zero is

2.4 $\quad V = \int\limits_{0}^{\infty} \exp\left(-R(t)\right) \left[p(t)F\{K(t), L(t)\} - w(t)L(t) - q(t)I(t)\right] \mathrm{d}t$

and, as has been shown in the previous section, the firm must choose $K(t)$, $L(t)$, $I(t)$ at each point in time to maximize this present value. There is a connection between the capital stock $K(t)$ and the rate of investment $I(t)$ which may be summarized as

2.5 $\dot{K}(t) = I(t) - \delta K(t).$

This simply states that the rate of change of the capital stock, $\dot{K}(t)$,[4] is equal to the purchases of new capital, $I(t)$, less the amount of capital depreciation, $\delta K(t)$.

Furthermore the firm is assumed to be initially in possession of an amount of capital stock K_0 so we have

2.6 $K(0) = K_0.$

Formally the firm will choose a production plan which maximizes V subject to the constraints given by equations 2.5 and 2.6. This maximizing production plan is in the form of sequences of capital input and labour input which must satisfy the necessary conditions

2.7 $p(t) \dfrac{\partial F}{\partial L} \{K(t), L(t)\} = w(t)$ for all $t \geqslant 0,$

2.8 $p(t) \dfrac{\partial F}{\partial K} \{K(t), L(t)\} = q(t)\{r(t) + \delta - \dot{q}(t)/q(t)\}$ for all $t > 0.$[5]

Equation 2.7 has an obvious interpretation, namely that at any point in time labour is hired up to the point where the marginal revenue product of labour is equal to the wage. Similarly, equation 2.8 implies that capital services are employed at any point in time up to the point where the marginal revenue product of capital is equal to the cost of capital. The term $q(t)\{r(t) + \delta - \dot{q}(t)/q(t)\}$ is the cost of capital in the sense that it is the cost of employing the services of one unit of capital stock for one time period. In other words it is the flow price of capital. The term $q(t) r(t)$ is the interest charge on $q(t)$ for one period, $q(t)\delta$ is the depreciation charge incurred because a proportion δ of the unit of capital has evaporated in the single time period and lastly $q(t) . \dot{q}(t)/q(t) = \dot{q}(t)$ is the rise in the price of the unit of capital stock during the course of the period. This term appears with a negative sign since a rise in the price of capital stock represents a capital gain for its owner and thus offsets the other elements of capital cost.

If this capital cost term is simply written as $c(t)$, then solving 2.7 and 2.8 simultaneously yields the firm's demands for factor services at every point in time, namely

2.9 $$K^*(t) = K\{c(t),\ w(t),\ p(t)\},\ t > 0$$

2.10 $$L^*(t) = L\{c(t),\ w(t),\ p(t)\},\ t > 0.$$

The most striking point is that the demand for factor services depends only upon current parameters. Thus, in order to maximize present value, the firm can determine its factor inputs at every point in time, as and when that time arrives, basing its calculation solely on the current observable prices and rates of change $p(t)$, $w(t)$, $r(t)$, $q(t)$, $\dot{q}(t)$. The problem which started out as apparently dynamic is revealed to be essentially static.[6] Moreover the necessary conditions 2.7 and 2.8 on which the demand functions 2.9 and 2.10 are based are readily seen to be the necessary conditions for the problem,

2.11   maximize $\Pi(t) = p(t)F\{K(t),\ L(t)\} - w(t)\ L(t) - c(t)K(t)$,

where $\Pi(t)$ may be termed the instantaneous profit, it being the difference between the revenue flow at time t and the cost of factor services at time t. Thus present value maximization is simply equivalent to maximizing the instantaneous profit at each point in time. The static nature of this problem arises because, as we have mentioned already, past decisions of the firm do not constrain present decisions. Exponential decay and the homogeneity of capital over time ensure that the age structure of capital stock is of no significance and the ability to adjust capital stock costlessly and instantaneously ensures that the correct amount of capital can be employed at each instant of time, independently of the capital purchased and employed during the previous instant. There is no question of expectations about the future influencing the present since the capital stock can be freely adjusted when the future arrives. This massively unrealistic result which flows from assumptions 4, 5 and 6 is probably the one, above all others, which makes these assumptions quite unacceptable as the basis of a model of firms' actual investment behaviour. However, since there has been a great deal of discussion in the literature of the investment behaviour (or lack of it) implied by this model, it is worth pursuing this point.

The rate of investment of the present value maximizing firm described in assumptions 1 to 7 may be derived from its demand for capital services via equation 2.5. By simply rearranging we have

2.12 $$I^*(t) = \dot{K}^*(t) + \delta K^*(t)$$

where $K^*(t)$ is given in equation 2.9. The basic problem, as has been pointed out most forcefully by Haavelmo and others,[7] is that a discontinuity in $c(t)$ at t_0, say, leads to a discontinuity in K^* at t_0 and to investment being undefined at this point. The following often quoted passage from Haavelmo (1960) provides a good basis for discussion.

> I do not . . . reject the possibility that an empirical relation may be found between the rate of interest and the rate of investment. What we should reject is the naive reasoning that there is a 'demand schedule' for investment which could be derived from a classical scheme of producers' behaviour in maximizing profit. The demand for investment cannot simply be derived from the demand for capital. Demand for a finite addition to the stock of capital can lead to any rate of investment, from almost zero to infinity, depending on the additional hypothesis we introduce regarding the speed of reaction of the capital-users. I think that the sooner this naive and unfounded theory of the demand-for-investment schedule is abandoned, the sooner we shall have a chance of making some real progress in constructing more powerful theories to deal with the capricious short-run variations in the rate of private investment.

Of course, in the context of this model, demand for any finite addition to the stock of capital cannot imply any rate of investment other than infinite because there are no costs of adjustment (assumptions 5 and 6). So what does this model tell us about the reactions of the firm's investment demand to parametric changes? First, simple comparative statics shows that $\partial K^*(t)/\partial c(t) < 0$. Consider then the reaction of the firm to a permanent fall in the rate of interest from r_1 to r_2 at time t_0, with all other parameters remaining constant for all time. The cost of capital would be some constant $c_1 = q(r_1 + \delta)$ for $t < t_0$ and some smaller constant $c_2 = q(r_2 + \delta)$ for $t > t_0$ (note $r_2 < r_1$). The firm would be investing at a constant rate $\delta K^*(c_1, \ldots)$, to cover depreciation, for all $t < t_0$. Then at time t_0 it would purchase an amount of capital stock $K^*(c_2, \ldots) - K^*(c_1, \ldots)$ and subsequently it would be investing at a higher constant rate $\delta K^*(c_2, \ldots)$. The rate of investment at time t_0 is not defined; however, it is clear that the fall in the rate of interest implies an increase in gross capital purchases on any time interval containing t_0. These are the consequences of a drop in the interest rate predicted by this model. The model does not provide an investment demand function of the form $I(r, \ldots)$ with a well-defined partial derivative. *In this sense, then,* the contention of Haavelmo that the demand for investment cannot be simply derived from the demand for capital is correct.

On the other hand, it may be argued, with some justification, that it is not admissible to ask questions of the type; what is the effect on the rate investment of a *ceteris paribus* fall in interest rates? If new capital goods are produced and supplied in a continuous flow then there could never be an instantaneous parametric change which would lead to an instantaneous aggregate demand for a block of capital since it could never be supplied. In other words, since new capital is supplied continuously, equilibrium would ensure that prices and interest rates could only change in such a manner that it was demanded continuously. On the basis of an assumption similar to that last mentioned, whereby price and interest rate changes are restricted to an 'admissible' set, Jorgenson (1967), using the model defined in this chapter, constructed a well-defined monotonic relationship between the rate of investment and the rate of interest.[8]

Unfortunately, casual empiricism would suggest that 'inadmissible' parametric changes in the above sense, such as *ceteris paribus* falls in the rate of interest, do occur. *Indeed,* some of the work that has been done on adjustment costs, involving the relaxation of assumption 6, has been motivated by a desire to construct a model where discontinuous changes in capital stock do not occur in response to such 'inadmissible' parameter changes. However, care must be taken to avoid going too far in devising theories of firms' investment which lead to continuous capital purchases since further casual empiricism would suggest that individual firms are observed to purchase capital stock in large blocks for reasons which are not entirely conditioned by the *physical* indivisibility of particular capital goods. The point is, although capital goods may be produced in a continuous flow, they may well not be supplied by one firm to another in a continuous flow; in fact there may be very good reasons for supplying them in discontinuous bundles, for example, because of returns to scale in transportation. Now, as far as the investment decisions of firms are concerned, the interest centres on when capital goods are purchased and, as we have seen, it may be desirable for them to be both purchased in blocks and delivered in blocks.[9] On the other hand, a macro-economic theorist is interested in the demand for investment goods in so far as it influences their production for this is what

14   THE INVESTMENT DECISIONS OF FIRMS

determines income and employment. Since production is a continuous process, it is clear that a theory of the production of investment
goods should have the property that such production is a continuous
function of the factors influencing the demand for investment goods.
Such a theory is not, however, necessarily in conflict with a theory of
the firm which implies that the firm would like to purchase capital
goods in blocks at discrete points in time.

Of course a model such as the one described in this chapter, which
predicts that firms purchase blocks of capital goods at *the same
instant* as a parameter change, is clearly open to objection. But it is
the instantaneous reaction which is objectionable, not the block
purchasing *per se*. More will be said on this point in subsequent
chapters, specifically when adjustment costs, time lags and neo-
Keynesian theories of investment are discussed.

More serious problems arise in the context of this model if we
consider the relationship between the demand for capital stock and
the price of capital goods. Suppose that all the parameters p, r, w,
are constant and that the price of capital goods, $q(t)$, follows the
time path,

2.13 $q(t) = q_1, t \leqslant t_0; \quad \dot{q}(t) > 0, t_0 \leqslant t \leqslant t_1; \quad q(t) = q_2, t \geqslant t_1.$

This path is illustrated in Figure 2.1 with the corresponding path for
the cost of capital directly beneath it.

It will be noted that the path for the cost of capital has a rather
peculiar pattern. The cost of capital is $c(t) = q(t)\{r + \delta - \dot{q}(t)/q(t)\}$. At
time t_0, $\dot{q}(t)$ jumps from zero to some finite positive number and
hence at this time $c(t)$ jumps downwards. After t_0, $q(t)$ and hence $c(t)$
increase until t_1 when $\dot{q}(t)$ jumps down to zero and $c(t)$ consequently
jumps up to its new higher level. The corresponding optimal path of
the capital stock is given by the mirror image of the path of the
capital cost since capital stock is inversely related to it. This path is
shown in Figure 2.2 and is intuitively very plausible. Capital stock
remains constant until t_0, at which point the price of capital goods
starts rising. The firm then purchases a large block of capital because
it scents the prospect of capital gains to be made. As the price of
capital gradually rises the firm slowly reduces its capital stock from
the new high level as a reaction to the increasing factor price. Then,
at t_1, the price of capital goods stops rising, the firm sells off its initial
large block purchase, collects the capital gain and settles down with
its new lower level of capital holdings. It is again, of course, assumptions 4, 5, 6, that make it profitable for the firm to manipulate its

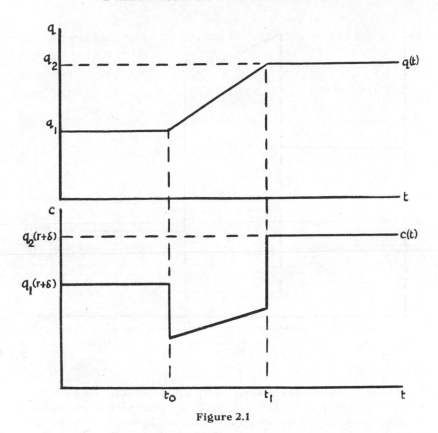

Figure 2.1

stock of fixed capital as if it were operating in paper assets. In some sense the model yields even more unrealistic results as the period t_0 to t_1 gets very small and the increase in capital goods prices becomes even steeper. The trough in $c(t)$ shown in Figure 2.1 becomes deeper and shorter and the purchases of capital goods for prospective capital gains become very much larger. As the rise in $q(t)$ tends towards an instantaneous jump, the purchases of capital goods at t_0 tend towards infinity.[10] Clearly the consequences of such instantaneous rises in q cannot be studied at all in the context of this model.

To summarize, the model based on assumptions 1 to 7 produces not implausible results within its limitations. These limitations show up very clearly and lead naturally to a relaxation of the assumption of

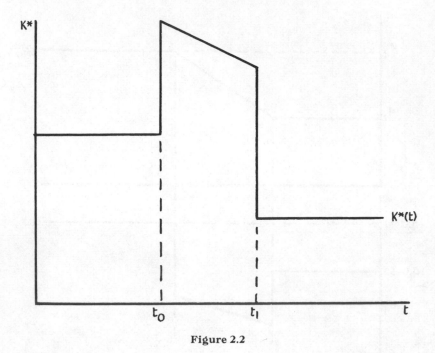

Figure 2.2

instantaneous and costless adjustment, for it is clearly this assumption which produces those results which are most open to objection. Before going on to consider these matters, however, it is worth spending a little time considering the consequences of replacing the assumption of price-taking behaviour (assumption 5) with the following:

Assumption 8. The firm faces a known downward sloping demand curve for its product, while taking factor prices as given.

We shall assume that the demand curve facing the firm at time t has the following separable form:

2.14 $z\{p(t)\}\beta(t)$ where $z_p < 0$.

The demand curve itself thus has a constant shape defined by $z\{p(t)\}$ and is shifted up and down by the time function $\beta(t)$. This separable form has the advantage that the elasticity of demand, ϵ, and the marginal revenue, M, are both functions of $p(t)$ *only*, time not entering as a separate argument.[11]

Assumption 8 also implies that diminishing returns to scale is no longer required to ensure a finite production plan. In fact this assumption will be replaced by

Assumption 3a. As assumption 3, except that there are constant returns to scale everywhere.

The firm will maximize present value as before but, in addition, we shall now assume that output is maintained in equality with demand. In other words we are supposing that the firm is both able and willing to adjust the price of output at each point in time to ensure that the current output flow is precisely what will be demanded. Such behaviour is patently unrealistic in the sense that it would imply more or less continuous price adjustments by the firm and no inventory holdings. Given that output price adjustments are costly both in a purely physical sense and because they add to uncertainty for customers, we would clearly expect such adjustments to be rather infrequent. However, any formal analysis of such a world would have to incorporate a number of additional elements, including a theory of inventory holdings, which would detract from the simplicity of the model which we consider without necessarily throwing a great deal of light on fixed capital investment decisions, which are essentially a longer run problem. We shall therefore generally persist in supposing that the firm's output price is perfectly flexible in the belief that it does not produce a gravely distorted picture of the world as far as fixed capital investment is concerned.[12]

As a result we have

$$2.15 \qquad z\{p(t)\}\beta(t) = F\{K(t),\ L(t)\}.$$

Solving for the output price we obtain

$$2.16 \qquad p(t) = p[F\{K(t),\ L(t)\}/\beta(t)]$$

where

$$\frac{\partial p}{\partial K} = \frac{F_K}{z_p\beta(t)} \qquad \text{and} \qquad \frac{\partial p}{\partial L} = \frac{F_L}{z_p\beta(t)}.$$

So the firm will maximize its present value,

$$\int_0^\infty \exp\{-R(t)\}(p[F\{K(t), L(t)\}/\beta(t)]F\{K(t), L(t)\} - w(t)L(t) - q(t)I(t))$$

subject to the constraints 2.5 and 2.6.

In this case the necessary conditions for a maximum are similar to those for the perfectly competitive firm (2.7 and 2.8), the marginal revenue function replacing the output price as one would expect. So, if we write this marginal revenue function as $M(p)$, we have

$$2.17 \qquad M\{p(t)\}\frac{\partial F\{K(t), L(t)\}}{\partial L(t)} = w(t),$$

$$2.18 \qquad M\{p(t)\}\frac{\partial F\{K(t), L(t)\}}{\partial K(t)} = c(t),$$

in addition to equation 2.15. As before, each factor of production is employed up to the point where its marginal revenue product just covers its cost.

The relationship between optimal capital stock, investment and cost parameters is much the same as in the perfectly competitive case and there is no point in reproducing it here. On the other hand, the relationship between investment and the exogenous demand parameter, $\beta(t)$, is a matter of considerable interest and, of course, only arises in the imperfectly competitive context. By making use of the necessary conditions and equation 2.5 it is possible to derive the following expression for the optimal investment path, where such a path exists, namely

$$2.19 \qquad \frac{I}{K} = \dot{\beta}/\beta + \delta + (1 - \epsilon_k)(\sigma + \epsilon_M)\dot{w}/w - \{(1 - \epsilon_k)\sigma - \epsilon_M\epsilon_k\}\dot{c}/c$$

where $\sigma(k)$ is the elasticity of substitution (defined to be positive), k is the capital labour ratio, ϵ_k is the elasticity of output/unit labour with respect to capital/unit labour and ϵ_M is the elasticity of the output with respect to marginal revenue.[13] Note that $0 < \epsilon_k < 1$, $\epsilon_M = (\partial z/\partial M) M/z < 0$ and that if the elasticity of demand $\epsilon\{p(t)\}$ is a constant then ϵ_M is equal to that elasticity.

The intuition behind this equation is clear. The left-hand side is the gross investment rate as a proportion of capital stock. The first two terms on the right show that this increases with the rate of growth of demand and with the rate of depreciation and the second two terms give the effect of changing factor prices. The effect of increasing capital costs is unambiguously negative, whereas the effect of increasing wage rates depends on the sign of $\sigma + \epsilon_M$. If the substitution effect dominates the output effect, $\sigma + \epsilon_M > 0$ and increasing wages yield a positive effect on gross investment. The converse is true if the output effect dominates the substitution effect.

If factor costs are constant then both the price of output and the capital labour ratio are constant (see Appendix, proposition 5, A10, A11). Equation 2.19 then reduces to a simple accelerator process where the rate of growth of capital stock is equal to the exogenous rate of growth of demand. Note that if the capital labour ratio is constant, then so is the capital output ratio and hence if Y is the output we have $K/Y = \alpha$, a constant. Then, since $\dot{\beta}/\beta - \dot{Y}/Y$, equation 2.19, reduces to

2.20 $$I = \dot{Y}/Y . \alpha Y + \delta K$$

or

$$I = \alpha \dot{Y} + \delta K,$$

where $\dot{Y}/Y$ is a demand determined exogenous variable. This is one method of rationalizing the popular accelerator model of investment, much used in empirical work.

Appendix

Proposition 1 (p. 5). If the rate of interest is constant at a rate r per unit of time, then one unit of money invested at time zero will grow to a sum exp (rt) units after time t, so long as the interest is compounded continuously.

Proof. If interest is only added at the discrete points in time $1/n$, $2/n, \ldots 1, (n+1)/n, \ldots, t-1/n, t$ where both n and nt are integers, then the interest which is added at each of these discrete points is r/n. Then one unit of cash invested at time zero will grow into a sum $(1 + r/n)^{nt}$ after t time units. So if interest is added continuously, one unit will grow into

$$\lim_{n \to \infty} \{(1 + r/n)^n\}^t = \{\lim_{n \to \infty} (1 + r/n)^n\}^t = \exp (rt).$$

Proposition 2 (p. 7). If there exists a perfect capital market and perfect certainty, and the owners of firms maximize the utility of their consumption streams, then firms will maximize present value.

Proof. Suppose Γ is the set of present values which result from all possible activities of the firm. Suppose that the firm has N owners, where the nth owner has a claim to a proportion α_n of the income stream produced by the firm. If $\{c(t)\}_0^\infty$ is a consumption stream and U^n is the nth owner's utility function representing his preferences defined over consumption streams, then the nth owner will maximize

$$U^n[\{c(t)\}_0^\infty]$$

subject to

$$\int_0^\infty \exp\{-R(t)\}\, c(t)\, \mathrm{d}t = V\alpha_n,\ V \in \Gamma$$

where V is measured in consumption units.

Suppose that a solution exists and is given by $\{c^*(t)\}_0^\infty$, V^*. Now suppose there exists a $V^{**} \in \Gamma$ with $V^{**} > V^*$.

Then define

$$\Delta c = \frac{(V^{**} - V^*)\alpha_n}{\int_0^\infty \exp\{-R(t)\}\, \mathrm{d}t} > 0.$$

Then the consumption stream $\{c^*(t) + \Delta c\}_0^\infty$ and the present value V^{**} are both feasible, and assuming non-satiation $U^n[\{c^*(t) + \Delta c\}_0^\infty]$ $> U^n[\{c^*(t)\}_0^\infty]$. This contradicts $\{c^*(t)\}$ as the solution and hence $V^* \geqslant V$ for all $V \in \Gamma$.

Proposition 3 (p. 10). A necessary condition for a firm to maximize present value as defined in equation 2.4 is that the streams of capital input $K(t)$ and labour input $L(t)$ satisfy

$$p(t)\, \frac{\partial F}{\partial L}\{K(t),\, L(t)\} = w(t) \text{ for all } t \geqslant 0$$

$$p(t)\, \frac{\partial F}{\partial K}\{K(t),\, L(t)\} = q(t)\{r(t) + \delta - \dot{q}(t)/q(t)\} \text{ for all } t > 0.$$

Proof. Consider the first condition.

Suppose an additional unit of labour is hired from time t to time $t + \mathrm{d}t$. Then the additional revenue is $p(t)F_L(t)\, \mathrm{d}t$, the additional cost is $w(t)\, \mathrm{d}t$. Now if $p(t)F_L(t) > w(t)$, $(p(t)F_L(t) < w(t))$, the hiring of one extra unit (one less unit) of labour will increase the net income flow from t to $t + \mathrm{d}t$ leaving it unchanged elsewhere, thereby increasing the present value of the firm. Hence $p(t)F_L(t) = w(t)$ is a necessary condition for a maximum.

Turning to the second condition the following argument may be used. Suppose an additional unit of capital is purchased at time t. Then the net addition to the present value of the firm is given by

$$\int_t^\infty \exp\{-R(s)\} \exp\{-\delta(s-t)\} \{p(s)F_K(s)\} \, ds - q(t) \exp\{-R(t)\}$$

and using the same argument as above it is necessary for maximizing the present value of the firm that this net addition be zero. Therefore,

A.1 $\quad \int_t^\infty \exp\{-R(s)\} \exp\{-\delta(s-t)\} \, p(s)F_K(s) \, ds - q(t) \exp\{-R(t)\}$
$$= 0 \text{ for all } t.$$

Taking d/dt of A.1 gives

A.2 $\quad \delta \int_t^\infty \exp\{-R(s)\} \exp\{-\delta(s-t)\} \, p(s)F_K(s) \, ds$

$$- \exp\{-R(t)\} \, p(t)F_K(t) + r(t)q(t) \exp\{-R(t)\}$$

$$- \dot{q}(t) \exp\{-R(t)\} = 0.$$

Substituting from A.1 and cancelling $\exp\{-R(t)\}$ gives

A.3 $\qquad\qquad p(t)F_K(t) = q(t)\{r(t) + \delta - \dot{q}(t)/q(t)\},$

namely the second condition.

Proposition 4 (p. 17). If a demand function is separable, taking the form $z\{p(t)\}\beta(t)$, then the elasticity of demand $\epsilon\{p(t), t\}$ and the marginal revenue function $M\{p(t), t\}$ are functions of $p(t)$ only.

Proof

$$\epsilon\{p(t), t\} = \frac{p(t)}{z\{p(t)\}\beta(t)} \frac{\partial z\{p(t)\}\beta(t)}{\partial p(t)} = \frac{p(t)}{z\{p(t)\}} \frac{\partial z\{p(t)\}}{\partial p(t)} = \epsilon\{p(t)\}.$$

$$M\{p(t), t\} = p(t)\left[1 + \frac{1}{\epsilon\{p(t)\}}\right] = M\{p(t)\}.$$

Proposition 5 (p. 18). The necessary conditions defined by equations 2.15, 2.17 and 2.18 imply an investment path given by

$$I/K = \dot{\beta}/\beta + \delta + (1 - \epsilon_k)(\sigma + \epsilon_M)\dot{w}/w - \{\sigma(1 - \epsilon_k) - \epsilon_M\epsilon_k\}\dot{c}/c$$

Proof. Since $F(K, L)$ is homogeneous of degree one in K and L, we have $F(K, L) = Lf(K)$ where $k = K/L$. Furthermore we have the standard expressions $\partial F/\partial K = f'$ and $\partial F/\partial L = f - kf'$. The necessary conditions 2.15, 2.17, 2.18 may then be rewritten as

A.4 $$\frac{K}{k}f = z\beta,$$

A.5 $$M(f - f'k) = w,$$

A.6 $$Mf' = c.$$

Defining the elasticity of substitution $\sigma = -f'(f - kf')/kff''$, the the elasticity of output/unit labour with respect to capital/unit labour $\epsilon_k = f'k/f$ and the elasticity of output with respect to marginal revenue $\epsilon_M = \partial z/\partial M . M/z$, the log time derivatives of A.4, A.5, A.6 may be written

A.7 $$\epsilon \dot{p}/p = \dot{K}/K + (\dot{k}/k)(\epsilon_k - 1) - \dot{\beta}/\beta$$

A.8 $$\frac{\sigma}{\epsilon_M} \epsilon \dot{p}/p + \epsilon_k \dot{k}/k = \sigma \dot{w}/w$$

A.9 $$\frac{\sigma}{\epsilon_M} \epsilon \dot{p}/p + (\epsilon_k - 1)\dot{k}/k = \sigma \dot{c}/c$$

A.8, A.9 imply that

A.10 $$\dot{k}/k = \sigma(\dot{w}/w - \dot{c}/c)$$

A.11 $$\epsilon \dot{p}/p = \epsilon_M\{(1 - \epsilon_k)\dot{w}/w + \epsilon_k \dot{c}/c\}$$

Substituting into A.7 gives

$$\frac{\dot{K}}{K} = \dot{\beta}/\beta + (1 - \epsilon_k)(\sigma + \epsilon_M)\dot{w}/w - \{(1 - \epsilon_k)\sigma - \epsilon_M\epsilon_k\}\dot{c}/c$$

and using the definition of I, this gives the desired result.

Footnotes

[1] See Appendix, proposition 1.

[2] For a formal proof of this result see Appendix, proposition 2.

[3] We are implicitly assuming here that the flow of services from a given stock of capital is proportional to the stock. This point will be considered further when capacity utilization is discussed in the last section of Chapter 7.

[4] A dot over a variable always represents the time derivative, e.g. $\dot{K}(t) = dK(t)/dt$.

[5] The necessary condition 2.8 need not be satisfied when $t = 0$, since the capital stock K_0 is given at this point in time. For a formal proof of these results see Appendix, proposition 3.

[6] The static nature of the problem is very much a function of the fact that we are working in continuous time. The cost of capital in discrete time is $q(t)r + q(t+1)\delta - \{q(t+1) - q(t)\}$ and so if the basic time unit is one month, for example, then the cost of capital is a function of, among other things, the price of capital goods one month hence. If the future is not known but expectations are certain then this variable will have to be replaced by the expected price of capital goods and we are in the position where future expectations affect current investment decisions. But in a very real sense we are talking about a completely different model when we move into discrete time. In the case where the time interval is one month, we are in a world where capital goods are *effectively* fixed into place for one month and therefore it is hardly surprising that expectations about their price in one month's time are an important factor in current purchasing decisions. In continuous time on the other hand we are assuming that capital goods can be bought and sold at each *instant* and future expectations can therefore play no role.

[7] Notably Lerner (1944) and Witte (1963). The quotation from Haavelmo (1960) given below is taken from p. 216.

[8] See Jorgenson (1967), pp. 147–151.

[9] For example it would occasion no surprise if a firm ordered a block of capital goods from abroad so that it arrived on the day after a drop in the tariff on such goods. Such behaviour could well be optimal.

[10] They may, of course, arrive at infinity when the cost of capital becomes negative and before the rise in $q(t)$ becomes instantaneous depending on the specification of the production function. However, this point merely reinforces the argument in the text.

[11] See Appendix, proposition 4.

[12] The one exception to this supposition can be found in the discussion of capacity utilization in the final section of Chapter 7.

[13] For a formal derivation of equation 2.19, see Appendix, proposition 5.

Bibliographical Notes—Chapter 2

The models of investment decisions discussed in this chapter are based on the theories of Irving Fisher as expounded in his *Theory of Interest Rates* (Fisher, 1930)) and are clearly neo-classical in tone. A more modern and detailed exposition of the basic Fisherian theory may be found in Hirshleifer (1970) and in Jorgenson (1967). Haavelmo (1960) is a book which is in the neo-classical tradition though it argues strongly against the sort of crude analysis of investment pictured in this chapter. In *partial* opposition to this type of analysis there are a number of extensions of the Keynesian model of investment behaviour which first saw the light of day in the *General Theory* (Keynes, 1936). Some of the more interesting of these extensions are to be found in Lerner (1944), Witte (1963) and Marglin (1970). Some general surveys of competing theories of investment are to be found in Lund (1971), Kuh (1971), and Junankar (1972).

The flexible accelerator model which is mentioned in the last section of the chapter was suggested initially in Goodwin (1948) as an extension of the original simple accelerator formulation of Clark (1917). Further extensions are presented in Chenery (1952) and Koyck (1954).

CHAPTER 3

COSTS OF ADJUSTMENT

1. The Concept of Adjustment Costs

In the previous chapter the analysis of a firm's demand for capital goods was based on a number of assumptions including one which enabled the firm to purchase and install new capital both costlessly and instantaneously (and also to do the reverse). The consequence of this particular assumption was that the firm responded to changes in relevant parameters[1] with instantaneous changes in its capital stock, a most unappealing result given the nature of capital goods and one which is in little accord with casual observation. Further consequences, of possibly even less appeal, were that the firm could ignore the future in making optimal investment decisions and that it would buy and sell large amounts of fixed capital *solely* for the purpose of making capital gains. It is therefore clear that the model developed in the previous chapter is grossly inadequate as a basis for understanding a firm's investment decisions and as a consequence the assumption of instantaneous and costless adjustment of capital stock will be dropped.

There are two basic lines of approach which may be taken at this juncture depending on which of the two words, costless or instantaneous, is removed from the assumption first. It is the purpose of this chapter to discuss the consequences of removing the first of these two words. This is achieved by introducing the notion of 'adjustment costs' which are costs associated with the sale, purchase or productive implementation of capital goods over and above the basic price of these goods. The assumed existence of such costs is usually justified by reference to the reorganization and retraining involved in the absorption of new equipment and the myriad teething troubles experienced with new plant. To introduce these extra costs into the model, assumption 6 of the previous chapter is replaced by the following:

Assumption 6a. There are adjustment costs associated with changes in the capital stock. These costs are a function of gross investment, are

25

increasing with the absolute size of the rate of investment or disinvestment and furthermore rise at an ever-increasing rate. They are zero only when gross investment is zero.[2]

The type of adjustment costs implied by this assumption is illustrated in Figure 3.1.

The fact that the costs rise at an increasing rate as investment or disinvestment increases implies that the graph of the adjustment costs function is everywhere bowed upwards. Such a function is known as strictly convex and the adjustment costs described in assumption 6a will be subsequently referred to as strictly convex adjustment costs. For the moment the question as to whether

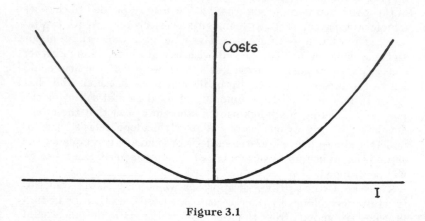

Figure 3.1

adjustment costs of this type are realistic or plausible will be left in abeyance; we look first at their consequences for the firm and its investment decisions.

Consider the firm described in the previous chapter and suppose that at time t_0 the rate of interest falls suddenly. Then it would instantaneously purchase and install a block of capital. However, if the firm was faced by strictly convex adjustment costs such an action would be extremely expensive. for the essence of such costs is that they penalize rapid change. A little experimentation with Figure 3.1 reveals that the total adjustment costs incurred by maintaining a given rate of investment for two periods is less than the cost of maintaining twice this given rate of investment for one period. Since the total change in capital stock is identical in both cases, there are clear cost advantages to moving from one level of capital stock to the other along the slower path. Indeed it can be demonstrated that the presence of strictly convex adjustment costs leads to the somewhat extreme result that a present value maximizing firm responding to a drop in interest rates would *never* reach its new higher equilibrium level of capital stock. This type of firm behaviour is often hypothesized in empirical work under the guise of the flexible accelerator mechanism. Here the equilibrium level of capital stock is referred to as the 'desired' capital stock which would be achieved instantaneously but for the costs of getting there. The firm then moves towards the 'desired' capital stock at a rate which is directly related to the difference between the desired stock and the actual stock. The larger this difference, the faster the firm closes the gap. As the gap becomes smaller the rate of net accumulation also declines in such a way that the gap is never closed in finite time.

2. A Formal Model

Turning now to a more formal approach, we require some additional notation for adjustment costs. Let these be represented by the expression $C\{I(t)\}$ which is a flow variable. Assumption 6a then implies that the function $C(\cdot)$ has the following properties,

3.1 $$C'(I) \lessgtr 0 \Leftrightarrow I \lessgtr 0, \; C(0) = 0, \; C''(I) > 0.$$

These restrictions should be checked against Figure 3.1, noting that the last mentioned, namely the positive second derivative, is the analytical representation of increasing costs at the margin. So, maintaining the previous notation, the firm will choose a production plan to maximize present value which is now given by

3.2 $$V = \int_0^\infty \exp\{-R(t)\}[p(t)F\{K(t), L(t)\} - w(t)L(t) - q(t)I(t) \\ - C\{I(t)\}] \, dt,$$

where, as usual, the plan is constrained by the capital accumulation equation

3.3 $$\dot{K}(t) = I(t) - \delta K(t).$$

The question now arises as to how the addition of adjustment costs affects the conditions which the optimal production plan must satisfy. First it is clear that, since there are no restrictions on the ability of the firm to adjust its labour force, it will always employ labour services up to the point where the marginal revenue product of labour services is equal to the wage, hence

3.4 $p(t) \dfrac{\partial F}{\partial L} \{K(t), L(t)\} = w(t)$ for all $t \geqslant 0$.

The difficult part is the necessary condition associated with the capital input and this will be dealt with in stages. Consider first the increase in revenue accruing to the firm at time s resulting from the purchase of an extra unit of capital stock at time t. This is given by the marginal revenue product of capital at time s corrected by a depreciation factor to account for the fact that one unit of extra capital at time t has diminished to $\exp\{-\delta(s-t)\}$ units of extra capital at time s. The revenue is thus given by the expression $\exp\{-\delta(s-t)\} p(s) (\partial F/\partial K)$. The present value (at time t) of the total additional revenue accruing to the firm is thus given by the expression

3.5 $\displaystyle\int_t^\infty \exp\{-r(s-t)\} \left[\exp\{-\delta(s-t)\} p(s) \frac{\partial F}{\partial K} \{K(s), L(s)\}\right] ds$

where the rate of interest, r, is assumed to be constant for the sake of simplicity. Consequently the *net* gain to the firm, $G(t)$ say, resulting from the purchase of one extra unit of capital, but excluding the costs of making this adjustment, is given by the above expression less the cost of the extra unit, namely,

3.6 $G(t) = \displaystyle\int_t^\infty \exp\{-(\delta+r)(s-t)\} p(s) \frac{\partial F}{\partial K} \{K(s), L(s)\} ds - q(t).$

Consider next the adjustment costs involved. These are simply the additional costs incurred by increasing the investment rate at time t by one unit for one time period[3] and are given by the expression $C'\{I(t)\}$. On the optimal production plan the costs of adjustment involved in installing one extra unit of capital stock must always balance the net gain of the adjustment. For if they did not balance in some period of time then either a unit increase or a unit reduction in the rate of investment in that period would lead to an increase in the present value of the firm (the argument here is identical to that given in proposition 3 in the Appendix to Chapter 2). Consequently we have as a necessary condition,

$$3.7 \quad C'\{I(t)\} = \int_t^\infty \exp\{-(\delta+r)(s-t)\}\, p(s)\, \frac{\partial F}{\partial K}\{K(s),\, L(s)\}\, ds$$
$$-q(t) \text{ for all } t > 0.$$

As it stands this condition is not very revealing, for the right-hand side is a function of the complete time path of capital stock from time t into the infinite future and the left-hand side is a function of the current rate of investment. Since the time path of capital stock depends upon, among other things, the current rate of investment, this condition does not, in general, give a decision rule for determining the current level of investment.

There is, however, one special case in which 3.7 does reduce to such a decision rule and that is the situation in which there are constant returns to scale in production. Because of this desirable property, this particular case will be discussed at some length. In spite of the fact that the constant returns assumption greatly simplifies the analysis, the resulting model nevertheless has many of the salient properties of more general models of this type and is not profoundly misleading. Consequently we assume constant returns in production (assumption 3a, p. 17).

In this case the marginal products of both labour and capital are functions *only* of the *capital labour ratio*. This ratio is thus determined for every time period in terms of prices by the labour productivity condition 3.4 and hence the marginal product of capital is a function of prices only along the optimal path. Condition 3.7 then determines the level of investment solely in terms of current and future prices.

More formally, if there are constant returns to scale, then $F(K, L)$ may be rewritten as $Lf(k)$ where k is the capital–labour ratio. Then 3.4 may be replaced by

$$3.4a \qquad f - \frac{k\partial f}{\partial k} = \frac{w(t)}{p(t)} \text{ for all } t,$$

using the well-known formulation of the marginal product of labour. Since the marginal product of labour is increasing in the capital labour ratio this equation may be solved to give

$$3.8 \qquad k(t) = g\{w(t)/p(t)\} \text{ where } g' > 0.$$

Noting that the marginal product of capital may be written as

$\partial f(k)/\partial k$, and using 3.8, the condition 3.7 may be replaced by

3.9 $\quad C'\{I(t)\} = \int\limits_{t}^{\infty} \exp\left\{-(\delta+r)(s-t)\right\} p(s)\, \dfrac{\partial f}{\partial k}\left\{g\left(\dfrac{w(s)}{p(s)}\right)\right\}\, \mathrm{d}s - q(t),$

or

3.10 $\quad C'\{I(t)\} = \int\limits_{t}^{\infty} \exp\left\{-(\delta+r)(s-t)\right\} p(s)\, f_k\{w(s)/p(s)\}\, \mathrm{d}s - q(t)$

$$\text{for all } t > 0,$$

in more compact notation. Here we have an investment decision rule in which the level of investment in any period is determined by the current and future values of prices. Since we have not relaxed our assumption of perfect certainty, or at least certain expectations (assumption 2), such a decision rule seems quite sensible. The important point to note is that the firm must look to the future when making current investment decisions, a result far more in accord with reality than the myopic investment rules resulting from the model without costs of adjustment. Before discussing exactly how future expectations influence current investment, it is worth showing how this model leads to the flexible accelerator model of net investment described at the end of section 1. Suppose that all prices are expected to remain constant; then 3.10 reduces to

3.11 $\qquad C'\{I(t)\} = p f_k\left(\dfrac{w}{p}\right) \int\limits_{t}^{\infty} \exp\left\{-(\delta+r)(s-t)\right\}\, \mathrm{d}s - q$

$$= \dfrac{p f_k(w/p)}{r+\delta} - q \text{ by integration.}$$

Now define the desired capital stock to be that quantity of capital which the firm would wish to use in long-run equilibrium at these constant prices. Since net investment must be zero at such an equilibrium, investment can only be for replacement purposes. The desired capital stock K^* requires a level of replacement δK^* to maintain itself and hence in equilibrium investment is given by δK^* which must satisfy

3.12 $\qquad C'(\delta K^*) = \dfrac{p f_k(w/p)}{r+\delta} - q \text{ from 3.11.}$

It is worth noting that, in spite of the presence of constant returns in production, this price-taking firm is of bounded size. The boundedness arises because the costs of adjustment are increasing at the margin and thus the costs of installing the replacement investment limit the size of the firm in equilibrium.

From 3.11 and 3.12 we have

$$C'\{I(t)\} = C'(\delta K^*)$$

and hence

3.13 $$I(t) = \delta K^*.$$

But from 3.3.

$$I(t) = \dot{K}(t) + \delta K(t)$$

and so 3.13 implies

3.14 $$\dot{K}(t) = \delta\{K^* - K(t)\}.$$

Thus the rate at which the firm accumulates capital stock is directly proportional to the difference between its desired capital stock and its current capital stock which is precisely the flexible accelerator mechanism. Because this particular view of the capital accumulation process of the firm is so popular in empirical work it is worth trying to extend it to the case where prices are changing (or expected to change). We must therefore return to equation 3.10 which defines the rate of investment in this particular case. If we define the firm's desired capital stock in a fashion analogous to the constant price case (3.12) we have $K^*(t)$ satisfying

3.15 $$C'\{\delta K^*(t)\}$$

$$= \int_{t}^{\infty} \exp\{-(\delta + r)(s - t)\} \, p(s) \, f_k\{w(s)/p(s)\} \, ds - q(t)$$

and using 3.10, this immediately gives the flexible accelerator formulation once again since equation 3.13 still holds. In this case, however, the desired capital stock $K^*(t)$ varies over time and we have the equation

3.16 $$\dot{K}(t) = \delta\{K^*(t) - K(t)\}.$$

The problem here is that there does not seem to be any good reason why $K^*(t)$ should be considered 'desirable'. $K^*(t)$ is that quantity of capital stock which requires that quantity of replacement investment which gives rise to a marginal adjustment cost which just balances the current marginal net gain. This is hardly the quantity of capital which would spring to mind as the desired capital stock. On the other hand it is difficult to conceive of any quantity of capital which would fill the bill in a regime of variable prices, particularly in the context of this particular model. This is a major problem with the whole concept of desired capital stock which has led most of the economists who use it in empirical work to assume, either explicitly or implicitly, constant prices or static expectations.[4]

Returning now to the main thread of the exposition, it is possible, by using equation 3.10, to see how changes in current and expected future prices or interest rates will affect the firm's investment plans. Consider first the effects of a permanent fall in the rate of interest from r_1 to r_2 at time t_0, assuming the fall to be *unexpected*. Then prior to t_0, the optimal level of investment I_1 satisfies,

$$3.17 \qquad C'(I_1) = \frac{pf_k(w/p)}{r_1 + \delta} - q$$

and after t_0 it satisfies the equation

$$3.18 \qquad C'(I_2) = \frac{pf_k(w/p)}{r_2 + \delta} - q.$$

The fact that C' is an increasing function implies that $I_2 > I_1$ and there is a permanent rise in the level of investment at t_0. This is rather a satisfying result and contrasts strongly with the behaviour of the firm in the same situation when there are no adjustment costs, which was discussed in the previous chapter.

Perhaps more interesting is the effect on current investment decisions of a change in the rate of interest which is expected to occur at some time in the future. Suppose that at time t_0 the firm expects the rate of interest to fall permanently from r_1 to r_2 at some future time t_1. Then we might suspect that at t_0 the expected future fall in interest rates would increase current investment above I_1, which is the optimal level under constant interest rate expectations. The reason for this suspicion is that a fall in future interest rates increases the present value of the revenue accruing over time to the marginal unit of capital stock without affecting its cost. Investment is therefore more profitable and increases. Furthermore, the closer is the present to the time at which the decline is expected to occur, the stronger should be the effect on current investment plans. All these intuitive conclusions are confirmed by the analysis as the level of investment during the interval from t_0 to t_1 is given by the equation

$$3.19 \quad C'\{I(t)\} = C'(I_1) + \exp\{-(\delta + r_1)(t_1 - t)\}\{C'(I_2) - C'(I_1)\}$$

which is derived in the Appendix (proposition 1). After the interest rate has declined at t_1 investment remains at the constant level I_2 as before.

To bring home the importance of future expectations in determining current investment plans, Figure 3.2 illustrates the various investment paths which will be followed from time t_0, given various different expectations concerning the timing of the future interest rate fall.

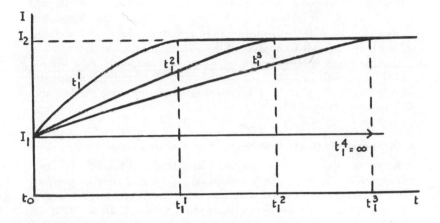

Figure 3.2
$t_1{}^i$ is the expected time when the interest rate falls.

Figure 3.2 shows four *investment* paths for four different expectations concerning the timing of the fall in the interest rate. It should be particularly noted that during the period t_0 to t_1^1 the *current* levels of all variables which affect investment plans are *identical* in every case.

Similar results may be obtained for changes in the other prices. It can easily be shown that the level of current investment is directly related to the current and future expected output price and inversely related to the current and future expected wage rate[5] (see Appendix, proposition 2). The only price, the future expected value of which has no effect on present plans is the price of capital goods (see equation 3.10). This is surprising and is in fact a very special result which follows from the constant returns assumption, for in this case the labour force is always adjusted so that the marginal product of capital is independent of the amount of capital employed. In more general cases this result does not hold.

In the analytically more complex case where diminishing returns to scale in production are prevalent (assumption 3, p. 8), the two equations which determine the production and investment plan of the firm are 3.4 and 3.7. In the case of static expectations it is possible to derive an approximate flexible accelerator equation from these conditions and also to show that an expected permanent reduction in the rate of interest or the price of capital goods will cause a permanent increase in the rate of investment (see Appendix, proposition 3). When expectations are not static the model becomes rather more difficult to analyse and we shall not deal with it here.

Having dealt with adjustment costs in a perfectly competitive world it is worth just glancing at the equivalent problem when the firm is not assumed to be a price taker in the product market and this we do in the next section.

3. Adjustment Costs and Imperfect Competition

As in the previous chapter we shall briefly consider the consequences of dropping the assumption of competition in product markets, supposing instead that the firm faces a downward sloping demand curve for its product (assumption 8, p. 16). In addition we shall revert again to constant returns to scale in production (assumption 3a, p. 17). The main point of considering such a model is to enable us to investigate how current and expected changes in demand will influence current investment decisions. The formal structure of the model is much the same as that considered in the previous section with the crucial difference that the output price is everywhere replaced by the marginal revenue function. In the light of this we shall not dwell on formal methods in this section but simply look at the more interesting results, the analysis underlying which may be found in proposition 4 of the Appendix.

Consider first a firm which is in equilibrium facing factor prices which are expected to remain fixed. The demand for its product then increases both sharply and unexpectedly. Because of the costs involved in making capital stock adjustments it will not immediately purchase a block of capital to give it the necessary capacity to satisfy this new level of demand at long-run marginal cost but will only gradually increase its stock of fixed capital towards this higher level. The gap between capacity and the higher level of demand is then closed, at least temporarily, by simultaneously raising the output price and taking on more labour. Then, as time goes on, the output price reverts towards its long-run equilibrium level as the firm's capacity catches up. In the case where the firm has some expectation that demand will increase at some point in the future, the existence of adjustment costs will provide an incentive for the firm to anticipate this demand increase by raising its current rate of investment, very much in the way that is illustrated in Figure 3.2 for the response of the competitive firm to expected falls in the interest rate.

Both types of firm response, the sluggish response to current changes and the anticipatory response which we have just described, are rather appealing descriptions of firm behaviour as indeed are the types of investment behaviour discussed in the previous section. They tie up closely both with casual empiricism and the distributed lag response of investment to demand changes so beloved of applied workers in this field. The question remains however as to whether the assumption of strictly convex costs of adjustment can be considered a plausible hypothesis or whether one should look elsewhere for an explanation of the rather sluggish and hesitant behaviour commonly observed when it comes to decisions about investing in fixed capital. This question is the topic of the next section.

4. The Importance of Adjustment Costs

At the beginning of this chapter, the notion of adjustment costs was introduced with only a brief word as to how such costs might arise in reality. It is the purpose of this section to consider whether these costs are likely to be important and particularly whether they are likely to be of the strictly convex type illustrated in Figure 3.1.

Reverting now to the perfectly competitive model of section 2 we shall first consider an interpretation of the adjustment cost function $C(\cdot)$ which arises out of the discussion of investment decisions in Keynes's *General Theory* (1936). Let $C\{I(t)\}/I(t)$ represent a premium which must be paid per unit, over and above the basic price, in order to acquire new capital goods. The existence of such a premium may be justified by assuming that the firm's demand for this particular type of capital is a significant proportion of the total demand and thus, as the firm's rate of investment and hence demand for new capital goods increases, the price it has to pay rises above the basic price.[6] The fact that a considerable proportion of all capital goods are highly specific to the firms purchasing them gives this interpretation some degree of plausibility. In addition, since the price paid rises with the rate of investment, the total premium $C\{I(t)\}$ could well be rising at the margin. Thus the strict convexity assumption does not seem unreasonable and, with this interpretation in mind, we may rewrite equation 3.10 as

3.20

$$\int_t^\infty \exp\{-r(s-t)\} \left[\exp\{-\delta(s-t)\}\, p(s) f_k \left\{\frac{w(s)}{p(s)}\right\}\right]\, ds = q(t) + C'\{I(t)\}$$

or defining the term in parentheses as $Q(t, s)$, the return at time s on an additional unit purchased at t, this reduces to

3.21 $$\int_t^\infty \exp\{-r(s-t)\}\, Q(t, s)\, ds = q(t) + C'\{I(t)\}.$$

This equation is very much a Keynesian formulation of the investment decision for a firm. The constant returns assumption removes the objection of Arrow and Leijonhufvud to the Keynesian formulation, namely that without constant returns, the s period marginal return $Q(s, t)$ depends on the capital stock at time s which depends on investment at time t thus invalidating 3.21 as an investment decision rule.[7]

This interpretation of $C(\cdot)$ is in line with Keynes' view that the most important reason for a declining marginal efficiency of capital schedule in the short run is the supply price rising with demand.[8] What is more, this model was constructed expressly to overcome the unrealistic nonsense of myopic investment decision rules and to accord an important role to future expectations. Here again the Keynesian parallel is striking for the discussion of investment decisions in *The General Theory* emphasizes this point above all else.[9]

If there are monopsonistic elements in the market for the capital goods purchased by the firm under consideration, then the strictly convex adjustment cost function $C(\cdot)$ may capture this point quite adequately. But it is difficult to argue that such monopsonistic elements always exist at the firm level and consequently other possible reasons for the existence of adjustment costs should be considered. First of all there may be costs associated with the installation of new capital goods, for example the reorganization of production lines, the training of workers to use the new equipment and the like. Unfortunately, in spite of some assertions to the contrary,[10] there seems to be no very good reason why such costs should be increasing at the margin. In fact it seems very much more plausible that reorganization and training processes are subject to large indivisibilities and consequently give rise to diminishing costs over a considerable range. Furthermore these processes use information as an input and this is a well-known cause of decreasing costs. Thus, once one has determined how to reorganize one production line, one has determined how to reorganize any number of similar ones. Lastly, there may well be fixed costs associated with the installation of new capital equipment such as the costs of stopping the plant while it is installed.

A more general line of argument purporting to give good reason for the strict convexity of $C(\cdot)$ has been that it is more expensive to do things quickly than slowly. This *may* be true for the installation

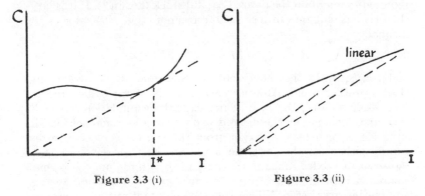

Figure 3.3 (i)   Figure 3.3 (ii)

of very large units of machinery over very short periods of time. For example, it is probably cheaper to install a new production line in a month than in a day. But it is not clear that it is more expensive in terms of adjustment costs to install a new production line in a month than to install it in fifty years, which is the implication of strict convexity.

In the light of these arguments, if monopsonistic elements in the capital goods market are not of overwhelming importance, it would seem reasonable to assume an adjustment cost function for positive investment (negative investment is dealt with later) which has a fixed cost element and is strictly concave up to a certain level after which it is linear[11] or strictly convex. Two such functions are illustrated in Figure 3.3.

What are the implications for investment decisions of the two types of adjustment cost function illustrated above? Consider first that shown in Figure 3.3 (i). With these adjustment costs it is cheaper to install capital at a rate I^* than at any other rate since the *average* installation cost is minimized at I^*. So in a situation of static expectations when the desired capital stock is greater than the current capital stock, the optimal rate of investment will always be greater than or equal to I^*. It could never be less than I^* since, if it were, an increase in the investment rate would lead to *both* lower average adjustment costs *and* a higher present value, exclusive of adjustment costs, because of the faster approach to the desired capital stock level. Whether or not this situation is very different from that with strictly convex adjustment costs depends crucially on whether or not I^* is large compared with the rate of replacement required to maintain the desired capital stock (i.e. δK^*). If it is large then the current rate of net capital accumulation $\dot{K}(t)$ satisfies the inequality

3.22 $$\dot{K}(t) = I(t) - \delta K(t) > I^* - \delta K(t) \gg 0$$

and consequently the movement from current to desired capital stock is rather rapid. Alternatively, if I^* is of the same order of magnitude as δK^*, the rate of net capital accumulation would be slow and declining as the desired capital stock is approached. The situation is then little different from the strictly convex case discussed earlier. So the outcome turns on whether the amount of replacement needed to maintain the firm at its optimum size is small compared with the rate of investment at which increasing average adjustment costs set in. Where there are constant returns in production, it is these adjustment costs themselves that determine the optimum firm size under perfect competition (see equation 3.12). So, in this situation, the initial non-convexity of adjustment costs would make no difference. However, if the optimum firm size was determined at a much lower level by decreasing returns in production or by the size of the accessible product market, the initial non-convexity of adjustment costs could lead to an investment response in which capital stock adjusted rapidly to its new higher equilibrium level in response to a favourable parametric change.[12]

The type of adjustment costs illustrated in Figure 3.3 (ii) shows the average cost of installation becoming ever smaller as the rate of investment increases. In this case jumps in the capital stock may be the optimal response to parameter changes since these will minimize the average installation costs. Then the only difference between this situation and one in which there are no adjustment costs at all is that in the former there may be no investment response to a small favourable parameter change because the fixed costs involved in making the response may outweigh the potential gains.[13] Indeed the existence of large fixed costs of adjustment of this type will be enough to drive a considerable wedge between the observed marginal rate of return on capital and the cost of capital as ordinarily measured. Only if this differential is above a certain critical size will it be worth investing so as to close the gap. However, the really important point to note is that the inclusion of these more plausible adjustment costs in the model does not rule out the possibility of large instantaneous investment responses, even to totally unforeseen parametric changes. This was one of the less appealing aspects of the original model[14] but it would appear that in the current context only the unacceptable assumption of strictly convex adjustment costs can reduce the immediate investment response to suitably small proportions. In fact the use of the word 'unacceptable' here may be a little strong since it will be argued in Chapter 8 on finance that the behaviour of loan markets in a world of uncertainty and bankruptcy is such as to have an effect on firms' investment decisions very much *as if* the firm was faced with strictly convex costs of adjustment. This is rather jumping ahead, however, and at the present juncture it is worth looking in other directions to increase the realism of our model.

At the beginning of the chapter it was decided to excise the assumption of costless and instantaneous adjustment of capital stock from the model and during the course of the chapter we have concentrated on the removal of the word *costless*. The final result has not been particularly satisfactory and consequently it is natural to turn our attention to the word *instantaneous*, not least because in all the empirical work in this field the lags between parametric changes and capital stock response are taken to be of fundamental importance. As a natural extension of the model we shall therefore introduce a specific time lag between the ordering of new capital goods and their installation. The effects of such a lag will be an important topic of the next three chapters.

Before closing this chapter, some mention must be made of those adjustment costs associated with the sale of old capital goods by the firm. Now it is quite clear that there is a large class of capital goods which are, in reality, almost impossible to sell other than as scrap.

The major exceptions to this are vehicles (including ships, planes, etc.) and certain types of buildings (e.g. offices), for which a ready secondhand market exists; but for capital goods not in these categories, such markets are few and far between. Prior to discussing the implications of this lack of markets we should first consider whether or not the existence of take-overs and the trade in complete subsidiary companies effectively offsets the dearth of more obvious second-hand markets by providing a means of trading in second-hand capital goods under a different guise. Here we shall argue that this is not the case. Such transactions simply imply a change of ownership for the productive unit as a whole. They cannot be used to make those marginal and frequent adjustments in the capital stock of the firm which would occur in a situation where there were proper markets for second-hand capital goods of all types and do occur for example, in the typical firm's stock of vehicles.[15] For capital goods where there are active second-hand markets it seems quite plausible for the adjustment costs to be more or less symmetric, that is $C(I) \simeq C(-I)$ where $C(\cdot)$ is the type of function illustrated in Figure 3.3. However, for the majority of capital goods, which are not in this category, it seems that the most obvious way of incorporating the situation described above into the model is to constrain gross investment to be non-negative. Firms are then simply not allowed to sell this type of capital.

In the next chapter we shall discuss models which specifically incorporate both lags and the type of irreversibility assumption discussed above. It is now becoming clear that as the models discussed become more 'realistic' they become less general. For example, the main models of this chapter may be a rather good description of the investment decisions involved in the purchase of trucks or tractors but not for the majority of other capital goods. A second point is that not only do the models become less general but they also become more difficult to analyse. This means that in order to study particular aspects of the investment decision problem it may be desirable to make simplifying assumptions concerning other aspects which are not being directly investigated. Thus in this chapter some insight was gained into the consequences of adjustment costs by assuming constant returns in production. So long as it is clear what the effects of the special assumptions are on the problem in hand, this simplifying technique is extremely useful and will in fact be vital in future chapters in order to make some rather difficult problems tractable.

Appendix

Proposition 1 (p. 33). A constant returns to scale firm maximizing present value as defined in 3.2 forms a certain expectation at time t_0 that at some future time t_1, the interest rate will fall from r_1 to r_2, all other prices remaining constant. Then for all t such that $t_0 \leqslant t \leqslant t_1$, the firm's investment path will satisfy,

$$C'\{I(t)\} = C'(I_1) + \exp\{-(\delta + r_1)(t_1 - t)\}\{C'(I_2) - C'(I_1)\}$$

where

$$C'(I_i) = \frac{pf_k(w/p)}{r_i + \delta} - q.$$

Proof. For $t_0 \leqslant t \leqslant t_1$, $I(t)$ satisfies the necessary condition

A.1 $\quad C'\{I(t)\} = pf_k(w/p) \int\limits_{t}^{\infty} \exp\left\{-\delta(s-t) - \int\limits_{t}^{s} r(\tau)\,d\tau\right\} ds - q$

which is the appropriate generalization of 3.11 for a variable interest rate. A.1 implies

$$C'\{I(t)\} = pf_k(w/p) \int\limits_{t}^{t_1} \exp\left\{-\delta(s-t) - \int\limits_{t}^{s} r(\tau)\,d\tau\right\} ds - q$$

$$+ pf_k(w/p) \int\limits_{t_1}^{\infty} \exp\left\{-\delta(t_1-t) - \int\limits_{t}^{t_1} r(\tau)\,d\tau\right\}$$

$$\times \exp\left\{-\delta(s-t_1) - \int\limits_{t_1}^{s} r(\iota)\,d_\iota\right\} ds$$

$$= pf_k(w/p) \int\limits_{t}^{t_1} \exp\{-(\delta + r_1)(s-t)\}\,ds - q$$

$$+ pf_k(w/p) \exp\{-(\delta + r_1)(t_1 - t)\}$$

$$\times \int\limits_{t_1}^{\infty} \exp\{-(\delta + r_2)(s - t_1)\}\,ds$$

since $r(t) = r_1$ for $t < t_1$ and $r(t) = r_2$ for $t \geqslant t_1$.

$$= \frac{pf_k(w/p)}{\delta + r_1}[1 - \exp\{-(\delta + r_1)(t_1 - t)\}]$$

$$+ \frac{pf_k(w/p)}{\delta + r_2} \exp\{-(\delta + r_1)(t_1 - t)\} - q$$

by integration

$$= C'(I_1) + \exp\left\{-(\delta + r_1)(t_1 - t)\right\}\{C'(I_2) - C'(I_1)\}.$$

Proposition 2 (p. 33). If a firm which is identical to that described in proposition 1 forms a certain expectation at time t_0 that at some time $t_1 \geqslant t_0$ either the wage rate will fall or the output price will rise with all other prices constant, then the current investment rate will rise.

Proof. Since the marginal product of capital is decreasing in the capital labour ratio, it follows from 3.8 that

A.2 $$\frac{\partial f_k}{\partial w}\left(\frac{w}{p}\right) < 0 \quad \text{and} \quad \frac{\partial f_k}{\partial p}\left(\frac{w}{p}\right) > 0.$$

Suppose that $w(t) = w_1$ for $t < t_1$, $w(t) = w_2$ for $t \geqslant t_1$ where $w_2 < w_1$ and let $I_1(t_0)$ be the level of investment which would have occurred if the wage had been expected to remain constant at the level w_1 as opposed to $I_2(t_0)$ which is the level of investment under the certain expectation of the future wage path described above.

Then from 3.11 we have

A.3 $$C'\{I_1(t_0)\} = p \int_{t_0}^{\infty} f_k\left(\frac{w_1}{p}\right) \exp\left\{-(\delta + r)(s - t_0)\right\} ds - q$$

and from 3.10 we have

A.4 $$C'\{I_2(t_0)\} = p \int_{t_0}^{t_1} f_k\left(\frac{w_1}{p}\right) \exp\left\{-(\delta + r)(s - t_0)\right\} ds$$

$$+ p \int^{\infty} f_k\left(\frac{w_2}{p}\right) \exp\left\{-(\delta + r)(s - t_0)\right\} ds - q$$

A.3 and A.4 imply that

$$C'\{I_2(t_0)\} - C'\{I_1(t_0)\}$$

$$= p \int_{t_1}^{\infty} \left\{f_k\left(\frac{w_2}{p}\right) - f_k\left(\frac{w_1}{p}\right)\right\} \exp\left\{-(\delta + r)(s - t_0)\right\} ds$$

> 0 from A.2.

Since $C'' > 0$, then $I_2(t_0) > I_1(t_0)$ thus proving the first part of the proposition. The second part follows from A.2 in a similar manner.

Proposition 3 (p. 34). Consider a firm with diminishing returns to scale which maximizes present value as defined in 3.2. (i) If K^* is the equilibrium level of capital stock at constant prices then the capital accumulation path of this firm will follow a flexible accelerator rule, $\dot{K}(t) = \lambda_1 \ (K^* - K\{t\})$, in the neighbourhood of this equilibrium. (ii) If the optimal investment path for this firm from some initial capital stock $K(0)$ is $I_i^* \ (t)$ when the interest rate is r_i for $i = 1, 2$, then $r_1 > r_2$ implies $I_1^* \ (t) < I_2^* \ (t)$ for all t. (iii) r_i may be replaced by q_i, the price of capital goods, in statement (ii).

Proof. (i) We start by converting 3.7 into a flow condition. Differentiating 3.7 with respect to t and using 3.7 itself gives

A.5 $\qquad pF_K\{K(t), L(t)\} = q(r + \delta) + C'\{I(t)\}(r + \delta) - C''\{I(t)\}\dot{I}$

for constant prices.

Solving the labour productivity condition 3.4, for the labour input gives

A.6 $\qquad L(t) = G\{K(t), w/p\}$ where $G_K = -F_{LK}/F_{KK}$.

Using A.6, A.5 may be rewritten as a second-order differential equation in $K(t)$, namely

A.7 $\quad \ddot{K} + \delta\dot{K} - \dfrac{C'(\dot{K} + \delta K)(r + \delta)}{C''(\dot{K} + \delta K)} + \dfrac{pF_K(K, \ G)}{C''(\dot{K} + \delta K)} - \dfrac{q(r + \delta)}{C''(\dot{K} + \delta K)} = 0$

Now in equilibrium $\ddot{K} = \dot{K} = 0$ and so K^* satisfies

A.8 $\qquad C'(\delta K^*)(r + \delta) + pF_K(K^*, G^*) - q(r + \delta) = 0.$

If we linearize equation A.7 in the neighbourhood of K^* we get, using A.8,

A.9 $\quad \ddot{K} - r\dot{K} - \left\{(r + \delta)\delta - \dfrac{p}{C''(\delta K^*)} \ (F_{KK}^* + F_{KL}^* G_K^*)\right\}(K - K^*) = 0$

Now the concavity of F guarantees that $F_{KK}^* + F_{KL}^* G_K^* < 0$, and hence the roots of this equation are real and opposite in sign, indicating a saddle point in the neighbourhood of K^*. The unique optimal path for $K(t)$ will be that one which converges on K^* and has the form

A.10 $\qquad K(t) = K^* + (K(0) - K^*) \exp(-\lambda_1 t); \ \lambda_1 > 0,$

where $-\lambda_1$ is the negative root of A.9.

Taking the time derivative of A.10 and using A.10 itself gives

A.11 $$\dot{K}(t) = \lambda_1 \{K^* - K(t)\}$$

which is the required flexible accelerator formulation.

(ii) We first note that an analysis of the phase diagram in the $(\dot{K}, K)$ space reveals that on the optimal path $K(t)$ approaches K^* monotonically.

Secondly, taking the derivative of A.8 with respect to r reveals that $\partial K^*/\partial r < 0$ and hence if $K^*(r_i)$ is the equilibrium capital stock when the rate of interest is r_i, then $K^*(r_1) < K^*(r_2)$ since $r_1 > r_2$.

Let $K_1(t)$, $K_2(t)$ be the optimal paths for the two rates of interest and suppose that they cross in the $(\dot{K}, K)$ plane. Then the crossing point must lie outside the interval $(K^*(r_1), K^*(r_2))$ since within this interval $\dot{K}_1(t) < 0$ and $\dot{K}_2(t) > 0$. Let K' be the crossing point nearest

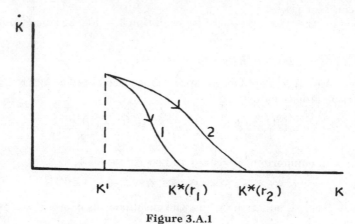

Figure 3.A.1

to $K^*(r_1)$ and below it. Now at this crossing point, it is clear from the diagram that the following holds,

A.12 $$\frac{\partial \dot{K}_1}{\partial K_1} \lessgtr \frac{\partial \dot{K}_2}{\partial K_2},$$

when evaluated at K'.

Now from A.7 we have

A.13 $$\frac{\partial \dot{K}_i}{\partial K_i} = \frac{\dot{K}_i}{\dot{K}_i} = \frac{q(r_i + \delta) + (r_i + \delta)C'(\dot{K} + \delta K) - pF_K}{\dot{K}C''(\dot{K} + \delta K)} - \delta$$

again evaluated at the crossing point K'. Note that at this point $K_1 = K_2$ and $\dot{K}_1 = \dot{K}_2$.

A.12 and A.13 then imply that $r_1 \leqslant r_2$ which is a contradiction. Similar arguments may be applied for the interval above $K^*(r_2)$ and consequently the two optimal paths cannot cross in the phase space. The optimal path in the phase space must then move uniformly upwards as the rate of interest decreases and consequently $\partial \dot{K}(t)/\partial r < 0$ and hence $\partial I^*(t)/\partial r < 0$. The result in (ii) follows.

(iii) Apply the same argument as in (ii).

Proposition 4 (p. 34). An imperfectly competitive firm with constant returns in production which faces strictly convex costs of adjustment of the type specified in assumption 6a (p. 34) will exhibit the following types of investment behaviour in response to changes in demand. (i) If the firm is in long-run equilibrium and demand changes unexpectedly then the rate of investment will be such as to shift the capital stock of the firm gradually towards its new equilibrium level with output price and labour input adjusting to close the gap between capacity and demand. (ii) If the firm is in long-run equilibrium and it decides that demand will change at some future date it will anticipate such a change by immediately altering its current level of investment in such a way as to shift the capital stock towards the equilibrium level corresponding to the expected demand change.

Proof. (i) By arguing in precisely the same fashion as we did to derive the necessary conditions for the competitive firm (3.4 and 3.7) we can derive equivalent conditions for the firm facing a downward sloping demand curve, namely

A.14 $$z\{p(t)\}\beta(t) = F\{K(t), L(t)\},$$

A.15 $$M\{p(t)\}F_L\{K(t), L(t)\} = w(t),$$

A.16 $$C'\{I(t)\} = \int\limits_{t}^{\infty} \exp\{-(r+\delta)(s-t)\} \times M\{p(s)\}F_K\{K(s), L(s)\}\, ds - q(t).$$

The notation is standard with $z\{p(t)\}\beta(t)$ as the demand for the firm's output and $M\{p(t)\}$ as the marginal revenue function. A.14 states that output is maintained in equality with demand, A.15 that labour is employed up to the point where its marginal revenue product is equal to the wage and A.16 that the marginal cost of adjustment is equal to the net present value returns on a marginal unit of capital stock. A.14 and A.15 may be solved for $L(t)$ and $p(t)$ in terms of $K(t)$, $w(t)$ and $\beta(t)$ at each point in time and then we may write the marginal revenue product of capital as

$$M(p)F_K(K, L) = M[p\{K(t), \beta(t), w(t)\}]F_K[K(t), L\{K(t), \beta(t), w(t)\}]$$

$$= G\{K(t), \beta(t), w(t)\} \text{ say.}$$

Straightforward differentiation reveals that $G_K < 0$ and A.16 can then be written as

$$\text{A.17} \quad C'\{I(t)\} = \int_t^\infty \exp\{-(r+\delta)(s-t)\} G\{K(s), \beta(s), w(s)\} \, ds - q(t).$$

By taking the time derivative of A.17 and using the definition of I in terms of $\dot{K}$ this may be transformed into the flow condition

$$\text{A.18} \qquad C''(I)\ddot{K} + C''(I)\delta\dot{K} - (r+\delta)C'(I) + G(K, \beta, w) = c$$

where c is the standard cost of capital. Then in a stationary state with constant demand and factor prices the equilibrium capital stock $K^*(\beta)$ must satisfy,

$$\text{A.19} \qquad\qquad G(K^*, \beta, w) - (r+\delta)C'(\delta K^*) = c.$$

Now suppose there is an unexpected jump in demand at time t_0 from β_0 to β_1 say with K^* jumping upwards from $K^*(\beta_0)$ to $K^*(\beta_1)$. Then for $t \geqslant t_0$, $K(t)$ satisfies the differential equation

$$\text{A.20} \qquad C''(I)\ddot{K} + C''(I)\delta\dot{K} - (r+\delta)[C'(I) - C'\{\delta K^*(\beta_1)\}]$$

$$+ G(K, \beta_1, w) - G\{K^*(\beta_1), \beta_1, w\} = 0$$

with $K(t_0) = K^*(\beta_0)$. This follows from A.18 and the definition of $K^*(\beta_1)$. Converting A.20 into a pair of first-order differential equations in K and I gives

$$\text{A.21} \qquad\qquad\qquad \dot{K} = I - \delta K$$

A.22

$$\dot{I} = \frac{(r+\delta)[C'(I) - C'\{\delta K^*(\beta_1)\}] - \{G(K, \beta_1, w) - G(K^*, \beta_1, w)\}}{C''(I)}$$

The optimal path of K is shown with the double-headed arrow in the phase diagram below. It is immediately clear that following the jump in demand investment increases and capital stock moves gradually

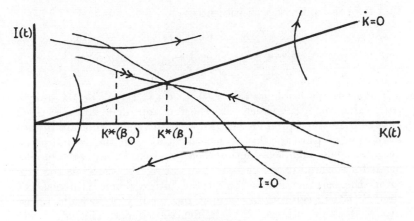

Figure 3.A.2

from $K^*(\beta_0)$ to $K^*(\beta_1)$, though of course it does not reach $K^*(\beta_1)$ in finite time. Also at t_0 there is a jump in the output price which thenceforward only gradually reverts to its original lower level.

This completes the proof of (i).

(ii) Suppose now that at some time $t' < t_0$ the firm expects demand to jump from β_0 to β_1 as before. Again for $t \geqslant t_0$ the optimal path for the firm's capital stock will be given by A.20, and will be described by the double-headed arrow in the phase diagram above. Prior to

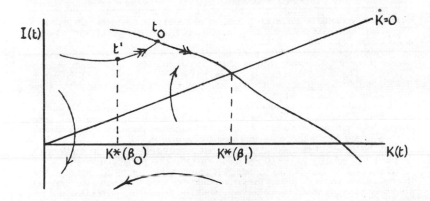

Figure 3.A.3

that time the optimal path will satisfy

A.23 $C''(I)\ddot{K} + C''(I)\delta\dot{K} - (r+\delta)[C'(I) - C'\{\delta K^*(\beta_0)\}]$
$$+ G(K, \beta_0, w) - G\{K^*(\beta_0), \beta_0, w\} = 0$$

with $K(t') = K^*(\beta_0)$.

The actual path followed by $K(t)$ for $t' \leqslant t \leqslant t_0$ will be the unique path satisfying A.23 which hits the final optimal path described above at the appropriate capital stock with the appropriate investment rate at time t_0. This path is illustrated in the second-phase diagram. The complete optimal path is shown by the double-headed arrow and it can be seen that at time t', as soon as the firm forms the certain expectation of the future demand increase at time t_0, it will raise its investment rate and start to build up its capital stock in anticipation of the demand change. This effectively completes the proof of (ii).

Footnotes

[1] These parameters include the rate of interest, the prices of output and capital goods, and the wage rate.

[2] Throughout this chapter we shall assume that adjustment costs are a function of gross investment and nothing else. A large number of other possibilities have been investigated in the literature, notably making them a function of net investment or expressing the costs in output, as opposed to money, terms. As far as the dynamic structure of the investment process is concerned the consequences of all these formulations are more or less the same. The equilibrium possibilities are rather different, however. As we shall see, the assumption of gross investment adjustment costs will imply that a firm with a constant returns to scale technology will be of bounded size, which is not the case with net investment costs, for example. In reality one might expect adjustment costs to be a mixture of many different types, but since the dynamic effects are the major point at issue it seems a perfectly acceptable limitation to consider only the one type.

[3] Strictly speaking the time period under consideration is the infinitesimal period $[t, t+dt]$. The net gain is then $G(t)\,dt$ and the adjustment cost is $C'\{I(t)\}\,dt$. The dt will then cancel to give the formula 3.7 in the text. However, it is preferable for exposition, if not strictly rigorous, to replace the infinitesimal interval by a unit interval.

[4] A solution to this problem which is geared towards empirical work is presented in section 4 of Chapter 11. The capital stock to be 'aimed at' turns out to be a convex combination of all the different 'desired' capital stocks corresponding to the different expected future prices.

[5] The latter is not completely general but simply reflects the strength of the output effect relative to the substitution effect in this particular model.

[6] Eisner and Strotz (1963) pursue this point rather forcefully, arguing that the influences which make one firm in an industry wish to expand (or contract) are likely to apply to all the others and that the firms will realize this and will thus recognize that they are, de facto, facing an upward sloping supply curve for capital goods.

7 This argument was discussed in the text following on from equation 3.7. It is put forward in Arrow (1968, p. 4) and in Leijonhufvud (1968, p. 139, section (2)).

8 Keynes formulates his model in a slightly different way by defining the so-called 'Marginal Efficiency of Capital' which is the rate of discount at which the future returns on the marginal unit of capital have a present value equal to the current price of the marginal unit. The rising supply price is emphasized in Keynes partly because he was interested in more aggregate models.

9 See Keynes (1936, Chapters 11 and 12), and especially the following quote from Chapter 11, 'It is important to understand the dependence of the marginal efficiency of a given stock of capital on changes in expectation, because it is chiefly this dependence which renders the marginal efficiency of capital subject to somewhat violent fluctuations which are the explanations of the trade cycle'.

10 See particularly Eisner and Strotz (1963).

11 Linearity could only be an approximation to the truth since this would give rise to jumps and obviously blocks of capital *cannot* be installed instantaneously. However, it may well be just as easy to install a machine in a week as in a year and a week is to all intents and purposes an instant.

12 A *favourable* parametric change refers to one which raises the equilibrium capital stock.

13 The fixed costs referred to here are clearly independent both of the rate of investment and of the time over which it continues. This does not emerge clearly from Figure 3.3.

14 Except possibly with reference to investment in some types of vehicles which are quickly and easily purchased.

15 In the years 1970–73 inclusive the aggregate acquisitions of plant and machinery in UK manufacturing industry was some £7077·4 million compared with disposals of a mere £286·3 million in the same period. On the other hand, for capital goods with more active second-hand markets, UK aggregate manufacturing industry acquisitions of land, existing buildings and vehicles in the same years comes to £1112·9 million with disposals at £681·7 million. The source is the *UK Census of Production 1973*, Pamphlet PA 1000, Table 2.

Bibliographical Notes—Chapter 3

The first formalization of the notion of strictly convex adjustment costs in relation to the demand for investment goods was presented in Eisner and Strotz (1963), although an analysis of the optimal policy of firms when investment is bounded is given in Arrow (1962). Further analyses of the effects of strictly convex costs of adjustment on the demand for investment using a variety of different models may be found in Lucas (1967a, b), Gould (1968), Treadway (1969, 1970) and Mortenson (1973) (the constant returns model in this chapter is essentially due to Gould). Rothschild (1971), on the other hand, presents an interesting discussion of the possible effects of non-convex costs of adjustment. Theoretical work on delivery lags in a world of certainty is rather rare, as might be imagined, though both Thalberg (1960) and Maccini (1973) treat this topic.

CHAPTER 4

DELIVERY LAGS AND IRREVERSIBLE INVESTMENT DECISIONS

1. Irreversible Investment Decisions

As our analysis of a firm's investment decisions proceeds it is desirable to emphasize more strongly the effects on these decisions of current and expected future changes in the demand for the firm's output. Such a shift in emphasis is indeed more or less obligatory given that both casual observation and current econometric work strongly suggest that these demand changes play an absolutely crucial role in determining the rate of investment. So, whereas in previous chapters both price taking and imperfectly competitive firms were discussed, in the bulk of what follows consideration will be restricted to the latter for it is only in this case that a direct analysis of the effects of demand fluctuation may be readily presented.

In the last chapter we discussed the effects of adjustment costs in the imperfectly competitive case, in particular emphasizing the smoothing effects of these costs when they are strictly convex. Such costs were, however, considered to be somewhat unrealistic, particularly in the direction of increasing capital stock and so, for the purposes of this chapter, we shall assume that they are linear in this direction. As far as the costs of disinvestment are concerned, it was pointed out in the final section that there exists a large number of capital goods in which investment is, to all intents and purposes, an irreversible process and it is these goods that will be considered in this chapter.[1] Again, following the discussion at the end of the previous chapter, a specific time lag will be assumed between the ordering of new capital goods and their installation. To incorporate these new additions into the model, assumptions 6 and 6a of the previous chapters are replaced by

Assumption 6b. (i) There are linear costs of adjustment associated with gross additions to the capital stock. (ii) Gross investment is constrained to be non-negative. (iii) There is a fixed time lag of m time units between the ordering of new capital goods and their productive implementation. Furthermore, new orders cannot be cancelled.

In order to keep the notation simple, the linear costs of adjustment of assumption 6b (i) are simply incorporated into the price of new capital goods, $q(t)$. In a world of certainty, or one where expectations about the future are held with certainty, the importance of the time lag of assumption 6b (iii) is very limited. The reason for this is that new capital goods can simply be ordered m periods before they are required and consequently any investment plan can be carried out exactly as if there were no lag. The lag is only important when expectations prove to be incorrect, in which case the firm must formulate a new production plan based on new expectations but is forced to receive capital goods ordered for the old plan for a further m periods. The really interesting effects of the time lag will only arise when uncertainty is introduced (see Chapters 5 and 6) and consequently in this chapter the main topic of analysis will be the role of irreversibility. The fact that investment decisions are irreversible is clearly going to affect a firm's attitude to the future and indeed the very word 'irreversible' when used to describe decisions suggests the necessity of taking great care to avoid mistakes. A profit-maximizing firm will have to consider the expected profitability of potential new capital goods over the whole of their lifetime if, once purchased, they cannot be resold. A particular worry will be the possibility of a fall in demand at some future date leaving the firm with a lot of expensive new equipment and little demand for the potential product of this new capacity. Clearly any such expectation could induce considerable cuts in current investment programmes which would not occur in a firm which is freely able to unload capital stock whenever it finds itself with an excess. These, and other consequences of the irreversibility of investment decisions will emerge very clearly from the formal model which we now discuss.

Consider the production and investment plan of an imperfectly competitive firm facing a known downward sloping demand curve for its product which is expected to shift in some known manner in the future. It has constant returns to scale (assumption 3a, p. 17) and all its investment decisions are irreversible (in fact assumption 6b holds). Formally its plan will be the solution to the following maximization problem.

4.1 Maximize $\displaystyle\int_0^\infty \exp\{-R(t)\}\,[p(t)F\{K(t),\,L(t)\}-w(t)L(t)-q(t)I(t)]\,\mathrm{d}t$

4.2 subject to $z\{p(t)\}\beta(t)=F\{K(t),\,L(t)\}$,

4.3 $$\dot{K}(t) = I(t) - \delta K(t),$$

4.4 $$I(t) > 0,$$

4.5 $$K(t) \text{ given for all } t < m.$$

4.1, 4.2, 4.3 is precisely the problem discussed in the final section of Chapter 2. 4.1, is the present value of the firm, 4.2 constrains the output of the firm to be equal to the demand for its product and 4.3 is the usual equation of capital accumulation. This problem has the standard solution that at each point in time the marginal revenue products of capital and labour are equated to the costs of capital and labour respectively (equations 2.17 and 2.18). In addition we now have the constraint that gross investment cannot be negative (4.4) and the fact that since capital stock must be ordered m periods in advance, there will be a predetermined flow of new capital goods accruing to the firm up until time m (4.5). In order to avoid complications, it will be assumed that this flow is 'correct', that is to say, during the period from time $-m$ to time zero, expectations about demand during the period from time zero to time m were precisely the same then as they are now. The firm has not revised its expectations during the last m periods.

The question now arises as to the difference which the irreversibility constraint on investment will make to the firm's plans. Suppose that equating the marginal revenue products of capital and labour to their respective costs yields an investment plan on which gross investment is never negative. Such a result could arise if, for example, demand is always growing. Then it is clear that this plan would also be optimal for the firm with irreversible investment, for the plan solves the problems 4.1 to 4.3 and also satisfies the constraint 4.4.

In such a situation the irreversibility constraint would be of no significance since it would never 'bite', that is the firm would never be constrained by it. Consequently it is plain that the irreversibility constraint will only have important consequences for the firm in a situation where, if it were not constrained, it would divest itself of some of its capital stock. It may be imagined that this is only likely to occur in cases where the demand for its product is falling at a faster rate than its capital stock is depreciating and a glance at equation 2.19 reveals that this is indeed the case, at least if factor prices remain fixed.

Turning now to a more rigorous analysis, we may divide the firm's optimal plan into two distinct phases, those periods where the irreversibility constraint does not bite and investment is positive (phase I) and those periods where the firm is constrained and gross investment is zero (phase II). From the analysis of Chapter 2, we know that when gross investment is positive, the firm must equate factor marginal revenue products to factor costs and consequently during such periods we have:

Phase I : $I(t) > 0$

Necessary conditions

4.6 $$z\{p(t)\}\beta(t) = F\{K(t), L(t)\}$$

4.7 $$M\{p(t)\} \frac{\partial F\{K(t), L(t)\}}{\partial L(t)} = w(t)$$

4.8 $$M\{p(t)\} \frac{\partial F\{K(t), L(t)\}}{\partial K(t)} = c(t)$$

The conditions which must be satisfied in the periods when investment is zero are a little less straightforward. It is clear, however, that output must still be equal to demand and furthermore since there are no constraints on the adjustment of labour input, the marginal revenue product of labout must still be maintained in equality with the wage rate. It is the capital stock condition which is the difficult one and here we shall proceed in a number of stages. First consider the net gain to the firm arising from the delivery of one extra unit of capital stock at time τ. This is given in equation A.16 of the Appendix to Chapter 3 as

4.9 $$G(\tau) = \int_{\tau}^{\infty} \exp\{-(\delta+r)(t-\tau)\} M\{p(t)\} \frac{\partial F}{\partial K}\{K(t), L(t)\} \, dt - q(\tau),$$

where the interest rate is expected to remain constant over time. During a zero investment period, it is plain that $G(\tau)$ cannot be positive otherwise the firm would wish to increase its capital stock. Suppose then that $G(\tau)$ is negative. This would imply that the firm would find it profitable to divest itself of some capital stock. But, of course, it is not in a position to do so because of the non-negativity constraint on investment. Thus during a zero investment period $G(\tau)$ may be negative and in fact in all probability is negative, although it could be zero. Furthermore, it is clear that during the positive investment periods $G(\tau)$ is always zero, otherwise the firm could make additional profits by moving the investment rate up (down) if $G(\tau)$ is positive (negative). Consequently, if we have a zero investment period from time n_0 to time n_1, then, since n_0 and n_1 themselves are the end and beginning respectively of positive investment periods, we have

4.10 $G(n_0) = 0 : G(\tau) \leqslant 0,\ n_0 \leqslant \tau \leqslant n_1 : G(n_1) = 0,$

and these imply

4.11   (a) $G(n_0) - G(\tau) \geqslant 0,\ n_0 \leqslant \tau \leqslant n_1,$

        (b) $G(n_0) - G(n_1) = 0.$

Since $G(\tau)$ may be rewritten in the following equivalent form,

$$G(\tau) = \int\limits_{\tau}^{\infty} \exp\left\{-(\delta+r)(t-\tau)\right\}\left[M\{p(t)\}\frac{\partial F}{\partial K}\{K(t),\ L(t)\}\right.$$
$$\left. -q(t)(r+\delta-\dot{q}/q)\right]\,dt$$
$$= \int\limits_{\tau}^{\infty} \exp\left\{-(\delta+r)(t-\tau)\right\}\left\{M\cdot\frac{\partial F}{\partial K}-c(t)\right\}\,dt,$$

where $c(t)$ is the cost of capital; 4.10 and 4.11 imply that the following conditions must hold on a zero investment interval.

Phase II : $I(t) = 0$ from n_0 to n_1

Necessary conditions

4.12   (a) $\displaystyle\int\limits_{n_0}^{\tau} \exp\left\{-(\delta+r)t\right\}\left(M\cdot\frac{\partial F}{\partial K}-c\right)\,dt \geqslant 0,\ n_0 \leqslant \tau \leqslant n_1$

      (b) $\displaystyle\int\limits_{n_0}^{n_1} \exp\left\{-(\delta+r)t\right\}\left(M\cdot\frac{\partial F}{\partial K}-c\right)\,dt = 0,$

and in addition the two conditions 4.6, 4.7 as before.

As they stand the above conditions appear to be somewhat obscure to say the least. It is, however, possible to use them in a very straightforward fashion. This is done in the next section.

2. The Optimal Investment Path Over a Demand Cycle

Suppose that the firm expects future demand to follow a single cycle before moving upwards on some continuous trend. Then it expects the function $\beta(t)$, which measures the position of the demand

curve (see 4.2), to move on a path of the type illustrated in Figure
4.1. Suppose furthermore that factor prices and the interest rate
are expected to remain constant. Then the firm will plan to have a
zero investment interval somewhere on this cycle if the slump in
demand between t_0 and t_1 is steep enough. More specifically, since
factor prices remain constant the investment rate on a positive

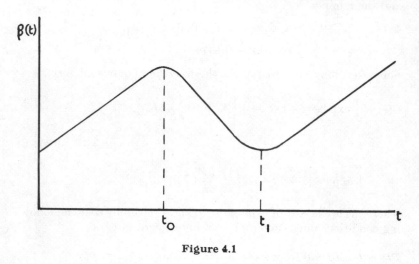

Figure 4.1

investment interval satisfies the following simplified version of
equation 2.19, namely

4.13 $$\frac{I}{K} = \dot{\beta}/\beta + \delta.$$

If during the slump the rate of decline in demand is greater than
the rate of depreciation of the capital stock, then $\dot{\beta}/\beta + \delta < 0$ and
consequently gross investment is negative. This is not allowed by
the constraint and therefore a zero investment interval must occur
somewhere around this time.

The problem then remains: how can we use the conditions 4.12
to determine precisely the length and position of this interval? We
know that the demand–supply equality 4.6 and the labour productivity condition 4.7 must hold throughout and from these two
conditions it is possible to derive (see Appendix, proposition 1) the
following equation for the rate of change of the marginal revenue

product of capital (MRPC), namely

$$4.14 \quad \frac{d}{dt} \log \left(M \cdot \frac{\partial F}{\partial K} \right) = \{ \dot{\beta}/\beta - \dot{K}/K + (1 - \epsilon_k)(\sigma + \epsilon_M) \dot{w}/w \}$$
$$\times \{ \sigma(1 - \epsilon_k) + | \epsilon_M | \epsilon_k \}^{-1}$$
$$= (\dot{\beta}/\beta - \dot{K}/K) \{ \sigma(1 - \epsilon_k) + | \epsilon_M | \epsilon_k \}^{-1}$$

if w is constant

$$= \left(\dot{\beta}/\beta + \delta - \frac{I}{K} \right) \{ \sigma(1 - \epsilon_k) + | \epsilon_M | \epsilon_k \}^{-1}$$

since $\dot{K} = I - \delta K$ as usual.

Note that as before σ is the elasticity of substitution, ϵ_k is the elasticity of output/unit labour with respect to capital/unit labour and ϵ_M is the elasticity of output with respect to marginal revenue.

If the zero investment interval lasts from n_0 to n_1, we know that at n_0 the MRPC is equal to the cost of capital and 4.12(a) shows that

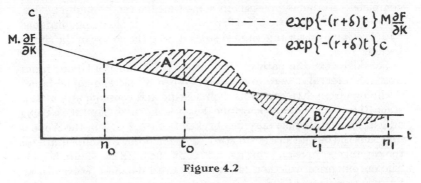

Figure 4.2

in the vicinity of n_0 the MRPC must rise above the cost of capital in order to make the integral positive. Consequently, at the start of the zero investment interval, $d/dt \log (M \cdot \partial F / \partial K) > 0$ and from 4.14, it follows that $\dot{\beta}/\beta + \delta > 0$, that is, demand is not falling faster than the rate of depreciation at this time. A similar argument shows this to be so at the end of the zero investment period as well and hence if, for example, demand is always falling faster than the rate of depreciation during the slump period t_0 to t_1, the above arguments immediately reveal that the period n_0 to n_1, must contain it, that is $n_0 < t_0 < t_1 < n_1$. This pattern can be illustrated on a graph of the MRPC and the cost of capital where both are discounted by the exponent $\exp \{ -(\delta + r)t \}$ and this is shown in Figure 4.2.

Outside the zero investment interval the two nelis (plain for capital cost and dashed for MRPC) coincide. Inside the interval the MRPC line first rises above the cost of capital and then, when demand starts to decline, it falls below the cost of capital rising back up to it when demand starts picking up again. The crucial point to note is that since the areas between the two graphs represent the integrals of 4.12 the position of n_0 is then arranged so as to make area A equal to area B, thus satisfying the condition 4.12(b). Note that 4.12(a) is then satisfied automatically since the positive area A (positive integral) comes first and the negative area B (negative integral) comes second. Any partial integral starting from n_0 must therefore contain a greater positive part than negative part and will hence be positive.

To summarize, it has been shown that if a firm is investing in capital goods which cannot be resold second-hand it must try to predict future slumps in demand since its optimal policy involves a complete cessation of investment some time before the slump begins. The reason for this is that the firm will wish to avoid being burdened with excessive unsaleable capital stock during the course of the slump period.

Consider next the path of the output price and the labour input over the interval of zero investment. When it starts, demand is not declining faster than capital is depreciating and consequently at this stage there is a capital shortage because no new capital is being added. This implies, as may be checked from A.2, A.3 in the Appendix, that the output price will start to rise in order to compensate for the capital shortage and this rise will continue until the slump begins. The output price will then fall steadily until demand returns to an upward trend at which point it turns up again. Again from A.2, A.3 it is easily seen that the capital/labour ratio moves in opposition to the output price. This means that during the slump itself the capital/labour ratio is rising and, since capital is depreciating, this clearly implies a falling labour input. The path of the labour input on the remainder of the interval is indeterminate since a falling capital/labour ratio is concomitant with either a rising or a falling labour input if the capital input is itself declining. In general, during the zero investment periods it is the output price which is used by the firm to adjust to demand variations with some help from the labour input. This is in stark contrast to the positive investment periods when the output price remains totally unaffected by demand variations.

The next matter of some interest concerns those expectational factors which influence the length of time which elapses between the cessation of investment and the start of the slump. Economic intuition would indicate that the duration of this period would depend on the expected length and depth of the slump, with the duration increasing as the expected slump becomes both longer and deeper. This is indeed the case as may be illustrated from Figure 4.2. If the slump is deeper, the decline in demand and therefore the decline in the MRPC is steeper (see equation 4.14) and consequently the dotted line of Figure 4.2 declines more steeply between t_0 and t_1. The consequence of this is to increase area B and decrease area A in the figure. The only way to restore equality between these areas is to move n_0 backwards in time, for this will provide an offsetting increase in area A and decrease in area B. Consequently the zero investment interval is increased. A precisely similar argument may be used to show that a lengthening of the slump, causing t_1 to move forward in time, increases area B and consequently again lengthens the optimal zero investment period. In fact it is possible to derive a fairly sharp result for a firm with a fixed coefficients technology facing a constant elasticity demand curve, namely that the length of time between the start of the zero investment interval and the start of the slump is given by the following expression.

4.15 $$t_0 - n_0 \approx \tfrac{1}{2} \left(\frac{\mu - \delta}{\delta + \gamma} \right) (t_1 - t_0)$$

where γ is the trend rate of growth of demand and μ is the rate of decline during the slump. Notice that since this rate of decline is greater than the rate of depreciation, $\mu > \delta$ and consequently the expression is positive. The positive relationship between the period of zero investment before the slump and the slump's steepness (μ) and length ($t_1 - t_0$) is clearly revealed.[2]

An important point to note is that the existence of the irreversibility constraint, as in the case of general adjustment costs, implies that changes in *expectations* about *future* levels of demand or other parameters may well effect current investment. Some examples were provided in the previous chapter but now the problem is complicated by the existence of the delivery lag because investment will follow the old plan for m time periods after the change in expectations. Consider the following example. The firm faces a slow increase in demand which it expects to be maintained. Then something happens to change the firm's predictions and it now expects a fairly serious slump in the near future. The firm would like to cease investing immediately but it is forced to accept the new capital goods from its previous orders for a further m periods. Of course it ceases to put in new orders as soon as its expectations change and there is a zero investment period after the m period lag has elapsed. If the firm has had no indication of the coming slump and does not recognize its existence until demand actually starts to turn down, then it could well be that the zero investment interval would not occur until the slump is over and demand has started to increase again. The firm would therefore receive new investment goods during the slump and cease investment during the subsequent boom. In contrast a firm with perfect foresight would always have its zero investment periods during slumps. This leads to a tentative argument that firms with imperfect forecasting and long lags are good for economic stability because such firms would still be investing in slump periods whereas firms with perfect foresight would never invest in a slump period thereby exacerbating the slump.[3]

3. Expected Price Changes

Another interesting example of the way in which changes in expectations induce adjustments to current investment plans is provided by the effects of future changes in the price of capital goods. Fairly dramatic changes in capital goods prices may occur because of tariff and tax changes or because of technical progress and these may have far-reaching effects if they are expected some time in advance. Suppose, for example, that the firm has good reason to believe that at some future date there will be a fairly sharp decline in the price of capital goods. Then we know that a firm that is not constrained in any way will sell capital goods just before the decline in price and repurchase them when the price has fallen. But the lack of a second-hand market prevents this from happening in the present case and one might therefore expect that the firm would cease buying capital goods for some period before the fall in price in order to acquire its new capital requirements more cheaply, albeit at a later date. That this will in fact be so can be illustrated by reverting to our simple diagram. Assuming capital goods prices are expected to decline quite sharply over the period from t_0 to t_1 then the consequent paths of the capital goods price, the cost of capital (see Chapter 2, Figure 2.1) and the MRPC are as shown in Figure 4.3.

The initial point of the zero investment period n_0 is adjusted so as to make area A = area B as before. Note also that a sharper decline

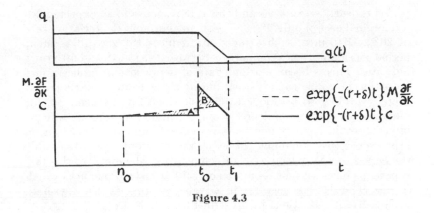

Figure 4.3

in the price of capital goods will raise the peak in the cost of capital, enlarge area B and therefore move the optimal position of n_0 backwards in time. Therefore the period during which investment ceases before the decline in price grows larger as the decline in price gets bigger; hardly an unexpected result. To give some idea of orders of magnitude, the following table gives a list of values of a *lower bound* on the zero investment period $(t_1 - n_0)$ for a variety of parameter values and for a fixed coefficients technology.[4]

Elasticity of demand	Rate of depreciation	Rate of interest	Rate of growth of demand	Decline in marginal cost[a]	Lower bound on $(t_1 - n_0)$ in years
−2·0	0·2	0·10	0	0·90	0·89
−1·5	0·2	0·10	0	0·90	0·87
−5·0	0·2	0·10	0	0·90	1·12
−2·0	0·2	0·05	0	0·90	1·00
−2·0	0·1	0·10	0	0·90	1·45
−2·0	0·2	0·10	0·1	0·90	0·77
−2·0	0·2	0·10	0	0·95	0·46

[a] The decline in marginal cost is the proportionate decline brought about by the fall in the capital goods price.

The first point to note is that, if the technology is not of the fixed coefficients type, the zero investment period can only increase because the firm copes more easily with capital shortages by substituting labour. The second point of interest is that the periods of time involved are by no means insubstantial. The lowest zero investment period is nearly six months and this is in response to an expected fall in marginal cost of only 5% and with an enormous depreciation rate of 20%. Of course, such a high rate reduces the zero investment period considerably as a comparison between the fourth and fifth rows indicates. This is because a high rate of depreciation implies a fast reduction in usable capital stock during the zero investment period thereby leading to a serious capital shortage for the firm. So, for more reasonable rates of depreciation, the minimum zero investment interval would be nine months in response to an expected 5% drop in marginal cost. Doubling the expected fall would roughly double the period to a very lengthy eighteen months. The moral of this tale is perhaps for governments not to reveal tax or tariff changes which reduce capital costs very far in advance if, that is, they wish to avoid current reductions in investment expenditures.

4. The Effects of the Delivery Lag

In this section we look at a very simple example of how the delivery lag effects the behaviour of the firm in response to unexpected changes in demand. Consider a firm which is facing static demand conditions which it expects to continue indefinitely. At time t_0 demand suddenly starts to increase. The firm has now to reformulate its expectations and in particular it must attempt to determine whether it expects demand to continue increasing, to flatten out at some higher level or to revert to its original level. These three possibilities are illustrated in Figure 4.4 and are labelled (a), (b) and (c) respectively.

If the firm decides that demand will follow the paths (a) or (b) it will order a block of capital to arrive at $t_0 + m$ which is large enough to move it back on to the appropriate optimal path. However, if it expects demand to follow path (c), then, since the level of demand is expected to revert to its current level *within* the period of the delivery lag, the firm will simply continue ordering at the same rate, thereby maintaining the existing capital stock. So, in spite of the minor boom in demand and the consequent temporary rise in 'desired' capital stock, the firm maintains an ordering policy identical to that which it would have followed if the temporary boom had not occurred. Of course this behaviour is a result of the combination of both a temporary unexpected boom and a long delivery lag. If either of these two elements, the unexpectedness or the delivery lag, were absent then the firm would react to the temporary boom with an increase in capital stock and investment. The implication of this analysis is to reveal that there are situations where an increase in 'desired' capital stock may not be accompanied by any increase in new investment orders by the firm. This is most likely to occur with capital goods that take a long time either to obtain or install and in response to changes of a temporary nature.

To sum up, the lack of second-hand markets for many capital goods has a strong influence on the firm's investment decisions. As with adjustment costs in general, firms are forced to look to the

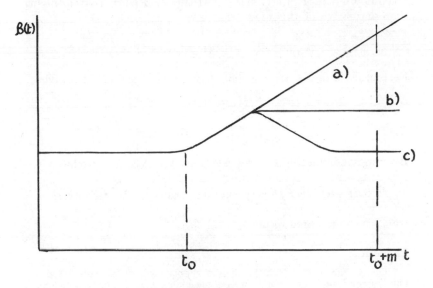

Figure 4.4

future and changes in expectations may seriously affect current decisions. The delivery lag affects the firm's response to unexpected events and the firm must decide whether current changes are of a permanent or merely temporary nature, in order to follow a correct ordering policy. However, the more subtle effects of a long delivery lag will only occur if a firm does not hold its expectations with certainty. Consequently in the following two chapters we shall discuss the whole range of problems which arise in considering investment decisions under uncertainty, in particular with reference to lags and the timing of decisions.

Appendix

Proposition 1 (p. 56). The conditions 4.6 and 4.7 imply that the rate of change of the marginal revenue product of capital satisfies

$$\frac{d}{dt} \log \left(M \cdot \frac{\partial F}{\partial K} \right) = \{\dot{\beta}/\beta - \dot{K}/K + (1 - \epsilon_k)(\sigma + \epsilon_M)\dot{w}/w\}$$
$$\{\sigma(1 - \epsilon_k) + |\epsilon_M| \epsilon_k\}^{-1}.$$

Proof. Since the firm has constant returns to scale, the marginal revenue product of capital may be written as $Mf'(k)$. Taking the log time derivative of this expression gives

A.1 $$\qquad \sigma \frac{d}{dt} \log Mf' = \frac{\sigma}{\epsilon_M} \epsilon \dot{p}/p + (\epsilon_k - 1)\dot{k}/k$$

Furthermore, taking the log time derivatives of 4.6 and 4.7 gives

A.2 $$\qquad \epsilon \dot{p}/p = \dot{K}/K + \dot{k}/k(\epsilon_k - 1) - \dot{\beta}/\beta,$$

A.3 $$\qquad \frac{\sigma}{\epsilon_M} \epsilon \dot{p}/p + \epsilon_k \dot{k}/k = \sigma \dot{w}/w.$$

By simply eliminating $\dot{k}/k$ and $\dot{p}/p$ from A.1, A.2, A.3, we have

$$\frac{d}{dt} \log Mf' = \{\dot{\beta}/\beta - \dot{K}/K + (1 - \epsilon_k)(\sigma + \epsilon_M)\dot{w}/w\}\{\sigma(1 - \epsilon_k) + |\epsilon_M| \epsilon_k\}^{-1}$$

which is the required result.

Footnotes

[1] The only goods for which this does not apply are vehicles, certain types of buildings and some very simple kinds of machinery, such as heavy-duty sewing machines.

[2] The proof of this result is too long to be usefully presented here, even in the appendix. Full details may be found in Nickell (1974a, pp. 8–11).

[3] There are many examples in economics of the destabilizing effects of perfect foresight. See for example Shell and Stiglitz (1967).

[4] The results are taken from Nickell (1974a, p. 12).

Bibliographical Notes—Chapter 4

The asymmetry between expansion and contraction of capital stock is one of the reasons underlying the reformulation of the accelerator model presented in Chenery (1952). A more formal analysis of the problems associated with the imposition of a strict irreversibility constraint on investment may be found in Arrow (1968) and this work is extended in Martirena-Martel (1971) and Nickell (1974a). The model discussed in this chapter is essentially that considered in Nickell (1974b).

CHAPTER 5

THE PROBLEM OF UNCERTAINTY

1. The Objective of the Firm in an Uncertain Environment

The stage in our analysis has now been reached where we must drop the assumption of certainty or certain expectations (assumption 2, p. 7) and try to discover how the firm's uncertainty about future events will affect its current investment decisions. This leads immediately to one particular problem which has not, as yet, been given a satisfactory solution, namely how to 'define the objective function of the firm in an uncertain world.[1] Corresponding to any investment plan, the firm receives a sequence of net income returns which are not known with certainty and are consequently random variables. The problem of defining the firm's objective function is essentially the problem of determining how it chooses the 'best' from a large number of different random income streams. It was shown in Chapter 2 that when future income streams are known with certainty, a perfect capital market ensures that the owners of the firm will always agree to choose the income stream with the highest present value, whatever their individual consumption preferences. Unfortunately, in the case of uncertain income streams, it is no longer possible to use the present value concept to separate the consumption and investment decisions. In other words, different individuals could prefer different investment plans solely because they have different consumption preferences.

To illustrate how this can happen, it is worth following through a simple example. Suppose there are two investment possibilities, labelled I and II, which yield the following random net returns for two periods.

Investment plan I yields:　　10, 10 with probability $\frac{1}{2}$,
　　　　　　　　　　　　　　20, 20 with probability $\frac{1}{2}$.
Investment plan II yields:　　15, 15 with probability 1.

The second plan therefore yields certain returns in both periods which are in fact equal to the expected (average) returns of the first plan. Now consider an individual with a utility function of consumption $U(c_1, c_2)$, where c_i is his consumption in period i, who is confronted with this investment choice. We shall assume that he acts in accordance with the standard rules of individual decision making under uncertainty and therefore chooses that investment plan which yields the higher expected utility of consumption.[2] If he chooses plan I and this plan turns out to yield the returns (10, 10), he will choose his consumption to solve the problem

5.1 $\max U(c_1, c_2)$

subject to

5.2 $$c_1 + \frac{c_2}{1+r} = 10 + \frac{10}{1+r}.$$

Notice that, once the plan yields a return of 10 in the first period, he can be certain that it will also yield 10 in the second period and consequently he can produce his optimal consumption plan by maximizing utility, subject to the constraint that the present value of consumption is equal to the known present value of income. Let the optimal consumption plan (the solution to 5.1, 5.2) be given by $c_1(10)$, $c_2(10)$. If, on the other hand, plan I happens to yield the returns (20, 20) then his consumption will be $c_1(20)$, $c_2(20)$ which solve the problem 5.1, 5.2 with 20 replacing 10. Then his *expected* utility of consumption, if plan I is chosen, is given by the sum of the separate maximum utilities for each outcome multiplied by their respective probabilities. Hence we have,

Expected utility for plan I,

5.3 $\{EU(\mathrm{I})\} = \frac{1}{2}U\{c_1(10), c_2(10)\} + \frac{1}{2}U\{c_1(20), c_2(20)\}.$

If plan II is chosen there is no problem because it yields a certain return and the optimal consumption plan will simply be $c_1(15)$, $c_2(15)$ in our standard notation. Thus the expected utility for plan II (which is the same as the actual utility) is simply given by,

5.4 $EU(\mathrm{II}) = U\{c_1(15), c_2(15)\}.$

So we can write down the individual's investment criterion as follows:

If $\frac{1}{2}U(c_1(10), c_2(10)) + \frac{1}{2}U(c_1(20), c_2(20)) > U(c_1(15), c_2(15))$ *then choose plan I. Otherwise choose plan II.*

To show how this criterion depends crucially on the form of the utility function, consider the following examples. Suppose U has the form $\log c_1 + \log c_2$. Then simple algebra reveals that $EU(\text{I}) = \log \{50(2+r)^2/(1+r)\}$ and $EU(\text{II}) = \log \{225(2+r)^2/4(1+r)\}$ and consequently plan II will be chosen. If, however, U has the form $c_1^2 + c_2^2$ then $EU(\text{II}) = 0{\cdot}9EU(\text{I})$ and thus plan I is chosen. We have thus confirmed that optimal investment decisions under uncertainty are not independent of the consumption preferences of the individuals who will benefit from such decisions, in particular the owners of firms.

One further point can also be illustrated on the basis of this example. Note that the expected net present values of the returns to the two investment plans are the same. For plan I, the expected net present value is $\frac{1}{2}\{10 + 10/(1+r)\} + \frac{1}{2}\{20 + 20/(1+r)\} = 15 + 15/(1+r)$ which is the expected net present value of plan II. Yet there was no question of the decision makers in the example being indifferent between the two plans. Consequently it is not possible, in general, to use the maximization of expected present value as a criterion for investment decisions.

Before considering exactly what can be done to provide some operational decision-making mechanism for firms in an uncertain world, it is worth discussing briefly the subject of attitudes towards risk. It may be noted that, in the example above, the individual with the logarithmic utility function preferred the investment plan with the certain outcome and conversely the individual with the squared utility function preferred the uncertain investment plan in spite of its having the same *expected* outcome as the certain one. Consider the logarithmic case and take just the first element, namely $\log c_1$. In Figure 5.1, we exhibit the graph of $\log c_1$ and for comparison we also plot the graph of the first element of the other utility function, that is c_1^2

It can be seen that the former function is bowed downward (strictly concave) and the latter is bowed upwards (strictly convex). Suppose that individuals with these two utility functions are asked to make a single period choice between (i) a gamble yielding c with probability $\frac{1}{2}$ and $\bar{c}$ with probability $\frac{1}{2}$; (ii) the certainty of the average outcome $(c+\bar{c})/2$. In both diagrams it is readily seen that AB represents the expected utility of the gamble (i) (i.e. $\frac{1}{2}U(c) + \frac{1}{2}U(\bar{c})$) and AC represents the (expected) utility of the certain average (ii) i.e. $U((c+\bar{c})/2)$.

So, as before, the choices differ with utility functions, the individual with the strictly concave utility function choosing the certain average (ii) and vice versa. It is also clear from the diagram that these choices would have been made for *any* strictly concave or strictly convex functions respectively. In fact, we can enunciate a general result that an individual whose utility function is strictly concave in consumption will always prefer the certainty of the average outcome (expected value) of a gamble to the uncertain gamble itself. Furthermore, the man with the strictly convex utility function always prefers the reverse. Not unsurprisingly the former kind of individual is referred to as risk averse and the latter as risk loving and the correspondence between risk aversion (risk loving) and strict

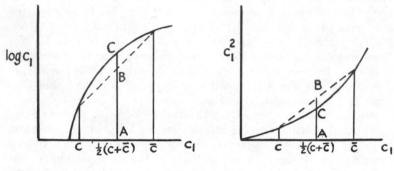

Figure 5.1

concavity (convexity) of utility functions is exact. The intuition behind all this is quite clear. Strict concavity of the utility function implies, as can be seen from the Figure 5.1, that as the individual receives more and more consumption goods, the utility increments accruing become smaller and smaller. Consequently, starting from any point, the increase in utility from the receipt of some additional quantity of consumption goods is smaller than the decrease in utility from the loss of precisely the same quantity. So, if the individual is confronted with the choice between remaining where he is or accepting an equiprobable chance of winning or losing a given amount, he will choose to remain where he is because more utility is lost if he loses the gamble than is gained if he wins it. A precisely similar argument may be used to explain the connection between risk-loving behaviour and strict convexity of utility. However, as might be imagined, in our discussions of firm behaviour it will usually be risk-averse behaviour that comes under scrutiny and this is generally considered to be the more normal case.[3]

Returning now to the mainstream of the discussion on the firm's objective under uncertainty, there are basically two possibilities available. The first is simply to assign arbitrarily some plausible objective to the firm possibly making use of the concept of risk aversion. The second is to make some probably implausible assumptions and use them to derive an objective for the firm from the underlying expected utility maximizing behaviour of the firm's owners. We start by exploring the first possibility in the context of a single period static model of the firm. We might assume that the firm maximizes expected profit and is therefore neither risk averse nor risk loving but risk neutral. The implication of this is that the firm would be indifferent between a certain profit of 100 and a gamble with a 50% chance of a profit of 300 and a 50% chance of a loss of 100. It may be argued that the owners of firms have a strong preference against bankruptcy and that, using the above example, the 50% chance of making an extra 200 profit would not compensate for the 50% chance of going bankrupt with 100 loss. The certain profit would therefore be preferred to the gamble and the firm would exhibit risk-averse behaviour.[4] This would be an argument in favour of assuming that firms maximize the expected value of some utility function of profits where the utility function is increasing in profits, but at a decreasing rate, that is, it is strictly concave. So if π is the profit, firms maximize $EU(\pi)$ where $U' > 0$, $U'' < 0$. Note that this formulation is consistent with the certainty case in the sense that maximizing $U(\pi)$ where U is increasing, yields precisely the same results as simply maximizing profits, π. In the remainder of this study some use will be made of this type of objective function but it is very difficult to extend to a dynamic formulation. It could be argued that the appropriate dynamic equivalent is for the firm to maximize the expectation of some concave utility function of present value. Unfortunately, as this objective is more or less impossible to use analytically, little can be done along these lines.[5]

A dynamic model of the firm is clearly most important for the present purpose since investment decisions are essentially intertemporal and consequently we must try to find some plausible intertemporal objective function. Following the path indicated by the second of the two possibilities mentioned above, we shall use some rather strong assumptions to derive a simple operational criterion. We shall couch the argument in terms of a single period for the sake of simplicity but it may easily be extended to many periods. Suppose there are a very large number of firms, each of which produces some profit of uncertain size. Furthermore, suppose that the distribution of profits is the same for every firm, although they are statistically independent. Assuming, for ease of exposition, that each firm distributes its profits entirely to shareholders because it operates for only a single period, the resulting distribution of returns on shares is the same for all shares although, of course, the distributions are independent if the shares are from different firms. This leads to all shares having the same price since they are indistinguishable. So we have a world where the random return on each share has the same mean, standard deviation, etc., but there is no correlation between the returns yielded by shares in different firms.

If an individual has a certain amount of wealth to invest in shares and if he is *risk averse*, he will clearly spread his investment over a large number of different shares, for all shares have the same mean return. By spreading his purchases he will reduce the variability of his total return, which is precisely the aim of such an individual.[6] In fact, he will buy equal numbers of all the different shares, thus getting the maximum spread and thereby the minimum variability. Suppose he has enough money to purchase w of each different type of share and there are n different types. Then what kind of total return can he look forward to from his stock market investment? Consider a group of n shares consisting of one of each of the n different types. Some will eventually yield more than the mean return and some will yield less. But since the returns on all of them are independent then, if n is a very large number, the average return across the whole group will have a very high probability of being very close to the common mean return on each individual share. Consequently for a very large value of n each individual is almost certain to receive on his investment an amount equal to the mean return times wn, his total number of shares. In other words, the outcome for each individual is almost certain. Consequently each and every individual can agree that the firm should choose an investment policy which maximizes the mean return on its shares and, since each firm has a fixed number of shares, this is equivalent to maximizing the mean profit. Thus under these circumstances, firms should maximize expected profits or, in a dynamic context, expected present value.[7]

This is rather an interesting result and it is important to realize that it does not depend crucially on all the assumptions. The firms may be of different sizes with different numbers of shares; this will have little impact. The important point is that there should exist a very *large* number of firms whose profits are more or less *uncorrelated* in any period. This will enable owners (i.e. investors), by means of spreading their investments, to reduce the variability of the return from their portfolio to a very low level in spite of the possibility of considerable variations in the profits of any particular firm. Consequently each individual will be interested in obtaining the highest possible mean return on his portfolio since the variance about this mean is negligible, and this is achieved by expected profit maximization on the part of firms. Now there are two very strong objections to all this. First, industry in advanced industrialized countries is very highly concentrated, whence a large proportion of total profit is produced by rather a small number of companies. Second, the profits of many companies, although they are random, are often highly correlated, moving up and down together over the trade cycle and in response to other common external events. These two objections together are enough to make the expected present value maximization assumption extremely dubious.

The question then arises as to whether we can do any better and derive a more satisfactory objective. The answer is certainly in the affirmative and in Chapter 8 we shall develop a more sophisticated model of the firm and its financial environment which will enable us to go a great deal further. Unfortunately, however, it will not allow us to derive an operational *intertemporal* objective function for any realistic specifications of uncertainty (see Chapter 8, section 3, for what is possible). So, in this and the following chapter we shall make do with what we have got, for in order to look at how uncertainty affects investment decisions we need to assume a simple operational objective function for the firm. It is arguable, however, that even if we take the most naive option and assume expected present value maximization, we shall not arrive at particularly misleading results. The impact of uncertainty on a firm's investment decisions can be (somewhat artificially) separated into two aspects—the effect of uncertainty about various future parameters on the *expected* returns of the firm and its influence on the rate at which these returns are to be discounted (this influence arises because of risk aversion on the part of the firm or its owners). If expected present value maximization is assumed, the second of these aspects is being ignored, although when we assume that the firm has a risk-averse utility function we are crudely trying to take account of it. But it is the first aspect that is really important when it comes to discerning the *qualitative*

effects of future expectations on investment decisions in the presence
of lags, adjustment costs and the like. In the light of this, it is clear
that, for present purposes, expected present value maximization is
not such a bad assumption particularly if one supposes that the rate
of interest which is utilized has been adjusted for risk (see Chapter 8,
p. 159, for a further discussion of this point).

2. Some Illustrative Examples of the Effects of Uncertainty on Investment Decisions

As should be clear by now, the analytical study of investment
decisions under uncertainty is by no means such a straightforward
problem as when expectations are held with certainty. For this
reason it is undesirable to take a monolithic approach and derive all
the results from a fully developed dynamic model of the firm, as was
done in previous chapters. Instead we consider a series of relatively
simple models, each of which illustrates some specific effect of uncertainty, and in this way try to build a fairly complete picture. To
start, we shall discuss a very crude model, simply to give the feel of
this type of analysis.

Example 5a. A firm faces a fixed selling price, p, for its output, a
fixed wage cost per unit of output, w, and a fixed cost of hiring
capacity, c per period, where one unit of capacity produces one unit
of output. At the beginning of the period the firm must determine
how much capacity to hire, and this amount is then fixed for the
period. During the period the demand for the firm's product is a
random variable $\tilde{x}$ which has a density function $f(\tilde{x})$.[8] A typical
example of a reasonable density function under these circumstances
is given in Figure 5.2.

In the figure a and b are the minimum and maximum conceivable
demands respectively and $\hat{x}$ is the most likely demand. Note that,
in the certainty case with demand x, the problem is trivial since the
firm will simply hire capacity x and make a profit $(p-w-c)x$. To
give the problem some substance, we assume $p-w-c>0$, otherwise
nothing would ever be produced. Now let y be the capacity chosen
and suppose it is chosen to maximize the expected profit for the
period. If the demand turns out to be $\hat{x}$, then the amount of output
produced and sold will be simply the lower of the two quantities y
and $\tilde{x}$, which is written as $\min(y, \tilde{x})$. Consequently the expected
profit to be maximized is given by[9]

5.5 $$E\pi = E\{(p-w).\min(y, \tilde{x}) - cy\}.$$

When expected profit is to be maximized, marginalist principles would lead us to expect that, at the optimal capacity, the expected net revenue gained by increasing capacity by one unit would just be offset by the additional cost. Indeed, if this were not the case and the expected gain was larger (smaller) than the cost, it is clear that an increase (decrease) in capacity would increase expected profit. So what is the expected gain if y is increased by one unit? If demand is less than capacity the gain is clearly zero, since the additional

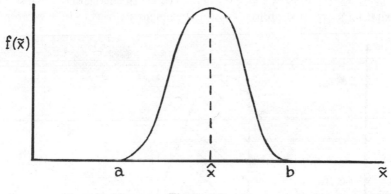

Figure 5.2

capacity is useless. On the other hand, if the demand is larger than capacity, the gain must simply be $p-w$. Consequently the expected revenue gain is $(p-w)$ multiplied by the probability of demand being greater than capacity. Since the increased cost is c, the necessary condition for expected profit maximization is then

5.6 $$(p-w) \times \text{prob}(\tilde{x} > y) = c.$$

In Figure 5.3 the shaded area shows the probability of $\tilde{x} > y$, and this is equal to $1 - F(y)$ where $F(y)$ is the distribution function given by $F(y) = \int_a^y f(\tilde{x}) \, d\tilde{x}$. This function is the probability that $\tilde{x} \leqslant y$ and is represented by the unshaded area under the curve. 5.6 thus shows that the optimal capacity y^*, satisfies the equation

5.7 $$F(y^*) = 1 - \frac{c}{p-w}$$

where note that since $p-w > p-w-c > 0$, than $1 > 1 - c/(p-w) > 0$ and thus y^* is well defined. This is a very sensible result. When demand is uncertain, capacity is pitched somewhere between minimum and maximum demand, the exact point depending on the unit profitability. If this is very low then $p - w$ is close to c, $F(y^*)$ is then close to zero and capacity is set close to the minimum possible demand. Alternatively, if net revenue is very much larger than capacity cost, $F(y^*)$ is close to one and consequently capacity is close to the maximum demand. Thus in general, a firm is likely to introduce larger increases in capacity in response to uncertain demand increases if it expects high profits per unit.[10] In this sense we can say that high expected profits are an inducement to firms to take greater

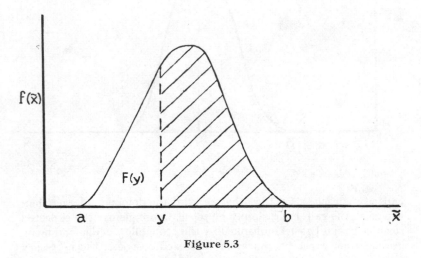

Figure 5.3

risks in expansion but note, however, that the firm in this example is assumed to be risk *neutral* with respect to profits.

In the next three examples we shall be comparing risk-neutral with risk-averse behaviour, but before turning to the details it is worth giving a general description of the sort of investment decisions on which they will hopefully shed some light. The idea here is that because of the existence of lags of one sort or another, the firm must determine future levels of capital stock some time before this capital stock will be needed. Since the examples given are static, they only apply to a world in which the capital stock decisions are independent in every period. Thus, if the lag is m, the capital stock for period t is determined in $t - m$, the capital stock for $t + 1$ is determined in $t-m+1$ and so on. The decisions are completely independent, which rules out any form of strictly convex adjustment cost including irreversibility,[11] and this should be borne in mind when looking at the examples. One further point is that the effects of *increasing* uncertainty are considered in some detail in what follows and this may be thought of as one of the consequences of increasing the lag between the investment decision and the outcome, for it is natural to assume that predictions become more uncertain as the events predicted become more distant.

Example 5b. A firm with a fixed coefficients technology faces a known downward sloping demand curve for its product but the position of the curve during any period is uncertain. As before, w and c are the wage per unit output and cost per unit capacity respectively. Capacity must be determined at the beginning of the period and the price of output then adjusts during the period to equate supply and demand.

More formally we have a demand function $\tilde{a}x(p)$ where $\tilde{a}$ is a random variable with density function $f(\tilde{a})$. Then, if y is capacity, the profit in a particular period is given by,

$$5.8 \qquad \pi = py - (w+c)y, \text{ where } p = x^{-1}(y/\tilde{a}),$$

and so, if we initially assume that the firm maximizes expected profit, it will maximize

$$E\pi = E\{y \cdot x^{-1}(y/\tilde{a}) - (w+c)y\}.$$

The necessary condition for the maximum is given by

$$5.9 \qquad EM(y, \tilde{a}) = w + c$$

where $M(y, \tilde{a})$ is the marginal revenue function. Note that the marginal revenue function is given by the equation

$$5.10 \qquad M(y, \tilde{a}) = p \left\{ 1 + \frac{1}{\epsilon(p)} \right\}$$

where p is defined in 5.8 and ϵ is the elasticity of demand, which in this case is a function of p only and not of $\tilde{a}$ (see Chapter 2, proposition 4). Furthermore, if the marginal revenue curve is to be downward sloping then the derivatives of M obey the relations,

$$5.11 \qquad M_y < 0, \ M_{\tilde{a}} > 0.$$

The expected profit maximizing condition, 5.9, is the fairly natural one that expected marginal revenue is equated to marginal cost thereby ensuring that any small change in capacity cannot raise the expected profit. Furthermore, since $(\partial/\partial y)EM = EM_y < 0$, this condition ensures that any increase in the wage or capital cost will reduce the optimal capacity, as might be expected. This is a very mundane result, however, and we shall now consider two rather more interesting, though considerably more difficult questions. These are, first, to determine whether it is possible to say anything about the actual effect of uncertainty itself on the optimal level of capacity and, second, to ask what is the effect of assuming risk aversion on the part of the firm.

Beginning with the former question, we must decide initially how to isolate the effect of uncertainty. Typically this is done by comparing the optimal situation in the uncertain case with the optimal situation in the certain case where the previously uncertain variables take on their mean values. In fact we would like to generalize this to a comparison between two uncertain situations where one is 'more' uncertain than the other and in order to do this, we make use of the notion of risk aversion which was discussed in the first section.

In deciding whether one situation is more uncertain than another, we are essentially comparing two distribution functions which have the same mean. These two distribution functions may be viewed as two different gambles where the *expected* winnings are the same in both cases. Then it seems natural to say that one gamble is less uncertain than the other *if and only if* it is preferred by any and every risk-averse individual.[12] This criterion is very intuitive since, if a risk-averse person is confronted with a choice between two gambles which yield the same expected return, we would naturally suppose that the one chosen would have a lower risk associated with it; that is, it would be less uncertain. So, more formally, if we have two random variables $\tilde{a}_1$, $\tilde{a}_2$ which have density functions $f_1(\tilde{a}_1)$ and $f_2(\tilde{a}_2)$ respectively and also have the same mean, then f_2 is more uncertain than f_1 if, and only if, *any* risk averse individual, with utility function $U(\cdot)$, prefers to receive $\tilde{a}_1$ units of consumption rather than $\tilde{a}_2$. That is, the expected utility of $\tilde{a}_1$ is greater than that of $\tilde{a}_2$ and thus

5.12 $$EU(\tilde{a}_1) > EU(\tilde{a}_2).$$

Writing out these expectations in full by multiplying each utility level $U(\tilde{a}_1)$ by its probability $f_i(\tilde{a}_i)\, d\tilde{a}_i$ and summing, gives

$$\int_{-\infty}^{\infty} U(\tilde{a}_1)f_1(\tilde{a}_1)\, d\tilde{a}_1 > \int_{-\infty}^{\infty} U(\tilde{a}_2)f_2(\tilde{a}_2)\, d\tilde{a}_2.$$

This must hold for any risk averse utility function U, that is, for any strictly concave increasing function. But it is easy to show that if it holds for any strictly concave *increasing* function, then it holds for any strictly concave function. So our natural definition of an increase in uncertainty in moving from $\tilde{a}_1$ to $\tilde{a}_2$ implies that inequality 5.12 must hold so long as the function U is strictly concave. We can now turn this round and say that the inequality 5.12 implies that if a function is strictly concave in an uncertain variable then an increase in uncertainty, as we have just defined it, will always lead to a fall in the mean value of the function.

Reverting to our original problem we can now say that if $M(y, \tilde{a})$ is strictly concave in $\tilde{a}$, then an increase in uncertainty keeping the mean level of demand fixed will diminish $EM(y, \tilde{a})$ and since EM is decreasing in y, this will imply a decrease in y in order to maintain EM in equality with the marginal cost (see equation 5.9). If, for example, the demand curve has constant elasticity $\epsilon < -1$,[13] then

5.13 $$M(y, \tilde{a}) = (1 + 1/\epsilon)y^{1/\epsilon}\tilde{a}^{-1/\epsilon}$$

which is certainly concave in $\tilde{a}$ so, in this case, increases in uncertainty definitely produce a drop in the optimal capacity. Unfortunately, it is not possible to show that this is always so and demand curves can be constructed where uncertainty increases lead to capacity *increases*, though this does not seem very likely.[14] It is worth just glancing at the intuition behind the constant elasticity case described above and to do this we may consider the marginal revenue function 5.13. Since this function is concave in $\tilde{a}$, an increase in demand above the mean level $E(\tilde{a})$ will yield an increase in revenue from the marginal unit of capacity which is *smaller* than the absolute drop in revenue occasioned by a corresponding decrease in demand below $E(\tilde{a})$. Consequently as uncertainty increases, the expected revenue from the marginal capacity unit declines since the increase in uncertainty implies, roughly speaking, that very high and very low values of demand are more likely to occur, and concavity ensures that the benefits of the high values are always *more* than offset by the low profits incurred at the low values. The fall in the expected revenue accruing to the marginal capacity unit will, of necessity, imply a decline in the optimal capacity.

Even though we cannot say anything in general about the effect of increasing uncertainty on capacity, it is possible to determine its effect on the maximum expected profit. It may be shown that the actual profit, defined in equation 5.8, is a strictly concave function of $\tilde{a}$ (see Appendix, proposition 2) and thus for any level of capacity, the expected profit declines as uncertainty increases. Consequently the maximum expected profit must also fall and, in this type of imperfectly competitive world, increasing demand uncertainty will therefore produce declining profit expectations.

Turning now to the second of the two questions which were originally asked of this model, we wish to know the effect on optimal capacity if the firm is assumed to be risk averse rather than risk neutral. We know that a risk-averse firm is excessively frightened of low profits or losses in comparison with a risk-neutral firm and we would therefore expect such a firm to be prepared to sacrifice some *expected* profit in order to reduce the likelihood of its earning profits which are exceptionally small. Since costs are not random and rise proportionately with capacity, it follows that as capacity increases so does the probability of a low profit or loss. On this basis we would predict that the risk-averse firm would install less capacity than the risk-neutral firm. Using more formal techniques we can confirm that this argument is correct. Since the firm is risk averse, we can assume that it maximizes expected utility of profit where the utility function is increasing in profit but at an ever-diminishing rate (i.e. it is strictly concave). Thus the firm maximizes the expression

5.14 $$EU(\pi) = EU\{y \,.\, x^{-1}(y/\tilde{a}) - (w+c)y\}$$

where $U > 0$, $U'' < 0$.

The necessary condition for the maximum is given in our usual notation, by

$$E\{U'(\pi)M(y, \tilde{a})\} = (w+c)EU'(\pi)$$

or

5.15 $$\frac{E\{U'(\pi)M(y, \tilde{a})\}}{EU'(\pi)} = w+c.$$

The aim now is to compare the left-hand side of this equation with the corresponding term in the risk-neutral case, namely the left-hand side of 5.9. We can show, in fact, that for any fixed level of capacity,

5.16 $$EM(y, \tilde{a}) - \frac{E\{U'(\pi)M(y, \tilde{a})\}}{EU'(\pi)} > 0$$

if U is strictly concave and increasing in π and this is proved in the Appendix, proposition 3. So if y^n is the optimal capacity of the risk-neutral firm and y^a is optimal for the risk-averse firm, then 5.16 along with 5.15, 5.9 imply

$$5.17 \qquad EM(y^n, \tilde{a}) = w + c = \frac{E\{U'(\pi)M(y^a, \tilde{a})\}}{EU'(\pi)} < EM(y^a, \tilde{a})$$

Since EM is monotonically decreasing in y, 5.17 must imply that $y^a < y^n$ for any risk-averse firm.

Having confirmed this important result, it now seems natural to ask whether the reduction in capacity due to risk aversion is larger the greater the degree of risk aversion itself. In order to throw some light on this problem, we require a suitable measure of the degree of risk aversion which clearly must be related to the degree of concavity of the utility function U. A suitable measure is the Arrow–Pratt concept of relative risk aversion which is measured by $-U''\pi/U' = R(\pi)$ where the negative sign is included to make the number positive.

Pratt (1964) has shown that if the index $R_1(\pi)$ for utility function U_1 is greater than $R_2(\pi)$ for U_2, then U_1 is more risk averse than U_2 in the sense that the risk premium is greater for U_1 than for U_2. This risk premium is defined as the maximum proportionate amount the producer would pay to avoid the risk associated with the random variable π and obtain its expected value with certainty, that is, $U\{E(\pi)(1 - \text{risk premium})\} = EU(\pi)$. In the Appendix (proposition 4) we show that if we have two utility functions U_1, U_2 such that for all π, $R_1(\pi) > R_2(\pi)$, the optimal capacity must be lower for the firm with utility U_1 than for the firm with utility U_2. Thus the more risk-averse firm has the lower optimal capacity. So not only is the optimal capacity lower for the risk-averse firm than for the risk-neutral firm but it also diminishes with the actual degree of risk aversion.

To summarize this particular example where the emphasis has been on demand uncertainty, we now know that for the risk-neutral firm it is not possible to say, *a priori*, what the effects of increasing demand uncertainty on capacity will be. However, we can say that with constant elasticity or linear or quadratic demand curves (see footnote 14), the optimal capacity is inversely related to the level of uncertainty. We also know that, when demand levels are uncertain, risk-averse behaviour is bound to lower capacity levels and the optimal capacity level is, in fact, a declining function of the degree of risk aversion.

The other obvious type of uncertainty which arises for the firm when it is planning future levels of capital stock is price uncertainty. In the context of an imperfectly competitive model where capital goods are ordered for the future at a known price, the future price the level of which will be worrying the firm most is the wage rate.[15] In order to study the effects of wage rate uncertainty it is desirable to extend the above model to include substitution and this is done in the following example.

Example 5c. Here we assume a firm with a constant returns to scale technology in exactly the same situation as the firm of the previous example except that the level of demand is now $x(p)$, which is certain, and the wage, $\tilde{w}$, is a random variable.

The firm chooses a quantity of capital stock, K, before the production period has begun and then, during the period when the wage is known, the firm clearly employs labour up to the point where the marginal revenue product of labour is equal to this known wage. So, during the production period, we have, using standard notation,

5.17 $$M(p)F_L(K, L) = \tilde{w},$$

and

5.18 $$F(K, L) = x(p),$$

where 5.17 is the marginal revenue product of labour condition and 5.18 simply states that supply is equal to demand. In order to determine the optimal value of K, the firm must first recognize that the size of the labour force which it will eventually employ and the output price which it will set are both going to depend on exactly which wage rate occurs and also on the level of capital stock already chosen. Precisely how this dependency works may be discovered by solving 5.17 and 5.18 for the quantity of labour and the output price in terms of K and $\tilde{w}$. That is 5.17 and 5.18 imply

5.19 $$L = L(K, \tilde{w}), \quad p = p(K, \tilde{w}).$$

The risk-neutral firm will then choose K to equate the expected marginal revenue product of capital to the cost of capital and thus the optimal K will satisfy

5.20 $$E_{\tilde{w}}[M\{p(K, \tilde{w})\}F_K\{K, L(K, \tilde{w})\}] = c.$$

Alternatively the risk-averse firm will equate the expected *utility* gain from the revenue accruing to the marginal unit of capital with the expected *utility* loss associated with the cost of this additional unit. So, in this case, K will satisfy

5.21 $$\underset{\tilde{w}}{E}[U'(\pi)M\{p(K,\tilde{w})\}F_K\{K, L(K,\tilde{w})\}]=\underset{\tilde{w}}{E}U'(\pi)c.$$

Proceeding as before, we may first ask what will be the effect on the optimal level of capital stock of increasing uncertainty about the future wage. The answer is derived in the Appendix (proposition 5) and is as follows. If the elasticity of substitution σ is less than the absolute value of the elasticity of demand $|\epsilon|$, then the optimal capital stock increases with increasing uncertainty. If, however, $\sigma > |\epsilon|$ then the optimal capital stock decreases with uncertainty.

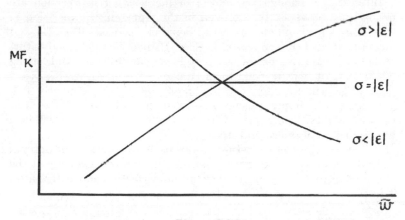

Figure 5.4

This is a rather satisfying result but it is by no means easy to see the intuition behind it. The best approach is to consider how the marginal revenue product of capital varies with the wage when the capital stock is fixed, so only the labour input is adjusted. Three examples appear in Figure 5.4 for three different levels of the elasticity of substitution. The analytical background is in the Appendix, propositions 5 and 6.

Consider first the case where the elasticity of substitution is low. When the wage falls the output effect dominates the substitution effect, and, if capital were a variable factor, its use would rise. Since it is fixed its marginal revenue product rises and, what is more, rises at an ever-increasing rate. It is this convexity which gives rise to an increasing level of capital stock when wage uncertainty increases.

Conversely, if there is a high degree of substitutability, then, as the wage level falls, the large substitution effect lowers the shadow price of capital (marginal revenue product), again at an ever-increasing rate. Since it is moving downwards, this makes the function concave thereby giving rise to a decreasing level of capital stock as uncertainty increases. Roughly speaking then, when there is high substitutability, large variability in wage expectations is best dealt with by having a low capital stock and employing large quantities of labour if the wage turns out to be low. On the other hand, if there is very little substitutability this strategy is not really feasible and higher levels of capital stock are required.

Interestingly enough the effects of increasing risk aversion are precisely the reverse. It is proved in the Appendix (proposition 7) that, as risk aversion increases, capital stock decreases if $\sigma < |\epsilon|$ and increases if $\sigma > |\epsilon|$. The reason is clear. If there is a lot of substitutability the main risk lies in having a lower capital stock and letting labour employment respond to the wage variation, for in this case a high wage will lead to very low profitability. Consequently risk avoidance will imply raising the fixed capital stock. With low substitutability the argument is reversed and risk avoidance will lead to a reduction of the capital stock.

In order to complete our study of this particular area of the optimal capital stock response to uncertainty it is worth just glancing at the effects of output price uncertainty on the perfectly competitive firm. This we do in the next example.

Example 5d. In this example the firm operates in a perfectly competitive market and has a decreasing returns production function of the usual form $F(K, L)$. It is uncertain about the output price which will prevail in the production period and must select its fixed capital stock before the period begins. As before, it is allowed to adjust its labour input after it knows the output price. We shall just discuss briefly the results which are proved in the Appendix, propositions 8 and 9. As far as increasing uncertainty is concerned, the risk neutral firm raises its capital stock in response to uncertainty increases if, and only if, the elasticity of substitution σ is less than $1/(1-\eta)$ where η is the returns to scale parameter. Otherwise capital stock is lowered. So, generally speaking, unless there is a massive degree of capital labour substitutability, uncertainty about the output price raises the level of capital stock. Why? Because even if there is no change in labour input. when the output price rises, the marginal product of capital rises linearly with the price. If the labour input is also increased, the marginal product of capital rises faster than linearly thus making the function convex and yielding the required result. A massive increase in labour input combined with very sharply diminishing returns could in fact lower the marginal product of capital, thereby having the opposite effect. This would be the case when $\sigma > 1/(1-\eta)$. The risk-aversion case is very straightforward for, as we show in the Appendix (proposition 9), increases in risk aversion always reduce the optimal capital stock. The usual result for the usual reasons.

In the introduction to these last three examples, we explained the general characteristics of the world which they were supposed to illuminate. We can now summarize our findings. For the risk-neutral firm, the effects of uncertainty are by no means clear cut. For reasonable levels of capital–labour substitutability ($\sigma \leqslant 1$), price uncertainty, both for output prices and substitute input prices, tends to raise the level of capital stock required. This is, generally speaking, because the high level of capital stock desired, should prices turn out favourably, *more* than offsets the lower level desired if they do not. If we can argue that longer lags lead to greater uncertainty, since predictions must be made further into the future, then this would imply a relatively higher planned capital requirement for capital goods with a longer gestation period. This is of course solely with reference to the *risk-neutral* firm responding to *price* uncertainty. The imperfectly competitive firm's response to demand uncertainty is not clear *a priori*, though the weight of the evidence would seem to support a lowering of capital stock orders relative to the certain case. And this cautious response to uncertainty will almost invariably be reinforced by any tendency on the part of the firm to risk aversion. A strongly risk-averse firm would therefore have a consistently lower capital stock and a more cautious investment policy than a risk-neutral firm.

In general, then, the firm confronted with the problem of determining its optimal capital stock in the face of uncertainty about the future economic climate is presented with a trade-off. A rather large capital stock would provide the firm with the flexibility in production to enable it to reap large profits in a world which turns out favourably. On the other hand this same large capital stock could well lead to disastrous profits or even losses should the economic climate turn out to be bad. The flexibility provided by a large capital stock is less necessary to the firm which is able to increase output easily by simply intensifying the use of its capital stock by employing more labour. In this case the *dangers* inherent in ordering a larger capital stock will tend to be the dominant factor and uncertainty will lead to lower investment orders, a tendency which is, of course, exacerbated in the case where the firm is excessively cautious about these dangers anyway. Alternatively, a firm which is not particularly concerned about losing money from time to time, if these losses can be offset by higher profits in other years, will be more concerned to preserve flexibility and will order more new capital in response to uncertainty, especially if such flexibility cannot be attained in other ways.

This completes our analysis of the static uncertainty problem and in the next chapter we turn to a consideration of the effects of uncertainty in a dynamic context, thus returning to the sort of world which was analysed in earlier chapters.

Appendix

Proposition 1 (p. 70). If there exist n firms with identically but independently distributed random profits, then as $n \to \infty$, any risk-averse investor will wish each and every firm to maximize its expected profit.

Proof. Let the density function of profit be $f(\pi_i)$ where π_i is the profit of the ith firm, $i = 1 \ldots n$. Furthermore, since all the distributions are identical we can write $E(\pi_i) = \bar{\pi}$ for all i. Now consider any risk-averse investor with utility function U, $U' > 0$, $U'' < 0$ and let θ_i be his share of the profits of the ith firm and K, a constant, be the sum total of his shares in all the firms. (Note that K is a constant since, in the share market, a share in firm i is exactly the same good as an equal share in firm j, all i, j.)

Then this investor will choose θ_i to maximize

$$EU(\sum_i \theta_i \pi_i) \text{ subject to } \sum_i \theta_i = K.$$

The necessary conditions are

$$EU'\pi_i = EU'\pi_j, \text{ all } i, j,$$

i.e.
$$\int_{-\infty}^{\infty} \ldots \int_{-\infty}^{\infty} U'(\sum_k \theta_k \pi_k) \pi_i f(\pi_1) f(\pi_2) \ldots f(\pi_n) \, \mathrm{d}\pi_1 \ldots \mathrm{d}\pi_n$$

$$= \int_{-\infty}^{\infty} \ldots \int_{-\infty}^{\infty} U'(\sum_k \theta_k \pi_k) \pi_j f(\pi_1) f(\pi_2) \ldots f(\pi_n) \, \mathrm{d}\pi_1 \ldots \mathrm{d}\pi_n$$

all i, j.

It is obvious that the solution to this set of equations is

$$\theta_i = \theta_j = K/n \text{ for all } i, j.$$

Consequently the investor's maximum expected utility is

$$EU\left(\sum_i \frac{K}{n}\, \pi_i\right) = EU\left(\frac{K}{n} \sum_1^n \pi_i\right).$$

Now since $1/n \sum_1^n \pi_i$ is a consistent estimator of $\bar{\pi}$ then $\lim n \to \infty$ $1/n \sum_1^n \pi_i = \bar{\pi}$ and consequently as $n \to \infty$ the maximum expected utility becomes $EU(K\bar{\pi}) = U(K\bar{\pi})$. Thus the investor will clearly wish for $\bar{\pi}$ to be maximized, that is for each and every firm to maximize its expected profit.

Proposition 2 (p. 78). So long as, for the given value of capacity, marginal revenue is positive and increasing in price for all positions of the demand curve which occur with positive probability, then the profit $\pi = py - (w+c)y$ where $x(p)\tilde{a} = y$, is strictly concave in $\tilde{a}$ over the relevant region.

Proof. The conditions of the proposition imply that (i) $\epsilon < -1$ and (ii) $d/dp \cdot p(1 + 1/\epsilon) > 0 = > p\epsilon_p - \epsilon < \epsilon^2$.
Then

$$\frac{\partial^2 \pi}{\partial \tilde{a}^2} = \frac{-p}{\tilde{a}^2 \epsilon^3}\,(p\epsilon_p - \epsilon - \epsilon^2) < 0 \quad \text{from (ii)}.$$

Thus π is strictly concave in $\tilde{a}$.

Proposition 3 (p. 79). In standard notation the inequality

$$EM(y, \tilde{a}) - \frac{E\{U'(\pi)M(y, \tilde{a})\}}{EU'(\pi)} > 0$$

holds if U is strictly concave and increasing.

Proof. Let $U'(\pi) = g(\tilde{a})$. Then $\partial g / \partial \tilde{a} < 0$ by concavity of U. Furthermore simple computation reveals that $M_{\tilde{a}} > 0$. Now define $\hat{a}$ as satisfying $g(\hat{a}) = Eg(\tilde{a})$.
Then

$$EM(y, \tilde{a}) - \frac{EU'M(y, \tilde{a})}{EU'}$$

$$= \int_{-\infty}^{\infty} f(\tilde{a}) \left(M - \frac{gM}{Eg}\right) d\tilde{a}$$

where f is the density function of $\tilde{a}$,

$$= \int\limits_0^\infty M\left(f - \frac{gf}{Eg}\right) \mathrm{d}\tilde{a} = \int\limits_0^\infty \{M(\tilde{a}) - M(\hat{a})\} \left(f - \frac{gf}{Eg}\right) \mathrm{d}\tilde{a}$$

since $\int f = \int fg/Eg = 1$,

$$= \int\limits_0^{\hat{a}} \{M(\tilde{a}) - M(\hat{a})\} \left(f - \frac{gf}{Eg}\right) \mathrm{d}\tilde{a} + \int\limits_{\hat{a}}^\infty \{M(\tilde{a}) - M(\hat{a})\} \left(f - \frac{gf}{Eg}\right) \mathrm{d}\tilde{a}$$

$$(-) \qquad\qquad (-) \qquad\qquad\qquad (+) \qquad\qquad (+)$$

> 0, the signs following from $M_{\tilde{a}} > 0$, $g_{\tilde{a}} < 0$.

Lemma 1. If U_1 and U_2 are two strictly concave increasing utility functions satisfying

$$\frac{-U_1''(\pi)\pi}{U_1'(\pi)} > \frac{-U_2''(\pi)\pi}{U_2'(\pi)}$$

for all π, where π is a function $\pi(y, \tilde{z})$ with $\pi_{yy} < 0$, and if y_i satisfies $E_{\tilde{z}} U_i'(\pi)\pi_y = 0$ for $i = 1, 2$, then $y_1 < y_2$ if $\pi_{\tilde{z}}$ and $\pi_{y\tilde{z}}$ have the same sign and $y_1 > y_2$ if $\pi_{\tilde{z}}$, $\pi_{y\tilde{z}}$ have opposing sign.

Proof. Since

$$\frac{-U_1''(\pi)\pi}{U_1'(\pi)} > \frac{-U_2''(\pi)\pi}{U_1'(\pi)} \quad \text{all } \pi$$

this implies

$$\frac{-\mathrm{d}}{\mathrm{d}\pi} \log U_1'(\pi) > \frac{-\mathrm{d}}{\mathrm{d}\pi} \log U_2'(\pi) \quad \text{all } \pi,$$

which implies

$$-\int\limits_a^b \frac{\mathrm{d}}{\mathrm{d}\pi} \log U_1'(\pi) \, \mathrm{d}\pi > -\int\limits_a^b \frac{\mathrm{d}}{\mathrm{d}\pi} \log U_2'(\pi) \, \mathrm{d}\pi \quad \text{if } b > a$$

and

$$-\int\limits_a^b \frac{\mathrm{d}}{\mathrm{d}\pi} \log U_1'(\pi) \, \mathrm{d}\pi < -\int\limits_a^b \frac{\mathrm{d}}{\mathrm{d}\pi} \log U_2'(\pi) \, \mathrm{d}\pi \quad \text{if } a > b,$$

and thus

A.1 $$\frac{U_1'(b)}{U_1'(a)} < \frac{U_2'(b)}{U_2'(a)} \quad \text{if } b > a,$$

and

$$\frac{U_1'(b)}{U_1'(a)} > \frac{U_2'(b)}{U_2'(a)} \quad \text{if } a > b.$$

In the statement of the theorem y_2 is defined to satisfy $EU_2'\pi_y = 0$.

Now define $\hat{z}$ to satisfy $\pi_y(y_2, \hat{z}) = 0$ and let $\pi_0 = \pi(y_2, \hat{z})$. Then we have

$$\frac{1}{U_1'(\pi_0)} \left. \frac{dEU_1}{dy} \right/ y_2$$

$$= \frac{1}{U_1'(\pi_0)} \left. \frac{dEU_1}{dy} \right/ y_2 - \frac{1}{U_2'(\pi_0)} \left. \frac{dEU_2}{dy} \right/ y_2,$$

by definition of y_2

$$= \int_0^{\hat{z}} \pi_y(y_2, \tilde{z}) \left[\frac{U_1'\{\pi(y_2, \tilde{z})\}}{U_1'\{\pi(y_2, \hat{z})\}} - \frac{U_2'\{\pi(y_2, \tilde{z})\}}{U_2'\{\pi(y_2, \hat{z})\}} \right] h(\tilde{z}) \, d\tilde{z}$$

$$+ \int_{\hat{z}}^{\infty} \pi_y(y_2, \tilde{z}) \left[\frac{U_1'\{\pi(y_2, \tilde{z})\}}{U_1'\{\pi(y_2, \hat{z})\}} - \frac{U_2'\{\pi(y_2, \tilde{z})\}}{U_2'\{\pi(y_2, \hat{z})\}} \right] h(\tilde{z}) \, d\tilde{z}$$

where $h(\tilde{z})$ is the density function of $\tilde{z}$.

Now A.1 and the definition of $\hat{z}$ imply that,

A.2 if $\pi_{\tilde{z}} > 0$ and $\pi_{y\tilde{z}} > 0$ $\left.\begin{array}{l} \\ \text{or} \\ \text{if } \pi_{\tilde{z}} < 0 \text{ and } \pi_{y\tilde{z}} < 0 \end{array}\right\}$ then the above expression is negative

if $\pi_{\tilde{z}} > 0$ and $\pi_{y\tilde{z}} < 0$ $\left.\begin{array}{l} \\ \text{or} \\ \text{if } \pi_{\tilde{z}} < 0 \text{ and } \pi_{y\tilde{z}} > 0 \end{array}\right\}$ then the above expression is positive.

By the strict concavity of U_i and π, U_i is strictly concave in y and consequently if

$$\left. \frac{dEU_1}{dy} \right/ y_2 > 0$$

then $y_1 > y_2$ and if

$$\left. \frac{dEU_1}{dy} \right/ y_2 < 0$$

then $y_2 > y_1$. Combining this with A.2 yields the required result.

Proposition 4 (p. 79). If the firm described in example 5b faces an uncertain level of demand then an increase in its aversion to risk will lower its optimal capacity.

Proof. Note that the derivatives of the profit function $\pi(y, \tilde{a})$ satisfy $\pi_{\tilde{a}} > 0$ and $\pi_{y\tilde{a}} > 0$. Now apply lemma 1.

Proposition 5 (p. 81). For an imperfectly competitive firm with constant returns to scale, an increase in uncertainty about the wage level will increase (decrease) the optimal capital stock if the elasticity of substitution is less (greater) than the absolute value of the elasticity of demand, assuming both of these are constant.

Proof. Consider the marginal revenue product of capital defined in 5.19, 5.20. That is $M\{p(K, \tilde{w})\}F_K\{K, L(K, \tilde{w})\} = X(K, \tilde{w})$ say. Then it is easily shown that $\partial X/\partial K < 0$ and some tedious manipulation reveals that

$$\frac{\partial^2 X}{\partial \tilde{w}^2} = \frac{Mf'(k)(1-\epsilon_k)k\sigma|\epsilon|\{1+\epsilon_k(|\epsilon|-1)\}(|\epsilon|-\sigma)}{\tilde{w}^2\{|\epsilon|\epsilon_k + \sigma(1-\epsilon_k)\}^3}$$

where $k = K/L$, $Lf(k) = F$ and $\epsilon_k = kf'(k)/f$ with $0 < \epsilon_k < 1$.

Thus X is convex (concave) in $\tilde{w}$ if σ is less than (greater than) $|\epsilon|$. This, when combined with the facts that $\partial X/\partial K < 0$ and $E_{\tilde{w}} X(K, \tilde{w}) = 0$ at the optimum, suffices to prove the proposition.

Proposition 6 (p. 81). The marginal revenue product of capital defined in 5.19, 5.20 is decreasing (increasing) in the wage if the elasticity of substitution is less (greater) than the absolute value of the elasticity of demand.

Proof. The equation below follows by simply differentiating the marginal revenue product of capital with respect to $\tilde{w}$, and using 5.17 and 5.18.

$$\frac{\partial MF_K}{\partial \tilde{w}} = \frac{Mf'(1-\epsilon_k)k_{\tilde{w}}}{k|\epsilon|} (\sigma - |\epsilon|)$$

where the unusual symbols are all defined in proposition 5.

The proposition follows directly.

Proposition 7 (p. 82). If the firm described in example 5c faces an uncertain level of wages then an increase in its aversion to risk will lower (raise) its optimal stock if the elasticity of substitution is less (greater) than the absolute value of the elasticity of demand.

Proof. If we define the profit $\pi(K, \tilde{w}) = p(K, \tilde{w})F\{K, L(K, \tilde{w})\} - \tilde{w}L(K, \tilde{w}) - cK$ then 5.17, 5.18 implies that $\pi_K = M\{p(K, \tilde{w})\} \times F_K\{K, L(K, \tilde{w})\} - c$. Then, trivially, we have $\pi_{\tilde{w}} < 0$ and proposition 6 implies that $\pi_{K\tilde{w}} < 0$ $(\pi_{K\tilde{w}} > 0)$ if $\sigma < |\epsilon|$ $(\sigma > |\epsilon|)$. The proposition then follows immediately from lemma 1.

Proposition 8 (p. 82). For a perfectly competitive firm with decreasing returns to scale, an increase in uncertainty about the price of output will increase (decrease) the optimal capital stock if the elasticity of substitution is less (greater) than $1/(1 - \eta)$, where η is the returns to scale parameter, assuming both parameters are constant.

Proof. The optimal level of capital stock will satisfy

A.3 $$\underset{\tilde{p}}{E}\left[\tilde{p}F_K\{K, L(K, w/\tilde{p})\} - c\right] = 0$$

where the function L is defined by the usual marginal productivity equation $\tilde{p}F_L(K, L) = w$. The notation is standard.

Rewriting A.3 more succinctly as

$$\underset{\tilde{p}}{E} G(K, \tilde{p}) = 0$$

then the fact that F has decreasing returns implies that $\partial G/\partial K < 0$.

Furthermore if we assume that F has the specific CES form $(aL^\nu + bK^\nu)^{\eta/\nu}$, some tedious manipulation reveals that the second derivative of G with respect to p is

$$\frac{\partial^2 G}{\partial \tilde{p}^2} = \frac{-(1-\eta)}{\tilde{p}\sigma^2\eta} \frac{F_K F_L^4}{F L^2 F_{LL}^3}\left(1 - \frac{LF_L}{F}\right)\left(\frac{1}{1-\eta} - \sigma\right)$$

Since $F_{LL} < 0$ and $1 - LF_L/F > 0$ this second derivative takes the sign of $\{1/(1-\eta) - \sigma\}$. The function G is thus convex (concave) in $\tilde{p}$ if $\sigma < 1/(1-\eta)\{\sigma > 1/(1-\eta)\}$. This fact when combined with $\partial G/\partial K < 0$ suffices to prove the proposition.

Proposition 9 (p. 83). For a perfectly competitive firm confronted with uncertainty about the price of output, an increase in its aversion to risk will always reduce the optimal level of capital stock.

Proof. If the profit is defined by

$$\pi(K, \tilde{p}) = \tilde{p}F\{K, L(K, w/\tilde{p})\} - wL(K, w/\tilde{p}) - cK$$

then it is trivial to show that $\pi_{\tilde{p}} > 0$ and $\pi_{K\tilde{p}} = G_{\tilde{p}} > 0$. Applying lemma 1 then proves the proposition.

Footnotes

[1] To acquire a flavour of some of the possibilities and problems involved in this area the reader should look successively at Bliss (1975, pp. 319–326), Borch (1968, pp. 166–210), Dreze (1974) and Leland (1974).

[2] It may be shown that, if an individual follows certain 'rational' rules when making choices under uncertainty, there will exist a utility function of his consumption such that he will always choose *as if* he were maximizing the expectation of this utility function. For a full description and critical evaluation of these 'rational' rules see either Luce and Raiffa (1957, pp. 23–24) or Borch (1968, pp. 20–33).

[3] The prevalence of insurance, hedging and so on provides casual evidence that risk-averse behaviour is widespread. This is not to say that risk-loving firms do not exist and indeed that some small percentage of them are not, by their very nature, extremely successful.

[4] The force of this argument is somewhat weakened by the fact that the limited liability laws which operate in a number of countries such as Britain or the United States have a tendency to insulate the owners of the firm from the consequences of the firm's going bankrupt. These laws restrict the liability of individuals for any losses which their firm may sustain to a fixed amount, thereby seriously reducing their fears of bankruptcy. On the other hand the managers of the firm will be very much concerned about the possibility of bankruptcy in so far as such an occurrence could well affect their livelihood. This may lead to owners and managers having conflicting views concerning risk taking with consequences for the firm's objective function which are difficult to determine on prior theoretical grounds.

[5] Another possibility is to use a certainty equivalent approach. That is, the criteria for judging a random income stream $\{\tilde{x}_t\}$ would be to compute the present value of the stream $\{\hat{x}_t\}$ where $U(\hat{x}_t) = EU(\tilde{x}_t)$ for some concave U and for all t. Again this criterion is difficult to use analytically unless U has some very simple form.

[6] Note that, whatever shares he buys, his total mean return will be the same, so his sole interest will be to minimize the variation.

[7] A formal presentation of this argument is provided in the Appendix, proposition 1.

[8] The density function $f(\tilde{x})$ describes the structure of probable outcomes for the random demand $\tilde{x}$. More formally $f(\tilde{x}) \, d\tilde{x}$ is the probability that the demand will lie in the small interval $[\tilde{x}, \tilde{x} + d\tilde{x}]$. Loosely speaking, the larger the value of $f(\tilde{x})$ for any particular value of $\tilde{x}$, the more likely it is that demand will turn out to be somewhere close to this particular value.

[9] As might have been gathered from the example in section 1, the expectation operator E operates on a random variable to give its mean or expected value. This is like an average in the sense that, if the firm under consideration operated by maximizing expected profit for a very large number of periods, then its average profit over all these periods would be equal to its maximum expected profit.

[10] Note that strictly speaking one should say high net revenue relative to cost rather than high profits, since a 100% increase in both net revenue $p - w$ and cost c will leave capacity unchanged in spite of doubling profit.

[11] If, of course, the firm is certain to be growing all the time, then any irreversibility constraint is irrelevant.

[12] It should be noted that this criterion produces only a partial ordering of gambles. In other words, there will be many gambles of which it is not possible to say that one is more uncertain than the other simply because some risk-averse individuals would prefer the one and some the other.

[13] $\epsilon < -1$ to make the marginal revenue positive.

[14] In fact the function is strictly concave if and only if

$$4\epsilon^4 + 3p^4 \frac{z^2 p_{pp}}{z^2} - 5\epsilon^2 p^2 \frac{z_{pp}}{z} - \frac{\epsilon p^3 z_{ppp}}{z} > 0$$

or

$$\left(2\epsilon^2 - \sqrt{3}p^2 \frac{z_{pp}}{z}\right)^2 + (4\sqrt{3} - 6)\frac{\epsilon^2 p^2 z_{pp}}{z} + \frac{p^2 \epsilon}{z}(\epsilon z_{pp} \quad p z_{ppp}) > 0.$$

A sufficient condition is that $pz_{ppp} > -|\epsilon z_{pp}|$ which is not very strong, e.g. it is always satisfied if z is linear or quadratic for then $z_{ppp} = 0$.

[15] Or, of course, the price of any other freely variable input.

Bibliographical Notes—Chapter 5

Concerning individual investment decisions under uncertainty, there are good discussions in Hirshleifer (1965, 1970). An elementary exposition of the concepts of risk-averse and risk-loving behaviour may be found in Friedman and Savage (1948), although as far as the quantification of risk aversion is concerned, the best references are Pratt (1964) and Arrow (1963). The seminal discussion of the effects of changes in the degree of uncertainty is to be found in Rothschild and Stiglitz (1970). A detailed bibliography for the firm's objective under uncertainty is presented at the end of Chapter 8; the justification of risk neutrality for the firm presented in this chapter follows from the ideas expressed in Malinvaud (1972).

Early work on the effects of uncertainty on investment behaviour was mainly concerned with the degree of excess capacity necessary to provide adequate flexibility in response to uncertain outcomes, typical examples being Stigler (1939), Manne (1961), Marschak and Nelson (1962) and Orr (1966). The work of K. R. Smith (1969, 1970) is in the same tradition. A slightly different approach is followed in an example in Rothschild and Stiglitz (1971) which is closer in spirit to the exposition in this chapter. Hartman (1972) provides a dynamic analysis of the problem which we discuss in the next chapter and Norstrom (1974) gives some rather sophisticated extensions of his results. A rather different dynamic model under uncertainty is discussed in the paper by Lintner in Marris and Wood (1971).

So far as the general theory of the firm under uncertainty is concerned, a discussion of the literature up to about 1969 is provided in Baron (1970). Proposition 1 in this paper also provides the basis for lemma 1 of the Appendix. Some further results in this area may be found in Sandmo (1971), Leland (1972) and Batra and Ullah (1974).

CHAPTER 6

UNCERTAINTY IN A DYNAMIC CONTEXT

1. A Simple Model of Uncertainty and Costs of Adjustment

The major drawback of the static approach to uncertainty described in the previous chapter is that the discussion was perforce limited to firms which take intertemporally independent capital stock decisions. That is, the optimal capital stock is determined period by period, albeit at some time prior to its actual utilization, and thus the firm is assumed to be able to plan capital stock adjustments of any size, either upwards or downwards, between each and every period. Only under these conditions, as we saw in Chapter 2, is the firm able to reduce its investment problem to a static one. If we introduce strictly convex adjustment costs we know from Chapter 3 that this is no longer the case and all periods must be looked at together. The introduction of uncertainty into such a world may be thought to present insuperable analytical problems but such is not the case if we are careful to keep the world simple or, alternatively, the form of uncertainty simple.

A particularly elegant method of introducing uncertainty into an adjustment cost model is displayed in the following example due to Hartman (1972). The underlying model, which we have looked at earlier in Chapter 3, consists of a perfectly competitive firm operating under constant returns to scale and facing strictly convex costs of adjustment. Then in every period, the capital–labour ratio and consequently the marginal revenue product of capital is determined by the labour productivity condition. Consequently all future net marginal returns to capital are determined independently of the current investment decision and we can immediately write down an investment decision rule stating that the marginal adjustment cost of introducing an extra unit of investment is just offset by the present value of the net returns to that investment. Thus, in our standard notation, we have investment at time t satisfying

$$6.1 \quad C'\{I(t)\} = \int_{t}^{\infty} \exp\{-(\delta+r)(s-t)\} \, p(s) f_k\{w(s)/p(s)\} \, \mathrm{d}s - q(t),$$

an equation which has already been derived more formally in Chapter 3 (see 3.10). This equation will now be used to determine the effect of uncertainty about the future prices w and p on the investment decisions of a risk-neutral firm. In order to do this it is much easier to convert the problem to a discrete time formulation by simply assuming that the prices $p(s)$ and $w(s)$ remain constant at p_s and w_s from time s to time $s+1$. 6.1 then reduces to

$$6.2 \qquad C'\{I(t)\} = \sum_{s=t}^{\infty} p_s f_k(w_s/p_s) \int_s^{s+1} \exp\{-(\delta+r)(\tau-t)\}\, \mathrm{d}\tau - q(t)$$

$$= \sum_{s=t}^{\infty} \alpha(s, t) p_s f_k(w_s/p_s) - q(t)$$

where the integral discount factor is written as $\alpha(s, t)$ and t is now an integer.

Suppose now that $\tilde{p}_s$ and $\tilde{w}_s$ are random variables which are independently distributed.[1] Then if the firm is risk neutral it will simply equate the marginal adjustment cost to the *expectation* of the present value net return on the marginal unit of capital and thus we have

$$6.3 \qquad C'\{I(t)\} = \sum_{s=t}^{\infty} \alpha(s, t) E\{\tilde{p}_s f_k(\tilde{w}_s/\tilde{p}_s)\} - q(t).$$

We show in the Appendix, proposition 1, that $\tilde{p}_s f_k(\tilde{w}_s/\tilde{p}_s)$ is convex in both $\tilde{p}_s$ and $\tilde{w}_s$ and consequently any increase in uncertainty concerning the prices in *any* future period is bound to stimulate the firm's current investment programme. This is, of course, a very special result since, as we noted in Chapter 3, the model is hardly one of great generality. It does however reinforce the conclusions concerning price uncertainty which were derived in the previous chapter and may be taken as suggestive, if nothing more.

2. The Effects of Uncertainty in the Timing of Demand Changes

We have finally reached a point in the discussion of uncertainty where it is worth trying, in a fully dynamic context, to relate the problems of uncertainty to those aspects of the world such as delivery lags and adjustment costs which we have already deemed to be important. The formal structure of the model which we shall use is almost identical with that discussed in Chapter 4 except that we shall assume a fixed coefficients technology, mainly for the sake of expositional simplicity. To fix the structure of the model and to relate it to the previous analysis it is worth setting out precisely what assumptions will be employed. Assumption 1 (p. 5) on perfect capital markets still holds but assumption 2 (p. 7) on certainty is replaced by

Assumption 2a. There may be uncertainty about the future values of some or all of the exogenous variables confronting the firm. The firm chooses a production plan to maximize the expectation of present value.

The technology of the firm is described in the next assumption which replaces assumption 3 (p. 8) or 3a (p. 17).

Assumption 3b. The firm has a fixed coefficients technology.

We retain assumption 4 (p. 8) on the exponential evaporation of capital and also assumption 8 (p. 16) on the imperfectly competitive market structure except that the firm may not know the various parameters with certainty. Assumption 6b (p. 51) of Chapter 4, which formalizes both the irreversible nature of the investment process and the delivery lag, is also maintained although irreversibility may be dropped from time to time. Finally there are still no taxes, assumption 7 (p. 8).

This model will be used to investigate the following sort of problem. Suppose the firm thinks that some relevant change will occur in its environment at some time in the future, the time itself being uncertain. How will this affect its investment plans? Clearly, if there is a delivery lag then it must try to anticipate the change rather than simply sitting back and waiting for it to happen, for if this latter policy is followed then, once the change has occurred, the firm may know *precisely* what it wants to do but cannot alter its production plan until the delivery period has elapsed. So, even if there are no direct costs of adjustment, the existence of uncertainty when combined with lags in response ensures that firms must try to anticipate future events. This is a very important point because if there are no costs of adjustment, *or* costs of adjustment are linear, then uncertainty alone, or delivery lags alone, does not imply any necessity on the part of the firm to look to the future. Only when they are combined does this necessity arise and this will emerge very clearly in the context of the model. We shall also consider how irreversibility of investment affects the firm's plans in this context and furthermore we shall discuss the influence of uncertainty about the size of the parametric change itself. On this latter topic we shall use some of the results which have already been derived.

Turning to more formal matters we first write down the maximization problem of the firm without specifying any particular variables as stochastic. The firm therefore derives its production plan by solving,

6.4   maximize $E \int\limits_{0}^{\infty} \exp\left(-rt\right) \left[\{p(t)-w(t)\}y(t)-q(t)I(t)\right] \mathrm{d}t$

6.5   subject to $z(p)\beta(t)=y(t)$

6.6 $\dot{y}(t)=I(t)-\delta y(t)$

6.7 $I(t)\geqslant 0$

$y(t),\ I(t)$ given for all $t\leqslant m$.

Here y is capacity output and investment, I, is in capacity units. w is the wage per unit of output and 6.5 states that capacity output is always maintained in equality with demand.[2] The rest of the problem is self-explanatory and the notation is standard.

Consider first a simple version of the general problem where the firm is uncertain about the timing of a particular change, but the size of the change itself is known with certainty. Furthermore, suppose that, after the change, the environment is certain for all subsequent periods. If the event occurs at time $\tilde{t}$, where $\tilde{t}$ is a random variable, then after $\tilde{t}$ the firm is in a world of certainty and after $\tilde{t}+m$ it can move on to its optimal path for the certain environment (it cannot do so before because of the lag). This optimal path may be defined by the solution to the problem

6.8   maximize $\int\limits_{t}^{\infty} \exp\left\{-r(s-t)\right\}\left\{(p-w)y-qI\right\} \mathrm{d}s$

subject to $y=z\beta$, $\dot{y}=I-\delta y$, $I\geqslant 0$ and $y(t)$ given, where $t=\tilde{t}+m$. Suppose the optimal production plan for this problem yields a present value at time t of $\pi\{y(t),\ t\}$.

Still without specifying the actual change that occurs at $\tilde{t}$, suppose that we define the instantaneous net income flow accruing at time t as $R^0\{y(t),\ I(t),\ t\}$ for $t<\tilde{t}$ and as $R^1\{y,(t),\ I(t),\ t\}$ for $\tilde{t}\leqslant t<\tilde{t}+m$. Then we can view the firm as being in receipt of the following pattern of net income.

Net income receipts at time $t = \tilde{R}(t) = R^0$ if $t < \tilde{t}$,

$$= R^1 \text{ if } \tilde{t} \leqslant t < \tilde{t} + m,$$

$$= \pi \text{ if } t = \tilde{t} + m.$$

What we have done here is to compress all the activities of the firm after $\tilde{t} + m$ into a single receipt by the firm at $\tilde{t} + m$ of the whole of the present value of all its subsequent income. This is clearly a legitimate procedure in the context of a perfect capital market. We

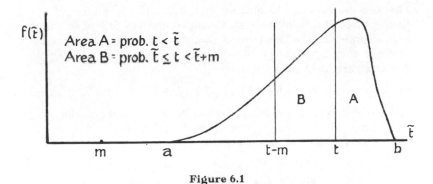

Figure 6.1

can now write down the expectation of the income flow at time t, and this is simply given by the expression,[3]

6.9 $\quad E\tilde{R}(t) = R^0 \times (\text{prob. } t < \tilde{t}) + R^1 \times (\text{prob. } \tilde{t} \leqslant t < \tilde{t} + m) + \pi$

$$\times (\text{prob. } t = \tilde{t} + m).$$

If we define the density of the random variable $\tilde{t}$ as $f(\tilde{t})$, where $f(t) = 0$ for $t \leqslant a \geqslant m$ and $t \geqslant b \leqslant \infty$, then the probabilities in the expression 6.9 can be illustrated as areas under certain segments of the density curve. The probability that $t < \tilde{t}$ is simply the area to the right of t and the probability that $\tilde{t} \leqslant t < \tilde{t} + m$ is equivalent to the probability that $t - m < \tilde{t} \leqslant t$ and is equal to the area between $t - m$ and t. These areas are shown in Figure 6.1. Note that a and b are the time limits outside which the firm considers the occurrence of the expected event to be inconceivable. Noting that area $A = \int_t^b f(\tilde{t}) \, d\tilde{t}$ and area $B = \int_{t-m}^t f(\tilde{t}) \, d\tilde{t}$, it is clear that the expression in 6.9 can be simplified to

$$E\tilde{R}(t) = R^0(t) \int_t^b f(\tilde{t}) \, d\tilde{t} + R^1(t) \int_{t-m}^t f(\tilde{t}) \, d\tilde{t} + \pi f(t - m).$$

If we let $\int_t^b f(\tilde{t})\,d\tilde{t} = G(t)$ and $\int_{t-m}^t f(\tilde{t})\,d\tilde{t} = G(t-m, t)$, then it further reduces to

6.10 $$E\tilde{R}(t) = G(t)R^0 + G(t-m, t)R^1 + f(t-m)\pi$$

and consequently the total expected present value to be maximized is

6.11 $$\int_0^\infty \exp(-rt)\,\{G(t)R^0 + G(t-m, t)R^1 + f(t-m)\pi\}\,dt.$$

This general formula will now be used to analyse a number of particular cases of special interest. Consider first the following simple type of problem. The firm expects some known change in demand to occur at time t, which may be formally expressed by defining the demand variable $\beta(t)$ as,

6.12 $\quad \beta(t) = \exp(\gamma t)\,\beta_0$ for all $t < \tilde{t}$, $\beta(t) = \exp(\gamma t)\,\beta_1$ for all $t \geqslant \tilde{t}$.

There is thus a trend growth in demand of rate γ and demand shifts instantaneously by some known amount at time $\tilde{t}$. For this case R^0 and R^1 may be defined as follows.

6.13 $$R^0 = ([z^{-1}\{y/\exp(\gamma t)\,\beta_0\} - w]y - qI),$$
$$R^1 = ([z^{-1}\{y/\exp(\gamma t)\,\beta_1\} - w]y - qI),$$

where we have substituted for $p(t)$ using the constraint 6.5. Using the simplifying notation, $N^i(y, t) = [z^{-1}\{y/\exp(\gamma t)\,\beta_i\} - w]y$ (the net revenue function), the problem for the firm is to maximize

$$\int_0^\infty \exp(-rt)\,\{G(t)N^0 + G(t-m, t)N^1 - G(t-m)qI + f(t-m)\pi\}\,dt.$$

Note that $G(t) + G(t-m, t) = G(t-m)$ by definition.

If we now factor out $G(t-m)$, the maximand becomes

6.14 $\displaystyle \int_0^\infty G(t-m)\exp(-rt)\,[g(t)N^0 + \{1 - g(t)\}N^1 + \phi(t-m)\pi - qI]\,dt$

where $g(t) = G(t)/\{G(t-m)\}$ and $\phi(t) = f(t)/G(t)$. Then, by noting that the discount factor $G(t-m)\exp(-rt)$ can be reformulated as

$$G(t-m)\exp(-rt) = \exp\{-rt + \log G(t-m)\}$$

$$= \exp\left[-\int_0^t \{r(\tau) + \phi(\tau-m)\}\,d\tau\right]$$

since $(d/dt) \log G(t) = -\phi(t)$, we see finally that the expected present value to be maximized can be written as

$$6.15 \quad \int_0^\infty \exp\left[-\int_0^t \{r(\tau)+\phi(\tau-m)\}\, d\tau\right] [g(t)N^0+\{1-g(t)\}N^1$$
$$+\phi(t-m)\pi-qI]\, dt.$$

This is now very much like a standard problem with $g(t)N^0+\{1-g(t)\}N^1+\phi(t-m)\pi$ as the firm's revenue net of wages and $r(t)+\phi(t-m)$ as the effective interest rate. Using standard arguments we can immediately see that at any point in time the firm will possess that level of capacity at which the net revenue accruing to the marginal unit is equal to the cost of the marginal unit, so long as this does not imply a negative rate of gross investment. The marginal net revenue in this problem is clearly given by $g(t)N_y^0+\{1-g(t)\}N_y^1+\phi(t-m)\pi_y$ and the marginal cost of capital is the usual one with the interest rate replaced by $r(t)+\phi(t-m)$. This then implies that the optimal capacity for the period m to $\bar{t}+m$ must satisfy

$$g(t)N_y^0+\{1-g(t)\}N_y^1+\phi(t-m)\pi_y=q\{r+\phi(t-m)+\delta-\dot{q}/q\}$$

or more simply

$$6.16 \quad g(t)N_y^0+\{1-g(t)\}N_y^1=q(r+\delta-\dot{q}/q)+\phi(t-m)(q-\pi_y),$$

which we may now use to derive results about the optimal capacity. Suppose first that the irreversibility constraint does not hold. We know that π_y is the value to the firm of having an extra unit of capacity at the beginning of the certainty period[4] (that is, it is the increase in present value following an increase in capacity of one unit) and since capital stock is freely adjustable, this can only be equal to q, the price of such a unit. Consequently the final term on the r.h.s. of 6.16 will disappear and, if we assume that the price of capital goods is constant, the optimal capacity must satisfy

$$6.16a \quad g(t)N_y^0+\{1-g(t)\}N_y^1=c$$

where c is the constant cost of capital. Thus with no irreversibility constraint we are left with an equation which states that the cost of capital must be equated to some convex combination of two net marginal revenue functions, the first being the marginal revenue which would accrue to the firm had the change in demand not occurred, the second being that which would accrue if it had. Indeed the weights of the convex combination are in fact the probabilities of the demand jump having occurred or not having occurred *conditional* on the date being before $\tilde{l}+m$ and so the left-hand side of 6.16a is a conditional expectation, as we might expect. Following on from this it should perhaps be noted that the disappearance of π_y from the optimality condition is simply a consequence of the fact that, with no irreversibility constraint, nothing that happens after $\tilde{l}+m$ can have any effect on the firm's optimal capacity before this date. Of course, after this date, optimal capacity is determined solely on the basis of the solution to the problem 6.8 and equation 6.16a will no longer apply.

In order to see the implications of equation 6.16a for optimal capacity before $\tilde{l}+m$ it is useful to list some of the more obvious properties of the functions N and g.

6.17   (i) $N_y^i = p^i \{1 + 1/\epsilon(p^i)\} - w$ where $p^i = z^{-1}\{y \exp(-\gamma t)/\beta_i\}$
      and consequently N_y^i is a function of $y \exp(-\gamma t)$ only, time
      not entering independently. The expression $y \exp(-\gamma t)$
      will be denoted by $x(t)$, which might be termed the growth
      discounted capacity.
    (ii) $N_y^0 \lessgtr N_y^1$ if and only if $\beta_0 \lessgtr \beta_1$.
  (iii) N_y^i is decreasing in x.
  (iv)   For $t < a$, $G(t-m) = G(t) = 1$, and thus $g(t) = 1$.
      For $a \leqslant t \leqslant b$, $G(t-m) \geqslant G(t)$ and thus $0 \leqslant g(t) \leqslant 1$.
      For $t > b$, $G(t) = 0$ and thus $g(t) = 0$.
      (Remember that a and b are the lower and upper limits of the
      density function of $\tilde{l}$.)
    (v) $\dot{g}(t)/g(t) = \phi(t-m) - \phi(t)$.
  (vi)   If $m_1 > m$, $G(t-m) = G(t-m_1) = 1$ for $a \leqslant t \leqslant a+m$ and
      $G(t-m) < G(t-m_1)$ for $t > a+m$. So $\{g(t)$ with lag $m\} = \{g(t)$ with lag $m_1\}$, for $a \leqslant t \leqslant a+m$ and $\{g(t)$ with lag $m\} > \{g(t)$ with lag $m_1\}$, for $t > a+m$.

The first property of the net marginal revenue, 6.17 (i), follows immediately from the fact that the marginal revenue function is a function only of the output price which in turn depends only on the growth discounted capacity, $x(t)$. The result of 6.17 (ii) is simply a statement of the fact that with a fixed capacity, marginal revenue will always be higher when demand is higher whereas 6.17 (iii) is the reverse result that it will always be lower when capacity is increased in the face of a constant demand. The properties of the probability functions in 6.17 (iv) and 6.17 (vi) can be easily checked by glancing at figure 6.1 and 6.17 (v) is a simple consequence of differentiating $g(t)$.

Turning now to the problem of deducing the path of optimal capacity from equation 6.16a, suppose first that $\beta_1 > \beta_0$, implying that an upward jump in demand is expected. Consequently, for any fixed x, the marginal revenue after the jump in demand is always greater than the marginal revenue before; that is $N_y^1 > N_y^0$ (see 6.17 (ii)). So, as $g(t)$ declines, weight is shifted from the smaller to the larger term on the left-hand side of 6.16a. But the cost of capital on the right is a constant and therefore, in order to keep the left-hand side equal to this constant, x must increase (see 6.17 (iii)). So now we can follow the path of x and consequently y, through the uncertain period. Before the period of uncertainty begins, $t < a$ and thus $g(t) = 1$ from 6.17 (iv). Thus x is a constant satisfying $N_y^0 = c$ and hence y moves up on the lower growth path determined by the β_0 level of demand.[5] During the first part of the uncertainty period, when $a \leqslant t < a+m$, 6.17 (v) implies that $\dot{g}/g = -\phi(t)$ and g is thus always diminishing. Consequently x is always increasing and capacity moves continuously up away from the lower trend path towards the upper trend path defined by the β_1 demand level. During the period $a+m \leqslant t < b$, which incidentally does not exist if $m > b - a$, capacity continues to move between the lower and upper trend paths, but not necessarily always *away* from the lower, for if $\phi(t-m) > \phi(t)$ then g is increasing and consequently x is falling. Then when we reach the end of the uncertainty period $t = b$ and $g(t) = 0$. Consequently x is a constant satisfying $N_y^1 = c$ and capacity moves on to the upper trend path.

The complete path we have just derived is, of course, only followed for $t < \hat{t} + m$. Once the demand jump actually occurs, a block of capital is ordered of such a size that, when it arrives m periods later, capacity will immediately jump on to the upper growth path. Note that if the jump occurs less than m periods before b, the end of the period of uncertainty, then the necessity of ordering a block of capital does not arise since planned capacity will already be on the upper growth path by the time such a block would have arrived.

A typical situation is illustrated in Figure 6.2 below, the demand jump actually occurring at $\hat{t}$. The continuous line illustrates the optimal policy when the lag is m and for comparison purposes we include the path of capacity if demand is *certain* to jump at $\hat{t}$ (the dotted line). Notice that the lag when combined with uncertainty forces the firm to anticipate the demand jump by increasing its capacity away from the path under certainty at time a, that is, as soon as there is any possibility of the demand jump occurring. Now suppose that the delivery lag is longer, m_1 periods say, where $m_1 > m$. Then it is clear from 6.17 (vi) that, from a to $a+m$, the optimal capacity path remains unchanged but from thereon the path for the longer delivery lag m_1 is higher.[6] This is shown by the dashed line in Figure 6.2. So, as might be expected, a longer lag implies that

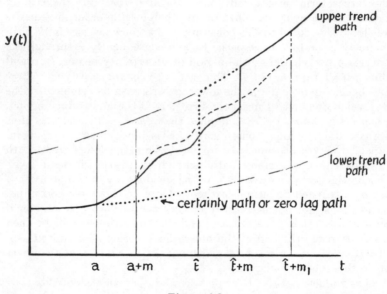

Figure 6.2

during the later part of the uncertainty period capacity is maintained closer to the final upper growth path. This is because, when the jump in demand actually occurs, the firm must wait longer before it can fully adjust. This is more costly and consequently it pays the firm to reduce the size of the necessary adjustment. Notice, of course, that if the lag is zero, $g(t)=1$ throughout and consequently the firm follows the lower trend path until the jump in demand occurs and then jumps instantaneously on to the upper trend path (the dotted line in Figure 6.2 again). Thus, as we emphasized before, in the absence of adjustment costs it is only the *combination* of lags and uncertainty which forces the firm to anticipate the future.

Returning to the point made earlier about the possibility of capacity moving back towards the lower trend path during the uncertainty period, it was pointed out that this would occur if $\phi(t-m) > \phi(t)$. $\phi(t)$, which is equal to $\{f(t)\}/\{G(t)\}$, is in fact the probability of the jump occurring at the instant t conditional on the fact that it has not already happened. Thus, if $\phi(t-m) > \phi(t)$, the firm imagined that the jump was more likely to have occurred around period $t-m$ than around period t, *given* in both cases that it had not already occurred. Thus, in some sense, the firm thinks that around time t the jump in demand is becoming less likely and that is why, at this time, the optimal capacity is falling back towards the lower growth path. This point may be clearly illustrated by considering the following rather special distribution function

6.18 $F(t) = 0$ for $t < a$,

$$F(t) = 1 - \exp\{-\lambda(t-a)^\eta\} \qquad \text{for } t \geqslant a.$$

Then

$$g(t) = \exp\{-\lambda(t-a)^\eta\} \qquad \text{for } t < a+m$$

$$= \exp[-\lambda\{(t-a)^\eta - (t-a-m)^\eta\}] \qquad \text{for } t \geqslant a+m.$$

This function g has the properties

6.19 $\dot{g}(t) < 0$ for $a < t < a+m$; $\dot{g}(t) \gtrless 0$ if $\eta \lessgtr 1$ for $t \geqslant a+m$.

So, after time $a+m$, the conditional probability of the demand jump is increasing (decreasing) if the parameter η is greater than (less than) unity and the demand jump is therefore felt to be conditionally more (less) likely to occur as time goes on. The dividing case where $\eta = 1$ is the situation where the demand jump is considered to be conditionally just as probable in any one time period as in any other and $g(t)$ is a constant, $\exp(-\lambda m)$, for $t > a+m$. These three possibilities are illustrated in Figure 6.3.

Before going on to consider the effects of irreversibility on these results it is worth summarizing and briefly commenting. The combination of lags and uncertainty has a partial smoothing effect on the demand for capacity. From the beginning of the period of uncertainty, capacity moves towards the path which will be followed m periods after the demand jump has in fact occurred. This movement continues throughout the uncertainty period unless the firm feels that the jump is becoming less probable in which case capacity will start to retreat towards the original path. Once the jump has occurred, enough new capacity is ordered so that, after the m period delay, capacity will jump on to the new certain path. A lengthening of the delivery lag will always bias capacity towards the final certain path and if this lag becomes longer than the uncertain period, the capacity path is completely smoothed and there are no jumps required at any time. Finally it should be emphasized that we have been continually describing what actually happens to capacity. The firm will always be ordering m periods in advance to make sure that capacity does indeed follow the paths described.

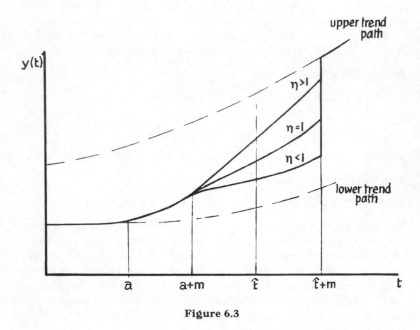

Figure 6.3

These optimal capacity paths are of some considerable interest, particularly when they are compared with the investment pattern of a firm faced with an expected demand increase when there are strictly convex costs associated with raising its investment rate. The discussion in section 3 of Chapter 3 indicates that such a firm will anticipate the demand increase by raising its current rate of investment and that the firm's capacity will follow a path very similar to those illustrated in Figure 6.2, although without the final jumps. So here we have an alternative explanation for what is, as we have already concluded in the section mentioned above, a rather realistic description of firms' investment behaviour. Furthermore, given that uncertainty and delivery lags are an incontrovertible reality which strictly convex adjustments costs most certainly are not, we can reasonably claim that the existence of the former factors provides a far more satisfactory explanation of observed investment behaviour than the latter hypothesis.

3. The Effects of Irreversibility

What are the likely effects on the above analysis of preventing the firm from selling any of its capital stock? If demand is expected to jump upwards, there is very unlikely to be any effect at all because, unless the firm considers that the jump in demand is becoming increasingly less probable at a very rapid rate (thus making g rise and hence x fall very fast), there is never any call for it to sell any capital goods. On the other hand, if the expected jump is downwards this is another story. In this case, when the downward jump actually occurs the firm would plan to sell off some capacity thereby suddenly lowering its capacity on to the new lower growth path after the m period delay.[7] This would not, of course, be allowed under an irreversibility assumption. What would have to happen instead would be a total cessation of new orders as soon as the jump occurs which would continue until m periods before capacity had depreciated of its own accord down to the required lower level. Since this is more costly to the firm than selling off the capital stock, it is clear that the firm would prefer to make the necessary adjustment rather smaller under irreversibility than it would be othersise. Consequently when the expected jump is downwards, we would expect that during the uncertainty period, the firm would move rather more quickly towards the lower capacity path under irreversibility. That this is indeed the case will be demonstrated using more formal analysis.

Turning back to our basic equation 6.16, we have, assuming that the capital goods price is constant, the following equation,

$$6.20 \qquad g(t)N_y^0 + \{1 - g(t)\}N_y^1 = c + \phi(t - m)(q - \pi_y).$$

If we continue to assume that, during the actual uncertainty period from a to $l + m$, the irreversibility constraint does not bite,[8] then this equation will still tell us the whole story. The difference in this situation is that if the capacity $y(t)$ is *above* the final certain path, then the present value of having an extra unit of capacity at the beginning of the certainty period, namely π_y, is *less* than the current cost of such a unit, namely q, the reason being that this extra unit cannot be sold immediately but must be kept and allowed to evaporate. Therefore the final term on the right-hand side of 6.20 is positive, provided the jump in demand is downwards (for only then will $y(t)$ be above the final certainty path) and provided also that $\phi(t-m) > 0$, i.e. that $t > a + m$. Thus for $t > a + m$, the cost of capital is effectively increased thereby lowering $x(t)$ and thus moving capacity closer to the final lower trend path. This effect of the irreversibility constraint is illustrated in Figure 6.4. Thus the effect of irreversibility is to bias

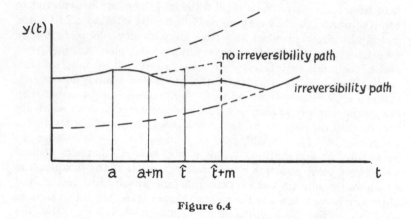

Figure 6.4

the optimal path towards its final certain level in the case of a downward jump. It is in fact possible to show that for adjustment costs in the upward direction the same thing will occur (see Nickell, 1975b) and so it is clear that the existence of adjustment costs will always tend to move the capacity level during the uncertainty period nearer to its final path.

4. Uncertainty about the Size of the Demand Shift

It is clearly unrealistic to assume that the firm is uncertain about the timing of some event but is completely certain about the character of the event itself. So it seems natural to extend the above model to the situation where the size of the demand shift is itself a random variable. Luckily this does not undermine any of the conclusions we have drawn from the previous model and in fact it makes very little odds altogether.

Suppose we assume that, instead of being known, the new demand level is in fact a random variable $\tilde{\beta}_1$ which is distributed independently of the timing of the jump. Then the expected revenue of the firm at time t, instead of being given by 6.10, is now given by

6.21 $$E\tilde{R}(t) = G(t)R^0 + G(t-m,\, t) \underset{\tilde{\beta}_1}{E}\,(R^1) + f(t-m) \underset{\tilde{\beta}_1}{E}\,(\pi).$$

What difference does this make? If there is no irreversibility constraint, we know that $\pi_y = q$, which is independent of $\tilde{\beta}_1$, and consequently the final term of the equation drops out as before. So, following the usual practice of comparing uncertain situations with the certain situation at the mean, all will depend on how the expectation of the net marginal revenue with uncertain demand compares with the certain net marginal revenue when demand is at the mean. That is, we must compare $E(N_y^1(\tilde{\beta}_1))$ with $N_y^1\{E(\tilde{\beta}_1)\}$ where N_y^1 is defined just below equation 6.13. But this problem has already been studied in example 5b (p. 75) of the previous chapter. If N_y^1 is concave in $\tilde{\beta}_1$, which it certainly is if the demand function is quadratic or has constant elasticity, $E(N_y^1)$ declines with increasing demand level uncertainty. Consequently, increasing uncertainty of this type will, under a concavity assumption, lower the level of optimal capacity (note 6.17 (iii)) and thus the capacity path will fall under these circumstances. However, since N_y^1 is always diminishing in x, then so is $E_{\tilde{\beta}_1}(N_y^1)$ and therefore the general structure of the optimal capacity path is completely unaffected by the additional dimension of uncertainty.

Suppose now that we have an irreversibility constraint on investment. Under these circumstances the *expectation* of the value of a unit of capacity added at the beginning of the certainty period, $E(\pi_y)$, will be less than the cost of such a unit, q, if, and only if, actual capacity is greater than the level of capacity which would be required at the *lowest possible* demand outcome. That is, if there is some possibility of the demand outcome being low enough to give the firm an excess of capacity. Consequently, if there is some positive probability that demand will decline, then the last term of 6.20 is positive after time $a + m$ and this pulls down the optimal capacity level during the uncertainty period. This is very much a natural extension of previous results and there is nothing much more to be said about it.

5. Some Other Forms of Uncertainty

Another possible objection to the foregoing analysis is that upward
or downward jumps in demand are somewhat unusual events,
though it may be argued that their analysis does offer a good insight
into the firm's response to any sort of relatively rapid demand shift.
However, just to show that very similar results hold in possibly more
realistic cases, we shall briefly touch on the possibility of uncertainty
in the timing of future changes in the rate of growth of demand. As a
typical example, consider the situation where the firm's demand is on
a shallow decline and at some uncertain future time it is expected to
turn upwards. We shall not analyse this situation formally since it

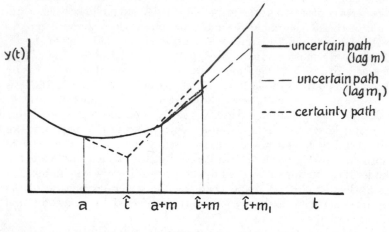

Figure 6.5

would be repetitious but simply restrict discussion to a statement of
results.[9] These are illustrated in the Figure 6.5. At the start of the
period of uncertainty the optimal capacity path (the continuous line)
moves above the certain path (the dotted line) in anticipation of the
possible upward change in the rate of growth. However, if the change
actually occurs at $\hat{t}$, then, when $\hat{t}+m$ arrives and the firm can jump
on to the certain path, the jump will always be upwards so long as
the growth rate has increased. If the delivery lag is longer, the
optimal capacity will be greater after time $a+m$, as in the previous
example. To summarize, the effect of uncertainty is to spread the new

investment over a longer period, anticipating any expected changes in the pattern of demand.

As a last example of the insights that may be gleaned from this kind of model, it is worth looking at the effects of uncertainty about future changes in the price of capital goods, particularly since the vagaries of technical progress could make such uncertainty extremely prevalent. There is, of course, some objection to looking at price effects in the context of a fixed coefficients technology, but since we only consider own price effects, where output and substitution effects typically reinforce each other, the results will not be misleading. In this situation there is no demand change so we may write $\beta(t) = \beta_0 \exp(\gamma t)$ for all t, but the price of capital goods changes at an uncertain time l from q_0 to q_1, say. Going back to the expected income expression, under these circumstances R^0 and R^1 may be defined as

6.22
$$R^0 = \{N^0(y, t) - q_0 I\},$$
$$R^1 = \{N^0(y, t) - q_1 I\},$$

and furthermore, in defining π, the present value income for the certainty period, q_1 is the appropriate price of capital goods. Substituting these into 6.11 leads to the firm maximizing

6.23
$$\int\limits^{\infty} \exp(-rt)\,[G(t-m)N^0 - \{G(t)q_0 + G(t-m,\,t)q_1\}I + f(t-m)\pi]\,dt$$

which leads naturally to the rather elegant result that during the uncertainty period capacity must satisfy

6.24
$$N_y^0 = \acute{q}(r + \delta - \dot{q}/\acute{q}) + \phi(t-m)(\acute{q} - \pi_y)$$

where $\acute{q} = q^0 g(t) + q_1\{1 - g(t)\}$, the expected price of capital goods conditional on the fact that the time is before $l + m$.

Suppose first that there are no adjustment costs. Then, as usual, $\pi_y = q_1$ and thus 6.24 becomes

6.25
$$N_y^0 = \acute{q}(r + \delta) - \dot{\acute{q}} + \phi(t-m)(\acute{q} - q_1).$$

If the price of capital goods is expected to fall, so $q_1 < q_0$, and further, if $g(t)$ is declining so the event is becoming conditionally more probable, then it is easily checked that $\acute{q} > q_1$ and $\dot{\acute{q}} < 0$. There are two forces pushing the firm in opposite directions here. One is the delivery lag which encourages the firm to anticipate the future need for increased capacity so that it does not have to wait so long when the need actually appears. This force operates by lowering $\hat{q}$ below the current price of capital q_0. Pulling in the opposite direction is the desire by the firm to delay its purchases in order to pick up the capital goods when they become cheaper and this comes in via the latter two positive terms in the cost of capital. This desire to delay capital purchases could have very important consequences if delivery lags are short and the firm is situated in an industry with a high rate of technical improvement leading to an expectation of large falls in the effective price of capital.

Things are very much the other way about if the price of capital goods is expected to rise. Under these circumstances $\hat{q} > q_0$, thus raising the cost of capital in anticipation of a reduction in future needs, but offsetting this is the fact that $-\dot{\hat{q}}$ and $\phi(t-m)(\hat{q}-q_1)$ are both negative, raising current demand in anticipation of capital gains when the price goes up. These capital gains fall into two categories. One is the very reasonable desire on the part of firms to buy up capital goods before they become more expensive. The other is the rather unrealistic possibility of buying up capital goods while they are cheap in order to *sell* them again when they become more expensive. Both these are included in this formulation if there is no irreversibility constraint but, if we introduce such a constraint, then we know from previous arguments that π_y is now less than q_1 so long as the firm has too much capital stock at the beginning of the certainty period. Since it certainly has if the price of capital goods is going up, this means that the second of the capital gains elements in the cost of capital, $\phi(t-m)(\hat{q}-\pi_y)$, is now considerably increased. So, if we remove the somewhat remote possibility of the firm actually *realizing* capital gains on fixed capital, then current purchases on the strength of future price rises are considerably diminished.

Finally, what of the effect of uncertainty about the actual size of the future change in capital goods prices? Using the previous arguments we can simply replace q_1 and π by their expected values since they occur linearly in the expression for the income of the firm. Then, in the case of no irreversibility constraint, equation 6.25 remains unchanged except that $\hat{q}$ is now equal to $q_0 g(t) + E(\tilde{q}_1) \times \{1 - g(t)\}$ which is not a very significant difference. Suppose, however, that we impose the irreversibility constraint. This has some interesting effects which are most easily illuminated by considering the case where the mean price of capital goods remains unchanged, that is, $E(\tilde{q}_1) = q_0$. In this case $\hat{q} = g(t)q_0 + \{1 - g(t)\}E(\tilde{q}_1) = q_0$. But the expected value of π_y is no longer simply $E(\tilde{q}_1)$ for, if the new price of capital turns out to be higher than q_0, then the firm has too much capacity and under these circumstances the value of an extra unit is lower than its price. If, on the other hand, the price of capital turns out to be such that there is too little capacity then the value of an extra unit is precisely equal to its price. When we take the mean of all these possibilities it is clear that this will be lower than the price. In fact, it can be shown (Appendix, proposition 2) that π_y is concave in $\tilde{q}_1$ for any given y and consequently its expectation becomes smaller as uncertainty about the new capital goods price increases. So in this case we have

$$N_y^0 = q_0(r+\delta) + \phi(t-m)\{q_0 - \underset{\tilde{q}_1}{E}(\pi_y)\}$$

where the last term increases with the uncertainty about the new capital goods price. Thus, after time $a+m$, current capacity declines because of this uncertainty and the decline becomes larger as this uncertainty increases. This happens in spite of the fact that the expected capital goods price is not expected to change. The reason is, of course, that the costs of adjustment for the firm are larger if the price of capital increases than if it decreases and, because of this asymmetry, the firm will reduce its current level of capacity.

6. General Conclusions about the Effects of Uncertainty

Suppose a firm faces a sudden and unexpected parametric change, a drop in the borrowing rate for example. We know that in a certain world with no lags and no adjustment costs, the response of the firm will be an immediate purchase of new capital stock. Now suppose we move into an uncertain world where there is a delivery lag and where investment is most probably irreversible. Then the first thing that the firm must do when there is a sudden drop in the borrowing rate is to start asking questions. Is this drop going to be permanent? Do we expect the rate to go back up again? Is there some positive probability that it will go up again? If so, when? Can we say when is the time we think it is most likely to change again?, etc. The firm must form some probability pattern about future movements of the rate. Having done so, it must reformulate its ordering policy in accordance with this subjective probability pattern. If the firm has some expectation that at some time the rate will rise again then it will not order so much capital as in a world of certainty and it will only change its capital stock position gradually. If it is risk averse it will be even more cautious about changing its capital position. Furthermore, no changes associated with the particular event can occur for at least the length of the delivery lag. So we have an image of the firm continually groping in the dark, forever peering into the future trying to formulate what it thinks will be most likely to happen. Its reaction to current events will be sluggish and strongly influenced by what it thinks will happen next. This pattern of behaviour is very much in accord with observation and typically the theoretical literature has formalized this sluggish and hesitant behaviour by introducing strictly convex costs of adjustment.[10] In the past few chapters we have indicated that this is a superficial formalization based on an inadequate theory. Costs of adjustment may be important but not in the role usually ascribed to them, for there are few good reasons for thinking of them as strictly convex.[11] If they are not they may well cause a considerable gap between the direct cost of capital and its marginal revenue product but they will not cause the sort of slow and cautious response to current events which is a feature of investment decisions. This, as we have emphasized in these last chapters, is more likely to be a result of uncertainty and lags allied with the irreversible nature of the investment process.

This really concludes the general theory of investment decisions and in the remaining theoretical chapters we shall consider a sequence of special topics starting with the problem of capital decay and replacement in the next chapter.

Appendix

Proposition 1 (p. 94). If $F(K, L)$ is a constant returns to scale production function and $f(k)$ is the corresponding function for output/head in terms of capital per head and if $k(w/p)$ is the solution to $f(k) - kf'(k) = w/p$ then $pf'\{k(w/p)\}$ is convex in p and w.

Proof. Let $k(w/p) = k^*$. Then k^* satisfies $pF_L(k) = w$.

Now $pf'\{k(w/p)\}K = pf'(k^*)K$

$$= pF_K(k^*)K$$

$$= pF(K, K/k^*) - pF_L(k^*)K/k^*$$

by Euler's theorem,

$$= pF(K, K/k^*) - wK/k^* \text{ by definition}$$

$$= \max_{L} \{pF(K, L) - wL\}$$

$$= g(p, w)K \text{ by homogeneity.}$$

But $g(p, w)K$ is a profit function and is therefore convex in p and w by the usual properties of such functions. Hence so is $pf'\{k(w/p)\}$.

Proposition 2 (p. 111). Let $\pi\{y(t), t\}$ be the solution to the problem:

$$\max \int_t^\infty \exp\{-r(s-t)\}\{(p-w)y-q_1 I\}\,ds$$

subject to $z\beta_0 = y$, $\dot{y} = I - \delta y$, $I \geqslant 0$, $y(t)$ given.

Then $\partial\pi/\partial y(t)$ is concave in q_1.

Proof. Let $M(p^*) - w = q_1(r+\delta)$ define $p^*(q_1)$. Let q_1^* satisfy $z\{p^*(q_1)\}\exp(\gamma t)\beta_0 = y(t)$.

Then for $q_1 \leqslant q_1^*$, $\partial\pi/\partial y(t) = q_1$ since there is then too little capital stock at time t and the irreversibility constraint does not bite. Now suppose $q_1 > q_1^*$. Then there is too much capacity at time t and investment will be zero on some period $(t, t+n)$. During this interval the price of output $\bar{p}(s)$ will satisfy

A.1 $\qquad z\{\bar{p}(s)\}\exp(\gamma s)\beta_0 = y(t)\exp\{-\delta(s-t)\}$

and this interval will continue until $\bar{p}(s) = p^*$ at time $t+n$ where

A.2 $\qquad z(p^*)\exp\{\gamma(t+n)\}\beta_0 = y(t)\exp(-\delta n)$.

After $t+n$, $\bar{p}(s) = p^*$, $y(s) = z(p^*)\exp(\gamma s)\beta_0$, $I(s) = (\delta+\gamma)z(p^*)\times \exp(\gamma s)\beta_0$. So

$$\pi\{y(t), t\} = \int_t^{t+n} \exp\{-r(s-t)\}\{\bar{p}(s) - w\}y(t)\exp\{-\delta(s-t)\}$$

$$+ \exp(\gamma t)\int_{t+n}^\infty \exp\{(\gamma-r)(s-t)\}z(p^*)\beta_0\{p^* - w - q_1(\delta+\gamma)\}\,ds$$

Thus

$$\frac{\partial\pi}{\partial y(t)} = \left(\exp\{-(r+\delta)n\}q_1 + \int_t^{t+n}\exp\{-(\delta+r)(s-t)\}\,[M\{\bar{p}(s)\} - w]\,ds\right)$$

using A.1, A.2.

Note that since $M\{\bar{p}(s)\} < M(p^*)$, $\partial\pi/\partial y(t) < q_1$.

Consider $\partial\pi/\partial y(t)\{q_1, n(q_1)\}$. Then from the definition of $\partial\pi/\partial y$, we have

$$\frac{\partial^2\pi}{\partial y\partial n} = 0, \quad \frac{\partial^2\pi}{\partial y\partial q_1} = \exp\{-(\delta+r)n\}$$

and hence

$$\frac{d^2}{dq_1^2}\left(\frac{\partial\pi}{\partial y}\right) = \left[-(r+\delta)\exp\{-(r+\delta)n\}\frac{\partial n}{\partial q_1}\right].$$

But from A.1 and A.2 $\partial n/\partial q_1 > 0$ and hence $\partial \pi/\partial y$ is concave for $q > q_1{}^*$. But since $\partial \pi/\partial y$ is non-increasing in q_1, and is linear in q_1 for $q_1 \leqslant q_1{}^*$, then $\partial \pi/\partial y$ is concave in q_1 everywhere.

Footnotes

[1] This assumption is merely made for expositional purposes and if p_s, w_s have some joint distribution, the result that is derived still holds good for a suitable extension of the definition of increasing uncertainty to multivariate distributions.

[2] This is rather a strong assumption since it implies that all the capacity is utilized, even if the marginal revenue falls below the wage cost per unit of output. This is clearly suboptimal if labour is freely adjusting and the firm should not utilize all its capacity at this time. We shall therefore assume that demand never falls low enough to bring about this situation.

[3] This expression is, in fact, not strictly accurate and there should be dt's multiplying the first two terms and the probability in the last term should be the probability of $t \leqslant \tilde{t} + m \leqslant t + dt$. However, the use of such loose mathematics causes little harm in this context and adds to the clarity of the analysis.

[4] The terms 'certainty period' and 'period of uncertainty' will be used to describe the periods after and before that point in time which in fact occurs *m periods after* the arrival of the uncertain event. So the 'certainty period' is shorthand for that period of certainty in which the capital stock decisions were taken after the occurrence of the uncertain event.

[5] Note if x is a constant, $y = x \exp(\gamma t)$ moves on a constant exponential growth path or trend path. There are two trend paths which bound capacity in this problem, the lower one where x satisfies $N_y^0 = c$, and the higher one where x satisfies $N_y^1 = c$.

[6] If the jump in demand is downwards, the path for the longer delivery lag is lower.

[7] There is, of course, an implicit assumption in the case of no adjustment costs that it takes m periods to sell off capital goods as well as to purchase them.

[8] If it does bite, then we must cope with a zero investment interval during the period of uncertainty, a problem which, though by no means insuperable, adds little and is therefore best avoided.

[9] Details may be found in Nickell (1977b).

[10] It has also been suggested, for example in Ando *et al.* (1974, p. 385, footnote 3), that the existence of *ex post* fixed coefficients (putty-clay) also helps to explain the sluggish behaviour of the investment response. In fact this will only explain a sluggishness in the response of the *capital–labour ratio* to relative *price* changes. In such a model investment will respond instantly to any price changes and, furthermore; capital stock will adjust fully and immediately to any *ceteris paribus* demand changes.

[11] Note, however, that in section 4 of Chapter 8, we suggest that capital market 'imperfections' may lead to a firm behaving as if it were faced with strictly convex costs of adjustment.

Bibliographical Notes—Chapter 6

Apart from the discussion of Hartman (1972) at the beginning, this chapter is almost entirely based on Nickell (1977b). There is no other work which concerns itself with delivery lags and uncertainty though some further results on uncertainty and adjustment costs can be found in Hartman (1973).

CHAPTER 7

REPLACEMENT AND DEPRECIATION

1. Mechanistic Decay and Replacement Investment

The investment plans of firms are inextricably bound up with decisions concerning whether or not to continue operating the oldest machinery and equipment. If at any point in time the firm decides to scrap (or sell) some of its old machinery, this may well entail an increase in current investment to compensate for the resulting loss of capacity. Up to this point in our study of investment we have neatly avoided consideration of such decisions by assuming that the firm keeps it capital for ever. This is a natural consequence of the exponential decay assumption 4 (p. 8) for, given the fact that capital evaporates in such a manner that what remains is completely indistinguishable from new capital, there is absolutely no point in the firm throwing any of it away at any time. There are two important aspects of this exponential decay assumption which we shall consider separately. The first is that it is completely mechanistic. Nothing the firm does can effect this decay, it goes on regardless of maintenance expenditure or intensity of use or in fact anything at all. In some sense, once capital has been purchased it is removed from the world of economics except that, if there is no irreversibility assumption, it can be sold again. The second aspect of the assumption is the specific form which the evaporation takes, namely exponential, and it is this aspect which will be discussed in this section. In later sections such things as maintenance costs, intensity of use of capital and scrapping will be considered, but for the moment we shall maintain the mechanistic view and simply consider the effects of non-exponential decay.

One of the very special consequences of exponential decay is the fact that old capital goods are completely indistinguishable from new ones. That is, a firm would be completely indifferent between possessing what is left out of one unit of capital purchased one year ago and $\exp(-\delta)$ units of new capital, where δ is the annual rate of decay. This indifference is quite independent of any external economic parameters and follows from a very special property of the exponential decay function. This is best seen by considering the following example. Suppose we take two units of capital and wait for them to decay to half a unit each. Then we put these two half units together. Clearly we now have one unit, but not only that. This unit will also decay in exactly the same way as a new unit and is thus completely identical to a new unit.[1] To bring home this point suppose we have some form of non-exponential decay, 'one hoss shay', for example, where there is no decay at all for a certain period of use and then the capital good simply disappears. Suppose that the useful lifetime of these goods is T. Then it might be thought at first glance that two of these goods with $T/2$ years of life remaining are precisely equivalent to one new good. The two old ones certainly cannot be any worse because if they are used sequentially they are precisely equivalent. But suppose the world is such that they can only be used to produce an output the demand for which drops to zero after $T/2$ years. Then clearly the two half used capital goods are far superior to the single new one because the single new good is entirely useless for the second half of its life. Consequently, if there is not exponential decay, the comparative *value* to the firm of old capital goods as opposed to new ones depends upon external economic circumstances even though their current productive capacities may be identical. The analytical consequences of this are very serious because it means that different vintages of capital goods must be kept separate in the analysis; that is, the age structure matters.

This is a matter of vital importance in considering so called replacement investment. Before plunging into this topic it is worth briefly defining exactly what is meant by the term replacement investment, for the existing literature contains a number of conflicting views on the subject. In order to do so we first define a quantity, which may not correspond to any actual purchases of investment goods, which we term potential replacement investment. *Potential replacement investment is defined to be that quantity of investment currently required to maintain capital stock constant.*[2] It is important to be quite clear how it is that potential replacement investment may not correspond to any actual purchases. For example, we know from Chapter 4 that when a firm faces an irreversibility constraint on investment it may well have a zero level of gross investment during slump periods. No purchases whatever are then being made and consequently, although capital stock is decaying and thus potential replacement investment is certainly positive, there is no actual investment of any description. Now we can define replacement investment itself and also expansion investment. *Replacement investment is equal to total (gross) investment if this is less than potential replacement investment. Otherwise it is equal to potential replacement itself and the remaining amount of total investment is expansion investment.*[3]

Looking at the standard accumulation equation when there is exponential decay, namely,

7.1 $$\dot{K} = I - \delta K,$$

we can immediately see that potential replacement investment in this case is simply equal to δK, for this is the quantity of investment required if capital stock is to be maintained at the current level (i.e. $\dot{K} = 0$). Now in empirical work it is often assumed that potential replacement investment is some fixed proportion of current capital stock and, since this assumption has been a serious bone of contention, it is worth looking to see if this can happen in circumstances other than those in which capital stock evaporates exponentially. In order to do this we first define a general evaporation function $\delta(\tau)$, which is the proportion of a unit of capital remaining after τ years in operation. So, if I is gross investment, the total quantity of capital stock in operation at time t is simply given by

7.2 $$K(t) = \int_{0}^{\infty} \delta(\tau) I(t-\tau) \, d\tau,$$

that is, the sum of what remains of all past investments. At this stage it is useful to define the concept of the age structure of the capital stock, so we let $A(t, \tau)$ be the proportion of the capital stock at time t which is of age τ. A is thus defined by

7.3 $$A(t, \tau) = \frac{\delta(\tau) I(t-\tau)}{K(t)}$$

where note that

7.4 $$\int_{0}^{\infty} A(t, \tau) \, d\tau = \frac{1}{K(t)} \int_{0}^{\infty} \delta(\tau) I(t-\tau) \, d\tau = \frac{K(t)}{K(t)} = 1,$$

and thus $A(t, \tau)$ is very much like a probability density function. In order to find out what potential replacement is in this case we note that by changing the variable in the integral of 7.2 we have

$$K(t) = \int_{0}^{\infty} \delta(\tau) I(t-\tau) \, d\tau = \int_{-\infty}^{t} \delta(t-s) I(s) \, ds$$

and then by differentiating we have

7.5 $$\dot{K}(t) = I(t) + \int\limits_{-\infty}^{t} \delta'(t-s)I(s)\,\mathrm{d}s$$

using the fact that $\delta(0) = 1$.

Potential replacement $PR(t)$ is then given by

$$PR(t) = -\int\limits_{-\infty}^{t} \delta'(t-s)I(s)\,\mathrm{d}s$$

$$= \int\limits_{0}^{\infty} \delta'(\tau)I(t-\tau)\,\mathrm{d}\tau \qquad \text{by a change of variable,}$$

$$= \int\limits_{0}^{\infty} \frac{\delta'(\tau)}{\delta(\tau)}\,\delta(\tau)I(t-\tau)\,\mathrm{d}\tau$$

$$= \int\limits_{0}^{\infty} \phi(\tau)\delta(\tau)I(t-\tau)\,\mathrm{d}\tau \qquad \text{where } \phi = -\delta'/\delta.$$

In order to study the conditions for the constancy of the potential replacement–capital ratio we simply divide PR by K to give

7.6 $$\frac{PR(t)}{K(t)} = \int\limits_{0}^{\infty} \phi(\tau)\,\frac{\delta(\tau)I(t-\tau)\,\mathrm{d}\tau}{K(t)} = \int\limits_{0}^{\infty} \phi(\tau)A(t,\tau)\,\mathrm{d}\tau,$$

and look for conditions which make this independent of t. By way of confirmation note that if $\delta(\tau)$ is an exponential function then $\phi(\tau)$ is a constant and thus

$$\frac{PR(t)}{K(t)} = \int\limits_{0}^{\infty} \phi(\tau)A(t,\tau)\,\mathrm{d}\tau = \text{constant} \times \int\limits_{0}^{\infty} A(t,\tau)\,\mathrm{d}\tau = \text{constant}$$

from 7.4.

More generally, if $PR(t)/K(t)$ is to be a constant for a general non-constant $\phi(\tau)$, then we have

$$\frac{\mathrm{d}PR/K}{\mathrm{d}t} = 0 = \int\limits_{0}^{\infty} \phi(\tau)\,\frac{\mathrm{d}}{\mathrm{d}t}\,A(t,\tau)\,\mathrm{d}\tau,$$

which will only hold in general cases if $(\mathrm{d}/\mathrm{d}t)\,A(t,\tau) = 0$ for all τ. Thus we can say immediately that for a general non-exponential decay function the potential replacement–capital ratio is constant if, and only if, the age structure of the capital stock remains unchanged over time. This is an extremely important result for it implies that if, in some particular case, we have good reason to believe that capital goods are not decaying exponentially then we have only to detect changes in the age structure of the capital stock and we can immediately say that the potential replacement–capital ratio must be changing.

However, we need not stop there. We can look for conditions under which the age structure remains constant. Suppose that gross investment is growing exponentially over time and thus we can write $I(t) = I(0) \exp(\xi t)$ for all t. Then the age structure is given by

$$A(t, \tau) = \frac{\delta(\tau)I(t-\tau)}{\int_0^\infty \delta(\tau)I(t-\tau)\,d\tau} = \frac{\delta(\tau)I(0)\exp\{\xi(t-\tau)\}}{\int_0^\infty \delta(\tau)I(0)\exp\{\xi(t-\tau)\}\,d\tau}$$

$$= \frac{\delta(\tau)\exp(-\xi\tau)}{\int_0^\infty \delta(\tau)\exp(-\xi\tau)\,d\tau}$$

which is independent of t and thus constant over time. Consequently, for non-exponential decay the potential replacement–capital ratio is constant if investment is and always has been growing on an exponential path. Furthermore, Feldstein and Rothschild (1974) have proved that this is the *only* case in which the age structure and hence PR/K remains constant. What is more, they show that if PR/K is to settle down to a constant level in the long run in the absence of exponential decay, investment must settle to an exponential growth path in the long run. This is, in fact the result of renewal theory which has been quoted in particular by Jorgenson[4] as a justification for assuming that the potential replacement–capital ratio is constant. Now, if investment was indeed moving on a fixed exponential growth path, a proliferation of investment equations would hardly be required to explain this movement and consequently any serious theoretical justification of the assumption of a fixed potential replacement–capital ratio for empirical work must fall back on exponential decay.[5]

It is worth briefly discussing the type of investment patterns which can be expected if decay is not in fact exponential so, just for illustrative purposes, we shall consider the 'one hoss shay' type mentioned above. Suppose that capital goods maintain their productivity for T years, after which they fall to pieces. Consider a simple fixed coefficients imperfect competition model with certainty, where the demand follows a known path $z(p)\beta(t)$ in usual notation, and the wage per unit output, w, the rate of interest, r, and the price of capital goods, q, are all constant. Furthermore, suppose that demand is such as to make gross investment positive at all times so that there is no problem of selling off capital stock. Then we know that on the optimal path the net return on any additional unit of capacity must balance its cost and this provides the natural optimality condition

7.7 $$\int_{t}^{t+T} \exp\{-r(s-t)\}\,[M\{p(s)\}-w]\,\mathrm{d}s = q \qquad \text{for all } t,$$

where $M(p)$ is the marginal revenue as usual. Since this holds for all t, it holds in particular for $t+T$, $t+2T$, etc., and, if we suitably discount and add all these conditions to 7.7, this gives

$$\int_{t}^{\infty} \exp\{-r(s-t)\}\,[M\{p(s)\}-w]\,\mathrm{d}s = q\{1+\exp(-rT)+\exp(-2rT)\ldots\}$$

7.8 $$= q\{1-\exp(-rT)\}^{-1}.$$

Taking the derivative of 7.8 with respect to t and substituting back yields the rather neat flow condition

7.9 $$M(p) = w + rq\{1-\exp(-rT)\}^{-1}.$$

Thus p is constant and the cost of capital is equal to the expression $rq\{1-\exp(-rT)\}^{-1}$, which is approximately equal to $q\{r+r\exp(-tT)\}$, whence we can say that the effective rate of depreciation in this case is $r\exp(-rT)$. Note that this shows that the effective depreciation rate depends on economic parameters, confirming the argument at the beginning of this section.[6]

Turning now to the capacity accumulation equation, note that capacity in this case is simply the sum of all the investments over the last T years. Thus we have

7.10 $$y(t) = \int_{t-T}^{t} I(s)\,\mathrm{d}s$$

which implies that the rate of change of capacity is

7.11 $$\dot{y}(t) = I(t) - I(t-T),$$

hardly a surprising result since it is simply the difference between new purchases and the quantity that falls to pieces. This means that potential replacement is $I(t-T)$, that is, the quantity of new investment purchased T years previously. This fact leads to an effect which is typical of non-exponential decay, namely the so-called echo effect.[7] This is where potential replacement is strongly influenced by the capital purchases made some T years before, T being the lifetime of the capital good in question. This effect is illustrated in Figure 7.1 below. Here we have demand showing an increase between t_0 and t_1 leading to a rise in investment between these two times. Then, at

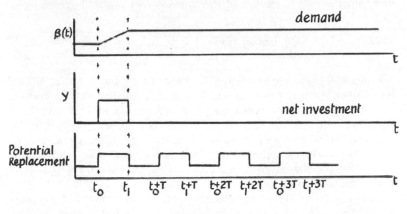

Figure 7.1

intervals of T units in the future, this additional investment is replaced leading to surges of replacement at regular intervals. These are the echoes.

In reality, of course, any echo effects would not be as clear-cut as those of Figure 7.1 for a variety of reasons, not least the fact that demand typically moves rather more randomly than in that picture thereby confusing the issue. It might be thought however that their existence would imply some systematic relation between the age structure of the capital stock and the amount of potential replacement. For example, it may be imagined that potential replacement would increase with the average age of the capital stock on the simple argument that the older the capital stock, the more needs replacing. Unfortunately, the existence of echo effects provides no such implication and consequently their existence is neither confirmed nor denied by the discovery that there is no systematic relationship between the average age of capital stock and the amount of potential replacement (or actual replacement, for that matter). To see that this is so we can simply note that from 7.6 the rate of change of the potential replacement–capital ratio is given by the equation.

7.12
$$\frac{\mathrm{d}}{\mathrm{d}t}\frac{PR(t)}{K(t)} = \int_0^\infty \phi(\tau)\,\frac{\mathrm{d}A}{\mathrm{d}t}\,(t,\,\tau)\,\mathrm{d}\tau,$$

and that the rate of change of the mean age of capital is given by

7.13
$$\frac{\mathrm{d}}{\mathrm{d}t}\,(\text{mean age}) = \int_0^\infty \tau\,\frac{\mathrm{d}A}{\mathrm{d}t}\,(t,\,\tau)\,\mathrm{d}\tau.$$

Since $\phi(\tau)$ is simply restricted to be positive and $\mathrm{d}A(t,\,\tau)/\mathrm{d}t$ can be more or less any function which is zero if integrated from zero to infinity, the relationship between the expressions of 7.12 and 7.13 is rather tenuous. In fact it is clear that $(\mathrm{d}/\mathrm{d}t)(PR/K)$ can be positive when $\mathrm{d}/\mathrm{d}t$ (mean age) is positive or negative and consequently we can conclude that there is no systematic relationship at all between changes in mean age and movements in the potential replacement–capital ratio.

This concludes the discussion of mechanistic forms of decay and we now consider the rather more interesting possibility that the rate of decay is itself an economic decision. This will take up the remainder of the chapter.

2. Determining the Optimal Maintenance Expenditure

At the beginning of this chapter two possible methods by which the firm might influence the rate of decay of its capital stock were suggested. These were the rate of maintenance expenditure and the intensity of use. In this section we ignore the latter and try to construct a simple model of the relationship between maintenance expenditures and the rate of decay. The general idea is that there is some trade-off for the firm between maintenance costs and the costs of capital decay and consequently the firm will choose a level of maintenance expenditures so that these two costs just balance at the margin. The problem is, however, slightly more complicated because the firm also has the choice of scrapping the good in question and the decision of when to scrap is, of course, related to the level of maintenance expenditures. For example, a firm is hardly likely, at least in a world of certainty, to scrap a piece of machinery just after it has been thoroughly overhauled. We shall now try and give these ideas some formal structure. Suppose $m(\tau, t)$ is the maintenance expenditure on one unit of capital of age τ purchased at time t. We must now define the relationship between the stream of maintenance expenditures and the rate of decay of the capital good, and this may be done in the following way. Let $\phi\{\tau, N(\tau, t)\}$ be the proportion of one unit of capital purchased at t which remains at age τ. The function N must be related in some way to the whole stream of past maintenance expenditures for the proportion of a capital unit remaining clearly depends on all past maintenance. Postponing briefly the discussion of how N is to be specified, it seems natural to suppose that ϕ increases in N but probably at a decreasing rate and thus $\partial\phi/\partial N > 0$ and $\partial^2\phi/\partial N^2 < 0$. Also one must assume that $\partial\phi/\partial\tau < 0$, that is, the capital good in fact decays if the level of 'total' maintenance is kept constant. Furthermore we may wish to assume that $\partial^2\phi/\partial\tau\partial N > 0$ implying that increasing the total maintenance level, N, has a stronger absolute effect later on in the life of the good.

Suppose now that we let $N(\tau, t)$ be defined by

$$7.13 \qquad N(\tau, t) = \int_0^t \psi(\tau - \nu, t)m(\nu, t)\,\mathrm{d}\nu.$$

The function N is thus some weighted sum of past maintenance expenditures where it would seem reasonable to assume that $\partial\psi/\partial(\tau - \nu) < 0$, that is, more recent expenditures have more effect on the current proportion remaining and are thus given a higher weight. This means, for example, that a unit of capital is more productive in the fifth year of its life if it has been overhauled in the fourth year rather than the second year, assuming the expenditure on the two overhauls is the same. To simplify matters the function ψ is assumed to be exponential, that is $\psi(\tau - \nu, t) = a(t)\exp\{-\eta(\tau - \nu)\}$ and this implies that, in some sense, the value of the accumulated maintenance expenditure decays over time at a rate η. If in some particular case this sort of decay is not very appealing then, of course, it is simply removed by letting η equal zero.

We may now graft this model on to a simple fixed coefficients imperfectly competitive model of the firm and write down the net present value return on an additional unit of capital stock purchased at time t. Assuming that it is scrapped at age $T(t)$, this is given by

$$7.14 \quad \int_0^{T(t)} \exp{(-r\tau)} \, [M\{p(\tau+t)\}-w(\tau+t)]\phi\{\tau, N(\tau, t)\} \, \mathrm{d}\tau$$

$$- \int_0^{T(t)} \exp{(-r\tau)} \, m(\tau, t) \, \mathrm{d}\tau$$

where the first term is the actual marginal return from selling the output less the wage cost and the second is the total present value of the maintenance expenditure. (Note that, as usual, M is the marginal revenue and w is the wage cost per unit of output.)

It is clear that for any fixed path of p and w, the firm will choose $T(t)$ and the maintenance expenditure $m(\tau, t)$ to maximize this expression.[8] This problem will not be treated formally because it is made somewhat difficult by the fact that it involves an implicit irreversibility constraint, namely $m(\tau; t) \geqslant 0$. On the other hand, it is possible to give some useful insights into the nature of the solution by using simple marginal analysis. Suppose at some age s, the firm spends an additional unit of income on maintenance. Then the accumulated N will be increased by $a(t) \exp{\{-\eta(\nu-s)\}}$ at age ν for all $\nu \geqslant s$, where remember that the effect of the additional unit of maintenance is 'decaying' at rate η. Consequently this will lead to an addition to the proportion of the marginal capital unit remaining of $\phi_N \exp{\{-\eta(\nu-s)\}} \, a(t)$ at age ν yielding an additional return of $\{M(\nu+t)-w(\nu+t)\}\phi_N a(t) \exp{\{-\eta(\nu-s)\}}$. On the optimal path the total addition to the present value return caused by the extra unit of maintenance expenditure must just balance the cost, giving

$$7.15 \quad \int_s^{T(t)} \exp{\{-(r+\eta)(\nu-s)\}} \, [M\{p(\nu+t)-w(\nu+t)]$$
$$\times \phi_N a(t) \, \mathrm{d}\nu = 1.$$

Taking the derivative with respect to s and using 7.15 itself gives the flow condition

$$a(t)\phi_N[M\{p(s+t)\}-w(s+t)]=\eta+r$$

which defines a value of N at each point of time.

Thus N is given by

$$7.16 \quad \phi_N\{s, N(s, t)\}=(\eta+r)([M\{p(s+t)\}-w(s+t)]a(t))^{-1}.$$

Note that since $\phi_{Ns}>0$ and $\phi_{NN}<0$, this shows that N increases with age (at least if p and w are constant). Before going on to further discussion of the maintenance problem we can very easily state the condition which will determine the scrapping age $T(t)$. The unit of capital will be thrown out when its net return just fails to cover the current maintenance expenditure and thus $T(t)$ satisfies the simple relation

7.17 $\left(M[p\{T(t)+t\}]-w\{T(t)+t\}\right)\phi[T(t),\ N\{T(t),\ t\}]=m\{T(t),\ t\}.$

If, of course, the net return is always greater than the current maintenance then the unit of capital is retained indefinitely.

The solution to the maintenance problem looks, on the face of it, rather straightforward. Just use 7.16 to compute the maintenance expenditure and then substitute into 7.17 to compute the scrapping age. Unfortunately it is not as easy as that and there is a sound intuitive reason why not. This type of solution would imply that the maintenance expenditure was entirely independent of the scrapping age, in the sense that it could be determined quite separately. This in turn, means that maintenance would continue right up to the point of scrapping. But this is counter-intuitive. Surely at some point close to the scrapping age further maintenance would be wasted and the machine should be left to die on its own, so to speak. This point may indeed be very close to the scrapping date but, as was pointed out before, a machine is not overhauled one day and scrapped the next. In fact this intuition is correct and the equation 7.16 only holds up to a certain point in time (technically because of the irreversibility constraint on $m(\tau, t)$. After this point maintenance is stopped and the machine is axed when it is useless, that is when ϕ becomes zero. However, this extra complication need not worry us too much because for the remainder of this section the model will be used only to make some rather informal points.

Briefly then, we can see immediately from 7.16 that maintenance expenditure is directly related to the output price p (remember $\phi_{NN}<0$ and $M_p>0$). Since $\phi_N>0$, an increase in N will increase ϕ at any point in time and because we now know that $\phi=0$ at the scrapping age, this implies a later scrapping date. Looking back over our past models we know that the output price increases at those times when capital purchases are held back in the face of increasing demand. This occurs, for example, when a firm making irreversible investment decisions faces a prospective slump (see Chapter 4) or because of adjustment costs when the firm faces a sudden increase in demand (see Chapter 3 section 3). The present analysis then tells us that at these times maintenance will be increased and scrapping postponed, thereby making greater use of the existing capital. This surely is a very sensible result. At times óf either voluntary or enforced capital shortage there will be a reduction in scrapping and an increase in expenditure on maintenance. In order to make some more detailed explorations of such matters and also to consider the role of technical progress in determining the rate of scrapping it is clear that we require a rather simpler model but one constructed along the same sort of lines. This will be the topic covered in the next section.

3. A Complete Model with Maintenance Costs

In order to construct a complete but manageable model with maintenance costs and scrapping, the level of maintenance expenditure on any unit of capital is assumed to follow a pre-ordained path as the unit ages. Furthermore, it is assumed that the maintenance expenditure increases without bound thereby ensuring that the capital good is eventually scrapped. From the analysis of the last section it is easy to see that these assumptions are somewhat arbitrary since, in reality, maintenance expenditure is a variable determined within the firm simultaneously with all the other operational variables. Nevertheless it seems not unreasonable to hope that the results which will be obtained will not point entirely in the wrong direction, and that the exercise is therefore worth carrying out. Unfortunately the technical difficulty of the model is about as severe as anything else in this book but that is an inevitable consequence of the structure of a model in which the different vintages of capital must be kept separate.

To be more precise about the structure of the model we shall set out in detail those assumptions which are being employed. Both assumption 1 (p. 5) on perfect capital markets and assumption 2 (p. 7) on certainty (or certain uniform expectations) are retained. The technology of the firm is slightly different from anything that has gone before because of the addition of technical progress and this is set out as

Assumption 3c. The firm has a fixed coefficients technology with simple capital augmenting technical progress.[9]

This type of technical progress simply means that the firm requires less capital to produce a unit of output as the capital employed becomes more modern. On the other hand if wages remain constant, then so does the wage cost per unit of output.

Clearly we must now reject assumption 4 (p. 8) on exponential evaporation and replace this by some assumption concerning maintenance costs. This is done as follows.

Assumption 4a. Capital goods are assumed to decay exponentially at a constant rate but, in order to restrict decay to this rate, the firm is required to make some expenditure on maintenance. The expenditure per unit increases as the capital good ages and becomes infinitely large as the capital good becomes infinitely old.

The imperfectly competitive framework described in assumption 8 (p. 16) is retained and investment is assumed to be an irreversible process, assumption 6b (p. 51). However, as there is no lag, part of assumption 6b must be dropped. Finally, there are no taxes, assumption 7 (p. 8).

The general strategy will be to look at the necessary conditions for present value maximization and then to discuss the situation where the scrapping age remains constant over time. We look at the effects of various parameter changes on the scrapping age, especially changes in the rate of technical progress which we might expect to be of some importance in this connection. Finally, we shall discuss the rate of scrapping and of actual replacement in response to booms and slumps in demand and also to changes in costs.

Formally the model has the following structure. If $n(t)$ is the birth-date of the last unit of capital scrapped, then the output $y(t)$ is defined by the equation,

7.18 $$y(t) = \int_{n(t)}^{t} \exp\left\{-\delta(t-s)\right\} \lambda(s)I(s) \, ds,$$

where y, I, δ are capacity, investment and the rate of decay respectively and $\lambda(s)$ is a technical progress coefficient which satisfies $\lambda' > 0$. Thus the current capacity is simply a suitably weighted sum of the previously purchased capital goods which are still in use. The total maintenance expenditure on the capital stock, which is designated as $A(t)$, is defined by

7.19 $$A(t) = a \int_{n(t)}^{t} \exp\left\{-\delta(t-s)\right\} m(t-s)I(s) \, ds$$

where $am(\tau)$ is the maintenance expenditure on a unit of capital goods of age τ (note that after τ years, only $\exp(-\delta\tau)$ of a unit remains). Then, if we assume that demand, $x(p)\beta(t)$ in our usual notation, is kept equal to capacity, we have the equality

7.20 $$y(t) = x\{p(t)\}\beta(t).$$

The firm will then maximize its present value

$$\int_0^\infty \exp\{-R(t)\}\{p(t)y(t) - w(t)y(t) - A(t) - q(t)I(t)\}\,\mathrm{d}t$$

subject to 7.18–7.20 plus the irreversibility constraint

$$I(t) \geqslant 0.$$

If we assume that the irreversibility constraint does not bite we may write down the necessary conditions immediately on the basis of simple marginal considerations. These conditions are two in number. The first states that on the optimal path the present value return on a marginal unit of capacity purchased at time t just balances the sum of its purchase price and the present value of the expenditure required to maintain it. So, if $T(t)$ is the age at which the marginal unit purchased at time t is scrapped, we must have

7.21 $$\lambda(t)\int_0^{T(t)} \exp\{-(r+\delta)\tau\}\,[M\{p(t+\tau)\} - w(t+\tau)]\,\mathrm{d}\tau$$

$$= q(t) + \int_0^{T(t)} \exp\{-(r+\delta)\tau\}\,am(\tau)\,\mathrm{d}\tau$$

where M is the marginal revenue, as before, and r is assumed constant for convenience.

The second necessary condition is rather simpler and states that a unit of capacity is scrapped when the return on it is completely offset by the necessary maintenance expenditure. That is,

7.22 $$\lambda(t)\big(M[p\{t+T(t)\}] - w\{t+T(t)\}\big) = am\{T(t)\}.$$

By differentiating 7.21 with respect to t and using both 7.21 and 7.22, we show in the Appendix (proposition 1) that the following flow condition holds, namely,

7.23 $\quad \lambda(t)[M\{p(t)\} - w(t)] = (r + \delta - \dot{q}/q + \dot{\lambda}/\lambda)q$

$$+ (r + \delta + \dot{\lambda}/\lambda) \int_{0}^{T(t)} \exp\{-(r+\delta)\tau\} \, am(\tau) \, d\tau$$

$$+ \exp\{-(r+\delta)T(t)\} \, am\{T(t)\}.$$

Before going on to make use of this condition it is worth spending a little time examining the intuition that lies behind it. The left-hand side is clearly equal to the current net revenue accruing to a marginal unit of capital. The right-hand side then ought to be the total cost of capital and this is indeed so, as the following discussion makes clear.

Consider first the expression $q + \int_0^{T(t)} \exp\{-(r+\delta)\tau\} \, am(\tau) \, d\tau$. This can be looked upon as the price of a capital unit which is combined with a guarantee that it will be maintained in good working order. The cost of using this unit for one period will then be made up of three elements of which the first two are simply the interest and depreciation charges, namely $(r+\delta)[q + \int_0^{T(t)} \exp\{-(r+\delta)\tau\} \, am(\tau) \, d\tau]$. The final element is the decline in value of the unit and this is rather more complicated. Suppose first that after one period of use the unit of capital was as good as new. Then even if the price of capital goods was also unchanged it would still decline in value by a proportion $\dot{\lambda}/\lambda$ because the new capital goods would be precisely that much more efficient. If the price of capital goods had changed however, then its value would have further declined by $\dot{q}$. But, of course, the unit of capital is in fact one period old, so it only has a maintenance guarantee with $T(t) - 1$ periods left to run and this is clearly worth $\exp\{-(r+\delta)T(t)\} \, am\{T(t)\}$ less than a full $T(t)$ year maintenance guarantee, the difference being the present value cost of the last period's maintenance expenditure.

Adding all this up gives a total cost of capital

$$(r + \delta + \dot{\lambda}/\lambda)\left[q + \int_{0}^{T(t)} \exp\{-(r+\delta)\tau\} \, am(\tau) \, d\tau\right]$$

$$- \dot{q} + \exp\{-(r+\delta)T(t)\} \, am\{T(t)\},$$

which is precisely the expression on the right-hand side of 7.23.

Using the conditions 7.22, 7.23 it may be shown that, if q, $\dot{\lambda}/\lambda$, w are all constant and these equations do not imply negative gross investment, the optimal scrapping age is given by a constant T^* which satisfies

7.24 $\quad am(T)[\exp{(\eta T)} - \exp{\{-(r+\delta)T\}}] - (r+\delta+\eta)$

$$\times \left[q + a \int_0^T \exp{\{-(r+\delta)\tau\}}\, m(\tau)\, \mathrm{d}\tau \right] = 0$$

where η is equal to the constant rate of technical progress $\dot{\lambda}/\lambda$ (see Appendix, proposition 2, for a proof). To see how this determines a complete solution, note that 7.22 shows that the price at time t must satisfy

7.25 $\qquad \lambda(t-T^*)[M\{p(t)\} - w] = am(T^*)$

and the demand condition 7.20 then gives the optimal capacity at time t. Using the derivative of 7.18 we find that the optimal rate of investment at time t must satisfy

7.26 $\quad \dot{y}(t) = \lambda(t)I(t) - \delta y(t) - \lambda(t-T^*)\exp{(-\delta T^*)}\, I(t-T^*)$

where the middle term is the amount of capital decay and the final term represents the rate of scrapping. It is worth noting from 7.26 that we shall again have the kind of echo effects discussed in the previous section because the rate of scrapping at any point in time depends directly on the level of gross investment some T^* periods previously.

Reverting to the optimal lifetime of the capital goods, T^*, we see from 7.24 that this depends on a number of parameters, in particular the rate of technical progress, η, the price of maintenance, a, and the price of capital goods, q. As far as technical progress is concerned it is generally asserted that higher rates of technical progress imply a shorter optimal economic life for capital goods and this is borne out by the model where indeed $\partial T^*/\partial \eta < 0$.[10] This is only to be expected in the sense that there is a clear incentive for firms to scrap capital goods earlier if there are much superior goods readily available. Arguing along similar lines we would also expect earlier scrapping if the price of maintenance were increased, for this would again shift the balance away from the old capital goods towards the new. Finally, a rise in the price of capital goods themselves should clearly imply a longer life as the firm economizes on new capital goods by maintaining the old ones for a longer time. Given the fact that maintenance costs are at least partly accounted for by wages, this is a form of substitution which can occur even in a fixed coefficients model of this type. Again, both these results are confirmed by the analysis.

Turning now to a consideration of the effects of booms and slumps in demand on general investment policy, we shall consider first the situation where the firm has been satisfying a stable level of demand for a long period and then enters a 'shallow' slump, that is to say a slump which is not severe enough to imply a negative rate of gross investment. The fact that demand has been constant for a considerable time implies that the rate of investment has been more or less uniform in the past and since the slump is shallow the scrapping age remains constant at T^*. Furthermore, we shall now assume away technical progress, and hence we can put $\lambda(t) = 1$ for all t, which implies that the output price remains constant at p^* satisfying

7.27 $$M(p^*) - w = am(T^*)$$

from 7.25. Then, throughout the slump, capacity simply follows the level of demand, maintaining equality 7.20 with $p(t) = p^*$. Consequently, the capital accumulation equation 7.26 reduces to

$$\dot{y}(t) = x(p^*)\beta = I(t) - \delta y(t) - \exp(-\delta T^*) I(t - T^*)$$

or

7.28 $$I(t) = x(p^*)\beta + \delta y(t) + \exp(-\delta T^*) I(t - T^*).$$

Note that throughout this shallow slump, the rate of scrapping remains constant because past investment has been maintained at a constant level. The firm adjusts for the slump simply by lowering the level of replacement investment during the period when demand declines and then, when demand starts to pick up again, replacement reverts to the level of potential replacement $\delta y(t) + \exp(-\delta T^*) \times I(t - T^*)$ and there is some expansion investment as well. The path of demand, expansion investment, replacement investment and scrapping are illustrated in Figure 7.2.

In contrast to this pattern of investment policy, we have something very different if the slump in demand is steep enough to imply a negative rate of gross investment, that is, if β is negative and large enough in absolute value to make the right-hand side of 7.28 negative. The problem is then rather more complicated and at this juncture we shall simply argue from past experience of such matters (especially Chapter 4).[11] We know that if a firm whose investment decisions are irreversible is confronted by a slump in demand its investment ceases completely sometime before the slump and only restarts on the upswing. This implies that when investment ceases, the output price will first rise to maintain demand in equality with the declining capacity, then fall again as demand actually slumps, finally rising again when demand recovers. We can now see what this implies for the optimal scrapping age given by 7.22. In order to

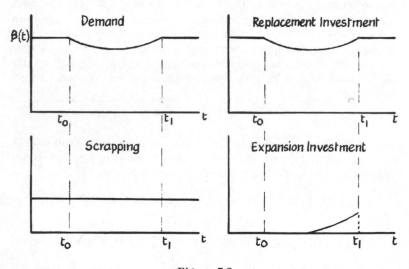

Figure 7.2

make clear exactly what is happening it is desirable to rewrite the scrapping rule 7.22 as it appears at time t, namely,

$$7.29 \qquad M\{p(t)\} - w = am\{t - n(t)\}$$

where remember that $\lambda = 1$ and that $n(t)$ is the birthdate of the capital goods currently being scrapped. Differentiating 7.29 with respect to t gives the relationship between price changes and changes in the age of the oldest capital, thus we have

$$7.30 \qquad M_p \dot{p} = am' . (1 - \dot{n}).$$

Note that both M_p and m' are positive and therefore $1 - \dot{n}$ takes the same sign as $\dot{p}$. So, if the output price increases, $1 - \dot{n}$ is positive $t - n(t)$ is increasing and thus the age of the oldest capital goods in use increases. The opposite applies if the output price declines. This is eminently reasonable since it implies that when there is a shortage of capacity which causes the output price to increase the existing capital is employed to a greater age, and vice versa. Consider the effect of this on the capital accumulation equation. Directly differentiating 7.18 gives (with $\lambda = 1$)

$$\dot{y}(t) = I(t) - \delta y(t) - \exp\{-\delta n(t)\} I\{n(t)\}\dot{n}$$

and thus the rate of scrapping is given by $\exp(-\delta n) I(n)\dot{n}$. Assuming, as before, that past investment was more or less constant, the rate of scrapping then depends directly on $\dot{n}$. When the output price is increasing $\dot{n} < 1$ and when it is decreasing $\dot{n} > 1$ and, consequently, the rate of scrapping is inversely related to output price movements. On the basis of this analysis we can now illustrate all the firm's investment activities during the steep slump and compare then with those for the shallow slump illustrated in Figure 7.2. This is done in Figure 7.3.

Note how the firm adjusts to the deep slump by ceasing investment altogether for the period from n_0 to n_1 and adjusting both its output price *and* its scrapping rate to deal with the demand fluctuations. This is in complete contrast to its reaction to a shallow slump where all adjustments were made by variations in the current rate of investment. It is interesting to compare also the reaction of the firm in this case with the reaction of the firm described in Chapter 4 (section 2) where there was no scrapping but there was capital labour substitution. In the current situation the firm ceases investment some time before the slump and then, to compensate for the lack of new capital, it raises the output price and slows down the scrapping rate thereby devoting more resources, including presumably labour, to maintenance activities. When demand does slump it lowers the price, scraps capital rather quickly and spends less on maintenance. The firm with substitution but no scrapping responds in a precisely similar fashion, the variations in scrapping and maintenance expenditure being mirrored by variations in labour input in production. In reality, of course, one would predict that there would be a combination of both effects.

Next we shall go on to consider the general investment and replacement policy in response to a boom in demand, supposing, first of all, that there are no strictly convex costs of adjustment. In this case the problem is very straightforward. The output price and the scrapping age remain fixed and, if previous demand and gross investment were more or less constant, then during the boom itself scrapping remains uniform and new investment simply increases to

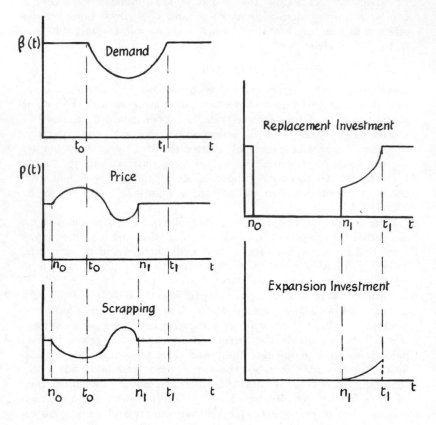

Figure 7.3

provide new capacity as required (see equation 7.28). However, if the boom was expected and there are strictly convex costs of adjustment as defined in assumption 6a (p. 25) the situation becomes rather more interesting. Again we shall argue from past experience, notably Chapter 3 (section 3).[12] In this case we know that the new investment is spread out because of the adjustment costs, and consequently new expansion investment expenditures are made in anticipation of the actual boom itself. These expenditures continue throughout the demand increase and even beyond and this yields a pattern of

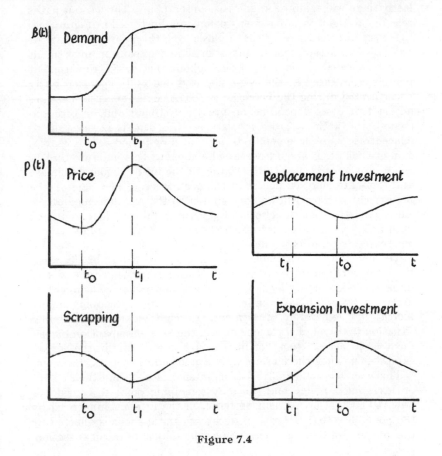

Figure 7.4

variation in output price whereby there is an initial decline as capacity is brought in to anticipate the boom, followed by a strong increase during the boom itself as demand overtakes capacity and finally a decline again back to the normal level of price as capacity eventually regains the correct level. So, from our previous analysis, we can immediately say that the rate of scrapping will follow a diametrically opposite path to the output price. Before the boom actually starts, scrapping will increase and maintenance will in fact decline. Then during the boom itself this trend will be reversed and lastly there will again be an increase in scrapping. The various paths relevant to the total investment policy are illustrated in Figure 7.4.

A very interesting point that follows from this analysis is that the path of actual replacement investment and expansion investment move somewhat in opposition throughout the period, replacement being concentrated at the beginning and end and expansion being concentrated during the boom itself.[13] This arises because there are adjustment costs depending on gross investment and, in order to smooth the path of gross investment, the firm is attempting to concentrate its replacement activities in those periods where expansion is weakest. It should perhaps be noted at this juncture that, if the firm is uncertain as to the timing of the future demand increase and there are delivery delays in the acquisition of new capital, the investment pattern will be very similar to the one described above since we know that the effects of such uncertainty when combined with delivery lags are very much the same as the effects of strictly convex costs of adjustment.

To conclude this particular section it is worth just briefly mentioning the effects of a reduction in costs, in particular the rate of interest.[14] This simply leads to a decline in output price as might be expected, leading to both an increase in the rate of scrapping and an increase in expansion investment. In contrast to the previous situation the level of replacement and the level of expansion investment both increase together in response to a decline in the cost of capital even when there are strictly convex adjustment costs.

This completes the analysis of maintenance costs and their effects on investment policy and the only remaining point to consider is how the general investment activities of the firm are influenced by the possibility that the rate of decay of capital goods is affected by the intensity of their use. This will be the subject of the next section.

4. Capacity Utilization and the Rate of Decay

In the foregoing analysis no use has been made of the notion that capital may be used at differing levels of intensity. On the contrary it has simply been assumed that capital is either used or it is not used. We shall now discuss this new notion in rather general terms, not by constructing any formal models (apart from a brief attempt in the Appendix) but rather by simply trying to see how it may be conveniently fitted into the previous analysis.

The effect of the intensity of use of capital goods on their rate of decay and thus on the effective cost of capital was briefly discussed by Keynes in *The General Theory*[15] in terms of providing a link between the present and the future. Since then this idea has been the subject of a certain amount of analysis but has never really found its way into the mainstream of discussion about investment decisions, although the cost of capital is often termed the 'user cost', presumably with this notion implicitly in the background. The idea is, however, intimately connected with the concept of capacity utilization which is much used in applied work and for which a variety of actual measures exist. In fact, one may argue that the degree of intensity of use of capital goods is synonymous with the degree of capacity utilization, the trouble being that both are somewhat elusive concepts. In a fixed coefficients technology there is no problem because it is clear that if there is irreversibility, for example, and demand declines very sharply then, when the shadow price of capital drops to zero, some of the capital will not be used at all and, consequently, the change in the level of capacity utilization is there for all to see. It would then seem not unreasonable to assume that the capital which is not being used does not decay as fast as the capital which is, thereby clearly affecting investment decisions. If, on the other hand, there is substitution between capital and labour, the concept of capacity utilization is a little more difficult to grip on to. It might be argued that the degree of utilization bears some relationship to the amounts of other factors which are employed with the capital and thus, for example, the rate of decay of capital should depend on the labour input per unit of capital stock. Surprisingly enough, a number of the studies that have analysed this matter have assumed that there is no relation between the rate of utilization and the employment of other factors, but have instead assumed that the rate of capacity utilization can be turned up or down quite independently, merely occasioning thereby a faster or slower rate of decay.[16] Unfortunately, the analytical and conceptual problems which arise if capacity utilization is not treated as a completely independent variable are really formidable and, simply to provide a flavour of these difficulties, we give an attempted formalization of the problem in the final part of the Appendix to this chapter.

As we pointed out at the beginning of this section we have no intention of discussing investment decisions in the context of a *formal* model which includes the effect of capacity utilization on the rate of decay, partly because of the difficulties we have already mentioned and partly because the major consequences of this notion can be discussed in the context of models already at our disposal, of which there are now a considerable number. One thing to note about these models is the fact that, when imperfect competition is assumed, the firm always adjusts its output price instantaneously to balance its demand with existing capacity. In fact, the very essence of many of our truly dynamic models of investment is that such price adjustments are being made continuously because the firm does not adjust capacity to demand variations for a whole host of reasons such as irreversibility, adjustment costs, delivery lags, uncertainty and the like. In a sense this is a thoroughly objectionable model of the world because, like many other economic variables and even more than most, the output prices of firms do not adjust at the flick of a switch. The firm uses many other mechanisms to keep demand in line with supply and one of these is by varying its rate of capacity utilization. This may involve bringing old machines in and out of operation, employing existing capital for more or less hours of the day or a whole host of other possibilities, most of which imply a change in the use of other factors. Nevertheless it seems quite reasonable to suppose that in those situations where variations in *demand* imply an increase or decrease in the output price, they also imply an increase or decrease in the rate of capacity utilization and thus in the intensity of use of existing capital. These variations in capacity utilization will naturally imply an overall reduction in the amplitude of price variations.

As an example of the sort of thing that can occur, consider again the standard response of the imperfectly competitive firm to a demand cycle when its investment decisions are irreversible. We know that some time before the expected slump the firm will cease investing and will maintain equality between demand and the now declining capacity by raising its output price and, if there is substitutability between capital and labour, by increasing its employment of labour. Furthermore, the analysis of the preceding section shows that the firm will also simultaneously reduce its rate of scrapping and increase its level of maintenance expenditure. We can say, in addition, that the firm will increase its rate of capacity utilization. In some sense this latter mode of adjustment is rather a catch-all which includes, among other things, elements of some of the other modes. For example, an increase in labour input clearly implies an increase in capacity utilization when capital stock is not increasing and the increases in maintenance expenditure may be thought of as compensating for the faster rate of decay. On the other hand, the introduction of capacity utilization as an instrument of adjustment for the firm may affect the simple inverse relationship between scrapping rates and output price variations which was derived in the last section. This may occur because increases in the rate of capacity utilization will cause faster decay of capital under more intensive use which will tend to reduce the productivity of all capital goods including the oldest, thereby tending to raise the scrapping rate. Nevertheless, in so far as variations in the rate of capacity utilization form an independent adjustment mechanism for the firm, it is quite clear where they fit into previous models.

Thus in the present example of the demand cycle, it is clear that, following the increase in capacity utilization just before the slump, it will fall during the actual slump itself only to rise again when demand picks up.

Turning to some other models, in the presence of adjustment costs capacity utilization will fall before an *expected* boom in demand but will rise rapidly during the boom itself, falling away again afterwards. Again, for example, if there was an unexpected rise in demand and also a delivery lag, we would expect a very large rise in capacity utilization until capacity had time to adjust. These examples can be continued indefinitely but the general principle is clear. In so far as the concept of capacity utilization is something which is independent of the other factors we have considered, then, in response to demand variations, it will rise and fall with the output price level, the level of labour input, and the level of maintenance expenditure. Its relationship with the rate of scrapping is somewhat ambiguous because, although scrapping is inversely related to these other variables in the absence of changes in capacity utilization, these changes can themselves pull the rate of scrapping in the opposite direction by affecting the productivity of the oldest capital units.

This completes the discussion of capacity utilization in particular and replacement problems in general and all that remains is to provide a summary of the findings. This we do in the final section.

5. Some Concluding Remarks on Replacement

The essential aim of this chapter has been to deal with the problems which arise when we get away from a purely mechanistic view

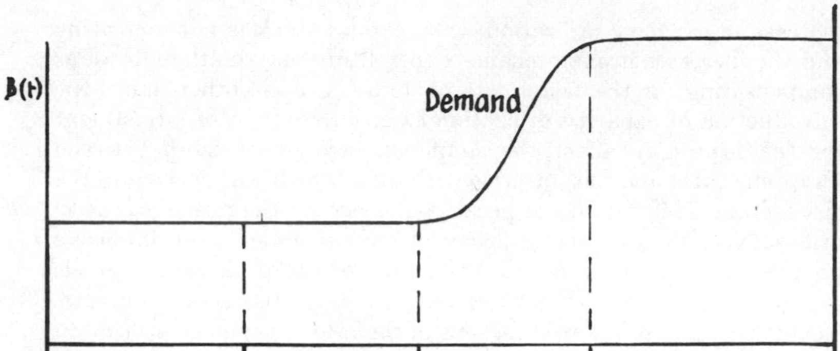

	Anticipation Period	Boom Period	Catching up Period
Gross Investment	↑	↑↑	↑
Output Price	↓	↑	↓
Labour Input	↓	↑	↓
Capacity Utilization	↓	↑	↓
Maintenance Expenditure	↓	↑	↓
Scrapping*	↑	↓	↑

*Exclusive of the possible effects of capacity utilization.

Figure 7.5

of capital stock decay and replacement. The replacement of mechanics by economics in this context gives rise to a whole new battery of instruments which the firm can use to manipulate its capital stock in response to changes in factor prices and demand. These are the rate of expenditure on maintenance, the rate of scrapping and the rate of utilization of existing capacity which are added to the sole instrument utilized to date, namely the rate of new capital purchases. All these four rates are determined simultaneously by the firm with the output price and the level of labour input. From these decisions, there emerges a rate of replacement and a rate of expansion but it is clear that these are in no sense basic decision variables.

As a final summary it is worth rounding up the results on the firm's response to a boom in demand where new purchases of capital respond in a sluggish manner. This is just the situation which arises with strictly convex adjustment costs in response to a certain expected boom or, perhaps more realistically, this is the response of the firm to a boom of uncertain size and timing when there is a lag in the delivery of capital goods. The adjustments of the variables under the firm's control are illustrated in the diagram opposite (Figure 7.5). In the figure we see that, during the anticipation period, the firm starts to accumulate capacity in response to the certain or uncertain expected boom. During this period capacity is beginning to outstrip demand and there is therefore an offsetting change in all the other instruments with output price, labour input, capacity utilization and maintenance declining and scrapping increasing. When the boom actually occurs the movements of all these other instruments will reverse as there is considerable pressure on capacity and this will continue until the final catching up period when the boom is over and the firm is making its final adjustments to the new higher demand level. It is worth noting that, in the case where the boom occurs at short notice, the adjustments of the boom period will start straightaway except that gross investment will not adjust at all for some time if there are lags. This will throw all the burden of the adjustment on to the other variables with consequent rapid increases in maintenance and capacity utilization, for example, with new capacity only arriving later to relieve the situation.

This more or less completes the theoretical study of the dynamic investment response of the firm. We have reached a point where we have a fairly good idea of how the firm will react to changes and expected changes in demand and factor prices and how it will utilize the various instruments at its disposal to adjust its capital stock. The next step is to make a deeper analysis of the crucial factor price in this context, namely the cost of capital, and to do this we must consider in greater detail the financial options open to the firm. This will be our concern in the next chapter.

Appendix

Proposition 1 (p. 128). If, in the usual notation

$$(1) \quad \lambda(t) \int_0^{T(t)} \exp\left\{-(r+\delta)\tau\right\} \left[M\{p(t+\tau)\} - w(t+\tau)\right] d\tau$$
$$= q(t) + \int_0^{T(t)} \exp\left\{-(r+\delta)\tau \, am(\tau) \, d\tau\right.$$

and

$$(2) \quad \lambda(t)\big(M[p\{t+T(t)\} - w\{t+T(t)\}\big) = am\{T(t)\} \qquad \text{for all } t,$$

then it follows that

$$\lambda(t)[M\{p(t)\} - w(t)] = (r + \delta - \dot{q}/q + \dot{\lambda}/\lambda)q$$
$$+ (r + \delta + \dot{\lambda}/\lambda) \int_0^{T(t)} \exp\left\{-(r+\delta)\tau\right\} am(\tau) \, d\tau$$
$$+ \exp\left\{-(r+\delta)T(t)\right\} am\{T(t)\}.$$

Proof. (1) may be written as,

$$\lambda(t) \int_t^{t+T(t)} \exp\left\{-(r+\delta)(\tau - t)\right\} \left[M\{p(\tau)\} - w(\tau)\right] d\tau$$
$$= q(t) + \int_0^{T(t)} \exp\left\{-(r+\delta)\tau\right\} am(\tau) \, d\tau$$

by changing the variable in the left-hand integral.

Differentiating with respect to t gives

$$(\dot{\lambda}/\lambda + r + \delta)\lambda \int_t^{t+T(t)} \exp\left\{-r + \delta)(\tau - t)\right\} \left[M\{p(\tau)\} - w(\tau)\right] d\tau$$
$$+ \lambda(t) \exp\left\{-(r+\delta)T(t)\right\} \big(M[p\{t+T(t)\}] - w\{t+T(t)\}\big) \left(\frac{dT}{dt} + 1\right)$$
$$- \lambda(t)[M\{p(t)\} - w(t)]$$
$$= \dot{q} + \exp\left\{-(r+\delta)T(t)\right\} am\{T(t)\} \frac{dT}{dt}.$$

Using (1) and (2) then gives the result.

Proposition 2 (p. 130). If q, λ/λ and w are all constant then the equations

i) $$\lambda(t)(M[p\{t+T(t)\}]-w\{t+T(t)\})=am\{T(t)\}$$

nd

(ii) $\lambda(t)[M\{p(t)\}-w(t)]$

$$=(r+\delta-\dot{q}/q+\lambda/\lambda)q+(r+\delta+\lambda/\lambda)\int_0^{T(t)}\exp\{-(r+\delta)\tau\}\,am(\tau)\,\mathrm{d}\tau$$

$$+\exp\{-(r+\delta)T(t)\}\,am\{T(t)\}$$

have a solution for the function $T(t)$ given by $T(t)=T^*$ which satisfies,

$$am(T)\,[\exp(\eta T)-\exp\{-(r+\delta)T\}]-(r+\delta+\eta)$$

$$\left[q+a\int_0^T\exp\{-(r+\delta)\tau\}\,m(\tau)\,\mathrm{d}\tau\right]=0$$

where $\eta=\lambda/\lambda$.

Proof. If q, w, $\lambda/\lambda=\eta$ are constant then (i) and (ii) may be written,

A.1 $$\lambda(0)\exp(\eta t)(M[p\{t+T(t)\}]-w)=am\{T(t)\}$$

and

A.2 $\lambda(0)\exp(\eta t)[M\{p(t)\}-w]$

$$=(r+\delta+\eta)\left[q+\int_0^{T(t)}\exp\{-(r+\delta)\tau\}\,am(\tau)\,\mathrm{d}\tau\right]$$

$$+\exp\{-(r+\delta)T(t)\}\,am\{T(t)\}.$$

Rewriting A.2 at time $t+T(t)$ gives

A.3 $\lambda(0)\exp[\eta\{t+T(t)\}](M[p\{t+T(t)\}]-w)$

$$=(r+\delta+\eta)\left[q+\int_0^{T\{t+T(t)\}}\exp\{-(r+\delta)\tau\}\,am(\tau)\,\mathrm{d}\tau\right]$$

$$+\exp[-(r+\delta)T\{t+T(t)\}]\,am[T\{t+T(t)\}].$$

Eliminating $M[p\{t+T(t)\}]$ from A.1 and A.3 gives

$a\exp\{\eta T(t)\}\,m\{T(t)\}$

$$=(r+\delta+\eta)\left[q+\int_0^{T\{t+T(t)\}}\exp\{-(r+\delta)\tau\}\,am(\tau)\,\mathrm{d}\tau\right]$$

$$+\exp[-(r+\delta)T\{t+T(t)\}]\,am[T\{t+T(t)\}]$$

which has a constant solution $T(t)=T^*$ for all t where T^* satisfies the required equation.

Proposition 3 (p. 130). If T^* satisfies the equation

(1) $am(T)\left[\exp\left(\eta T\right)-\exp\left\{-(r+\delta)T\right\}\right]-(r+\delta+\eta)$

$$\times\left[q+a\int_0^T \exp\left\{-(r+\delta)T\right\}m(\tau)\,\mathrm{d}\tau\right]=0$$

where $m'>0$ and $\eta>0$ then $\partial T^*/\partial\eta<0$, $\partial T^*/\partial a<0$, $\partial T^*/\partial q>0$.

Proof. Write (1) as $\psi(T,\,\eta,\,a,\,q)=0$
    Then

$$\psi_T=a(m_T+\eta m)\left[\exp\left(\eta T\right)-\exp\left\{-(r+\delta)T\right\}\right]>0$$

$$\psi_\eta=\exp\left(\eta T\right)am(T)\,T+(r+\delta+\eta)^{-1}\left(\exp\{-(r+\delta+\eta)T\}-1\right)$$

$$\psi_a=\exp\left(\eta T\right)m(T)\left[1-\exp\left\{-(r+\delta+\eta)T\right\}-(r+\delta+\eta)\right.$$

$$\left.\times\exp\left(-\eta T\right)\int_0^T \exp\left\{-(r+\delta)\tau\right\}\frac{m(\tau)}{m(T)}\,\mathrm{d}\tau\right]$$

$$>\exp\left(\eta T\right)m(T)\left[1-\exp\left\{-(r+\delta+\eta)T\right\}-(r+\delta+\eta)\right.$$

$$\left.\times\int_0^T\exp\left\{-(r+\delta+\eta)\tau\right\}\mathrm{d}\tau\right]$$

$$=0$$

$$\psi_q=-(r+\delta+\eta)<0$$

Thus

$$\frac{\partial T^*}{\partial\eta}=-\frac{\psi_\eta}{\psi_T}<0,\ \frac{\partial T^*}{\partial a}=-\frac{\psi_a}{\psi_T}<0,\ \frac{\partial T^*}{\partial q}=-\frac{\psi_q}{\psi_T}>0.$$

Some Notes on Formalizing the Concept of Capacity Utilization

To keep things simple we shall assume that the firm only employs two factors of production, capital and labour. So, when it is deciding how it should operate on any particular day, it has essentially four things to consider. First, the size of the *stock* of capital which it should employ, second the total number of employees who are to work with this stock of capital at some time during the day, third the number of hours to be worked by each of these employees and, lastly, the number of hours during the day when the stock of capital is to be used. It is already clear that even with just two factors, a specification of the production possibilities is quite tricky given that output will depend on the number of workers using the capital at any given time and also on the number of hours worked by each worker. However, if we assume that all workers are employed for the same number of hours, a reasonable way to proceed would be the following.

Let N be the number of men actually employed during the course of one day's operation, H_n be the number of hours worked by each of these men, K be the capital stock and H_K be the number of hours during the day in which it is in operation. Now let $g(H_n)$ be the number of 'standard' hours worked by an employee who works for H_n actual hours, where this number is the length of time it would take the employee to complete the work he or she actually does by working at some constant 'standard' rate. Presumably because of tiredness and general loss of efficiency, $g'(H_n) < 1$ and $g''(H_n) < 0$ for H_n greater than a 'normal' working day. If we denote an employee working at the 'standard' rate as a 'standard employee', then $\{Ng(H_n)/H_K\}$ is the average number of 'standard employees' working at any particular time during the period when the capital stock is being used. It seems reasonable to assume that the day's output can be represented by a production function to the form

$$F\left\{K, \frac{Ng(H_n)}{H_K}, H_K\right\}$$

which could arguable be specialized to

$$G\left\{K, \frac{Ng(H_n)}{H_K}\right\} H_K.$$

The rate of decay in any one period could then be written as

$$\delta\left\{\frac{Ng(H_n)}{H_K}, H_K\right\}$$

where we take no account of maintenance activities and so δ is increasing in both arguments. Given that the average daily wage for the employees would be a function of the form $w(H_n, H_K)$ with w strictly convex in both arguments because of overtime payments, anti-social hours payments, etc., this formalization could certainly be used to discuss quite sensibly the interrelationships between output demand, hours of work, hours of operation, wage structures, and the like, though it might be more illuminating to impose a greater degree of institutional structure as do Winston and McCoy (1974) for example.

Unfortunately, this sort of model is far too complex to analyse fruitfully investment paths with adjustment costs and such like and so in the body of the chapter we simply present an informal discussion of the issues involved.

Footnotes

[1] Note that if we take two pieces of capital of age τ^* where $\exp(-\delta\tau^*)=\frac{1}{2}$ and put them together we have an amount $2\exp(-\delta\tau^*)=1$. Now consider the amount that is left s periods later. This is $2\exp\{-\delta(\tau^*+s)\}=2\exp(-\delta\tau^*) \times \exp(-\delta s)=\exp(-\delta s)$ which is the same quantity as would be left from one new unit of age s.

[2] Since we are dealing solely with mechanistic decay and there is no technical progress, this definition is unambiguous. New and old capital have the same productive characteristics and so maintaining capital stock constant simply implies acquiring enough new capital to keep output constant given any fixed labour input. This in no sense implies keeping the *value* of the firm's capital stock fixed, indeed far from it.

[3] The other two terms which are commonly used and, in fact, have been used in this book are gross and net investment. Gross investment is equal to the sum of replacement and expansion investment. Net investment is equal to gross investment less potential replacement investment.

[4] See in particular Jorgenson (1974).

[5] It is worth noting that if capital goods (like light bulbs) fail randomly after some period of their life, then this is exactly equivalent to exponential decay if, and only if, the probability of failure in any time period is independent of the age of the good.

[6] It is worth noting that in the general case of mechanistic decay we know that equation 7.7 will take the form

$$\int_t^\infty \exp\{-r(s-t)\}\ \delta(s-t)\ \{M(p)-w\}\ ds=q,$$

and, in the situation where prices remain fixed, this implies that

$$M(p)=w+q\left[\int_t^\infty \delta(s-t)\ \exp\{-r(s-t)\ ds\right]^{-1}$$

The cost of capital is thus given by the final term

$$q\left[\int_t^\infty \delta(s-t)\ \exp\{-r(s-t)\}\ ds\right]^{-1}$$

of which the expression in equation 7.9 is a special case.

[7] Note that with exponential decay there are no echo effects since potential replacement is simply equal to the rate of decay times the *current* capital stock.

[8] Note that we are trying to determine optimal maintenance expenditure on the capital that is actually purchased. This is only one half of the problem, the other half being the decision to purchase itself. However, it is quite legitimate to divide the whole problem in this manner for it is clear that the decision to purchase capital can only be made assuming that we know the consequences of optimally maintaining it.

[9] This is the first formal introduction of technical progress. We have avoided this problem in previous chapters because it necessitates the use of vintage models which adds a great deal in terms of complexity without shedding much light on the problems with which we have, up until now, been concerned.

[10] All the effects of parameter changes on the optimal life of capital goods are proved in the appendix, proposition 3.

[11] Details may be found in Nickell (1975, p. 65).

[12] Again, details may be found in Nickell (1975, pp. 72–75).

[13] So long as the scrapping is not outweighed by the decay element of replacement $\delta y(t)$ which clearly follows the level of capacity.

[14] Yet again all the details may be found in Nickell (1975, pp. 75–76).

[15] See Keynes (1936, pp. 66–73).

[16] See for example Taubman and Wilkinson (1970) and K. R. Smith (1969, 1970). Winston and McCoy (1974) on the other hand present a very interesting model in which capacity utilization is closely related to the quantity of labour employed.

Bibliographical Notes—Chapter 7

A general discussion of mechanistic decay models can be found in Arrow (1964b), Smith (1966) and Coen (1975). An analysis of this problem with particular reference to the hypothesis of a constant potential replacement–capital ratio occurs in Jorgenson (1974) and Feldstein and Rothschild (1974).

Work on scrapping times and non-mechanistic models of capital decay in general is to be found in a classic paper by Hotelling (1925) which has been extended in Terborgh (1949), Smith (1957, 1966), Feldstein and Rothschild (1974), Malcomson (1975) and Nickell (1975). A standard reference on the replacement of stochastically failing equipment is Jorgenson, McCall and Radner (1967).

Theoretical work on the effects of capacity utilization on the rate of decay is presented in Taubman and Wilkinson (1970) and K. R. Smith (1969, 1970), and a deeper analysis of the concept of capacity utilization itself is to be found in Marris (1964a) and Winston and McCoy (1974).

CHAPTER 8

FINANCE, INVESTMENT AND THE COST OF CAPITAL

1. An Introduction to the Modigliani–Miller Theorem

In this chapter our major concern will be the relevance of financial decisions in determining the cost of capital to the firm. If the financial position of the firm is germane to this matter then clearly it cannot be ignored in any theory which purports to explain the firm's investment decisions. This question of financial policy is, of course, intimately related to the structure of taxation but, since the complexities of the corporate tax system obscure the basic issues, their examination will be held over until the next chapter.

As a first step it is worth giving some indication of the standard financial options open to a firm, and we shall do this by a simple example. Suppose the owners of a firm purchase some capital input this year which will produce some output next year and then disappear. Suppose, furthermore, that if the input level is y, next year's output, which for the sake simplicity may be assumed to consist of the same good, is $\theta f(y)$, where θ is some parameter which may be a random variable. Consider the following two financing possibilities open to the owners of the firm. They can borrow an amount y this year, pay back $(1+r)y$ next year, where r is the rate of interest, and keep the residual, namely $\theta f(y) - (1+r)y$. Alternatively, they can sell a claim to some portion of next year's output up to a value of y and then, when next year's output is produced, they can settle the claim and keep whatever is left. For example, they can divide next year's output into n equal lots of $\{\theta f(y)\}/n$ and start selling them. If the present value of a claim to θ units of output next year is p, then each lot of $\{\theta f(y)\}/n$ will sell for $\{pf(y)\}/n$. The owners will then sell k lots, where $\{pf(y)\}/n \cdot k = y$ and use the money to acquire y units of input. Next year the firm's owners will be able to keep $\{(n-k)\theta f(y)\}/n$ units of output for themselves which, substituting for k, gives a quantity $f(y) - \theta y/p$. Thus we have two possible methods of finance which apparently yield two different returns to the owners. The first of these is called debt financing (or bond

149

financing) and the second equity financing, where the lots of $\{\theta f(y)\}/n$ are, of course, shares (or equity) in the firm. The first important point to note is that, if θ is not a random variable, it is obvious that a claim to θ next year, which was priced at p, is currently worth its present value, namely $\theta/1+r$. Hence $p = \theta/1+r$ and the residual gains accruing to the current owners, namely $\theta f(y) - (1+r)y$ for bond finance and $\theta f(y) - \theta y/p$ for equity finance, are identical. We can immediately conclude that in a world of certainty the method of finance is of no consequence in making investment decisions. As we saw in Chapter 2, the present value is all that matters.

In a world of uncertainty, however, it is not at all obvious that this is the case, for here we have no easy method of determining the present price of a future claim to the random quantity of output, θ. So it is not clear at first sight whether the owners of the firm will prefer to receive the random variable $\theta f - (1+r)y$ or the random variable $\theta f - \theta y/p$. What is more it is also not clear how y is to be chosen, although it does seem that the choice of y could well depend on which mode of finance is preferred.

There is, however, a most important theorem concerning this matter which was first proved by Modigliani and Miller in 1958.[1] This states that, under certain circumstances, the owners of the firm will be quite indifferent between the outcomes under different financial policies and, furthermore, that the investment decisions of the firm can be taken quite independently of its financing decisions. This is, in fact, a theorem of considerable subtlety and to provide an initial illustration of how it works we present the following tale.

One day an individual with some entrepreneurial pretensions had an idea for a new product. After a few calculations he decided that he required some £1,000,000 to bring his idea to fruition and that, having made this initial investment, the company thus formed would yield a total annual net return of some £1,100,000θ in perpetuity, where θ is a random variable with an expectation of 0·1. Noting from his knowledge of the securities market that the right to a perpetual random income stream of £θ per annum was worth about £1, he reckoned that he could sell 1,000,000 of these income streams, thereby acquiring the million pounds, and then sit back and enjoy the remaining annual return of £100,000θ for himself.

Before starting out on his career as an entrepreneur he decided that he would talk things over with a friend of his who was a bit of an expert in financial matters, just to check that everything was all right. His friend listened carefully as the plan was unfolded and at the end remarked that it was a good job that he had been consulted because, if his advice were followed, our entrepreneur could do even better for himself. The trick was to take advantage of 'leverage', about which our entrepreneur had heard not a word, but which very simply boiled down to the following. First go along to the bank and borrow £200,000 at 5% which was the going rate at the time. This implies paying out £10,000 per year in interest charges. Then, instead of offering to the public 1,000,000 sets of income streams of £θ per annum, offer them income streams which pay £$(\theta - 0.01)$ per annum. A quick check soon reveals that after the interest charges and income streams have been paid out each year this still leaves £100,000θ per annum for the entrepreneur to enjoy. But the advantage is the following. Consider how much the public will pay for an income stream of £$(\theta - 0.01)$ per annum. They will pay £1 for an income stream of £θ per annum which has an expectation of £0·1, so for £$(\theta - 0.01)$ per annum which has an expectation of £0·09 and has almost the same risk they will surely pay about 90p or maybe a fraction under. So, for a million of these, they will pay a little under £900,000 and with the £200,000 from the bank this yields nearly £1,100,000. £1,000,000 to set the project going and nearly £100,000 free bonus for the entrepreneur because he had taken good financial advice.

When the entrepreneur heard this he was stunned. To him it seemed like money for nothing. However, he could see nothing wrong with the plan so next morning before putting his income streams (or shares) on the market he called into the bank and collected his £200,000. The bankers were only too happy to lend him this sum since they saw great merit in his plan and their opinions about the variability of θ were such that they saw no possibility of default on the loan. Then, after booking a world cruise at the travel agents in expectation of the extra bonus due to his friend's financial wizardry, he went down to the market and offered his million income streams for sale. There was a lot of discussion about his offer and he was gratified to hear that everyone agreed that £θ per annum in perpetuity was worth £1, so his original calculation was correct. However, when people started buying the £$(\theta - 0.01)$ income streams he was a little shocked to discover that they were selling for only 80p and consequently the whole lot sold for only £800,000 and not close on £900,000 as he had been led to expect by his financial friend. Thus with the £200,000 from the bank he had just £1,000,000 to launch the project, exactly the same as if he had never heard of 'leverage' and simply carried out his original plan. He was a little bit irritated because he had to cancel his world cruise but on the other hand he had always thought it was a bit too good to be true. However, he still could not quite understand where the arguments of his expert acquaintance had been wrong so he decided to ask one of the people who had bought at $£(\theta-0.01)$ stream why it was only worth 80p. The buyer replied as follows, 'It's obvious! For 80p I can make up a $£(\theta-0.01)$ stream for myself. I borrow 20p at 5%, the going rate, and then, with an additional 80p of my own, I buy a $£\theta$ income stream which can be had on the market for £1. The interest on 20p is £0.01 per annum and thus for 80p of my own I have purchased a security which pays $£(\theta-0.01)$ per annum. So obviously 80p is what one of your income streams was worth. Didn't you realize that?'

So after a little thought our entrepreneur recognized that, however little or much he had borrowed from the bank, it would all have come to the same thing and he might just as well not have bothered. He found this rather comforting in a way since it seemed rather unnatural to him that such a simple manoeuvre should yield him such a large bonus. He then decided to learn more about such matters so he purchased a book on finance and discovered in the following quotation[2] both why his friend had given him the advice he had and also that there were some financial experts in existence who would have accurately predicted the results of following that advice.

The traditional view . . . is that the stockholder's value per share can be increased by judicious use of debt. The other position (expounded by Modigliani and Miller) implies that, in the absence of taxes on corporate income, the value of a firm is independent of the proportion of debt to total capitalization.

In this tale the entrepreneur attempts to increase the wealth accruing to him via the firm by judicious use of debt and this policy conspicuously fails. The essential reason why it fails is that all he has to sell is a million $£\theta$ income streams. If this is split into one million certain £0.01 income streams and one million risky $£(\theta-0.01)$ income streams, there seems to be no particular reason why they should be any more valuable *in toto* than the basic one million $£\theta$ streams. If only $£\theta$ streams are on sale and an individual has a particular penchant for $£(\theta-0.02)$ streams, he can simply borrow 40p at 5%, spend 60p of his own money and buy a $£\theta$ stream. He has then created for himself a $£(\theta-0.02)$ stream, and he would be quite indifferent between doing it this way and the firm selling £($\theta - 0{\cdot}02$) streams directly. The point is that, by dint of judicious use of debt, an *individual* can create a stream for himself which is any combination of θ and a certain return, whatever combination of θ and a certain return the firm happens to sell. So there can be no advantage to the firm in bundling up special combinations of θ and a certain return and hoping that these will go down especially well with the public.

There is, however, one very strong implicit assumption in all of this and that is that members of the public have as ready an access to the capital market as the firm and at the same rate of interest. If one looks back at the story, it is immediately clear that the entrepreneur will gain from his bank borrowing if the rate at which individuals can borrow is 6%. Under these circumstances, the £($\theta - 0{\cdot}01$) income streams would fetch $83\frac{1}{3}$p and thus the entrepreneur would gain a bonus of about £33,333. Later on in this chapter we shall return to such considerations, which are in fact extremely important, but before then it is worth looking at the Modigliani–Miller proposition in a more formal manner.

2. A Simple Formal Model

It is unfortunately necessary, in studying the financial decisions of the firm, to include the rest of the economy in the analysis. This necessity derives, as we shall see in due course, from the fact that the concept of price-taking behaviour is more or less self-contradictory in the market for financial capital in a world of uncertainty. Indeed, in any analysis of such markets, it is more or less essential to know, in a paraphrase of the last line of a famous limerick, 'who lends what, and how much, and to whom'.[3]

Consider the following very simple two-period general equilibrium model which is based on that of Diamond (1967).

Firms—With a little loss of generality, and a considerable reduction in subscripts, we shall assume there is only one firm. If in the first period it utilizes a quantity of (capital) input y, then in the second period a quantity $\phi(\theta)f(y)$ of this same good is produced as output and the original input disappears. The variable θ is a random variable which describes the state of the world[4] prevailing in the second period and f has diminishing returns and hence $f' > 0$, $f'' < 0$.

The firm can issue shares in the first period which consist of the right to some proportion of the firm's output after its debt obligations have been fulfilled. In addition the firm can also issue bonds in the first period which it redeems in the second period paying a constant rate of interest r^*. *There is no possibility of default on the bonds and thus no possibility of bankruptcy.*

In order to procure the initial output y, the firm issues bonds to the value of λy, $0 \leqslant \lambda \leqslant 1$, and finances the remainder by issuing shares. Let $\pi(\theta, y, \lambda) = \phi f - (1 + r^*)\lambda y$, the total payout on shares by the firm. Then if M is the total market value of these shares, the return per unit of invested income is simply π/M.

Individuals—There are I individuals numbered $1 \ldots i \ldots I$. The ith individual has an initial endowment consisting of w_i units of the good and an ownership right α_i which is the initial fraction of the firm owned by i, where note that $\sum_i \alpha_i = 1$. The ith individual is solely concerned with maximizing the expected utility of his consumption in the second period and receives no income except the returns on his various investments. These investments consist solely of shares in firms and of bonds which may be issued by firms or individuals and which all pay an interest rate r^*. Thus individuals may borrow and lend among themselves, and, as with firms, *there is no possibility of default on these loans.* Then if b_i is the total value of bonds and s_i is the total value of shares purchased by individual i, his budget constraint consists of

8.1 $$b_i + s_i = w_i + \alpha_i\{M - (1 - \lambda)y\}$$

where note that the term $M - (1 - \lambda)y$ is the total value of the shares in the firm excluding the value of the new shares issued. It is this quantity multiplied by α_i which gives the value of the ith individual's original shareholding. The total consumption of the ith individual is given by

8.2 $$c_i(\theta) = (1 + r^*)b_i + s_i M^{-1}\pi$$

where remember that the return per unit income investment in the firm's shares is $M^{-1}\pi$. The individual will now choose b_i and s_i to maximize the expected utility of consumption subject to the budget constraint 8.1, taking the parameters M, λ, r^* and y as given. Equilibrium in financial markets will then imply that

8.3 $$\sum_i b_i = \lambda y$$

8.4 $$\sum_i s_i = M$$

and note that if we sum all the budget constraints over i and use $\sum_i \alpha_i = 1$, we have after some rearrangement

8.5 $$(\Sigma b_i - \lambda y) + (\Sigma s_i - M) + (y - w_i) = 0.$$

This merely states that the sum of the excess demands for bonds, shares and goods is zero which is, of course, Walras' law, and this will guarantee equilibrium in the goods market, given equilibrium in the financial sector.

Now consider the Modigliani–Miller proposition, which states, in this context, that a change in the value of λ, the proportion of new investment financed by bonds, has no significant consequences. Suppose the firm reduces λ to zero, thereby making no use whatever of bond financing, and let the variables in the new situaion be designated with hats ($\hat{b}_i$, etc.). The total payout on shares in the new situation will be given by $\hat{\pi} = \phi f$ and so individual i's consumption is now given by

8.6 $$\hat{c}_i(\theta) = (1 + r^*)\hat{b}_i + \hat{s}_i \phi f \hat{M}^{-1}.$$

Previously this same individual's consumption was given by

8.7 $$c_i(\theta) = (1 + r^*)b_i + s_i\{\phi f - (1 + r^*)\lambda y\}M^{-1}$$

from 8.2 and the definition of π.

Now suppose that in the new situation individual i reduces his bond holdings from b_i to $\hat{b}_i = b_i - s_i \lambda y M^{-1}$ and increases his shareholdings from s_i to $\hat{s}_i = s_i + s_i \lambda y M^{-1}$, thereby leaving his total financial holdings the same and hence remaining within his budget constraint. Then, since $\hat{b}_i = b_i - s_i \lambda y M^{-1}$, 8.6 and 8.7 reveal that his *ex ante* consumption opportunities remain unchanged if and only if $\hat{s}_i \phi f \hat{M}^{-1}$ and $s_i \phi f M^{-1}$ are identical, that is if

8.8 $$(s_i + s_i \lambda y M^{-1})\phi f \hat{M}^{-1} = s_i \phi f M^{-1}$$

or

$$\hat{M} = M + \lambda y.$$

(Note that if this holds, the individual's total wealth given by the right-hand side of the budget constraint 8.1 remains unaffected by the reduction in the firm's bond issues.)

But the new share valuation of the firm, $\hat{M}$, will be determined in the financial markets and so, if we assume that individuals shift their portfolios in the manner described, then equilibrium in the financial sector will imply $\sum_i \hat{s}_i = \hat{M}$ and $\sum_i \hat{b}_i = 0$, for *net* bond issues for the economy are now zero.

Equilibrium in the share market thus implies

$$\hat{M} = \sum_i \hat{s}_i = \sum_i s_i(1 + \lambda y M^{-1})$$
$$= M(1 + \lambda y M^{-1})$$
$$= M + \lambda y,$$

and equilibrium in the bond market follows automatically from 8.3 and 8.4 and the definition of $\hat{b}_i$. So the resulting equilibrium in the market for shares yields a new share valuation which is precisely the one which leaves all individual *ex ante* consumption opportunities unchanged and therefore the reduction to zero by the firm of the proportion of its investment financed by bond issues turns out to be of no real consequences to individual investors.

So the Modigliani–Miller proposition holds and individuals, by manipulating their private portfolios, can offset any changes in the quantity of bonds sold by firms and leave their consumption opportunities unaffected. At a later stage we shall go on to discuss some very serious drawbacks to this analysis and develop a rather more general view, but for the moment we shall consider the investment decisions of the firm in this kind of world, that is, the problem of how the firm sets about choosing the appropriate value of y. Looking back to the budget constraint 8.1, it can be seen that, as far as the individual shareholders are concerned, they would like the firm to choose y so as to maximize the total value of the original shares in the firm, namely $M - (1 - \lambda)y$, for in this manner the total original wealth of all individuals will be maximized. This seems to be a fairly natural objective for firms and is one which is commonly recommended as being equivalent in an uncertain world to present value maximization in a world of certainty.

In order to discuss the implications of this objective for the firm we must first look at the results of the consumers' choice of their optimal portfolios. Consumer i will make his choice so as to maximize the expected utility of consumption, that is, he will choose s_i to maximize

$$E_i U_i\{c_i(\theta)\}$$

where $c_i(\theta)$ is given by the expression

$$c_i(\theta) = \{\pi - M(1 + r^*)\}s_i/M + [w_i + \alpha_i\{M - (1 - \lambda)y\}](1 + r^*)$$

which is derived by eliminating b_i from 8.1 and 8.2. E_i here indicates that the expectation is taken relative to individual i's own subjective probability density over states of the world θ, which may of course be quite different from that of other individuals. The result of this maximization is that s_i must satisfy the simple necessary condition

$$E_i(U_i{}'\pi)/M = (1+r^*)E_iU_i{}'$$

which states that at the optimum a unit increase in bond investments will yield the same increase in expected utility as a unit increase in shareholdings. This condition can be rewritten in more convenient form as

8.9
$$\frac{E_i(U_i{}'\pi)}{E_iU_i{}'} = (1+r^*)M,$$

and using this and the definition of π, the firm's objective function can be expressed as

$$M - (1-\lambda)y = (1+r^*)^{-1}\left\{\frac{E_i(U_i{}'\phi)}{E_iU_i{}'}f(y) - (1+r^*)y\right\}$$

by simply eliminating M. Consequently the firm should choose its investment y in order to maximize

8.10
$$\frac{E_i(U_i{}'\phi)}{E_iU_i{}'}f(y) - (1+r^*)y$$

which is independent of λ, as we might have expected from the foregoing analysis. Note that the expression $\{E_i(U_i{}'\phi)\}/E_iU_i{}'$ is, in spite of appearances to the contrary, independent of i because it is the same for all individuals (from 8.9). The next problem which arises concerns the ability of the firm actually to solve the maximization of the objective, 8.10, for any change in y will change the whole equilibrium structure of the economy, notably the expression $\{E_i(U_i{}'\phi)\}/E_iU_i{}'$. The assumption which is typically used to deal with this problem is, as might be expected, one of the perfect competition type. It is assumed that, for any firm which produces a particular pattern of returns across the states of nature, there exist a large number of other firms (or linear combinations of other firms) which produce the same pattern, such a group of firms being known as a risk class.

So, if we now pretend that there are a large number of other firms in the same risk class as the firm in our economy, that is, all producing a pattern of returns $\phi(\theta)$, our firm can take as given the price of a security which yields a return $\phi(\theta)$. Suppose this price is p. Then, by definition, the gain in expected utility by any individual on receipt of p, namely $pE_iU_i{}'$ must be identical to the gain on receipt of a promise to pay ϕ one period hence, namely $\{E_i(U_i'\phi)\}/(1+r^*)$. This implies

8.11
$$p = \frac{E_i(U_i'\phi)}{E_i U_i'} \cdot 1/(1+r^*), \text{ all } i.$$

So, using 8.10 and 8.11 we can now see that the firm will choose its level of investment, y, to maximize

8.12
$$pf(y) - y$$

where the firm can take p as given. Furthermore, if we assume that all individuals have identical expectations, we can give the formulation 8.12 a simple discount rate interpretation. For, if p is the value of a security which pays ϕ in the next period, we may ask at what rate the (common) expected returns produced by this security are effectively discounted by the market? This discount rate ρ clearly satisfies the relationship $p = E(\phi)/1+\rho$. From 8.12 we can now see that in this case the firm will choose y so as to maximize

$$E(\phi)f(y) - (1+\rho)y$$

where $1/1+\rho$ is the present value of a security which has unit expectation and has the same pattern of returns as the firm across all the states of nature. The discount rate ρ can thus be viewed as the rate at which the market discounts the *mean* returns of the firm, taking due allowance for uncertainty. Furthermore, if the firm issues no bonds at all its shares would yield $\phi(\theta)f/M$ per unit income and ρ would be the rate at which the market discounts the expected returns on such shares, since they have the appropriate pattern of returns. Firms which issue no bonds are sometimes termed *unlevered* firms, where the degree to which the firm issues bonds relative to its total value is the degree of *leverage*. So, bearing in mind our definition of risk class, ρ is the rate at which the market discounts expected returns on securities in the same risk class as the firm, which is also the rate at which the market discounts the returns on the shares of the firm itself, so long as it is unlevered.[5] ρ is thus the appropriate rate of discount for the firm and its cost of capital is then $(1+\rho)$ since the rate of depreciation is equal to unity, as is the price of capital goods (cf. the usual expression for the cost of capital, p. 10). To maximize its objective function, the firm will clearly solve,

8.13
$$E\phi . f'(y) = 1 + \rho$$

thereby equating the expected marginal product of capital to the appropriate cost which may be taken as given.

One of the interesting points which arises from this analysis is that it can be used to justify the assumption of expected present value maximization which we used extensively in our discussion of uncertainty. This assumption is clearly valid in the sort of world we have just considered provided that we use the appropriate rate of discount, namely ρ. Furthermore, we can deduce something about the size of this discount factor, by noting that the outcome for the case of a single firm, as given by ϕ, will be positively correlated with the consumption of individuals, since the higher the returns of the firm, the better off will be the investors. Risk aversion will then imply that this level of consumption is negatively related to marginal utility, implying that the covariance of ϕ and U' will be negative. It is then simple to demonstrate that $\rho > r^*$ (see Appendix, proposition 1), and consequently the cost of capital in these circumstances is likely to be somewhat higher than would be derived using the safe rate of interest r^*, but the pattern of investment response will be much the same.[6]

Unfortunately there are several serious objections to the above analysis. The first concerns the assumption incorporated into the model, of the existence of borrowing and lending at the safe rate of interest, r^*, without any limitation. This rules out any possibility of bankruptcy and the consequent defaulting on loans, something which, as we shall see later, is an *essential* part of capital markets in a world of uncertainty and cannot be ignored. Second, the conclusion that the appropriate rate of discount, ρ, is given exogenously to the firm depends crucially on the existence of 'risk classes', each of which contains a large number of firms.[7] If this were not the case, the pattern of returns yielded by any particular firm would be quite distinctive and the rate at which such returns would be discounted in the market would depend on the quantity which the firm makes available. The discount rate would then depend on the level of investment and the foregoing analysis would be invalidated. The final objection concerns the assumption of value maximization as the objective of firms, an assumption which is rather natural at first sight, but which, on closer inspection, may be shown to be open to strong objections. However, before going on to discuss these matters, we shall first look at a particular case of the previous model where it is possible to derive an objective function for the firm in dynamic form. This will then be used to compare optimal policies with some of those derived in the chapters on uncertainty which were based on less rigorously formulated objectives.

3. The Mean–Variance Valuation Model and Some Dynamic Extensions

The particular model we shall look at assumes that individual preferences concerning risky returns are based solely on the mean and variance of these returns and on no other characteristics. This is a very crude assumption[8] but it has the advantage of great analytical tractability and leads to some extremely appealing results.

Suppose that there are I individuals and that individual i has a utility function $U_i(e_i, v_i)$ where e_i is the expected cash flow generated by his asset portfolio one period hence and v_i is the variance of this cash flow. It is assumed quite naturally that $\partial U_i/\partial e_i > 0$ and $\partial U_i/\partial v_i < 0$, with available assets consisting of the shares in J un-levered firms and personal borrowing or lending at the safe rate of interest r^*. Let $\tilde{x}_j$ be the total random return paid to the owners of firm j, w_{ij} be the fraction of firm j held by individual i and b_i be individual i's net borrowing. Then if $E(\tilde{x}_j) = \bar{x}_j$, var $(\tilde{x}_j) = \sigma_{jj}$, cov $(\tilde{x}_j, \tilde{x}_k) = \sigma_{jk}$ where all investors have the same expectations regarding these variables, we have that the mean and variance of the cash returns accruing to the ith individual are given by

8.14 $$e_i = \sum_j w_{ij}\bar{x}_j - (1+r^*)b_i,$$

8.15 $$v_i = \sum_j \sum_k w_{ij}w_{ik}\sigma_{jk}.$$

The ith individual will thus choose w_{ij}, b_i to solve

$$\max U_i(e_i, v_i) \qquad \text{subject to } \sum_j w_{ij}V_j - b_i = w_i,$$

where V_j is the market value of the jth firm and w_i is the individual i's initial wealth. Writing down the Lagrangian for this problem and differentiating with respect to w_{ij} and b_i, we have, after eliminating the Lagrangian multiplier, the necessary conditions,

8.16 $$\frac{\partial U_i}{\partial e_i}\{\bar{x}_j - (1+r^*)V_j\} + 2\frac{\partial U_i}{\partial v_i}\sum_k w_{ik}\sigma_{jk} = 0 \qquad \text{all } j,$$

which holds for all individuals.

Utilizing these conditions and the fact that in equilibrium the fractions of the firms held by investors must sum to unity, that is,

8.17 $$\sum_i w_{ij} = 1 \qquad \text{for all } j,$$

it is possible to derive the following expression for the equilibrium market value of the jth firm.[9]

8.18 $$V_j = (1+r^*)^{-1} \{\bar{x}_j - \tau \sum_k \text{cov} (\tilde{x}_j, \tilde{x}_k)\}$$

where

$$\tau = \frac{\sum_k \bar{x}_k - (1+r^*) \sum_k V_k}{\sum_k \sum_l \sigma_{kl}}.$$

At first sight, this looks rather a forbidding result but, in reality, it is both simple and intuitively sound. Consider first the meaning of τ. If there were no risk in the economy it would be natural to suppose that the value of each firm would be equal to its future discounted return, that is $V_k = (1+r^*)^{-1}\bar{x}_k$. But there is risk and so there is a difference between the value of the firm and its discounted future *mean* return, the former being typically smaller. The difference in current value terms, $\bar{x}_k - (1+r^*)V_k$, is a measure of how much the risk costs in the sense that it is the amount the market would be prepared to pay in current value terms to remove the risk and have the certainty of the expected return. Thus $\sum \bar{x}_k - (1+r^*) \sum V_k$ is the current total cost of the risk to the market. The denominator of τ is equal to the total variance in the economy; it is in fact equal to var $(\sum_k \tilde{x}_k)$ and may therefore be deemed to be the total quantity of 'risk' in the market. The quantity τ is thus equal to the total cost of risk divided by its total quantity and is called the 'price' of risk. It is the amount that any individual in the market would be prepared to pay to be rid of one unit of 'risk' (one unit of variance).

We now have an obvious interpretation of the expression for the firm's value, 8.18, for it is equal to the present value of the expected return of the firm minus the total risk inherent in the firm, $\sum_k \text{cov} (\tilde{x}_j, \tilde{x}_k)$, multiplied by the price of that risk, τ. Looking more closely at the risk term we see that it is equal to the variance of the return of firm j plus the covariances of this return with the returns of all the other firms in the economy. Consequently, if we take a firm whose returns are highly correlated with most of the other firms in the economy then it will have a high-risk term and a correspondingly low value in relation to its mean return. The reason for this is that the firm is not very attractive to risk-averse investors because it provides very little help to them in spreading their risks. On the other hand a firm whose returns are highly *negatively* correlated with the returns of most of the other firms in the economy could have a risk term which is in fact negative and it would thus be worth more than its present value mean return. This is because risk-averse investors would find its shares a very desirable property because it would help to offset the riskiness of the majority of the other shares in their portfolios. For example, if all firms are involved in producing agricultural products and the vast majority do well when the weather turns out to be good, a firm which produces a product which does well in bad weather would be extremely valuable since all the risk-averse investors would flock to invest in it as an insurance against the weather turning out to be bad. The consequence of this is that firms which tend to do well when most other firms in the economy do badly and vice versa would typically face a lower cost of capital than the majority.

However, the main point of introducing this mean–variance model is to show how it may be used to produce a simple dynamic objective function for the firm in a world of uncertainty, at least under certain circumstances. In order to dynamize 8.18, we may argue that the final return to the investors of firm j, $\tilde{x}_j$, is equal to the total dividend paid out by firm j plus the value of firm j at the end of the period. Thus we can write the return with time arguments as

$$8.19 \qquad \tilde{x}_j(t) = \tilde{d}_j(t) + \tilde{V}_j(t+1)$$

where $\tilde{d}_j(t)$ is the total dividend paid out by firm j in period t. Writing 8.18 in dynamic discrete time form gives

$$8.20 \qquad V_j(t)\{1 + r^*(t)\} = E\tilde{d}_j(t) + E\tilde{V}_j(t+1)$$
$$- \tau(t) \sum_k \text{cov}\,[\{\tilde{d}_j(t) + \tilde{V}_j(t+1)\},$$
$$\{\tilde{d}_k(t) + \tilde{V}_k(t+1)\}]$$

which holds for all t. There are clearly going to be great problems in dealing with this type of difference equation if the safe rate of interest, $r^*(t)$, and the price of risk, $\tau(t)$, are random variables. But if they are known with certainty then all the $V_j(t)$ are non-random and consequently 8.20 reduces to the simple difference equation

$$8.21 \qquad V_j(t)\{1 + r^*(t)\} = E\tilde{d}_j(t) + V_j(t+1) - \tau(t) \sum_k \text{cov}$$
$$\{\tilde{d}_j(t), \tilde{d}_k(t)\},\ \text{all } t.$$

If we now assume for simplicity that r^* is constant, then it is easily checked by straightforward substitution that this difference equation has the solution

8.22 $$V_j(t) = \sum_{s=t}^{\infty} \frac{1}{(1+r^*)^{s-t}} [E\tilde{d}_j(s) - \tau(s) \sum_k \text{cov}\, \{\tilde{d}_j(s),\, \tilde{d}_k(s)\}]$$

In particular, if we write 8.22 in continuous time and put $t=0$, we have a simple expression for the value of firm j at time zero, namely,

8.23 $$V_j(0) = \int_0^{\infty} \exp\,(-r^*s)\,[E\tilde{d}_j(s) - \tau(s) \sum_k \text{cov}\, \{\tilde{d}_j(s),\, \tilde{d}_k(s)\}]\,\mathrm{d}s$$

where the dividend flow $\tilde{d}_j(s)$ is simply the random net earnings flow (that is, net of investment expenditures) generated by the firm j at time s. The value of the firm is then equal to the expected present value of the future income stream produced by the firm less the total cost of the 'risk' associated with that particular income stream. The objective of the firm at time zero will then simply be to choose a production plan which maximizes the firm's value at time zero, $V_j(0)$.

Before we can try out this objective function on one or two investment models we must first deal with the problem of how the firm takes account of the future behaviour of other firms, this problem arising because of the covariance terms in 8.23. In fact we shall sidestep the problem somewhat arbitrarily by assuming that firm j treats the prospective future dividends of other firms as being simply related to its own dividend by the series of relationships

8.24 $$\tilde{d}_k(t) - E\tilde{d}_k(t) = \alpha_k(t)\,\{\tilde{d}_j(t) - E\tilde{d}_j(t)\} + \tilde{\beta}_k(t) \text{ all } k \neq j,$$

where cov $\{\tilde{d}_j(t),\, \tilde{\beta}_k(t)\} = 0$ and $E\tilde{\beta}_k(t) = 0$.

The idea of this is that firm j sees that all the other firms are affected by the same sort of events (business cycles, etc.) and so expects their dividend variations to be simply related to its own. For example, an ice-cream seller might give an ice-cream manufacturer a large positive α and an umbrella manufacturer a negative α.

This implies that 8.23 may be rewritten as

8.25 $$V_j(0) = \int_0^{\infty} \exp\,(-r^*s)\,[E\tilde{d}_j(s) - \hat{\tau}(s)\,\text{var}\,\{\tilde{d}_j(s)\}]\,\mathrm{d}s$$

where $\hat{\tau}(s) = \tau(s)\{1 + \sum_{k \neq j} \alpha_k(s)\}$. In general $\hat{\tau}(s)$ will be positive but for those firms which tend to do well when most other firms do badly, and vice versa, it could be negative.

We shall now utilize this objective function to investigate the simplest truly dynamic model of investment with uncertainty, namely the Hartman model discussed in section 1 of Chapter 6. In this model there are strictly convex costs of adjustment facing a perfectly competitive firm operating under constant returns to scale with wage and output price uncertainty. As before, the labour input is chosen when prices are certain and so the dividend $\tilde{d}_j$ is given by

$$8.26 \qquad \tilde{d}_j = \max_{L} \{\tilde{p}F(K, L) - \tilde{w}L\} - qI - C(I)$$

in standard notation. But in the proof of proposition 1 in the Appendix to Chapter 6, it was shown that $\max_{L} \{\tilde{p}F(K, L) - \tilde{w}L\} = g(\tilde{p}, \tilde{w})K$ in every time period, where g is convex in $\tilde{p}$ and $\tilde{w}$. So the dividend is given by,

$$8.27 \qquad \tilde{d}_j = g(\tilde{p}, \tilde{w})K - qI - C(I)$$

again in standard notation. Consequently, the value of the firm at time zero may be written as

$$V_j(0) = \int_{0}^{\infty} \exp(-r^*s)\,[K(s)\,Eg(\tilde{p}, \tilde{w}) - \hat{r}K(s)^2 \operatorname{var} g(\tilde{p}, \tilde{w}) - q(s)I(s) - C\{I(s)\}]\,ds.$$

On the optimal production path a unit increase in investment at time s must have the property that the additional costs incurred in bringing it about must just offset its additional contribution to the value of the firm. So, on the optimal path, we have[10]

$$8.28 \quad C'\{I(s)\} + q(s) = \int_{s}^{\infty} \exp\{-(r^* + \delta)(t - s)\}[Eg\{\tilde{p}(t), \tilde{w}(t)\} - 2\hat{r}K(t) \operatorname{var} g\{\tilde{p}(t), \tilde{w}(t)\}]\,dt$$

where δ is the rate of depreciation. The important point to note is that if the firm were maximizing expected present value, then the only difference would be the omission of the final term in the right-hand integrand (cf. Chapter 6, section 1). Since this final term takes the sign of $\hat{r}$ and since C' is increasing in I, it is clear that the rate of investment in the present case of market value maximization is always lower than under expected present value maximization if $\hat{r}$ is positive and always higher if $\hat{r}$ is negative.

This is hardly an unexpected result for if $\hat{r}$ is positive it would be natural to describe the objective function 8.23 as risk averse where risk in these circumstances is synonymous with variance. What is more, we know from past experience that risk aversion has a strong tendency to lower the optimal level of investment (see Chapter 5) and that is precisely what is happening here. It is possible to apply this objective function to the other dynamic investment model of Chapter 6 where the uncertainty applies to the timing of events and here again one can show in a number of cases that the level of investment is uniformly lower if $\hat{r}$ is positive and higher if it is negative.

In general then, we have some tentative theoretical evidence to argue that, if investors are risk averse, this will be reflected in the behaviour of most firms but not necessarily in all firms. As we have seen, it is possible for firms which yield returns which tend to be inversely correlated with the majority of other firms in the economy to have a risk-loving objective function in spite of the risk aversion of all individual investors. It must be recognized, however, that this theoretical evidence is very tentative. There are many strong objections to the mean–variance model itself not to mention the assumption of certainty about the future values of the interest rate and the price of risk. Unfortunately, if any of these assumptions are dropped the whole problem becomes analytically intractable and at the present time this is just about as far as we can go.

4. Bankruptcy and the Risk of Default

We mentioned at the end of section 2 that there were very serious drawbacks associated with any model of a capital market under uncertainty which assumes that individuals borrow freely at a risk-free rate of interest and, more generally, which assumes that securities are bought and sold at a price which takes no account of the identity of the buyer and seller. In order to highlight this point it is worth looking back at the model of section 2 in order to demonstrate that upon close analysis it has some rather extraordinary properties. When this model was analysed we glossed over the problem of whether or not the individual's holdings of shares were restricted to be positive[11] and the difficulties that such a restriction would cause for the necessary conditions for utility maximization. If we now assume that negative shareholdings are not allowed, it is clear that if an individual holds zero shares then the marginal expected utility provided by the income from a unit investment in shares must not be more than that provided by the income from a unit investment in bonds, otherwise bonds would be sold and shares purchased. This implies that $E_i(U_i'\pi)/M$ is not more than $(1+r^*)E_iU_i'$ and thus we have

8.29
$$\frac{E_i(U_i'\pi)}{E_iU_i'} \leqslant (1+r^*)M$$

which is simply the necessary condition 8.9 with an inequality sign.

Now suppose that one of the individuals in this economy is risk neutral, all others are risk averse, all investors have the same subjective probabilities over states of the world and the returns on shares are such that all risk-averse investors require a positive risk premium to hold any at all. Then, if any risk-averse individual holds shares, we have that

8.30
$$\frac{E(U_i'\pi)}{EU_i'} = (1+r^*)M$$

for some i. But since the risk premium for the firm must be positive this implies from proposition 1 of the Appendix, that $E(U_i'\pi)/EU_i'$ $< E\pi$ and thus $E\pi M^{-1} > (1+r^*)$ from 8.30 and the expected return on a unit investment is shares is greater than the return on bonds. The risk-neutral person would clearly not be in equilibrium if this were so, since he is only interested in expected returns and he clearly has a strong incentive to borrow at the rate of r^* and purchase more shares in the firm. Thus there can be no equilibrium in which any risk-averse individual holds any shares. Consequently, in equilibrium, the single risk neutral individual holds *all* the shares in the firm and inequality 8.29 holds strictly for all the other individuals. This is hardly surprising since the risk-neutral person, being totally unconcerned with the risk attached to any asset, is always going to value a risky asset more highly than a risk-averse person. So, given that he has the resources, and since he can borrow freely at the safe rate this is never a problem, he will always buy up all the risky assets. This will happen even if his initial wealth is zero. It immediately follows from this that the value of the discount rate ρ will always be r^* since the expected return on shares is equal to $(1+r^*)$. Thus the entry of a single risk-neutral person with zero wealth into this economy will immediately imply that the firm uses the safe rate of interest for discounting purposes.

This result will still hold even if there are a *large number* of risky firms in the economy, for, using the same arguments as above, the risk-neutral individual will hold all the shares in every risky firm, however many there may be. All the risky firms will then discount at the safe rate of interest.[12]

But this is not the most extraordinary property of this model by a long way. Suppose that the firm has a pattern of returns of the type

$$\phi(\theta)=1,\, 0 \leqslant \theta \leqslant 1;\, \phi(\theta)=0,\, \text{all other values of } \theta.$$

Then suppose that the risk-neutral individual has a subjective probability over states of the world such that he believes that prob.$[0 \leqslant \theta \leqslant 1]=1$ and that all the other individuals imagine that prob.$\lceil 0 \leqslant \theta \leqslant 1\rceil=0$. Then it is clear that the risk-neutral individual will purchase all the shares and that the firm will maximize its expected present value discounting at the safe rate of return and *using the risk-neutral individual's subjective probabilities to form its expectation*. This, in spite of the fact that all other individuals in the economy think that the firm will yield a *certain* return of zero and that all real investment in such a firm is completely wasted. Thus this model implies that an individual with zero wealth can borrow and invest as much as he wishes in a company which everyone else in the economy thinks is entirely worthless. This is clearly the height of absurdity and it follows from assuming a perfect market in risk-less bonds. In reality, of course, no one would lend an individual with zero wealth anything if it was to be invested in this way.

So it is now clear that we cannot avoid investigating a model in which the possibility of bankruptcy for both firms and individuals is taken into account for the simple reason that the assumption of 'perfection' for a capital market in a world of uncertainty is clearly liable to lead to absurdity.[13] Indeed, it seems reasonable to argue that such capital markets are *inherently* imperfect and, as we shall see, these 'imperfections' are non-trivial in their effects.

Take first the case which we have just been discussing in which all individuals have identical expectations but only one is risk neutral. It is clear that if such an individual borrows too much from the others in order to invest in a risky firm, there is a strong possibility that he will go bankrupt if the firm does badly. This risk of bankruptcy implies that the other individuals will not lend him the money he requires at the safe rate of interest because there is a probability that he will default on at least some of the loans. In order to compensate for this possibility, he will be charged a rate of interest in excess of the safe rate and consequently the marginal cost of borrowing for the individual, and hence the marginal cost of capital for the firm, will be above the safe rate. The size of the 'risk premium' will depend not only on the degree of risk aversion of lenders but also on the amount borrowed, for the risk of default will clearly rise with the total size of the loan. But this in its turn will be dependent on the initial wealth of our risk-neutral investor, for the more money of his own which he can invest in risky shares, the less he need rely on borrowing from others. So it seems not unreasonable to conclude that the marginal cost of capital to the risky firm will depend, among other things, on the initial wealth of the risk-neutral investor who is in fact the sole owner of the firm. This being so, we can immediately say that the level of investment by the risky firm will be an increasing function of this initial wealth, a result which will clearly be reinforced if the risk-neutral investor is also more optimistic about the risky firm's prospects.

This is an important result for it implies that the investment decisions of firms could be affected by the wealth of their owners. An important element of this wealth may well consist of the profits earned by the firm in the previous period and consequently there is the possibility of a direct link between current investment and past profits, a link which is more or less non-existent in a world of 'perfect' capital markets unless variations in past profits influence individual expectations about future returns. Since it has often been maintained[14] that there is no such link other than via expectations and that capital market 'imperfections' are of little consequence, it is vital to recognize how the link can arise from the essential structure of capital markets under uncertainty.

This is such an important issue that we must pursue a formal analysis despite the considerable difficulties involved. The problems arise from the fact that, if one individual lends money to another, he cannot know what interest to charge without knowing both the risks of default on the loan and also what returns he will receive in case of such default. This implies a knowledge of the debtor's complete portfolio, the structure of his debts to other individuals and also of the rules of payment which will be followed should the debtor become bankrupt. In reality, there are innumerable institutional and legal rules which are used to deal with these problems, though the incidence of law suits concerned with such matters indicates how complicated and uncertain the whole business can become. Consequently, in order to construct a formal model, we must clearly make some drastic simplifications although we shall not utilize the notion of risk classes, for this in some sense evades the issue. Their existence in reality may indeed weaken the impact of the effects with which we shall be concerned but, in any discussion of capital markets, it seems vital to look closely at the relationship between borrowers and lenders, a relationship which the perfectly competitive concept of the risk class is designed to avoid. In addition we shall also investigate the status of the Modigliani–Miller proposition in a world of bankruptcy since it does not seem very likely that it can be preserved, given the differences in the structure of individual and company borrowing. In other words, it seems improbable that individual and company borrowing are perfectly substitutable, which is one of the essential preconditions of the Modigliani–Miller theorem.

Turning then to a more formal approach we first consider the following very simple general equilibrium model.

Firms—There are two firms, one of which has constant returns to scale and, for an input of y_1 in the first period, produces an output of $(1+r^*)y_1$ in the second period. This effectively anchors the safe rate of interest at r^*. The second produces $\theta f(y_2)$ units of output in the second period for an input of y_2 in the first. In both cases the input disappears in the second period and there is only one good involved in the economy. θ is a random variable, as before.[15] The first firm issues only (safe) bonds and the second firm issues both shares and bonds.

Individuals—There are two individuals, one of whom is a risk averse with utility function U and is called A (subscript a) and the other who is referred to as N (subscript n) and is risk neutral.

Initially we shall assume that both individuals have the same subjective probability densities on θ, namely $g(\theta)$, and that $g(\theta) \geqslant 0$ for all $0 \leqslant \theta \leqslant \Lambda$ where Λ is large, and otherwise is zero. Let w_i be the initial wealth and let k_i, b_i, s_i respectively be the holdings of safe bonds, bonds in the risky firm and shares by the two individuals, for $i = a$, n. Assume that all asset holdings are restricted to be non-negative. Suppose first that the risky firm is unlevered and consequently issues no bonds. Then there are effectively three kinds of asset in the economy:

(1) Safe bonds which yield a return of $(1+r^*)$ per unit of income invested.

(2) Shares in the second firm which yield $S(\theta) = \theta f / M_2$ per income unit invested, where M_2 is the total value of all the shares in the firm.

(3) Loans from A to N which are rather more difficult to characterize. Suppose that the amount of the loan is l and the rate of interest charged is r_l. Then N's consumption will be given by $s_n \theta f / M_2 + k_n(1+r^*) - l(1+r_l)$ so long as this is non-negative. If θ turns out

less than $\hat{\theta}$ given by

8.31 $s_n \hat{\theta} f / M_2 + k_n(1+r^*) = l(1+r_l),$

then N is unable to pay off his loan plus the interest and is declared bankrupt, forfeiting all his wealth to A. Consequently, the return per unit of income loaned by A to N can be defined as

$$L(\theta) = (1+r_l) \qquad \text{for } \theta \geqslant \hat{\theta}$$

$$= \{s_n \theta f / M_2 + k_n(1+r^*)\}/l \qquad \text{for } \theta < \hat{\theta}.$$

We now consider the equilibrium possibilities in this economy but before doing so we must clarify precisely what each of the two individuals takes as given when making portfolio decisions. We shall try to keep as closely as possible to a competitive formulation and it will therefore be assumed that both A and N take y_2, M_2, r_l as given. On the other hand, we shall assume that when A is determining his optimal supply of loans he recognizes that the shareholdings of N depend on the size of these loans. The next step will be to narrow down the equilibrium possibilities of the economy which we shall do by considering a series of points.

Point 1: In equilibrium it is not possible to have $r_l < r^*$. If $r_l < r^*$, the expected return on a loan to N from A is clearly less than $(1+r^*)$. Since A can invest as much as he wishes at a safe return $(1+r^*)$ he will clearly not be prepared to make any loans to N under these circumstances. Equally under such circumstances N will demand a loan simply to invest in the safe asset and consequently there will be an excess demand for loans.

Point 2: If $r_l \geqslant r^*$ it is not possible for N to hold safe bonds and to borrow from A. Suppose $r_l > r^*$ and N borrows to buy safe bonds. By reducing his safe bond holdings by one unit and his loan by one unit, N gains an additional $(r_l - r^*)$ in all states in which he is not bankrupt. Furthermore, he is less likely to go bankrupt and consequently under these conditions he will never borrow and hold safe bonds. On the other hand, if $r_l = r^*$ then loans to N are completely safe otherwise A would not make the loan. Therefore we have a situation of A lending to N at the safe rate so that he may buy safe bonds. Such trivial lending may safely be ruled out by assumption.

Point 3: In equilibrium, A will never hold shares. There are four possibilities to consider.

(a) *N holds only shares and safe bonds.* The expected return on shares must then be equal to the return on safe bonds. But A is risk averse and will never hold a risky asset when a safe asset with the same expected return is also available. So in this situation he will never hold shares.

(b) *N holds only safe bonds*. Consequently A must hold shares which thus have a higher expected return than safe bonds. N will thus demand some and this cannot be an equilibrium.

(c) *N holds shares and borrows from A*. This is rather more difficult and we must now consider A's portfolio choice problem. From point 2, we know (and A knows) that $L(\theta)$, the return on loans, has the form:

$$L(\theta) = 1 + r_l \qquad \text{for } \theta \geqslant \hat{\theta}$$

$$= \frac{s_n \theta f}{l M_2} \qquad \text{for } \theta < \hat{\theta}.$$

Furthermore, A realizes that $s_n = l + w_n$ from N's budget constraint and so A's consumption pattern is given by

$$c^a(\theta) = l(1 + r_l) + (w_a - s_a - l)(1 + r^*) + s_a S(\theta), \qquad \text{for } \theta \geqslant \hat{\theta},$$

$$= l\left\{ \frac{(l + w_n)\theta f}{l M_2} \right\} + (w_a - s_a - l)(1 + r^*) + s_a S(\theta), \qquad \text{for } \theta < \hat{\theta}.$$

Let us now write down the gain in expected utility achieved by A if he increases his shareholdings or his loan to N by one unit. In the former case this gain is simply $E_\theta[U'\{c^a(\theta)\}S(\theta)]$ whereas in the latter it is $E_\theta[U'\{c^a(\theta)\}L(\theta)]$ where $L(\theta)$ is the marginal increase in consumption opportunities following a unit increase in l, which is given by simple differentiation as,

8.32 $$\qquad L(\theta) = 1 + r_l \qquad \text{for } \theta \geqslant \hat{\theta}$$

$$= \theta f / M_2 \qquad \text{for } \theta < \hat{\theta}.$$

So, at the margin, A's loans to N are equivalent to securities of the form $L(\theta)$. We will now show that A will always prefer these securities to shares and in order to do this we must consider the portfolio problem faced by N. Since he is risk neutral it is clear that in portfolio equilibrium N must receive equal increments in expected consumption from a unit increase in shareholdings and a unit reduction in his debt to A. Furthermore, for all values of θ less than $\hat{\theta}$ he is bankrupt and can consume nothing so we need only consider expectations over values of θ not less than $\hat{\theta}$ which are denoted by $E_{\theta \geqslant \hat{\theta}}$. In equilibrium we must have

8.33 $$\qquad\qquad E_{\theta \geqslant \hat{\theta}} S(\theta) = E_{\theta \geqslant \hat{\theta}} (1 + r_l).$$

But, since for all $\theta < \hat{\theta}$ the securities $\bar{L}(\theta)$ and $S(\theta)$ are identical, both yielding $\theta f/M_2$, and for $\theta \geqslant \hat{\theta}$, $\bar{L}(\theta)$ is equal to the right-hand side of 8.33, then it is clear that 8.33 implies

8.34 $$\underset{\theta}{E}\, S(\theta) = \underset{\theta}{E}\, \bar{L}(\theta).$$

So, for N to be in portfolio equilibrium, the securities $S(\theta)$ and $\bar{L}(\theta)$ must have the same expectation. Looking at Figure 8.1 we can see that $S(\theta)$ and $\bar{L}(\theta)$ have the further property that for some θ', $\bar{L}(\theta) \geqslant S(\theta)$ for $\theta \leqslant \theta'$ and $\bar{L}(\theta) < S(\theta)$ for $\theta > \theta'$, and in this well-defined sense we can say that shares are more risky than securities

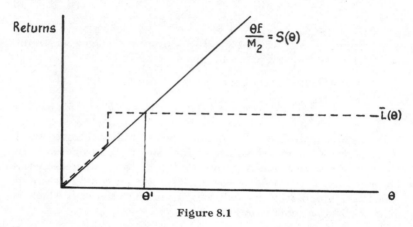

Figure 8.1

$\bar{L}(\theta)$. Since, in addition, shares must have the same expected return as $\bar{L}(\theta)$ securities, we can show that A always prefers to lend to N rather than hold shares because the marginal gain in expected utility is always higher on loans, that is $E_\theta U'\{c^a(\theta)\}S(\theta) < E_\theta U'\{c^a(\theta)\}\bar{L}(\theta)$ for all $s_a \geqslant 0$. (This last is proved formally in the Appendix, proposition 3.)

To sum up, we can argue that if N borrows to buy shares then his expected returns on shares must be equal to his expected marginal cost of borrowing. This equality of expectations, combined with the fact that shares are more risky than loans, leads to A minimizing his risk at any given level of expected returns by refusing to hold any shares at all.

(d) *N holds only shares.* Since N is not borrowing the expected marginal cost of borrowing must clearly be greater than or equal to the return on shares. But in this case A would rather lend than hold shares which are more risky and yield a lower expected return than loans. Consequently, in equilibrium A could not hold shares under these circumstances.

The upshot of these three points is that there are only two possible equilibrium patterns. The first is that A holds safe bonds and N holds safe bonds and shares, the second is that A holds safe bonds and lends to N and N holds shares and borrows from A.[16] Since N holds all the shares it is clear that the first possibility arises when N's initial wealth is greater than the value of the risky firm and the second when it is not. The first type of equilibrium is rather trivial. In this case N holds all the shares and some safe bonds. Consequently, the expected return on shares must be equal to that on safe bonds and this determines the value of the risky firm M_2 as

$$M_2 = E(\theta)f(y_2)/(1+r^*).$$

The original shares are clearly valued at $M_2 - y_2$ and consequently in this case the firm will maximize

$$(1+r^*)^{-1}\{E(\theta)f(y_2) - (1+r^*)y_2\}$$

where the cost of capital is thus given by the safe rate of return. In the second type of equilibrium where N has not the wealth to purchase all the shares without borrowing, things are a little more complicated. In this case the value of the risky firm, the total loan from A to N and the rate of interest on the loan are determined simultaneously.

A's willingness to supply loans results from his expected utility maximization which, for the purposes of defining equilibrium, may be taken as conditional on a zero holding of shares. This yields a supply function of the form

8.35 $\qquad\qquad\qquad l = l(r_l, y_2, M_2)$

where note again that the average return on loans is defined by

8.36 $\qquad\qquad L(\theta) = 1 + r_l \qquad$ for $\theta \geqslant \hat{\theta}$,

$$= \frac{(l+w_n)\theta f}{lM_2} \qquad \text{for } \theta < \hat{\theta},$$

with $\hat{\theta}$ defined by

8.37 $\qquad\qquad\qquad (l+w_n)\hat{\theta}f = lM_2(1+r_l).$

We know that N's portfolio equilibrium requires that the expected return on shares equals the expected marginal cost of borrowing which, from 8.34 requires that

8.38
$$E_{\theta}\{S(\theta)\} = E_{\theta}\{\bar{L}(\theta)\}$$

where $\bar{L}(\theta)$ is defined by 8.32. In addition, of course, N's budget constraint implies that the total shareholding is equal to his initial wealth plus the amount of his loan, thus

8.39
$$M_2 = l + w_n.$$

The three equations 8.35, 8.38 and 8.39 suffice to determine r_l, l and M_2 for any given level of y_2, in the case where N's initial wealth is less than the total value of the shares. In this case we have from 8.38 that

$$M_2 = E(\theta)f(y_2)/E\{\bar{L}(\theta)\}]$$

and hence the value of the original shareholding in the risky firm is

8.40
$$M_2 - y_2 = E\{\bar{L}(\theta)\}^{-1}[E(\theta)f(y_2) - E\{\bar{L}(\theta)\}y_2].$$

The important point to note is that the cost of capital is now higher than the safe rate $(1+r^*)$. The reason for this is that, since A effectively holds some of the risky security $\bar{L}(\theta)$, its expectation must be greater than the safe return.[17] Consequently, in a model where bankruptcy is specifically included, it no longer follows that the introduction of a risk-neutral person into the economy implies that all firms discount at the safe rate, though they will if he is rich enough. The investment decision of the firm therefore does indeed depend crucially on the initial wealth position of its ultimate owners, confirming our previous intuitive arguments.

The next step is to see whether the Modigliani–Miller theorem holds in this sort of world. In the first type of equilibrium discussed above, it clearly does hold. If the firm issues bonds, all the bonds will be purchased by N who will thus receive the same gross receipts from the risky firm as before. What is more, at the return on bonds required by N, A will not demand any since they will be risky with the same expected return as the safe asset. Hence nothing will change. This is not, however, true of the second type of equilibrium and in order to discuss this we must look at the characteristics of bonds more closely.

If the risky firm issues B bonds then the return on bonds $B(\theta)$ may be written as

$$B(\theta) = 1 + r_b \qquad \theta \geqslant \theta^*,$$

$$= \theta f / B \qquad \theta < \theta^*,$$

where θ^* satisfies the equation

$$\theta^* f - (1 + r_b)B = 0.$$

θ^* is the value of θ below which the risky firm goes bankrupt. In other words, for any outcome $\theta < \theta^*$, the returns to the firm are not enough to cover its debts and therefore it defaults. In this situation all of its assets go to the bond-holders and the shareholders receive nothing.[18] The return on shares, $S(\theta)$, is consequently given by

$$S(\theta) = \frac{\theta f - (1 + r_b)B}{M_2'} \qquad \theta \geqslant \theta^*,$$

$$= 0 \qquad \theta \leqslant \theta^*,$$

where M_2' is the total value of the shares.

Suppose initially that bonds and shares *must be held* in the proportions $B : M_2'$ by both A and N. Then one unit of this combined risky asset yields a return

8.41 $$\frac{1}{B + M_2'} \{B . B(\theta) + M_2' . S(\theta)\} = \frac{\theta f}{B + M_2'} \qquad \text{for all } \theta.$$

This risky asset is thus precisely the same as a share in the original model where the risky firm issued no bonds. Consequently, the equilibrium in the new situation where the firm is levered will be precisely identical to that in the original situation so long as shares and bonds are always held in the proportions $B : M_2'$. It will again be described by equations 8.35, 8.38 and 8.39 with $B + M_2'$ replacing M_2 and N will hold all the bonds as well as all the shares. Having arrived at this position suppose we now relax the constraint on the proportion of bonds to shares that may be held and determine whether A can be made better off if the total value of the firm and N's utility are both maintained at the same level. Suppose one unit of bonds is transferred from N to A at the same time reducing N's loan by one unit. The expected gain to N of reducing his loan by one unit is given by $E\{\bar{L}(\theta)\}$ where $\bar{L}(\theta)$ is now defined by replacing M_2 by $B + M_2'$ in 8.32. Since we are moving from a constrained equilibrium position this expectation must be equal to the expected return on the risky asset combination, that is

8.42 $$E\{\bar{L}(\theta)\} = E\left(\frac{\theta f}{M_2' + B}\right)$$

and consequently, in order to maintain N's utility, the expected return on the transferred bond must satisfy[19]

8.43 $$E\{B(\theta)\} = E\left(\frac{\theta f}{M_2' + B}\right).$$

Since A's loan to N yields a return which is equivalent at the margin to a security $\bar{L}(\theta)$, this transfer implies a gain to A of a unit of bonds yielding $B(\theta)$ and a loss of a unit of loan yielding $\bar{L}(\theta)$ where from 8.42 and 8.43 the expected returns on these units are identical.

Now compare the structure of the returns $B(\theta)$ and $\bar{L}(\theta)$ which are related below for convenience.

$$B(\theta) = 1 + r_b \quad \theta \geqslant \theta^*, \qquad \bar{L}(\theta) = 1 + r_l \quad \theta \geqslant \hat{\theta},$$
$$\quad\quad = \theta f / B \quad \theta < \theta^*, \qquad \quad\quad = \theta f / (B + M_2') \quad \theta < \hat{\theta}.$$

It is clear that if M_2' is positive and $r_b < r_l$, then there exists a θ' such that $B(\theta) > \bar{L}(\theta)$ for $0 < \theta < \theta'$ and $B(\theta) < \bar{L}(\theta)$ for $\theta > \theta'$. $\bar{L}(\theta)$ is then more risky than $B(\theta)$ and, since they have the same expected return, A will experience an increase in expected utility by losing one unit of the former and gaining one unit of the latter (see again proposition 3 of the Appendix for a proof). It simply remains to show that the firm can choose B such that M_2' is positive and $r_b < r_l$. If we make B small enough, θ^* will be less than $\hat{\theta}$ and M_2' will be positive since $B + M_2'$ remains constant. But if $r_b \geqslant r_l$ it follows that $B(\theta) \geqslant \bar{L}(\theta)$ for all θ (with $>$ for some θ) and so the two assets could hardly have the same mean return. Consequently $r_b < r_l$ and for small enough bond issues by the risky firm A will be made better off when a unit of bonds is transferred from N with a simultaneous unit reduction of N's loan. Since N is indifferent and the transfer is performed from the same equilibrium position as that arising when the firm is unlevered, it is clear that the introduction of bonds by the risky firm has increased the *ex ante* consumption possibilities of investors.

If the bond issue, B, is very small, it is obvious that A will be made better off if *all* the bonds are transferred from N with a concomitant reduction in the loan. Indeed, if N had still more of this type of bond, further transfers would make A even better off. So, if the firm were to issue more bonds, investors' *ex ante* consumption possibilities could be increased further and the firm's cost of capital would be reduced even more. But there is clearly a limit to this process, for suppose the firm were to issue bonds up to the point where B was close to the original value of the firm. Then M_2' would be very small and the securities $B(\theta)$ and $L(\theta)$ would be almost identical, with $B(\theta)$ only slightly less risky. Then, starting from the point where N holds all the bonds, the expected gain to A on receipt of the first unit of such bonds with a corresponding reduction in his loan would be negligible and the effective cost of capital to the firm would be higher than it would have been with a somewhat lower bond issue.

Clearly then, the Modigliani–Miller theorem no longer holds and the cost of capital to the firm decreases with leverage up to a certain point, in spite of the fact that the rate of interest to be paid out on

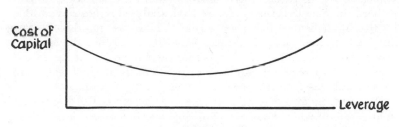

Figure 8.2

bonds, r_b, is a rising function of the number issued because of the increasing risks of bankruptcy. So, for any given level of investment and initial wealth position, the cost of capital is a U-shaped function of the degree of leverage as illustrated in Figure 8.2. This is in fact the shape of the cost of capital curve as it is drawn in most textbooks on finance, although it is usually drawn this way for different reasons, namely those which were discussed in the story of the entrepreneur in section 1. The correct reason is that the introduction of risky bonds into the economy by the firm creates a new risky asset which could not have been readily created by the individuals concerned without making some very peculiar contractual arrangement. It is, of course, theoretically possible for any individual or firm to create any risky asset he or it chooses, and put it up for sale, but in practice the problems and costs of doing so are not usually worth the effort.[20] Thus, in a trivial sense the Modigliani–Miller theorem will always hold, for individuals can always recreate for themselves the bonds of a firm. The point about the world as illustrated in this particular model is that these bonds cannot be created by individuals out of readily available standard assets like shares and private loans and consequently, if they are created naturally by the firm, the firm will gain from the widening of individual *ex ante* consumption possibilities.[21]

In some senses this is a bit of a blow for the investment theorist since it means that the financing decision and the investment decision are interdependent. For practical purposes this implies that the cost of capital to the firm cannot be taken as a given number independent of the firm's decisions. This is hardly surprising when one remembers that the first question a bank manager always asks, in response to a request for a loan, is "What for?' Its analytical consequences are, however, a little hard to take. Furthermore, it should be borne in mind that the model we have analysed is most favourable to the Modigliani–Miller proposition. There are no direct costs involved in bankruptcy and, since any such costs would influence the firm's choice of its degree of leverage, their inclusion in the model would tend to reinforce our results particularly if these costs are considerable (as indeed one suspects they are, in reality).

Two other points are worth noting at this juncture. The first is that in any kind of equilibrium a rise in the exogenously given safe rate, r^*, will always lower the optimal investment in the risky firm. This follows because the rate required by A for any sort of loan will always be higher for loans of a given size and so if A does any lending to the risky firm, either directly or indirectly, a rise in the safe rate increases the cost of capital for any given level of investment. On the other hand, if all investment is financed by N, the safe rate is used as the direct discount rate and so it follows directly that risky investment is inversely related to it.

The other, perhaps more important, point which is worth re-emphasizing is that the optimal level of debt incurred by the risky firm depends crucially on the initial wealth of N, the firm's owner.[22] Indeed, if N is wealthy enough, no debt will be incurred at all. This is, of course, related to the fact, which was noted earlier, that the optimal investment of the risky firm is higher if N has enough wealth to purchase all the firm without either the firm or himself going into debt than it is otherwise. So the initial wealth of N is a significant factor in determining both the investment and debt policy of the risky firm, a stark contrast to the no bankruptcy model of section 2.

Furthermore, as we have already mentioned, in a dynamic context it is not unreasonable to suppose that N is also the original owner of the risky firm and that a significant contribution to N's initial wealth could have been made by its previous profits. Strictly speaking, it is not permitted to put this model in a dynamic context without explicitly considering the consumption decisions of individuals in the previous period. Nevertheless, we can reasonably suppose that if the profits of the risky firm were higher in the previous period, N would have more wealth both to consume and to carry over to the next period and thus he would arrive with a higher initial wealth. Indeed, in reality, the firm itself can keep some of this wealth in the form of retained profits but it is still, of course, the wealth of the firm's owners in the final analysis.[23]

So we can conclude from this that high past profits, by increasing the funds available to the firm's owners, will have a tendency to lower the combined firm and owner level of debt and, since the debt must be procured from individuals who are more averse to the risks of the firm than the owners, such a reduction will lower the effective cost of capital schedule and raise the optimal level of investment. In reality it is not clear how significant this effect will be but there is another possibility which is probably more important. So far, within this model we have assumed that the subjective probability distributions about future events are the same across individuals. It seems very unlikely that this will be so and what seems more likely is that different individuals will be more or less 'optimistic' about the returns of particular risky firms. It is then natural to suppose that the owners of the firm will be that group which is most optimistic about the firm's prospects. It is clear also that the greater the wealth of this group, the less they will have to borrow to finance the firm's investments. But, since they are borrowing from individuals who are less optimistic, the less they have to borrow, the lower will be the effective cost of capital schedule and thus the higher will be the firm's investment. Thus we again have a direct link from past profits to greater wealth for the owners to higher investment (and lower debt).

In order to illustrate this point consider the following very simple adaptation of the previous model. Instead of A and N we have two risk-neutral individuals N_1 and N_2 who have different subjective density functions on the random variable $\theta > 0$, namely $g_1(\theta)$ and $g_2(\theta)$ where $g_i \geqslant 0$ for $0 \leqslant \theta \leqslant \Lambda_i$ and $\Lambda_2 \geqslant \Lambda_1$. The firms are exactly the same as previously and N_2 is assumed to be more 'optimistic' about the risky firm than N_1. More 'optimistic' is defined in the following way. *If $G_i(\theta)$ is equal to the distribution function $\int_0^\theta g_i(\nu)\, d\nu$ for $i=1, 2$ then N_2 is more optimistic than N_1 if $g_2(\theta)/1-G_2(\theta) < g_1(\theta)/1-G_1(\theta)$ for $0 < \theta < \Lambda_1$.*

This is a natural definition in the following sense. $\{g_i(\nu)/1-G_i(\nu)\}\, d\nu$ is the probability that the random variable θ will fall in the interval $[\nu, \nu+d\nu]$ conditional on the fact that it is not lower than ν. So if we ask the two individuals about the probability that the output of the firm will lie in any interval $\{\nu f, (\nu+d\nu)f\}$, assuming that it is no lower, N_1 will always give a higher probability than N_2. That is, as we move up the output scale N_1 will always think that the output is more likely to be in the next interval if it has not come already and N_2 will think it less likely to be in the next interval and so more likely to be in some higher interval. In some sense, therefore, N_2 is uniformly more optimistic all the way up the scale of possible outputs.

It will be assumed from the start that all the shares in the risky firm are owned by N_2, who borrows directly from N_1 if necessary. We are thus completely identifying N_2 with the firm, which is not such a serious assumption as it sounds since it can be quite easily shown that in equilibrium N_1 would not demand any shares in the risky firm. It is clear that if the total input required by the risky firm is less than the initial wealth of N_2, then he will not borrow from N_1 and his final wealth will be given by the expression

$$\theta f(y_2) + (1+r^*)(w_2 - y_2)$$

where w_2 is his initial wealth and $w_2 - y_2$ is the amount he has left to invest in safe bonds (which is positive). The amount of investment in the risky firm, y_2, is then chosen by maximizing the expectation of this expression and satisfies

8.44 $$E_2(\theta)f'(y_2) = (1+r^*).$$

Thus the expected marginal product of capital is equated to the safe return where the expectation is based solely on the more optimistic expectations of N_2. Turning now to the other case, suppose that N_2's initial wealth is less than the value of y_2 satisfying 8.44. Then he is forced to borrow from N_1, and the question arises as to the terms under which he can acquire a loan. Here we shall assume that N_2 presents N_1 with the following information: (i) that N_1 is N_2's only creditor, (ii) that he is not holding any safe bonds, (iii) the technical details of the production process and the amount of input used, i.e.

$f(y_2)$, (iv) the amount which he wishes to borrow, namely B. N_1 then sets the rate of interest on the loan so that his expected return over all states of nature including those in which N_2 defaults on the loan is equal to the safe return $(1+r^*)$. In a sense N_2 asks for the loan at the same time offering the output of the firm as collateral in case of default.[24]

So, if the rate of interest required by N_1 is equal to r, the return on the loan may be defined as

$$B(\theta) = (1+r) \qquad \theta \geqslant \theta^*,$$
$$= \theta f / B \qquad \theta < \theta^*,$$

where B is the size of the loan and θ^* is the bankruptcy point defined, as usual, by

8.45 $$\theta^*/f = B(1+r).$$

The size of r is then determined by equating the expected return on the loan to the safe rate using N_1's 'pessimistic' probability distribution. This gives

8.46 $$(1+r)\{1 - G_1(\theta^*)\} + \int_0^{\theta^*} g_1(\theta)\theta \, \mathrm{d}\theta . f/B = 1 + r^*$$

and substituting r from 8.46 gives

8.47 $$\left[\theta^*\{1 - G_1(\theta^*)\} + \int_0^{\theta^*} g_1(\theta)\theta \, \mathrm{d}\theta\right] f(y_2) = B(1+r^*).$$

Before going on to discuss N_2's optimal investment plan it should first be noted that N_1 may actually impose a borrowing limit for any given level of y_2. This arises because the maximum value of the term in parentheses on the left-hand side of 8.47 is $E_1(\theta)$, the expected value of θ in the opinion of N_1. This will yield a borrowing limit of $E_1(\theta)f(y_2)/(1+r^*)$, above which it is not possible for N_1 to earn an expected return of $(1+r^*)$ on his loan to N_2 for any borrowing rate r. We shall assume in what follows that N_2 never has such optimistic expectations as to be constrained by such a limit. Turning now to N_2's investment plan we can first note that N_2 will not hold any safe bonds and his final wealth will be given by

$$\theta f - (1+r)B \qquad \theta \geqslant \theta^*$$
$$0 \qquad \theta \leqslant \theta^*,$$

where $y_2 = w_2 + B$ is his budget constraint. N_2 will then maximize his expected final wealth subject to his budget constraint and the definition of θ^* in 8.47.[25] Using this reduces the problem to one of maximizing.

$$\left[\int_{\theta^*}^{\infty} \theta g_2(\theta)\, \mathrm{d}\theta - \theta^*\{1 - G_2(\theta^*)\} \right] f$$

subject to

$$\left[\theta^*\{1 - G_1(\theta^*)\} + \int_{0}^{\theta^*} g_1(\theta)\theta\, \mathrm{d}\theta \right] f = (y_2 - w_2)(1 + r^*).$$

In the Appendix, proposition 4, we show that this yields the necessary condition

$$H(\theta^*)f'(y_2) = (1 + r^*)$$

where

$$H(\theta^*) = \frac{1 - G_1(\theta^*)}{1 - G_2(\theta^*)} \int_{\theta^*}^{\infty} \theta g_2(\theta)\, \mathrm{d}\theta + \int_{0}^{\theta^*} \theta g_1(\theta)\, \mathrm{d}\theta.$$

This result is very much in accord with common-sense. $H(\theta^*)$ is a mixture of the means of θ under the two different probability distributions. It reduces to the common mean if they are identical, in which case N_2's initial wealth clearly makes no odds. Furthermore, it is easy to show that $H(\theta^*)$ is decreasing in θ^*, implying an increase in the effective cost of capital as the probability of bankruptcy increases. Most importantly, however, it is shown in the Appendix, proposition 5, that, because N_2 is more optimistic than N_1, the optimal level of investment is increasing in the initial wealth of N_2, that is $\partial y_2/\partial w_2 > 0$. This confirms all that we would expect. The less wealth there is available to the optimistic owners of the risky firm, the more they must borrow from the pessimists which automatically raises the cost of capital schedule.

Summarizing these last results we note that, even in the context of a perfectly functioning capital market with no transaction costs, additional costs of bankruptcy or any other such factors, we are forced to conclude that the firm's effective cost of capital schedule is not independent of its recent level of profitability. The higher the recent profit flow, the smaller the reliance which the firm has to place on borrowing from individuals who are bound to be both more pessimistic about the firm's prospects and more averse to the risks inherent in the firm's returns than the firm's owners (otherwise these outside individuals would themselves be co-owners of the firm). It is most important to bear in mind, however, that these results have emerged from models in which there is only one risky firm and this could be misleading. The fact that the supply of funds to the individual firm is not very elastic with respect to rates of return does, of course, depend crucially on the firm having a pattern of future returns across states of nature unlike that of other firms. If this were not the case and there were a large number of firms in the same 'risk class' then, since investors would be indifferent between investment in different firms, the supply of funds to any individual firm would be very elastic. On the other hand, although the existence of large risk classes would flatten the relationship between the rate of investment and the cost of funds, it would not necessarily lessen the impact of recent profits on capital costs. The reason for this is that if one firm in a risk class makes high profits, then *all* firms in the risk class must do so, for if the outcome is a favourable state of nature for one firm in the class, then it is obviously favourable for all. Consequently, high profits in one firm will, by our previous arguments, lower the cost of capital schedule to the risk class as a whole, and will thus imply a lower cost of capital to each individual firm.

The question of the existence of risk classes is, of course, an empirical matter. Casual observation, however, seems to go against the notion, for there is an enormous variation in profitability from one firm to another, even in the same industry, and in addition there are considerable changes in the ranking of firms by rates of return from one period to the next.[26] Given that profits must move together for firms in the same risk class, this would seem to throw some doubt on their plausibility.

Two further arguments of a slightly different nature may be adduced to justify a link between recent and current profits and the level of investment. One is that shareholders who are involved in the firm may well have considerably more information concerning the firm's future prospects than outsiders and will therefore perceive a lower risk associated with these prospects. The other, perhaps more forceful, argument is that a higher profit earned by the firm may actually influence prospects in the direction of optimism, thereby lowering the effective cost of capital. This could well be an extremely important effect and may possibly be the dominant reason why current profitability would influence a firm's investment plans. If this were the case, and assuming that such expectational effects are adequately captured by the price of the firm's equity or some other measures of its expectations concerning the future values of relevant parameters, then we would expect to find no independent influence of current profits on investment once these other variables are taken into account. We shall be returning to this issue when we come to study the evidence provided by empirical investment studies.[27]

Returning to the mainstream of our discussion it is clear from the above model that the profit flow also influences the optimal debt of the firm. If the profit flow is very large and the firm distributes these profits to the shareholders, at the same time issuing debt to finance

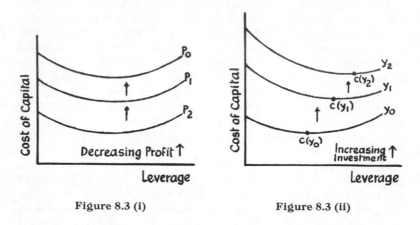

Figure 8.3 (i)   Figure 8.3 (ii)

new investment, these very same shareholders will use their wealth to purchase the debt and the firm is in precisely the same position as if it had retained the profits to finance the investment. If, however, the profit flow is not large enough to make these two possibilities the same (and remember that shareholders also wish to consume), then, as we have seen, there is an optimal quantity of debt to be issued which depends on the actual size of the profit flow. So, to summarize, we have, for any given level of investment, a series of U-shaped curves relating the cost of capital to the degree of leverage where the height of the curve depends on the level of recent profits. These are illustrated in Figure 8.3(i).

Then, as the level of investment is increased, these curves all shift upwards because of the greater reliance on finance from more pessimistic and more risk-averse agents. Thus, *for any given level of profits*, there exists another set of U-shaped cost of capital curves corresponding to different levels of investment as shown in Figure 8.3(ii). The minimum points on these curves will therefore determine an upward sloping cost of capital schedule for the firm, the height of which is inversely related to its past profit flow and the steepness of which is inversely related to the availability of close substitute investments. This schedule may then be used to determine the optimal level of investment, given a knowledge of expected future returns.[28] The 'cost of capital' which emerges is thus determined simultaneously with the level of investment and the degree of leverage. This last point is important because it is frequently claimed that there exists an independent 'optimal' degree of leverage which a firm should be aiming at. In the light of our analysis, it is not quite clear how this should be interpreted, since both the level of past profits and the available investment opportunities will influence the firm's correct degree of leverage in each period.

Lastly, it is worth noting that because we have a cost of capital schedule which is increasing in the level of investment we may possibly be able to justify the assumption of strictly convex costs of adjustment which was extensively discussed in Chapter 3. This justification has nothing to do with adjustment costs as such, but is simply based on the fact that as investment increases the costs of financing it are rising at the margin and these financing costs could well cause the firm to behave *as if* it were faced with strictly convex costs of adjustment of the usual type. That is to say, if the firm had static expectations and was moving towards some 'desired' level of capital stock, it would spread out its new capital purchases over time, so as not to have too high a rate of investment in any one period which would incur very heavy capital costs. Furthermore, since the cost of capital schedule shifts with the level of current profitability we would expect the rate at which the firm adjusts to its long-run equilibrium to depend on this very same level, with higher levels of current profitability leading to faster rates of adjustment. Indeed, we can go further and argue that the main effect of current profits is on this rate of adjustment and not on the long-run equilibrium level of capital stock itself, for *in the long run* the firm can generate enough wealth for its owners to finance its fixed equilibrium level of capital stock without recourse to expensive borrowing from less optimistic or more risk-averse economic agents.[29]

5. The Objective of the Firm

As a final point it should be noted that until now we have had very little to say about the separation of management and ownership and it may well be that this is important. Consideration of the possible effects of this separation have lead to various *ad hoc* criteria for firm behaviour such as maximizing growth (and perhaps, thereby, the manager's importance and salary)[30] subject to a firm valuation constraint. In a sense this may make the flow of profits even more vital in investment decisions because a large profit flow gives managers more money to play with without a great deal of external control (see footnote 27). On the other hand, it has been pointed out that firms which do not maximize stock market valuation are liable to be taken over by other firms, which could profit by doing so by the amount by which the stock market valuation was off its maximum. Typically such takeovers are not in the interests of the managers since they may well be sacked in the process and thus there is a strong encouragement for them to maximize the firm's stock market valuation. Unfortunately, this last argument is not correct and the following two rather negative propositions have been proven under quite weak assumptions.

There exist production plans which are unanimously agreeable to shareholders which are different from the production plan which maximizes stock market valuation (or the price of shares).

The production plan which maximizes the share price is not the same as that which minimizes the risk of being taken over.

No formal proof will be given of these propositions but it is worth giving some general idea of why they might be true.[31] Suppose we have a firm with N identical shareholders which has S shares outstanding. Suppose the two demand curves illustrated in Figure 8.4 are the demand curves of a shareholder for the shares of the firm under two different policies, (1) and (2). First of all, it is clear that the total value of the shares is maximized under policy (1). On the other hand, the consumer surplus of the shareholder is maximized under policy (2) and consequently the shareholders will be unanimous in their preference for policy (2). Now suppose some outside entrepreneur wishes to gain control of this company by purchasing 51% of all the shares. If the rules of take-overs are such that he must offer the same price to all shareholders, he must clearly pay $T(2)$ per share if the firm is pursuing policy (2) and $T(1)$ per share if it pursues policy (1). Consequently, (2) is also the policy to minimize the probability of take-over.

The fact that this sort of thing can occur is clearly dependent on the existence of downward sloping individual demand curves for the shares of a particular firm. So, as with the upward sloping cost of capital schedule, these problems would not arise if the firm was part of a large risk class, for then the demand for the shares of an

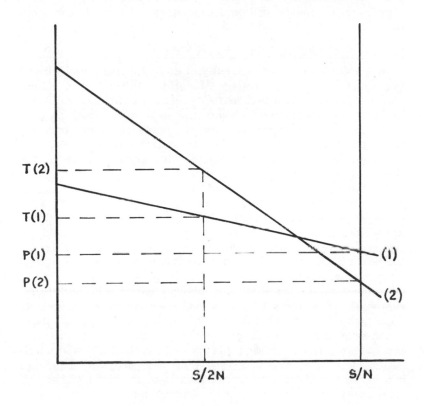

Figure 8.4

individual firm is perfectly elastic. But, if we are not prepared to accept this rather dubious assumption, we are still confronted with the very serious problem of the objective of firms under uncertainty, especially since it may be shown that under general kinds of uncertainty, shareholders will most certainly not be unanimous about the best policy for the firm to pursue.[32] This leads into problems of group decision-making where it seems clear that the institutional and legal structure of the firm cannot be ignored.

There is little more that can be said. The introduction of uncertainty has moved us from the clear certainties of present value maximization into the foggy realms of group decision-making in a very complex economic and institutional framework. The question remains open.[33]

6. Some Concluding Remarks on Finance

In a world without the possibility of default on loans and with no taxes and transaction costs the Modigliani–Miller theorem holds. The firm is quite indifferent as to its method of finance and it can make its investment decisions independently of its financing decisions. The rate at which the firm discounts its future expected returns for the purposes of making investment decisions is that rate at which the market would discount the expected returns on the firm's shares if the firm issued no debt.

As we have seen, however, a world without the possibility of bankruptcy is absurd and typically the introduction of default risks negates the Modigliani–Miller result, largely because the firm's bonds are a risky asset which it is most improbable that individuals can reproduce privately. The introduction of such a new risky asset by the firm will automatically reduce the firm's cost of capital since it improves the position of investors (in the sense of Pareto). On the other hand, even if the Modigliani–Miller theorem holds with bankruptcy, the wealth of a firm's shareholders may be of considerable importance in determining the cost of capital schedule, particularly if non-shareholders are less optimistic about the firm's future prospects. Since the firm's past profits are an important contribution to shareholders' wealth, this is clearly an argument for the direct influence of profits on investment behaviour. It should perhaps be emphasized that assigning a role to earnings in the determination of the cost of capital is in no sense incompatible with the Modigliani–Miller theorem being valid, so long as default risk is not assumed away. Thus, if there is default risk and the Modigliani–Miller theorem still happens to remain valid, then the rate at which the market discounts the expected returns on unlevered shares is still the appropriate discount rate for the firm.[34] The point is that, unless the firm's shares are highly substitutable for those of other firms, this rate is going to be crucially dependent on the wealth of existing shareholders and indeed on the actual level of investment undertaken, for it depends either on the expectations of the least optimistic shareholder or on the expectations of the least optimistic of the firm's creditors. In the absence of default risk such matters would be of no consequence since the most optimistic individuals could always borrow enough at the *safe rate* to control the firm. Consequently, even if the Modigliani–Miller theorem holds, default risks ensure that there is an upward sloping cost of capital schedule (with respect to investment), the height of which will be inversely related to the current earnings of the firm. The importance of these effects for investment decisions then depends on the degree to which the pattern of returns on the firm's productive assets across states of nature are distinct from the pattern of returns produced by other firms. If there are a large number of firms in the same 'risk class' the slope of the cost of capital schedule of any one of them will be very small, although the influence of current earnings may still be important because earnings will move together for all firms in the same class. Furthermore, the fact that the Modigliani–Miller theorem is unlikely to hold anyway means that there corresponds to each point on the cost of capital schedule some optimal degree of leverage. So the quantity of debt and the level of investment are chosen simultaneously on the basis of this schedule.

These then are the final conclusions of our theory. They are typically reinforced by the introduction of transactions costs about which we shall have almost nothing to say,[35] but perhaps more importantly they are also reinforced by the typical tax structure and it is this topic which will be considered in the following chapter.

Appendix

Proposition 1 (p. 159). If

$$\frac{1}{1+\rho} = \frac{E(\phi U')}{E\phi E U'} (1+r^*)^{-1}$$

then $\rho > r^*$ if and only if cov $\phi U' < 0$.

Proof

$$\text{cov } (\phi U') = E(\phi U') - E\phi E U'$$

Thus cov $(\phi U') < 0 \Leftrightarrow E(\phi U') - E\phi E U' < 0$

$$\Leftrightarrow \frac{E(\phi U')}{E\phi E U'} < 1$$

$$\Leftrightarrow \rho > r^* \text{ by definition.}$$

Proposition 2 (p. 161). Given the equations

$$(1) \qquad \frac{\partial U_i}{\partial e_i} \{\bar{x}_j - (1+r^*)V_j\} + 2 \frac{\partial U_i}{\partial v_i} \sum_k w_{ik}\sigma_{jk} = 0 \qquad \text{all } i, j,$$

and the equilibrium conditions

$$\sum_i w_{ij} = 1 \qquad \text{all } j,$$

then

$$V_j = (1+r^*)^{-1} \{\bar{x}_j - \tau \sum_k \text{cov}\,(\tilde{x}_j, \tilde{x}_k)\}$$

where

$$\tau = \frac{\sum_k \bar{x}_k - (1+r^*) \sum_k V_k}{\sum_k \sum_l \sigma_{kl}}.$$

Proof. From

$$(1) \qquad \frac{\bar{x}_j - (1+r^*)V_j}{\sum_k w_{ik}\sigma_{jk}} = -2 \frac{\partial U_i/\partial v_i}{\partial U_i/\partial e_i} \qquad \text{all } i, j.$$

Thus for all pairs (j, t) we have

$$\left(\sum_k w_{ik}\sigma_{tk} \right) \frac{\bar{x}_j - (1+r^*)V_j}{\bar{x}_t - (1+r^*)V_t} = \sum_k w_{ik}\sigma_{jk} \qquad \text{for all } i.$$

Summing over i and using $\sum_i w_{ij} = 1$ all j gives

$$\left(\sum_k \sigma_{tk} \right) \frac{\bar{x}_j - (1+r^*)V_j}{\bar{x}_t - (1+r^*)V_t} = \sum_k \sigma_{jk} \qquad \text{all } (t, j),$$

or

$$\text{A.1} \qquad \frac{\bar{x}_j - (1+r^*)V_j}{\sum_k \sigma_{jk}} = \frac{\bar{x}_t - (1+r^*)V_t}{\sum_k \sigma_{tk}} \qquad \text{all } (t, j).$$

Denoting this common ratio by τ gives

$$\tau = \frac{x_t - (1+r^*)V_t}{\sum_k \sigma_{tk}} \qquad \text{all } t,$$

$$= \frac{\sum_t \bar{x}_t - (1+r^*) \sum_t V_t}{\sum_t \sum_k \sigma_{tk}}.$$

Substituting back into A.1 and solving for V_j gives the required result.

Proposition 3 (p. 172). Consider a risk-averse individual holding non-negative amounts of two risky assets A_1 and A_2, with returns per unit invested $a_1(\theta)$ and $a_2(\theta)$ defined on states of the world θ. The individual's subjective density is $g(\theta)$. Suppose the following conditions hold

   (i) A_1 and A_2 have the same expected return.
  (ii) A_1 is at least as risky as A_2 in the sense that there exists a θ' such that

$$a_1(\theta) \leqslant a_2(\theta) \qquad \text{for } 0 \leqslant \theta \leqslant \theta'$$

$$a_1(\theta) \geqslant a_2(\theta) \qquad \text{for } \theta \geqslant \theta'.$$

 (iii) $\partial a_1/\partial \theta \geqslant 0$, $\partial a_2/\partial \theta \geqslant 0$.
 (iv) For some interval $[\underline{\theta}, \bar{\theta}]$ we have $g(\theta) > 0$, $\partial a_1/\partial \theta > 0$ and either $a_1(\theta) > a_2(\theta)$ when $\theta > \theta'$ or $a_1(\theta) < a_2(\theta)$ when $0 < \theta < \theta'$.

In portfolio equilibrium the individual will not hold asset A_1 and, if he does hold asset A_1, he will be better off if he receives one unit of A_2 in return for one unit of A_1.

Proof. Suppose the risk-averse individual has a utility function $U\{c(\theta)\}$ with $U' > 0$, $U'' < 0$. Then, from (iii) and the fact that $U'' < 0$ we have

A.1 $\qquad\qquad U'\{c(\theta)\} - U'\{c(\theta')\} \geqslant 0 \qquad \text{for } \theta \leqslant \theta',$

$\qquad\qquad\qquad U'\{c(\theta)\} - U'\{c(\theta')\} \leqslant 0 \qquad \text{for } \theta \geqslant \theta',$

if the individual's holding of A_1 is positive.

If $a(\theta) = a_1(\theta) - a_2(\theta)$, then (i) implies that

A.3 $\qquad\qquad\qquad\qquad \int g(\theta) a(\theta) \, \mathrm{d}\theta = 0,$

and (ii) implies that

A.4 $\qquad\quad a(\theta) \leqslant 0 \qquad \text{for } \theta \leqslant \theta', \; a(\theta) \geqslant 0 \qquad \text{for } \theta > \theta'.$

In addition (iv) and the fact that $U'' < 0$ imply that on some interval $[\underline{\theta}, \bar{\theta}]$ we have

A.5 $\qquad\qquad g(\theta) > 0 \text{ and } a(\theta)[U'\{c(\theta)\} - U'\{c(\theta')\}] < 0$

if the holding of A_1 is positive.

Consider now the expression

$$\int\limits_0^\infty g(\theta)a(\theta)U'\{c(\theta)\}\,\mathrm{d}\theta$$

for any positive holding of A_1,

$$=\int\limits_0^\infty g(\theta)a(\theta)[U'\{c(\theta)\}-U'\{c(\theta')\}]\,\mathrm{d}\theta \qquad \text{from A.3,}$$

$$=\int\limits_0^{\theta'} g(\theta)a(\theta)[U'\{c(\theta)\}-U'\{c(\theta')\}]\,\mathrm{d}\theta$$
$$+\int\limits_{\theta'}^\infty g(\theta)a(\theta)[U'\{c(\theta)\}-U'\{c(\theta')\}]\,\mathrm{d}\theta$$

<0 from A.2, A.4 and A.5.

So, for any positive holding of A_1, we have

$$\int g(\theta)U'\{c(\theta)\}a_1(\theta)\,\mathrm{d}\theta < \int g(\theta)U'\{c(\theta)\}a_2(\theta)\,\mathrm{d}\theta.$$

That is to say that the contribution to expected utility of an additional unit of A_2 is always greater than the contribution to expected utility of an additional unit of A_1, if the individual holds a positive quantity of A_1. The theorem follows immediately.

Proposition 4 (p. 182). Maximizing the expression

$$\left[\int\limits_{\theta*}^\infty \theta g_2(\theta)\,\mathrm{d}\theta - \theta*\{1-G_2(\theta*)\}\right]f(y_2)$$

subject to

$$\left[\theta*\{1-G_1(\theta*)\}+\int\limits_0^{\theta*} \theta g_1(\theta)\,\mathrm{d}\theta\right]f(y_2)=(y_2-w_2)(1+r*)$$

with respect to $\theta*$ and y_2 yields the single necessary condition,

$$H(\theta*)f'(y_2)=(1+r*)$$

where H satisfies,

$$H(\theta*)=\frac{1-G_1(\theta*)}{1-G_2(\theta*)}\int\limits_{\theta*}^\infty \theta g_2(\theta)\,\mathrm{d}\theta + \int\limits_0^{\theta*} \theta g_1(\theta)\,\mathrm{d}\theta$$

Proof. The constraint implies that

A.6 $\quad \dfrac{\partial \theta^*}{\partial y_2}\{1-G_1(\theta^*)\}f=(1+r^*)-\theta^*\{1-G_1(\theta^*)\}f'-\displaystyle\int_0^{\theta^*}\theta g_1(\theta)\,\mathrm{d}\theta f'$

by simply differentiating.

Differentiating the objective function with respect to y_2 and equating to zero yields the necessary condition,

$$\left[\int_{\theta^*}^{\infty}\theta g_2(\theta)\,\mathrm{d}\theta+\{1-G_2(\theta^*)\}\theta^*\right]f'(y_2)=\{1-G_2(\theta^*)\}f\frac{\partial\theta^*}{\partial y_2}$$

Substituting for $\partial\theta^*/\partial y_2$ from A.6 gives the result.

Proposition 5 (p. 182). Suppose θ^* and y_2 satisfy the equations

(i) $\quad \left[\theta^*\{1-G_1(\theta^*)\}+\displaystyle\int_0^{\theta^*}g_1(\theta)\theta\,\mathrm{d}\theta\right]f(y_2)=(y_2-w_2)\,(1+r^*),$

and

(ii) $\qquad\qquad H(\theta^*)f'(y_2)=(1+r^*),$

where

$$H(\theta^*)=\frac{1-G_1(\theta^*)}{1-G_2(\theta^*)}\int_{\theta^*}^{\infty}\theta g_2(\theta)\,\mathrm{d}\theta+\int_0^{\theta^*}\theta g_1(\theta)\,\mathrm{d}\theta.$$

If $G_2(\theta)$ is a more 'optimistic' distribution function than $G_1(\theta)$ in the sense that $g_2(\theta)/1-G_2(\theta)<g_1(\theta)/1-G_1(\theta)$ for all $\theta>0$, then $\{\partial H(\theta^*)/\partial\theta^*\}<0$ and $\partial y_2/\partial w_2>0$.

Proof. First note the following inequalities,

A.7 $\qquad\qquad g_2(\theta^*)\{1-G_1(\theta^*)\}-g_1(\theta^*)\{1-G_2(\theta^*)\}<0$

since G_2 is more optimistic than G_1.

A.8 $\qquad\qquad \theta^*\{1-G_2(\theta^*)\}-\displaystyle\int_{\theta^*}^{\infty}\theta g_2(\theta)\,\mathrm{d}\theta$

$\qquad\qquad <\theta^*\{1-G_2(\theta^*)\}-\theta^*\displaystyle\int_{\theta^*}^{\infty}g_2(\theta)\,\mathrm{d}\theta=0.$

Taking the derivative of H with respect to θ^* gives

$$\frac{\partial H}{\partial \theta^*} = \frac{1}{\{1 - G_2(\theta^*)\}^2} \left[\int_{\theta^*}^{\infty} \theta g_2(\theta) \, d\theta - \theta^* \{1 - G_2(\theta^*)\} \right]$$

$$\times [g_2(\theta^*) \{1 - G_1(\theta^*)\} - g_1(\theta^*) \{1 - G_2(\theta^*)\}]$$

< 0 from A.7 and A.8.

Differentiating (i) and (ii) with respect to w_2 and eliminating $\partial \theta^* / \partial w_2$ gives

$$\left[-\frac{H(\theta^*) f''}{\partial H / \partial \theta^* . f'} \{1 - G_1(\theta^*)\} + f' \theta^* \{1 - G_1(\theta^*)\} \right.$$

$$\left. + f' \int_0^{\theta^*} g_1(\theta) \theta \, d\theta - (1 + r^*) \right] \partial y_2 / \partial w_2$$

$$= -(1 + r^*)$$

The first term in parentheses is negative since $f'' < 0$ and $\partial H / \partial \theta^* < 0$. Substituting for $(1 + r^*)$ from (ii) reveals that the last three terms in parentheses are equal to

$$f' \left[\theta^* \{1 - G_1(\theta^*)\} - \frac{1 - G_1(\theta^*)}{1 - G_2(\theta^*)} \int_{\theta^*}^{\infty} \theta g_2(\theta) \, d\theta \right]$$

$$= f' \frac{\{1 - G_1(\theta^*)\}}{\{1 - G_2(\theta^*)\}} \left[\theta^* \{1 - G_2(\theta^*)\} - \int_{\theta^*}^{\infty} \theta g_2(\theta) \, d\theta \right]$$

< 0 from A.8.

Consequently $\partial y_2 / \partial w_2 > 0$.

Footnotes

[1] See Modigliani and Miller (1958) and also Modigliani and Miller (1963).

[2] See Robichek and Myers (1965, p. 21).

[3] See p. 99 of *The Lure of the Limerick* by W. S. Baring-Gould (Rupert Hart-Davis, London, 1969).

[4] It is worth digressing briefly on the concept of the 'state of the world' for it is most important in the economics of uncertainty. A state of the world simply refers to an objectively describable state of affairs. θ then refers to that aspect of the state of affairs which is relevant in the particular context with which we are concerned. For example, suppose the output of wheat from a particular field depends on the quantity of seed which the farmer sows, s, the number of hours worked by the farmer in this particular activity, h, and the number of hours of sunshine while the wheat is ripening, θ. This last variable could then be described as that aspect of the future state of affairs

which is important in this case and the output of wheat may be written as a function $F(s, h, \theta)$. θ is the random variable describing the state of the world. There are two important points to note. First, the production relationships which are conditional on states of the world are *objectively given* and there can be no question of individuals disagreeing about them. Differences in expectations about the future arise because individuals have different *subjective* views about future values of θ (i.e. about the likelihood of different states of the world), not because they disagree about the consequences which follow any particular value of θ. Second it is clear from this discussion that a production relation of the form $\phi(\theta)f(y)$ is rather special because the uncertainty is multiplicative, so the pattern of output across the various states of nature (values of θ) is always the same whatever the level of output.

[5] For a security to be in the same risk class as the firm, it must have a pattern of returns of the form $k\phi(\theta)$ where k is constant. It is clear that the shares of the firm, which yield $\{\phi(\theta)f(y) - (1+r^*)y\lambda\}/M$, are only in this risk class if $\lambda = 0$, that is, the firm is unlevered.

[6] The difference $\rho - r^*$ is quite naturally referred to as the *risk* premium. It is possible for some firms in a many firm economy to have a negative risk premium if their returns are strongly negatively correlated with the returns on the majority of the firms in the economy. Examples of this possibility are provided in the context of the mean–variance model discussed in the next section.

[7] This is an overly strong condition, for all that is basically required is that there exist a set of competitive markets for securities, a linear combination of whose patterns of returns gives the pattern of returns produced by the firm concerned. The market then possesses the so-called *spanning* property *vis-à-vis* the firm in question. In fact, a recent paper by Oliver Hart (Hart, 1977) indicates that even this condition is not necessary in a world in which there are a very large number of investors each holding a very small number of shares in the firm relative to the value of their total portfolio. Under these circumstances, variations in $E_i U_i{}' \phi / E_i U_i{}'$ are very small when the firm changes its level of output and consequently this term and hence the discount rate may be taken as exogenously given to the firm.

[8] The relative merits and demerits of this approach are hotly debated in Borch (1969), Feldstein (1969), Tobin (1969) and Samuelson (1971).

[9] See Appendix, proposition 2, for the derivation.

[10] The current value contribution at time t of the marginal unit of capital stock purchased at time s is given by the derivative of the first two terms of the integrand of $V_j(0)$ with respect to K times the quantity of this marginal unit remaining at time t, namely $\exp\{-\delta(t-s)\}$ $(Eg - 2\hat{r}K \operatorname{var} g)$ and the right-hand side of 8.28 is simply the sum of all these contributions.

[11] An individual may effectively hold negative quantities of shares by selling 'short'. That is, by promising to sell shares at some future date which he does not currently own.

[12] Here we are implicitly assuming away the possibility that the returns on the shares of some firms are so negatively correlated with the returns of the majority of other firms that their risk premia are negative. If such firms are allowed then no firm will use a rate of discount which is higher than the safe interest rate, though some may use a rate of discount which is lower. This is still a fairly drastic result.

[13] We have glossed over some difficulties in this discussion concerning the boundedness of individual consumption sets. If we assume that no individual can hold a portfolio which yields negative consumption in any state of nature, the situations which we have described will not arise because the risk-neutral individual will be drastically constrained in the amount he can borrow, simply because negative consumption in any state of nature cannot be contemplated. So we are basically arguing that it is far more realistic to suppose that an

individual can hold a portfolio which yields some probability of negative consumption if all contracts are fulfilled and then does not fulfil his contracts if such an outcome occurs, rather than ruling out such possibilities by assumption. Such defaulting on contracts will, of course, be equivalent to the introduction of new risky securities in the economy, so there is every incentive for this to occur given that there do not already exist as many independent securities as there are states of nature. If the requisite number of securities exists (a somewhat unlikely occurrence) then the resulting equilibrium is a first best Pareto optimum and the introduction of further securities can yield no Pareto improvement (see Arrow, 1964a).

[14] For example in Jorgenson's (1971) survey of some US econometric studies of investment he concludes (p. 1133) 'where internal finance variables appear as significant determinants of desired capital, they represent the level of output. Where both output and cash flow are included as possible determinants, only one is a significant determinant. The preponderance of evidence clearly favours output over cash flow.'

[15] Note that we have now simplified matters by redefining the states of nature so that they refer directly to the output of the risky firm.

[16] Note the previous comment about trivial loans under point 2 (p. 170) which are ruled out by assumption.

[17] Remember that although the loan yields an average return of $L(\theta)$, the marginal return is $\underset{\sim}{L}(\theta)$ and it is this which determines A's portfolio choice.

[18] This description of the returns on bonds and shares assumes the existence of limited liability arrangements for shareholders. That is to say that shareholders are never liable for the debts of a bankrupt firm in the sense that the firm's creditors have no claims over any of the other assets of the shareholders. This arrangement implies that the assets of the 'firm' are not quite identifiable with the assets of the firm's owners. As we shall see, most tax systems tend to reinforce this distinction.

[19] Note also that 8.43 when combined with 8.41 reveals that $E\{B(\theta)\} = E\{S(\theta)\}$ and thus N remains in portfolio equilibrium during the transfer.

[20] This is not to say that a vast number of different risky assets are not created everyday. Probably the most impressive creators and sellers of such assets are bookmakers at race tracks or in betting shops, at least in terms of sheer volume created in any time period. For variety it would be hard to beat the combination of a large London bookmaking firm such as Ladbrokes or William Hill with Lloyds insurance, who between them will offer securities which pay out in almost any simply defined state of nature one can think of.

[21] For an excellent example of the Pareto improving possibilities implicit in the creation of new risky assets, see the example of the contractor and his assistant in Borch (1968, p. 103).

[22] In reality, of course, firms have more than one owner but this will make little difference to the argument. The combined wealth of all the owners is then the important variable in this context.

[23] The need to make a serious distinction between the firm's wealth and the owner's wealth will only arise when we consider the tax structure in the next chapter.

[24] This sort of negotiation is very much what is observed when firms or individuals borrow from banks, the information detailed in points (i) to (iv) above being typical of that required by creditors when lending money to support risky ventures.

[25] We are implicitly assuming that N_2 knows the rate of interest which N_1 will charge for any combination of loan size B and input level y_2 and uses this information to compute his optimal decisions. In this particular model we are thus according the monopoly power to the firm's owner rather than the 'bank'. If we take a more competitive model in which N_1 and N_2 determine their

supply and demand for loans taking the rate of interest, r, as given, then the same results may be obtained, in the sense that investment in N_2's firm increases with his initial wealth, provided that the equilibrium loan is determined at a point where N_1's supply curve is upward sloping. Perverse results may however result if equilibrium occurs on the backward bending portion of the supply curve.

26 For example, Singh and Whittington (1968, p. 31) reveal that the mean rate of return on net assets in the food industry between 1954 and 1960 is 15·9% with a standard deviation of 9·3%. The equivalent figures for clothing and footwear are mean 14·2%, s.d. 10·7% and for non-electrical engineering are mean 18·3%, s.d. 9·2%. In addition they find (p. 142) that for thirteen different firm subgroups of the three industries mentioned the rank correlation of pre-tax rates of return for the periods 1948–54 and 1954–60 is never greater than 0·692 and is significantly different from zero at the 5% level in only five of the thirteen groups.

27 The reasons we have adduced to justify the influence of recent profitability on the level of investment are, of course, strictly within the context of the assumption that the firm is operated in the interests of its owners. If we suppose that the managers of the firm undertake investment policies based on a different criterion, then high profits may influence investment by providing managers with retained earnings which they could use to *over-invest* from the owners' viewpoint. Superior access to relevant information could make this a feasible proposition. Details of theories of this type may be found in Marris (1964b) and Wood (1975).

28 Of course, with a truly dynamic investment model under uncertainty, analysing the optimal policies in detail is certainly easier said than done. For an interesting attempt, see Hochman, Hochman and Razin (1973).

29 For an interesting theoretical discussion of these issues, see Steigum (1977).

30 Typically managers at equivalent levels in different firms have salaries related to the size of the firm. See, for example, Lydall (1968).

31 These propositions are proved in Leland (1974) and King (1974c) respectively. The subsequent discussion is based on both these papers.

32 Notice, for example, that we have completely avoided the problems which arise if the firm can actually choose its pattern of returns across states of nature. This will cause no trouble if this choice simply refers to a small number of projects, each of which corresponds to some particular well-defined risk class, for then the firm knows the market valuation of each project. If this is not the case, however, then there will be serious difficulties which have not, as yet, been overcome. Hart (1976) provides the deepest study of this particular problem.

33 King (1977), chapter 5, has a very illuminating and extensive discussion of this problem.

34 Strictly speaking, we have not defined this market rate of discount when expectations are non-uniform, for whose expectations are to be used when measuring the 'expected' returns of the firm? In fact any *constant* set of expectations will do; those of the firm's managers, for example. In the case of non-uniform expectations the market rate of discount is only defined relative to a particular set.

35 For a discussion of some of the possible effects of transactions costs see Lintner (1962) and Baumol and Malkiel (1967).

Bibliographical Notes—Chapter 8

The original discussion of Modigliani–Miller financial theory may be found in Modigliani and Miller (1958, 1963). Elementary expositions of the basic theorem are provided in Baumol and Malkiel (1967) and Robichek and Myers

(1965) and the latter book also contains an analysis of the traditional theory of finance. Stiglitz (1969, 1974) contain the most general theorems of the Modigliani–Miller type accompanied by very simple and elegant proofs. Diamond (1967) provides a simple general equilibrium model in the context of which the basic theorem emerges with great clarity.

The mean–variance valuation model of section 3 is based on the work of Sharpe (1964), Lintner (1965) and Mossin (1966) and there is a thorough discussion of all its theoretical and empirical ramifications in Jensen (1972). The dynamic extension of this model follows closely the work of Stevens (1974).

The crucial importance of bankruptcy and its effects on Modigliani-Miller financial theory are discussed at some length in a very interesting paper by Stiglitz (1972a), and similar considerations are dealt with in V. L. Smith (1970, 1972a) Baron (1974, 1976) and Hagen (1976). A slightly different approach to the problems inherent in Modigliani–Miller financial theory can be found in Lintner (1962, 1964) and there is a good general analysis of the relationship between these problems and the level of investment in Lintner (1967).

The model of the two risk-neutral agents with different views about the future discussed in section 4 is in the tradition of studies of the availability of credit to firms. There is an early discussion of some of these matters in a seminal paper by Kalecki (1937) and some more recent theoretical analyses may be found in Quirk (1961), Jaffee and Modigliani (1969), Stiglitz (1972a), V. L. Smith (1972b) and Jaffee (1972).

Concerning the objective of the firm under uncertainty, Fama and Miller (1972) discuss the market value maximization criterion (on pp. 198–202) and this is analysed at some length in Stiglitz (1972b), King (1974c), Leland (1974), King (1977), Grossman and Stiglitz (1976), Grossman and Hart (1976). Dreze (1974) and Hart (1976), both very difficult papers, comprise the most sophisticated attempt to construct an objective for the firm based on strictly neoclassical assumptions. For a rather different approach one may consult some of the articles in Marris and Wood (1971), particularly those by Marris, Solow and Williamson and also a further book by Wood (1975).

CHAPTER 9

INVESTMENT DECISIONS AND THE CORPORATE TAX STRUCTURE

1. Taxation and the Price of Capital Goods

The structure of personal and corporate taxation in the majority of countries is enormously complex and it is possible that this very complexity has an influence on the investment decisions of firms comparable with any effects due to the actual rates of tax themselves. However, it is these latter which will be our major concern although in the final section of this chapter we shall discuss some of the more subtle aspects of government intervention in the investment decisions of the private sector, particularly those concerned with uncertainty and expectations.

There are two main ways in which the existence of taxation influences investment decisions, the first being via the actual price of capital goods and the second through the other elements of the cost of capital. The former effects are very straightforward to analyse and can be studied in the context of a simple perfectly competitive model. Suppose first that the firm's 'profits' are taxed at rate τ, where the term 'profits' is used in the accountants' sense of the difference between current revenue and current costs excluding capital costs. Consequently, the after-tax cash flow of the firm at time t is given, in standard notation, by

$$9.1 \qquad [p(t)F\{K(t),\,L(t)\} - w(t)L(t)]\,(1-\tau) - q(t)I(t).$$

Second, suppose that all income from lending is taxed at a rate $\theta\tau$ and, to avoid any form of double taxation on this type of income, all interest payments on loans can be offset against tax, again at a rate $\theta\tau$. This implies that the effective rate of interest is simply $r(1 - \theta\tau)$ where r is the rate before tax.

Let us now turn to some typical fiscal instruments which directly affect the price of capital goods, the most obvious being the direct investment grant which is a payment by the government to the firm of some percentage of the cost of all the capital equipment which it purchases. Supposing this grant to be $100\,g\%$, the effective price of

199

capital goods to the firm is then $q(t)\,(1-g)$. The other major fiscal instrument in this field is the depreciation allowance, which allows the firm to offset against profits tax a sum which may or may not be closely related to the actual amount by which the firm's capital has depreciated in any given period. In order to keep things very simple we shall assume exponential decay at a rate δ and then suppose that a proportion $\nu \exp\{-\nu(s-t)\}$ of expenditure on capital goods at time t is allowed against tax at time s. This is the so-called declining balance form of depreciation allowance, for it is easy to check that at time s a proportion $[1-\exp\{-\nu(s-t)\}]$ of expenditure has already been allowed against tax and thus a proportion $\exp\{-\nu(s-t)\}$ is still remaining to be allowed. Then a fraction ν of this remainder is allowed at time s, where the remainder itself is the declining balance. Clearly if this balance is to reflect accurately the physical quantity of capital remaining at time s, the parameter ν must be equal to δ, the true rate of physical decay. So, if $\nu > \delta$, the rate at which capital is assumed to depreciate for tax purposes is greater than the rate of physical decay and this is termed accelerated depreciation.

In order to incorporate this form of depreciation allowance into the model the simplest thing to do is to compute its present value at time t. This present value on one unit of expenditure is given by the discounted sum of all the future tax savings, namely,

$$\int\limits_{t}^{\infty} \exp\{-r(1-\bar{\theta}\tau)(s-t)\}\, \nu\tau \exp\{-\nu(s-t)\}\, \mathrm{d}s = \frac{\tau\nu}{\nu+r(1-\bar{\theta}\tau)},$$

assuming that ν, τ, r, $\bar{\theta}$ are all expected to remain constant. Consequently, the effective price of capital goods at time t which will be referred to as $\hat{q}(t)$, is given by

9.2 $$\hat{q}(t) = q(t)\,(1-g)\left\{1-\frac{\tau\nu}{\nu+r(1-\bar{\theta}\tau)}\right\}.$$

The after-tax effective dividend flow at time t may then be written as

$$p(1-\tau)F - w(1-\tau)L - \hat{q}I$$

and thus the firm will be maximizing

$$\int\limits_{0}^{\infty} \exp\{-r(1-\bar{\theta}\tau)t\}\,\{p(1-\tau)F - w(1-\tau)L - \hat{q}I\}\, \mathrm{d}t$$

subject to the usual constraints.

Using the analysis of Chapter 2 we can immediately write down the marginal revenue product conditions which must be satisfied at every point in time, and these are

$$pF_L = w,$$

$$p(1-\tau)F_K = \dot{q}\{r(1-\theta\tau) + \delta - \dot{q}/\dot{q}\},$$

From the second of these, noting that the constancy of g, τ, ν, r, θ implies that $\dot{q}/\dot{q} = \dot{q}/q$, we can see that the effective cost of capital at time t, $c(t)$, is given by

$$c(t) = \dot{q}\{r(1-\theta\tau) + \delta - \dot{q}/q\}(1-\tau)^{-1}$$

which implies, using 9.2 and rearranging, that

9.3 $c(t) = q(1-g)\left\{1 - \dfrac{\tau\nu}{\nu + r(1-\theta\tau)}\right\}(1-\tau)^{-1}\{r(1-\theta\tau) + \delta - \dot{q}/q\},$

or

9.4 $c(t) = q(1-g)\left\{\nu + r\dfrac{(1-\theta\tau)}{1-\tau}\right\}\left\{\dfrac{\delta - \dot{q}/q + r(1-\theta\tau)}{\nu + r(1-\theta\tau)}\right\}.$

It is immediately clear from 9.3 that $\partial c/\partial g < 0$ and $\partial c/\partial\nu < 0$ and thus, as we might expect, an increase in the investment grant or an increase in the rate of depreciation allowed for tax purposes lowers the cost of capital to the firm. Suppose now that interest income is taxed at the rate τ and thus interest payments by the firm are fully deductible against profits tax. Then $\theta = 1$ and 9.4 gives $c(t)$ as

9.5 $c(t) = q(1-g)(\nu + r)\left\{\dfrac{\delta - \dot{q}/q + r(1-\tau)}{\nu + r(1-\tau)}\right\}.$

It now follows that $\partial c/\partial\tau$ is positive if ν is less than $\delta - \dot{q}/q$ and is negative if ν is greater than $\delta - \dot{q}/q$.[1] Note that $\delta - \dot{q}/q$ is the true economic rate if depreciation which is only equal to the rate of physical decay if the price of capital goods remains constant. So it is possible for a rise in the corporate tax rate actually to lower the cost of capital if all firm borrowing is fully tax deductible and the rate of depreciation for tax purposes is greater than its true economic rate. Similarly, the corporate profits tax will have no effect on the cost of capital if depreciation for tax purposes is equal to true economic depreciation, again so long as all borrowing by the firm is fully tax deductible. The corporate profits tax will, under these circumstances, be simply equivalent to a lump sum tax on firms. Since non-distortionary taxation may well be considered desirable for efficiency reasons, it is perhaps worth looking a little more closely at this result which depends crucially on two points.

The first is the equality of depreciation for tax purposes with true economic depreciation. Even in the simple case described here this may be rather difficult to achieve, given the dependency of true depreciation on the rate of change of the price of capital goods. Clearly, when account is taken of all the factors considered in Chapter 7 concerning the decay of capital and the rate of scrapping, it is almost impossible to *define* the true rate at which capital is used up, let alone compute it in any practical sense. Consequently, equating the tax allowance with the economic value of the capital which is used up in any period can only be done very approximately. The other point is the tax deductibility of borrowing. In a wider context this is equivalent to the firm financing all investment, at least at the margin, from sources to which any 'interest' payments are tax deductible. As we shall see subsequently this is very unlikely to be the case, especially in a world of uncertainty.

Consequently, if one of the aims of a corporate profits tax is to be non-distortionary, then introducing the particular structure described above is clearly not the way to go about it. A very much simpler method which does not have these drawbacks is to have zero tax deductibility for interest payments on firm borrowing ($\bar{\theta}=0$) and to allow all capital expenditure to be immediately offset against tax ($\nu = \infty$). Then, from 9.3 we see that the cost of capital is given by,

$$9.6 \qquad c(t) = q(1-g)\,(r + \delta - \dot{q}/q)$$

which is completely independent of the rate of profits tax. In fact the effective price of capital goods is simply $q(1-g)\,(1-\tau)$ and thus the dividend flow of the firm at any time may be written as

$$\{pF - wL - q(1-g)I\}\,(1-\tau)$$

and it is hardly surprising that the size of τ is not relevant to the firm's investment decisions.[2]

This form of tax structure can be viewed as a method by which the government becomes a partner in the firm. The government is effectively providing a proportion τ of the firm's capital and collecting a proportion τ of all the future net returns on this capital. This is akin to partial nationalization except that all control is still vested in the management of the firm.

We have now seen how the government can effectively influence the price of capital goods by manipulating investment grants and depreciation allowances, and this problem has been analysed in the context of a very much simplified corporate tax structure. One *caveat* should be added. The effect of these tax measures has only been discussed in a partial equilibrium context. For example, the introduction of a universal investment grant will not necessarily reduce the effective price of capital goods in the same proportion in the new general equilibrium. The new equilibrium price will depend on both the demand and supply elasticities and, in the last analysis, on the complete general equilibrium structure. This point should always be borne in mind when considering the effects of any change in the tax structure on the *aggregate* rate of investment.

2. Taxation, Finance and Investment

The next stage in the analysis must be to look at the detailed effects of the corporate tax structure on the finance and investment decisions of the incorporated firm.[3] With the exception of investment in private housing and agriculture, the vast majority of private sector investment projects are initiated by such firms and so they should undoubtedly be the focus of our interest. In the previous chapter it was made clear that, in the absence of taxation, there is very little to distinguish wealth in the hands of the owners of the firm from wealth in the hands of the 'firm', since it can be freely transferred in either direction. The only thing which distinguishes the 'firm' from its owners are the limited liability arrangements whereby the 'firm' can go bankrupt without its owners following suit.

However, as we shall see, with a typical corporate tax structure the firm and its owners become very distinct entities because of the taxation barriers between them. Thus £1 in the 'firm' is not the same as £1 in the hands of the owners because typically it will be taxed on its way from the former to the latter. This necessitates a more detailed examination of the institutional structure of the firm than was required in the last chapter. Basically, at the beginning of any 'period', the firm has, on the financial side, some profit, some outstanding debt and some outstanding equity. It then has various decisions to make. It pays out some of its profit as dividends on the existing shares. The remaining profit is retained and is used either to pay off some debt or to spend on capital goods, or possibly to buy back outstanding shares. Alternatively, it may increase its debt and issue further shares, using the money to spend on capital goods. So, given the firm's level of profits from the previous period and its outstanding equity and debt, it must simultaneously determine its level of real capital expenditure, its total dividend payout and its new levels of debt and equity in the current period. If taxation is ignored and if P_{t-1}, B_{t-1}, S_{t-1} are the profits, debt and equity from period $t-1$, then the level of dividends, D_t, and real investment, I_t, in period t must satisfy

$$9.7 \qquad I_t = (B_t - B_{t-1}) + (S_t - S_{t-1}) + (P_{t-1} - D_t).$$

The last term on the right is the level of retentions and thus we can see that investment may be financed using either debt, equity or retentions. In the no tax (and transactions cost) case of the previous chapter the last two were completely indistinguishable but with the introduction of taxation it is necessary to keep them separate.

We shall now introduce a simplified tax structure, starting with the personal sector.

τ_p is the personal tax rate on unearned income. That is to say on income from shares or loans. It is assumed to be constant for all levels of income.

τ_g is the tax rate on capital gains. Typically capital gains are taxed on realization but, for formal analysis, it is much simpler to assume that they are taxed on accruals. So, if an individual's shares go up in value, he is taxed on that increase whether he sells the shares and realizes his capital gain or not. There are complete loss offset provisions in the sense that for any capital loss incurred by the individual, the government pays him an amount τ_g times the loss.

Now suppose that r is the constant interest rate for private borrowing, that $V(t)$ is the value of a share in a firm at time t and that $D(t)$ is the after-tax dividend per share payed out by the firm at time t. $D(t)$ is thus the actual cash in the hand of the shareholder after all taxes have been paid on it. Then, in a world of certainty, equilibrium in the asset market will require that the after tax return on investing $V(t)$ in bonds or loans at a rate r is equal to the after tax return on purchasing a share. That is

$$9.8 \qquad (1 - \tau_p) r V(t) = D(t) + (1 - \tau_g)\{V(t+1) - V(t)\}.$$

A point to note is that, if the interest payments on personal borrowing are not tax deductible, the cost of borrowing is r, which is greater than the after-tax returns on lending and therefore greater than the after-tax returns on shares. We can immediately deduce that in this case no individual would simultaneously be in debt and own shares (remember we are in a world of certainty).

Since 9.8 holds for all t we can immediately solve the difference equation to deduce the value of the firm at time zero in terms of its future dividend payments. This is done in the Appendix (proposition 1) and gives

9.9
$$V(0) = \sum_{0}^{\infty} \frac{1}{1-\tau_g} \frac{D(s)}{\alpha^{s+1}}$$

where

$$\alpha = 1 + \frac{(1-\tau_p)r}{(1-\tau_g)}.$$

This formula reduces to the normal present value formula if the taxes are both zero, but when the tax rates are positive the effective rate of discount is given by $\{(1-\tau_p)r\}/(1-\tau_g)$, the tax adjusted rate of interest, and the whole stream is weighted by $1/(1-\tau_g)$.

Turning now to the tax situation in the corporate sector we introduce the following.

τ_c is the corporate profits tax. θ is the opportunity cost of retained earnings in terms of net dividends forgone. That is, if one unit of after tax earnings is used to pay dividends, the actual dividends received by the shareholders after *their* tax is θ. This is the tax variable which implies that £1 in the hands of the firm is not equivalent to £1 in the hands of the shareholders. For example, if profits are taxed at τ_c and in addition dividends are liable to income tax at τ_p, then $\theta = 1 - \tau_p$.

Having completed our specification of the tax structure we shall now consider the optimal financial policy of the firm in terms of the relative costs of the three methods of financing, that is, debt, equity and retentions. Remember that in a no tax certainty world, the firm is completely indifferent between all three methods. In order to concentrate on the financial problem we shall suppose that the real investment expenditures are given and that we are looking for the cheapest method of financing them. For simplicity of exposition we shall look at the problem in terms of three two-way comparisons, starting with the comparison between using retentions or issuing new equity, keeping the level of debt fixed.

Consider the choice in period zero between financing investment by retaining profits or by issuing new shares. Note that dividends and taxes are paid at the end of the period and that new shares are issued at the end of the period ex-dividend (after the dividend has been paid) and are thus sold at a price equal to the share value at the beginning of the next period. The alternative policies are:

(1) Retain profits and hold the number of shares constant at N, say.
(2) Issue ΔN new shares at a price $V^2(1)$ and increase net dividends per share from $D^1(0)$ to $D^2(0)$; note that the superscripts refer to the policy being pursued.

If (2) is followed instead of (1), the new issues raise an amount $\Delta N V^2(1)$ and net dividends, plus the extra tax paid, increase by $\{D^2(0) - D^1(0)\}N/\theta$. These two must be equal to each other and to the quantity of new investment, so we have

9.10 $$\Delta N V^2(1) = \{D^2(0) - D^1(0)\}N/\theta.$$

Both these policies lead to the same future profits stream since they finance the same level of investment and, consequently, the total equity value in period 1 is the same in both cases. Hence

9.11 $$V^1(1)N = V^2(1)(N + \Delta N).$$

From 9.8 we know that

9.12 $$V^i(0) = \frac{D^i(0)}{(1-\tau_g)+(1-\tau_p)r} + \frac{(1-\tau_g)V^i(1)}{(1-\tau_g)+(1-\tau_p)r}, \quad i = 1, 2,$$

and using this with 9.10, 9.11 gives, after some manipulation,

9.13 $$V^2(0) - V^1(0) = \frac{\Delta N}{N} \frac{V^2(1)(\theta + \tau_g - 1)}{(1-\tau_g)+(1-\tau_p)r}.$$

So, given that the objective of the firm is to maximize the value of the equity at time zero, then it is clear that retained profits are superior to share issues as a method of finance if, and only if, $\theta + \tau_g - 1 < 0$. The reason is obvious. By financing out of retained profits the extra dividends, which would have been paid out directly if shares were issued, are instead paid out effectively in the form of capital gains. Since the tax on capital gains τ_g, is lower than the penalty tax on dividends $(1 - \theta)$, this is clearly a superior method of finance. Indeed, if there are any retentions remaining after financing the necessary investment, the remainder should be used for buying back shares from the shareholders rather than paying out any dividends at all. This enables the high rate of dividend taxation to be avoided entirely and all funds which are transferred from the firm to the shareholders incur only the lower capital gains tax. Since many typical tax structures do indeed have $\theta + \tau_g - 1 < 0$ it is not surprising that buying back shares is often illegal (e.g. in the UK) or is prohibited if such a repurchase of shares appears to be equivalent to paying dividends (e.g. in the US).[4]

On the other hand, if $\phi + \tau_g - 1 > 0$ and capital losses are tax deductible, it clearly pays the firm to issue new shares, thereby incurring a tax deductible capital loss for existing shareholders, and to use the proceeds to pay dividends which are taxed at a lower rate than the rate at which the capital losses are offset. As might be expected this is also legally restrained by the law which forbids dividend payments in excess of current profits.

In the tax structure with which we shall be typically concerned (France, USA, UK until 1973, for example) the penalty taxation on dividends exceeds the capital gains tax and consequently the firm would never issue additional shares while simultaneously paying dividends since it is cheaper to retain the dividends and not issue the shares, as we have seen. In spite of this fact, such behaviour is not uncommon and it is probably safe to say that in reality the role of dividend payments is not very clearly understood. Actual firm behaviour suggests that the attitude to dividend payments is much less flexible than our analysis would indicate: thus, for example, firms seem very loth to reduce their dividends from one year to the next. This suggests that shareholders are not indifferent between dividend payments and capital gains and a variety of reasons have been put forward to explain this. Wood (1975) has an extensive discussion of this issue and one of the main arguments in his view arises from the difficulties of realizing capital gains at will in highly volatile equity markets. As he rather aptly puts it,

> In particular, shareholders do not regard dividend policy primarily in terms of the quantity of the company's marginal investment opportunities. Instead, they view the payout decision pre-eminently as a decision about how much of the bird is to be put into the hand and how much is to be left in the bush.[5]

It is also clear that dividends play some kind of signalling role which is required in an uncertain world where shareholders are rather short on information. As yet, however, there has been no formal analysis of this signalling mechanism and existing theory cannot be said to be entirely satisfactory on this point.

We turn now to the second of the two-way comparisons, that

between issuing shares and borrowing. The alternatives to be considered are:

(1) Issue new shares ΔN.
(2) Borrow at a rate r at the end of period zero, repaying the principal and interest one period later.

In both cases the dividends paid out in period zero will be the same and thus, from 9.8, we have

9.14 $$V^2(0) - V^1(0) = \frac{1}{\alpha} \{V^2(1) - V^1(1)\}$$

where α is defined in 9.9.

Since the two policies finance the same investment, policy (2) involves borrowing $\Delta N V^1(1)$ which is repaid, together with the interest, at the end of period 1. This total repayment is equal to the difference in total dividends plus taxes for the two policies. So, assuming that debt interest payments are tax deductible for the firm, we have

9.15 $$(\Delta N + N) \frac{D^1(1)}{\theta} = \frac{N D^2(1)}{\theta} + \{1 + (1 - \tau_c)r\} \Delta N V^1(1).$$

As before, the value of the equity in period 2 is identical in both cases and consequently

9.16 $$V^1(2)(N + \Delta N) = V^2(2)N.$$

Then, using 9.14, 9.15, 9.16 and 9.8 with $t = 1$, we have, after some manipulation

$$V^2(0) - V^1(0) = \frac{1}{\alpha^2(1 - \tau_g)} \frac{\Delta N}{N} V^1(1)[\alpha(1 - \tau_g) - \theta\{1 + (1 - \tau_c)r\}].$$

Thus debt finance is superior to equity finance if, and only if,

$$\alpha(1 - \tau_g) - \theta\{1 + (1 - \tau_c)r\} > 0$$

or

9.17 $$(1 - \tau_g) + (1 - \tau_p)r > \theta\{1 + (1 - \tau_c)r\}.$$

Again the intuition behind this result is clear. If the firm borrows and uses its own income to pay off the interest and the principal, this is cheaper than the individual borrowing then giving money to the firm and then using the taxed dividends from the firm to pay off his interest and principal. Note that, if $\theta = 1$ and there is no capital gains tax, the comparison between debt and equity finance depends only on which form of borrowing is tax deductible at the higher rate, firm borrowing or private borrowing. Therefore, in a sense, it is not so much the tax deductibility of firm interest payments which favours debt finance as the penalty tax on dividends, since firm borrowing and personal borrowing are more or less substitutable. Of course, if firm borrowing is not tax deductible and personal borrowing is, then the penalty tax on dividends would have to be quite high in order to swing the balance towards firm borrowing. Often, however, complete tax deductibility on personal borrowing is not available. For example, in the UK the rules change from time to time although, typically, personal borrowing for house purchase is always tax deductible but personal borrowing for washing machine purchase rarely is, unless there is a Tory government in power and a bank loan is used. All these considerations tend to reinforce the superiority of debt finance in a typical tax structure.

The final two-way comparison which must be made is between retentions and debt. The alternative policies are:

(1) Retain profits and pay out $D^1(0)$ net dividends per share.
(2) Borrow at rate r, repaying the principal and interest one period later, and pay out $D^2(0)$ dividends per share.

Since these policies finance the same outlay, the amount borrowed under (2) is $\{D^2(0) - D^1(0)\} N/\theta$ and thus the difference between the dividends per share payed out in period 1 satisfies

9.18 $(1/\theta)\{D^1(1) - D^2(1)\} = (1/\theta)\{D^2(0) - D^1(0)\}\{1 + (1 - \tau_c)r\}.$

As usual the value of the equity in period 2 must be the same under both policies and thus

$$V^1(2) = V^2(2).$$

Using this fact in combination with 9.18 and 9.8 at $t = 0, 1$, gives

$$V^2(0) - V^1(0) = \{D^2(0) - D^1(0)\} \frac{[\alpha - \{1 + (1 - \tau_c)r\}]}{1 - \tau_g}.$$

Thus we can conclude that debt finance will be superior to retentions if, and only if,

$$\alpha - \{1 + (1 - \tau_c)r\} > 0$$

or

9.19 $$1 - \tau_p > (1 - \tau_g)(1 - \tau_c).$$

The capital gains term in this expression appears because, with retentions as opposed to debt, the capital gain occurs one period earlier. If we ignore capital gains 9.19 reduces to

9.20 $$\tau_c > \tau_p.$$

This implies that it is better for the firm to borrow rather than the individual because interest payments are tax deductible at a higher rate. Note that if there is a variable personal tax rate, those shareholders with a very high marginal tax rate may well prefer retentions to debt whereas those on the standard tax rate will prefer the opposite. This leads to the possibility of shareholders in different income tax brackets 'specializing' in the shares of different firms operating different finance policies.

Generally speaking, however, in the typical tax system (e.g. UK or USA), as it applies to the average shareholder, debt is preferable to retentions and retentions are preferable to new share issues. In the UK the following were the percentage rates of capital income tax for incorporated firms using the three types of finance.[6]

	1960–65	1965–73	1973–
Debt finance	38·75	41·25	30 00
Retentions	53·75	51·13	53·75
Equity finance	53·75	66·22	54·50

In subsequent discussion we shall assume that this ordering is correct.

3. The Consequences of Taxation for the Cost of Capital

In a world of certainty it is clear that all investment is financed by debt and all earnings are paid out as dividends. Then, assuming that the depreciation allowance is equal to the true economic depreciation, the tax deductibility of the firm's interest payments on the debt ensures that the effective cost of capital is simply $q(r + \delta - \dot{q}/q)$, the same as if there were no taxes. This is precisely one of the cases described in section 1.

Suppose now that we have uncertainty but no bankruptcy. Again it is clear that the marginal unit of investment is entirely financed by debt and so all rental payments on this unit are tax deductible. We are thus back in the Modigliani–Miller world described in section 2 of the previous chapter. The rate of discount, instead of being the safe rate r, is equal to the rate at which the market discounts the income stream of the firm with no taxes and no debt, which was called ρ. The cost of capital is still independent of taxation, apart from individual income effects which may change the value of ρ. Modigliani–Miller themselves propose a rate of discount of $\{\rho(1 - \tau_c L)\}/(1 - \tau_c)$ on pre-tax earnings where L is the long-run optimal proportion of debt finance. But we know that if there is no bankruptcy all the marginal units of investment are financed by debt and L is therefore 1. The Modigliani–Miller formula then reduces to ρ. On the other hand, if there is bankruptcy, it is not obvious what meaning can be attached to the 'long-run' optimal proportion of debt finance, L. The proportion of debt used to finance the marginal unit of investment depends, as we have seen in the previous chapter, on the investment opportunities and the current level of earnings of the firm. Furthermore, we have also seen that in the bankruptcy case the value of ρ may depend on the firm's current earnings. This is because of their crucial impact on the funds available for investment which are in possession of that group of individuals who are most optimistic about the firm's prospects, namely the current shareholders.

Since, in the absence of bankruptcy, all marginal investments are financed entirely by debt, it is clear that the non-existence of bankruptcy is rather an absurd assumption, for this is precisely the financial policy most likely to lead to a high bankruptcy probability. It is this fact which will limit the firm's dependence on debt in an uncertain world. Thus bankruptcy risks will ensure that, after a certain level, the costs of debt will be rising at the margin fast enough to offset any tax advantages. We are thus back with the familiar U-shaped cost of capital curve discussed in the previous chapter. Indeed, there may even be effective quantity restrictions on debt, either because, above a certain level of debt, there exists no interest rate which will give lenders an expected return above the safe rate, or because lenders may use such restrictions as a useful rule of thumb method of limiting bankruptcy risks in a situation where they do not have the information necessary to compute the appropriate lending rates. That is to say that the effective borrowing rate for the firm may rise rapidly to infinity above a certain level of debt. The firm will thus typically make use of retained earnings to finance some of its investment.

At the beginning of the period the firm has three possible uses for its current after-tax earnings. It can utilize them to pay off existing debt, to pay out as dividends or to spend on investment goods. It is clear that the optimal policy will imply that the marginal benefits are the same at all three margins. Utilizing this fact and the discussion in section 2, we can now summarize the influences of the following exogenous variables which act on the level of investment through the rate of interest term in the cost of capital.

The after tax earnings from the previous period: An increase in this variable will lower the effective cost of capital basically by providing more investible funds for that group of investors who are most optimistic about the firm's prospects and who are least averse to the risks inherent in the returns of the firm (this point was analysed in great depth in section 4 of the previous chapter). The mechanism by which an increase in after-tax earnings affects the cost of capital is via increased retentions which will lead to a lower final cost of debt at the margin and will also probably shift the cost of debt schedule by increasing the equity value, thereby reducing the degree of leverage. Typically transactions costs and the tax system will reinforce these effects by providing an incentive to the shareholders to encourage the firm to utilize earnings in this way because of the tax penalties incurred by pay-outs in the form of dividends.

In addition, higher current earnings may actually change individual expectations about the firm in the direction of greater optimism, and in so far as the individuals concerned are among the firm's current or potential creditors, this will lower the cost of debt and raise the price of shares. Such arguments may also imply that not only profits in the previous period but also profits in the recent past have an effect on the cost of capital.

The rate of interest on safe bonds: An increase in the safe rate of interest raises the opportunity cost of all funds invested in risky shares and bonds, which will clearly raise the cost of finance from whatever source (see again the previous chapter, section 4).

The initial degree of leverage: An increase in the initial debt equity ratio will raise the effective cost of capital by raising the initial marginal cost of debt. This is because the firm is initially at a point which is higher up the rising portion of the U-shaped cost of capital curve.[7]

The ratio $(1 - \tau_p)/(1 - \tau_g)(1 - \tau_c)$*:* This ratio measues the cost of retentions relative to debt (see 9.19), the marginal cost of which is not directly affected by tax parameters since it is fully tax deductible (except in so far as the rate of interest to be paid on safe bonds changes with the rate of personal income tax). Clearly any rise in this ratio will effectively raise the cost of retentions and thereby raise the cost of capital as a whole.

The tax parameter θ: It is this parameter which measures the opportunity cost of retentions in terms of net dividends forgone and its effects on the cost of capital are somewhat tricky to determine *a priori.* King (1974b) argues rather forcefully that it should have no effect, but he ignores the possibility of equity finance. Clearly, from 9.13 (and what follows) and from 9.17, a fall in θ raises the cost of equity finance relative to both debt and retentions and, since the marginal cost of debt is unaffected by tax parameters, this implies an absolute rise in the cost of equity finance. Thus, in situations where the investment opportunities are so large that all current after-tax earnings are used up and the amount of debt used to finance investment is large enough to raise its marginal cost up to the cost of equity finance, a rise in this latter cost will raise the effective cost of capital and lower the level of investment. On the other hand, as we observed when comparing equity finance with retentions on p. 206, things do not appear to work quite like this in the sense that dividends are often paid even when equity finance is used and they appear to play rather an autonomous role. That is to say that the proportion of current earnings paid out in dividends often appears to be more or less independent of current investment opportunities. Then a fall in the value of θ (a rise in the penalty tax on dividends) gives the firm the incentive to reduce current dividend payments after tax and to try to pay out proportionately more to shareholders in the form of capital gains. But if the corporate profits tax rate remains constant, a fall in θ will imply an increase in total tax payments for any given level of dividends. So, even if this means a reduction in *after-tax* dividend payments by the firm, this could imply either a rise or a fall in the level of retentions available for investment and consequently an indeterminate effect on investment.

Other relevant variables: It is clear that the cost of capital will also depend both on the general level of market risk aversion and the market view of the firm's riskiness; two variables which are extremely difficult to measure. The influence of both is, of course, incorporated in the rate which the market uses to discount the expected earnings generated by the firm, namely ρ, and so in spite of doubts about its exogeneity, it is worth considering as a relevant variable in this context. Obviously an increase in ρ will raise the cost of capital to the firm.

This completes our list of variables which affect the total cost of capital via the 'rate of interest' term and we shall postpone discussion as to precisely how the cost of capital should be specified in any actual situation until section 5 of Chapter 11. In the remainder of this chapter we shall be concerned with some of the more subtle aspects of the relationship between the tax structure and the firm's investment decisions and it is to these issues that we turn next.

4. Some Examples on Taxation and Uncertainty

As we have already seen, tax rates and the structure of allowances can crucially influence both the effective price of capital goods and the cost of capital. If we suppose that capital stock decisions are not independent over time, it is clear that expectations about future changes in the tax structure can also influence current investment decisions via their expected effects on the future price and cost of capital. In order to analyse these effects we can simply apply our previous results, particularly those in the relevant sections of Chapters 4, 5 and 6. In the light of this fact it is hardly worth detailing all the possible variations on this theme, so instead we shall restrict our discussion to some examples of particular interest.

Our first example is one where the government deliberately induces a certain expectation of a future tax adjustment simply by announcing a change in the corporate tax structure which will be maintained only for a limited period. Assuming that investment decisions are irreversible, then, if the proposed change involves a *temporary* alteration in the effective *price* of capital goods (as would ensue from a temporary rise in investment grants, for example) this would have a considerable impact on investment expenditures, even in comparison with the consequences of a *permanent* change of the same type. The crucial point here is that a certain *temporary* fall in the price of capital goods will lead to firms bringing forward capital purchases so as to take advantage of the low price. Such a rearrangement of the timing of capital purchases is clearly unnecessary if the fall in price is expected to be permanent, and so in this manner the government is able to influence quite markedly the time pattern of investment expenditure.[8] This example is based on a policy of inducing a certain expectation of a future tax change. An alternative situation which is probably not uncommon is that, either wittingly or unwittingly, the government induces uncertainty in the corporate sector about future variations in tax rates. We have already dealt with the effect of uncertainty about the future price of capital goods and the cost of capital in Chapters 5 and 6 and since an analysis of tax rate uncertainty is little more than a simple application of these results, we need only touch on the matter briefly. One point of particular interest in this regard concerns the neutrality of the corporate profits tax if interest payments are not tax deductible but all capital expenditure may be immediately offset against tax. In section 1 of this chapter we have already shown that the level of the corporate tax rate has no impact on investment if this tax structure prevails, provided that the tax rate remains constant. This result arises simply because the price of a capital good is subsidized at precisely the same rate as the returns on it are taxed, so the actual level of this rate is of no consequence. If, however, the firm thinks that there is some probability that the corporate tax rate will alter, then the neutrality property disappears. Suppose, for example, that the firm expects that the tax rate will rise at some stage. Then some of the returns on capital goods purchased currently will be taxed at a higher rate than that at which the purchase price is being subsidized, and the firm has an incentive to postpone capital expenditure until the tax rate has actually risen in order to acquire the higher subsidy. This effect can be quite considerable, for example in Nickell (1977a) we show, on the basis of the model discussed in Chapter 6, that if the firm thinks that there is a 60% chance that some time next year the corporate profits tax will rise from 40 to 50%, this will lead to an increase in the *current* cost of capital equivalent to a 10 *percentage* point rise in the real rate of interest.

In some ways the non-neutrality of this tax system, when the firm expects tax rates to change, is rather a strange business, for if the government can spring a change in the tax rate on completely unsuspecting firms then investment decisions will be unaffected because of the neutrality property. However, this clearly cannot be done too often or firms will be perpetually thinking there is a change in the offing and adjust their investment decisions accordingly. One point worth noting, however, is that the other form of neutral tax structure, namely depreciation allowances equal to the true economic rate of depreciation plus all interest payments tax deductible, remains neutral whatever firms think about future tax changes. This follows essentially because with this tax structure it is *current* costs and *current* returns which are respectively subsidized and taxed at the same rate; future tax rates are of no significance.

As a final example of the many interesting problems which arise in the realms of uncertainty and government policy, we may consider the following. It has been suggested by businessmen and others that frequent changes in the tax structure facing firms have a deleterious effect on investment simply by raising the level of uncertainty and irrespective of the actual changes themselves. In order to investigate such a proposition, we must first attempt to model the situation described and this we may do by supposing the firm to be in a state of 'pure uncertainty' about some tax parameter, where 'pure uncertainty' is defined in the following sense. Using the basic model of section 2, Chapter 6, we suppose first that in each period the firm has some conditional probability that the tax parameter will change, this probability remaining the same from one period to the next, and second that the change itself is random, with the expected value of the uncertain future tax rate identical to its current value. These assumptions attempt to capture the notion that the firm really does not know what is going to happen next, at least as far as the tax parameter is concerned. In addition, to keep the analysis fairly straightforward, we shall suppose that the firm imagines that the world will remain unchanged after the uncertain tax change has occurred.

Turning now to a more formal analysis we shall consider a firm that has a fixed coefficients technology, makes irreversible investment decisions, and faces a downward sloping demand curve which may be written in inverse form as $p = h(y)\alpha$ where α is a combination of a demand and sales tax parameter and is the particular government instrument on which we focus attention in this example. This is rather an apt choice since it is frequent government manipulation of sales taxes and demand which has been a major source of complaint by leaders of the motor-car and electrical-goods industries in the UK in recent years. Assuming, as in Chapter 6, the existence of a delivery lag, m, and furthermore that the firm expects a change in α from α_1 to $\tilde{\alpha}_2$ to occur at an unknown time $\check{t}$, we may write the net income receipts of the firm at time t as,

$$9.21 \quad \tilde{R}(t) = R^0(t) = \{h(y)\alpha_1 - w\}y - qI \qquad \text{for } t < \check{t},$$

$$= R^1(t) = \{h(y)\tilde{\alpha}_2 - w\}y - qI \qquad \text{for } \check{t} \leqslant t < \check{t} + m,$$

$$= \tilde{\pi} = \max \int_{\check{t}}^{\infty} \exp\{-r(s-t)\}\left[\{h(y)\tilde{\alpha}_2 - w\}y - qI\right]\mathrm{d}s$$
$$\text{for } t = \check{t} + m.$$

The unexplained notation is in the standard form of Chapter 6 (particularly p. 96), there is no profits tax and the pure uncertainty assumption implies that $E\tilde{\alpha}_2 = \alpha_1$. Then, using the formula 6.11, the firm will choose a production plan between m and $l + m$ to solve the problem,

$$\max \int_0^\infty \exp\left(-rt\right)\left(G(t-m)\left[\{h(y)\alpha_1 - w\}y - qI\right] + f(t-m)\,\underset{\tilde{\alpha}_2}{E}\,\tilde{\pi}\right) dt$$

where note that $G(t) + G(t-m, t) = G(t-m)$ and $E\tilde{\alpha}_2 = \alpha_1$.[9] Using an argument similar to that utilized in deriving 6.16 we may deduce that the optimal capacity, $y(t)$, must satisfy

9.22 $$M(y)\alpha_1 = w + (r + \delta)q + \phi(t-m)\left\{q - \underset{\tilde{\alpha}_2}{E}\left(\frac{\partial\tilde{\pi}}{\partial y}\right)\right\}$$

where $M(y)$ is the marginal revenue function, ϕ is the conditional probability of the parametric change and $E(\partial\tilde{\pi}/\partial y)$ is the expectation of the value to the firm of an extra unit of capacity taken over all possible levels of the future tax rate. In this case of pure uncertainty f is chosen such as to make the conditional probability $\phi(.)$ a constant, so the value of $y(t)$ satisfying 9.22 is simply a constant. The question now arises as to whether this constant level of capacity is lower or higher than it would be if the firm was certain that α_1 was to remain fixed. The answer is very straightforward, for we show in proposition 2 of the Appendix that $\partial\tilde{\pi}/\partial y$ is concave in $\tilde{\alpha}_2$ and strictly concave over some interval. Its expectation is therefore less than q (which is its value if α_1 remains fixed) and, furthermore, is declining with increases in uncertainty about the tax change. So we can immediately say that any increase in the conditional likelihood of a sales or tax change and any increase in the degree of uncertainty about this change will lower the optimal capacity of the firm, even if it is risk neutral. The basic reason for this result is that over-capacity is more costly for the firm than under-capacity. When the tax change has occurred the firm can always purchase some additional capacity, albeit with some delay, if it has too little, but if it has too much then it is simply stuck with it.

Just to give some idea of the orders of magnitude involved, if it is assumed that the uncertainty about the new value of the parameter $\tilde{\alpha}_2$ takes the form of a uniform distribution with mean unity between limits $[1 - \bar{\alpha},\ 1 + \bar{\alpha}]$, then Table 9.1 gives the percentage drop in capacity from that which would obtain under certainty given various parameter values.[10]

The magnitudes are not very startling although they increase rather rapidly with increasing uncertainty, rising to a peak of an 8·5% drop in capacity if the interest rate and rate of depreciation are rather low and the firm thinks there is a 50% conditional probability of a change of somewhere up to 30% in sales tax in either direction in each year. This analysis does, of course, ignore risk aversion which would reduce capacity still further and it also assumes that the effective costs of over-capacity are simply those of being on the wrong point of the demand curve. That is, prices are always adjusted to utilize all the available capacity. In reality, output prices may not be as flexible as this and costs of over-capacity may

Table 9.1

Conditional probability of change (ϕ)	Elasticity of demand (assumed constant)	Interest rate (r)	Rate of depreciation (δ)	Degree of uncertainty ($\bar{x}$)	% drop in capacity
0·5	−1·5	0·1	0·1	0·1	0·32
0·5	−1·5	0·1	0·1	0·2	2·7
0·5	−1·5	0·1	0·1	0·3	5·3
0·5	−1·5	0·05	0·05	0·1	0·52
0·5	−1·5	0·05	0·05	0·2	4·7
0·5	−1·5	0·05	0·05	0·3	8·5

be relatively higher when account is taken of possible costs of lay-offs, redundancy payments, etc. This would tend to cause reductions in the optimal capacity which are larger than those shown in Table 9.1. Furthermore, increasing uncertainty is likely to raise the cost of capital to the firm and so there are several other factors all working in the same direction. Nevertheless, even as they stand, the percentage reductions in steady state capacity are not inconsiderable when it is borne in mind that this is an effect of uncertainty from only one source.

Another interesting aspect of uncertainty in this context is the way it can induce a slow response to exogenous changes when they do occur, if the firm imagines them to be impermanent. For example, if there is a government-stimulated increase in demand for the firm's output, the firm may well be initially rather sceptical that it is here to stay, especially if there have been frequent similar ups and downs in the past, and only after it has remained for some time will the firm be gradually convinced of its permanence. The effect of this kind of scepticism is clearly to make the firm's investment response to policy changes somewhat sluggish. Of course this sluggish responsiveness cuts both ways. If there is a decline in demand which the firm imagines is only temporary it will probably continue to replace some of its out of date capital stock, whereas, if the decline is viewed as permanent, the firm will cease investment completely until capacity has declined to the lower level required. The basic point is, however, extremely important. The more the government manipulates the demand or tax situation facing a particular firm, the less likely it is that the firm will view the change as permanent and the smaller and more sluggish will be the investment response. There will thus be a tendency for firms to develop a sort of 'tolerance' to changes in fiscal incentives. The more changes there are, the less effect any given change will have and so the greater will be the temptation to make the changes larger and larger as the government becomes more and more irritated with the lack of private sector responsiveness. All this succeeds in doing, of course, is to exacerbate the whole problem.

This last example completes our series of some of the interesting problems which can arise when considering how the corporate tax structure influences the level of investment and it more or less completes the strictly theoretical discussion of the firm's investment decisions. The remaining chapters are concerned with the specification of investment demand functions in the light of this theoretical analysis and with surveying the empirical evidence. However, we shall not plunge directly into the details of investment demand equations but in an interim chapter we shall comment briefly on the results of all this theorizing and then look at some of the general difficulties which arise in moving from the theory to hypothesis testing with the available data.

Appendix

Proposition 1 (p. 205). If the firm's value per share $V(t)$ satisfies the difference equation, $(1 - \tau_p)r V(t) = D(t) - (1 - \tau_g)\{V(t+1) - V(t)\}$, then the value per share at time zero, $V(0)$ is given by,

$$V(0) = \sum_{s=0}^{\infty} \frac{1}{1 - \tau_g} \frac{D(s)}{\alpha^{s+1}}$$

where

$$\alpha = 1 + \frac{(1 - \tau_p)r}{(1 - \tau_g)}.$$

Proof. $(1-\tau_p)rV(t)=D(t)-(1-\tau_g)\{V(t+1)-V(t)\}$ implies that

$$V(t)=\frac{V(t+1)}{\alpha}+\frac{1}{1-\tau_g}\frac{D(t)}{\alpha}$$

which holds for all t. Backward substitution then yields

$$V(0)=\frac{V(t+1)}{\alpha^{t+1}}+\frac{1}{1-\tau_g}\sum_{s=0}^{t}\frac{D(s)}{\alpha^{s+1}}$$

Then, so long as the value per share remains bounded, letting $t\to\infty$ gives the result.

Proposition 2 (p. 217). Consider the function $\pi\{y(t),t\}$ which is defined as

$$\pi\{y(t),t\}=\max\int_{t}^{\infty}\exp\{-r(s-t)\}\,([h\{y(s)\}\alpha-w]y(s)-qI(s))\,\mathrm{d}s,$$

subject to $\dot{y}=I-\delta y,\ I\geqslant0,\ y(t)$ given.

Then $\pi\{y(t),t\}$ has the property that $\partial\pi/\partial y$ is concave in α and strictly concave on some interval.

Proof. Since all the parameters in the maximization problem are constant, its solution is simply given by y^* satisfying

A1. $M(y)\alpha=w+(r+\delta)q,$

so long as $y^*\geqslant y(t)$. Under these circumstances π is given by

A.2 $\pi\{y(t),t\}=q\{y^*-y(t)\}$

$$+\int_{t}^{\infty}\exp\{-r(s-t)\}\,[\{h(y^*)\alpha-w\}y^*-q\delta y^*]\,\mathrm{d}s.$$

On the other hand, if $y^*<y(t)$ then because of the irreversibility constraint, there must be a zero investment interval during which capacity depreciates from $y(t)$ to y^*. Subsequently capacity is maintained at y^* as before. Suppose that the zero investment interval continues from t to $t+n$. Then n clearly satisfies

A.3 $y^*=\exp(-\delta n)\,y(t),$

and, furthermore, during the interval $[t,t+n]$ capacity $y(s)$ satisfies

A.4 $y(s)=\exp\{\delta(s-t)\}\,y(t).$

Thus in the case where $y(t) > y^*$ we have

$$\pi\{y(t), t\} = \int_{t}^{t+n} \exp\{-r(s-t)\}\left([h\{y(s)\}\alpha - w]y(s)\right) ds$$

$$+ \int_{t+n}^{\infty} \exp\{-r(s-t)\}\left[\{h(y^*)\alpha - w\}y^* - q\delta y^*\right] ds$$

Taking the derivative and noting from A.4 that $\partial y(s)/\partial y(t) = \exp\{-\delta(s-t)\}$ gives

A.5 $\quad \dfrac{\partial\pi}{\partial y(t)} = \exp(-rn)\{h(y^*)\alpha - w\}y^* \dfrac{\partial n}{\partial y(t)}$

$$+ \int_{t}^{t+n} \exp\{-(\delta+r)(s-t)\}[M\{y(s)\}\alpha - w]\, ds$$

$$- \exp(-rn)\{h(y^*)\alpha - w\}y^* \frac{\partial n}{\partial y(t)}$$

$$+ q\exp(-rn)\delta y^* \frac{\partial n}{\partial y(t)}$$

$$= \exp\{-(r+\delta)n\}\,q + \int_{t}^{t+n} \exp\{-(r+\delta)(s-t)\}$$

$$\times [M\{y(s)\}\alpha - w]\, ds.$$

From A.1 it is clear that for all

$$\alpha > \frac{w + (r+\delta)q}{M\{y(t)\}}, \; y(t) < y^*$$

and thus $d\pi/dy = q$, which is independent of α. For

$$\alpha < \frac{w + (r+\delta)q}{M\{y(t)\}}, \; y(t) > y^*$$

and $\partial\pi/\partial y$ is given by A.5.

Differentiating A.5 twice with respect to α, noting that n is a function of α via A.3 and A.1 gives

$$\frac{\partial^2}{\partial\alpha^2}\frac{\partial\pi}{\partial y(t)} = \exp\{-(r+\delta)n\}\, M(y^*) \frac{\partial n}{\partial\alpha}$$

where from A.3,

$$\frac{\partial n}{\partial\alpha} = \frac{\partial y^*}{\partial\alpha}\{\delta\exp(-\delta n)\,y(t)\}^{-1} < 0.$$

Hence $\partial\pi/\partial y(t)$ is strictly concave in α when

$$\alpha < \frac{w+(r+\delta)q}{M\{y(t)\}}.$$

Noting the $\partial\pi/\partial y(t)$ is non-decreasing and continuous in α everywhere then gives the required result.

Footnotes

[1] Note that

$$\frac{\partial c}{\partial \tau} = \frac{q(1-g)(\nu+r)}{\{\nu+r(1-\tau)\}^2}[-r\{\nu+r(1-\tau)\}+r\{\delta-\dot{q}/q+r(1-\tau)\}]$$

$$= \frac{q(1-g)(\nu+r)r(\delta-\dot{q}/q-\nu)}{\{\nu+r(1-\tau)\}^2}$$

[2] It should however be noted that if the firm expects the corporate tax rate to change at some time in the future, then neutrality is no longer preserved. This point is discussed fully in section 4.

[3] This section follows very closely the excellent analysis given in King (1974a).

[4] For an interesting discussion of some of the legal ramifications of this point, see Stiglitz (1973, p. 10, footnote 14).

[5] Wood (1975, p. 45).

[6] These figures are taken from Whalley (1974, p. 15). They incorporate a number of specific assumptions concerning actual tax rate levels which did not in fact remain constant over the years. 1965 and 1973 were, however, years when the corporate tax structure was almost entirely overhauled.

[7] Typically we would not expect a firm to be in a situation where it is on the downward section of the U-shaped curve because this would imply that an increase in debt would lower its capital costs. In this context, however, one must take a rather broad view of capital costs. For example, it may be that the managers have such a strong fear of bankruptcy that they hardly utilize any debt finance at all. To an outsider it may appear that the firm could reduce its capital costs by greater leverage and indeed the shareholders might well be in favour of such a step if they were fully aware of the situation. However, this is not the managers' view, and they take the decisions.

On the other hand, it is very easy for the firm to be in the situation where a reduction in the proportion of outstanding debt to equity would reduce the costs of capital in the absence of any costs involved in actually changing the degree of leverage. The problem is that such a change may well not be worth carrying out by issuing shares because of the transaction's costs and tax disadvantages of actually making the issue.

[8] It should be noted that this effect on the timing of investment decisions will not occur if the fiscal policy change only affects the cost of capital (by reducing effective interest rates, for example). Since such a policy only affects *current* flow costs, its timespan has no influence on the timing of expenditures though it may have some effect on their general level. See Nickell (1974b) for some extensive discussion of these issues.

[9] Just as a reminder, $f(t)$ is the density function of the uncertain future time at which the tax rate is due to change, $G(t) = \int_t^\infty f(\nu)\,d\nu$ and $G(t-m, t) = \int_{t-m}^t f(\nu)\,d\nu$, where these functions are illustrated in Figure 6.1.

[10] See Nickell (1977a).

Bibliographical Notes—Chapter 9

The influences of various forms of depreciation allowance and investment grant on the effective price of capital goods are considered in some detail in Hall and Jorgenson (1967), Coen (1971) and King (1972, 1975). Concerning the relationship between tax systems, finance and investment, discussions which only consider the corporate tax rate are to be found in Modigliani and Miller (1958, 1963) and Myers (1974). More detailed discussions, including capital gains tax and other elements of the personal as well as the corporate tax structure, are included in Lintner (1962, 1964, 1967), Stapleton (1972) and Pye (1972). The most complete analyses are probably those of Stiglitz (1973) and King (1974a).

The classic theoretical and empirical analysis of dividend payments is that of Lintner (1956) and there is also an extensive and lucid discussion of the issues involved in Wood (1975).

All the topics discussed in this chapter are dealt with in far greater detail in King (1977).

CHAPTER 10

FROM THEORY TO TESTING

1. A Summary of the Theory

Back in Chapter 2 we started with a simple model of investment decisions where the future is certain and capital stock can be freely and instantaneously adjusted at every point in time. This results in the firm determining its optimal capital stock at each instant independently of its past history or its future prospects, a conclusion which is clearly a travesty of reality. In the four subsequent chapters we modified this simple model by incorporating additional assumptions concerning the environment in which the firm's decision-makers operate. In particular, in Chapter 3 we considered the adjustment cost model which, although convenient analytically, does not always yield results in accord with casual observation nor does it possess a very convincing theoretical basis. Somewhat more appealing models were obtained by the successive introduction of irreversibility, delivery lags and uncertainty in Chapters 4, 5 and 6. These simple assumptions, which reflect three obvious and important aspects of reality, are quite adequate to generate the sort of hesitant and sluggish investment response which is such a crucial facet of observed behaviour.

Following these more general theoretical chapters we then considered the rather more specialized topics of replacement and decay in Chapter 7 and of financial policy in Chapter 8. One important aspect of investment behaviour which emerges from the former chapter concerns the ways in which firms may alter their productive capacity other than by the purchase of new capital goods. These include the scrapping of old capital, the expenditure of resources on maintenance and the use of existing capital goods for different proportions of the week. All these activities are direct substitutes for variations in the rate of investment and their optimal levels are, of course, determined simultaneously with it. In the chapter on financial policy we were essentially concerned with the opportunity cost of fixed capital investment. The crucial question is whether it is sensible to suppose that this opportunity cost is exogenous to the firm or, alternatively, to suppose that the firm is faced with a cost of funds schedule which rises with the rate of investment. The latter case would occur if the firm's uncertain returns were such that its equity had few, if any, close substitutes. Under these circumstances a firm's internally generated funds would be an important factor in determining investment policy, as indeed would its financial situation in general. In Chapter 9 we then went on to discuss how the corporate tax structure fitted into the picture, studying in particular its relationship with optimal financing and its consequent impact on real investment decisions.

2. Some Sins of Omission

This, briefly, is the coverage of our theoretical discussion. It has been, of necessity, somewhat selective and it is worth considering some of the important aspects of the firm's investment decisions which have been omitted. Throughout our analysis we have consistently assumed that the firm uses only one type of capital good.[1] This is hardly realistic but, on the other hand, extending the models to the case where the firm uses many different types of capital good would, in most cases, require little more than patience and subscripts, and yield equally little in the way of insight. It seems fairly clear that, for studying most of the interesting areas of investment decision-making, the assumption of a single capital good is innocuous. It does, however, imply that we cannot look at the question of substitution between different types of capital goods which may be important for a variety of reasons.[2] First, even if the relative prices of different capital goods remain fixed, this does not imply that they will always be used in fixed proportions. Indeed, the degree of substitutability between capital goods and labour may well depend on the degree to which one capital good may be substituted for another. Second, and perhaps more important, different capital goods may have different delivery times and this may, for example, imply that the firm orders different combinations of goods in response to the same expected demand change, depending on how far into the future it is expected to occur. Any analysis of this issue would probably be prohibitively complex, although it may be important for the specification of lags in empirical investment demand equations.

Another assumption which has been implicit in all our discussions is that production takes no time and consequently we have said nothing about 'work in progress' and the problems of allocating costs to output when prices are changing during the production process. Of course, the time between the purchase of the inputs and the sale of the output is an aspect of the utilized technology, and the consequent possibility of substitutability or complementarity between fixed capital and 'work in progress' may well be important in investment decisions, particularly in the firm's response to changes in the price of output relative to capital goods. A further important temporal aspect of investment decisions which we have ignored is the possibility of the firm shortening the delivery delay on a particular good by paying more. This would obviously be advantageous to a firm facing a sudden and unexpected increase in demand, for example, and casual observation suggests that it is not uncommon. Unfortunately, formal analysis of this would probably be quite tricky although, as with the problem of different delivery times for different capital goods, it may throw some light on the correct specification of lags in investment demand functions.

The omissions in our theoretical analysis of investment decisions which we have mentioned so far are probably of rather minor significance; something which cannot be said of our having paid no attention whatever to the relationship between investment in fixed capital, investment in research and development and, to a lesser extent, advertising expenditure. The latter two forms of expenditure by firms are a deliberate attempt to influence future costs or demand, both of which have been assumed exogenous in our work. Since these latter are the crucial determinants of investment expenditure, it is clear that a truly complete analysis of firm behaviour should explain the firm's expenditure on fixed capital, R and D and advertising simultaneously. The exclusion of advertising expenditure from the discussion can be justified by appeal to the observation that the firms seem unable to do much about major cyclical fluctuations in the demand for their products. They do not appear to use advertising expenditure as a counter cyclical measure, indeed quite the reverse.[3] R and D expenditure is another matter. Massive expenditure on the creation of new cost-saving techniques and on new products can, if it is successful, lead to enormous bursts of fixed capital investment and is clearly one of the driving forces behind a firm's secular growth. By treating both costs and demand as exogenous the whole issue has been sidestepped, and by way of exoneration it can only be pleaded that a detailed analysis of R and D investment would be a very lengthy and difficult business, and would be somewhat out of place in a study whose major focus is on investment decisions in response to short- and medium-term fluctuations rather than on the determinants of long-run secular growth. This issue, of course, ties up with the problem of the firm's objective function and, in particular, the notion that the managers have an incentive to choose policies which will imply that the firm grows faster than the shareholders might wish.[4] Here again, our assumption of exogenous demand more or less rules out any investigation of this issue, though it clearly cannot be done justice without a detailed examination of exactly how a firm can influence the demand for its products.[5]

Related to this issue of exogenous demand has been the omission of all reference to the problem of oligopoly. In so far as the firm's pricing strategy in particular, and its competitive activities in general, affect the demand for its products, these will clearly feed into its investment decisions. In their turn these decisions can also affect the firm's market position, for the degree of capital intensity of the firms within an industry can influence the likelihood of new firms entering.[6] Clearly this point also ties up with the question of R and D and advertising expenditure which we have already mentioned.

The final important area which we have failed to discuss in any great depth concerns the relationship between all the various adjustment mechanisms which are open to the firm as a response to changes in its environment. If the firm experiences an unexpected increase in the demand for its output it can do some or all of the following things: raise the price of its output, ration demand (increase delivery time), reduce stocks, employ the existing labour force for longer hours, hire new employees, utilize the existing capital stock for more hours of the week, switch employees from maintenance to production (or vice versa), reduce the rate at which old capital goods are scrapped, order new capital goods. The optimal strategy for the firm will clearly depend on its expectations about the permanence of the demand increase and the relative costs of all the possibilities we have mentioned. In Chapter 7 we have tried to analyse the relationships between some of these factors but throughout our work we have always assumed that output price and labour input are more or less freely adjustable. This can be justified on the grounds that this is true *relative* to the costs of capital adjustment and that for some sorts of problems the answers provided are not too misleading. Nevertheless it would clearly be interesting to try to investigate the problem in all its generality in order to analyse the relationships between the demands for various factors of production. Some pioneering attempts in this direction have already been made in the work of Nadiri and Rosen (1969) and Brechling (1975) on inter-related factor demand models, but these have been based on the somewhat mechanical adjustment cost approach about which we have already had our say. Unfortunately, as our analysis in Chapter 7 indicates, this whole problem is fraught with difficulties. One thing, however, is quite clear. Any analysis which purports to solve this problem must take *explicit* account of the actual time structure and time delays involved in the firm's operations and, furthermore, must cope with the problem of the influence on present decisions of different patterns of expectations about the future. No such analysis is presently available.

This then completes the list of sins of omission. The substantive questions we have just raised are typically more difficult to answer than those we have actually treated in the preceding chapters. Generally speaking, however, an understanding of the problems which have been dealt with is a necessary prerequisite of any attack on these further questions. Such an attack must be left to another time and place.

3. Some Empirical Problems

In the next two chapters we shall be considering some of the empirical studies which are so abundant in the field of investment. Before looking at the details, however, it is worth touching on some of the general difficulties which arise when trying to test empirically the hypotheses which flow from the theory. We shall identify three major problem areas in this context, namely aggregation, micro-macro relationships and measurement. All three are large and difficult topics so we shall do little more than point out why problems arise.

When considering empirical work in the field of production, even at the firm level, it is immediately striking that the attempt is being made to represent the multifarious productive activities which take place in an automobile plant, for example, by a mathematical function which has only two arguments. Indeed, more often than not, the function is taken to represent many different automobile plants plus a few making buses and trucks as well. Now it is clear that these plants produce many different outputs using many different types of machinery and many different qualities of labour. So the question arises as to whether one can construct aggregates for the outputs, the capital good inputs and the labour inputs so that it is possible to define a production function which gives aggregate output as a function of the aggregate capital and aggregate labour inputs. The answer, in any realistic case, is that it is not.[7] So how then can one justify the use, in empirical work, of pseudo-production relationships between value aggregates of output and capital and labour inputs? In particular, how can one justify their use in optimization conditions as if they were true production functions In answer to these questions there is little to be said. Any empirical work in this area is bound to be based on approximation and the role of economic theory is to suggest appropriate variables and possible structural relationships between them. One plausible way of using economic theory is to assume that the pseudo-production relationship relating aggregate values is in fact the true one and to specify appropriate optimality conditions on this basis. The resulting relationships between observable variables are then only approximations and great care must be exercised in interpreting the coefficients which are estimated, particularly those which purport to be parameters of production relationships. This does, however, seem to be the only sensible way of allowing theory to impose some structure on the empirical relationships.

This problem is serious enough at the level of the firm but even more difficulties arise when considering data at the industry or even higher levels of aggregation. Even if one supposes the empirical relationships at the firm level to be good approximations of reality, it becomes progressively harder to maintain much faith in the structure of these relationships at higher levels of aggregation, particularly if the basic structure is non-linear. In the linear case things are not too bad, particularly if the micro-units which are being aggregated are more or less identical, but in the non-linear case it is difficult to develop structural restrictions on the aggregate relationships corresponding to those which theory imposes on the micro-level equations.[8]

These are not the only problems which arise from attempts to study investment behaviour at the industry or still more aggregate levels. Once we move to these higher levels of aggregation it is then possible that the demand for investment goods by the group of firms under consideration forms a significant section of the relevant market. It is then clear that there will be problems of identifying the demand function when the rate of investment to be explained is being determined simultaneously with the price and delivery time of capital goods.[9] Chapter VII of Brechling (1975) provides a very good example of how misleading results can arise when a firm based model of investment demand is estimated using market data.

Finally, we come to problems of measurement. There are enormous difficulties associated with measuring investment and even greater ones with measuring capital stock. One of the problems with the former is that investment usually takes time. Investment data can thus be based on orders, deliveries or payments or some mixture of all three. So, for example, in the UK progress payments on large items of fixed capital investment are treated as part of fixed domestic capital formation.[10] It is clear, however, that these are not additions to a firm's capital stock and this can yield misleading results in empirical work particularly with respect to the interpretation of estimated lag structures. Generally speaking, however, investment data is more accurate than capital stock data with the British Central Statistical Office grading gross domestic fixed capital formation as accurate to between 3 and 10% and total gross capital stock at replacement cost as accurate to between 10 and 20%.[11]

Obviously, the key problem with measuring existing capital stock is the evaluation of old capital goods for which there exist no active markets. This will entail making assumptions about the rate at which particular capital goods decay and so we can easily reach the position where there are different measures of capital stock corresponding to different capital decay hypotheses and different specifications of investment demand functions. The measured data is thus dependent on the hypothesis which it is being used to test.

These, then, are just some of the difficulties which arise to a greater or lesser extent with all the empirical work in this field. They are serious problems and when we come to look at the empirical work which has been done in this field, we shall find that they are rarely considered. The reason is, of course, that given existing data there is little which can be done about most of them. Bearing this in mind we shall also forget about them, although it is always worth keeping them at the back of one's mind and maintaining a healthy scepticism about the results and procedures which we shall describe in subsequent chapters.

Footnotes

[1] This is not quite correct, for if one assumes non-exponential decay, as in Chapter 7, then old capital goods are no longer the same as new ones. This point also ties up with our having omitted, so far, all mention of the 'putty-clay' technology where there is *ex ante* but no *ex post* substitutability between capital and labour. This form of technology is analysed extensively in the next chapter.

2 See Boddy and Gort (1971) for an empirical study of this question.

3 For an extensive discussion of the evidence on this issue, see Schmalansee (1972).

4 The argument is based on the observation that managers of large firms are paid more than those of small ones. On the other hand, as Meeks and Whittington (1975) confirm, managers of more profitable firms are paid more than those of less profitable ones. The managers' optimal policy is not, therefore, absolutely clear.

5 It should perhaps be emphasized that it is the *demand curve* which is taken as exogenous; actual demand can, of course, be influenced by manipulating the output price. There are some alternative models of investment behaviour notably that described in Wood (1975). in which the output price influences *the rate of growth of demand* and this directly and permanently affects the rate of investment. The actual operating mechanism is not made clear, though a possible example of this sort of behaviour is provided by the markets for some new consumer durables where the rate of growth of demand is affected by the extent of existing ownership. The lower the firm sets the price, the faster the market becomes saturated. These sort of 'epidemic' demand processes are discussed in Glaister (1974).

Generally speaking the degree to which firms can control the demand for their products is rather a contentious issue although, given the extent of demand fluctuations for most products in recent years, they are certainly not much good at it. (See, for example, *The New Industrial State* by J. K. Galbraith (1967) and the review by R. M. Solow (1967).)

6 See in particular Spence (1976).

7 See Leontief (1947), Gorman (1968), Fisher (1969), or, most accessibly, Bliss (1975, Chapter 7), for the extremely stringent conditions under which this is possible.

8 See Theil (1954) for conditions necessary to aggregate linear relationships.

9 For example Engle and Foley (1975) explain aggregate investment by means of an equation which has as its arguments, GNP and a distributed lag of equity prices and which they claim to be essentially a supply relation. Many equations with similar, if not identical, independent variables have been estimated as demand relationships.

10 See Maurice (1968, p. 362).

11 See again Maurice (1968, p. 382).

Bibliographical Notes—Chapter 10

A large number of different topics are discussed in this chapter and so in these notes we shall simply mention a few studies which provide a broad overview and will themselves have extensive bibliographies. A detailed and informative study of advertising is Schmalensee (1972) and a good survey of the work on research and development is given by Kamien and Schwartz (1975). An interesting theory of investment decisions which tries to incorporate oligopolistic and related factors is that set out in Wood (1975). Brechling (1975) has an extensive theoretical discussion of the relationships between some of the various adjustment mechanisms open to the firm in response to exogenous changes.

As far as aggregation is concerned, a good survey is Green (1964) while Rowley and Trivedi (1975, Chapter 5) deals with some of the econometric aspects of the problem. Concerning data and measurement, Liesner (1975) is a good introduction to statistics on investment and capital stock and some very interesting discussion and examples of investment and capital stock measurement are provided in Christensen and Jorgenson (1969) and Boddy and Gort (1973).

CHAPTER 11

THE STRUCTURE OF INVESTMENT
DEMAND EQUATIONS

1. The Timing of the Investment Process

In order to confront a theory of the investment decisions of firms with the facts it is necessary to deduce from the theory some readily testable hypotheses. One of the most powerful methods of so doing is to write down a specific equation which explains the demand for a certain type of investment good by a firm in terms of a number of observable variables which are preferably exogenous. On the basis of such an equation it is then possible to test a large number of competing hypothesis concerning the relative importance of these explanatory variables using the standard techniques of multivariate statistical analysis.

It is the purpose of this chapter to discuss the structure of such investment demand equations in the light of both the previous theory and some of the very numerous equations that have been investigated by researchers in this field. Since it is the relationship between investment demand equations and theory which is the point at issue, most of the examples from existing empirical work have been chosen because they are derived more or less explicitly from some type of firm value maximizing behaviour, that is, from specific micro-economic considerations.[1] In addition we shall only be considering the deterministic specification of these demand equations and not the stochastic specification. This latter subject is of very great importance when it comes to hypothesis testing and is in some respects rather closely bound up with the deterministic specification. Since, however, it is a subject of some considerable technical complexity it would require a rather deep exposition of certain areas of econometric theory in order to do it full justice and consequently it will not be treated here.

There exist such an enormous variety of possible structures for an investment demand equation, especially in respect of lags, that it is very difficult to see the wood for the trees. As a first step, therefore, we shall look at the distributed lags that arise from the physical time

233

structure of the actual investment process, basically with a view to clearing them out of the way. In a close look at the investment decision process Lund (1971) has divided the lag between the time when the firm is faced with a situation in which it requires further capital expenditure and the time of the actual investment expenditure itself into no less than five separate components. These are:

(1) The time which elapses between the events which actually stimulate the desire for new investment and the firm's knowledge of these events. For example, the time taken to collect and absorb relevant statistical information.
(2) The time taken to draft investment plans and arrange finance.
(3) The time taken to place orders or make purchases.
(4) The time between the placing of an order and the commencement of work on the order, which is sometimes referred to as the queueing period.
(5) The time between the commencement of work on the order and its final production. Payment for the final product may be made on delivery or may be made in the form of progress payments during the production period. These payments may show up as actual investment expenditures.

In order to analyse how this rather complex process will affect the structure of investment equations we suppose first that the firm uses one specific type of capital good for which, at any point in time, there is a known lag between the ordering date and the delivery date. Let this known delay at time t be $m(t)$ and suppose that the total quantity of capital which the firm thinks at time t that it would like to possess at time $t + m(t)$ is $\bar{K}\{t, t + m(t)\}$.

Then, if $K\{t, t + m(t) - 1\}$ is the quantity of capital which the firm thinks at time t that it will possess at time $t + m(t) - 1$, $S\{t, t + m(t) - 1\}$ is the quantity of capital which the firm thinks at time t will be scrapped at time $t + m(t) - 1$ and $D\{t, t + m(t) - 1\}$ is the quantity of capital which the firm thinks at time t will evaporate at time $t + m(t) - 1$, it is natural for the firm to order at time t a quantity of new investment, $I_0(t)$, given by

11.1　$I_0(t) = \bar{K}\{t, t + m(t)\} - K\{t, t + m(t) - 1\}$
$$+ S\{t, t + m(t) - 1\} + D\{t, t + m(t) - 1\}.$$

Some comments on this equation are in order. First, the time lag $m(t)$ is the time between phase (3) and the end of phase (5) of the investment process described above. Second, if the time taken to draft investment plans is considerable, the size of the term $\bar{K}\{t, t+m(t)\}$ may in fact be determined some time before time t and consequently could not depend on any exogenous variables at time t itself. Third, the reason why $K\{t, t+m(t)-1\}$ is not precisely known at time t is because the quantity of capital which will be scrapped or will evaporate between t and $t+m(t)$ is not known with certainty.

The next question which arises is, how does the level of actual investment expenditures depend on past orders? If the level of investment expenditures at time t is given by $I(t)$ and if we assume that payments are always made on delivery, and no orders are cancelled, we have

11.2 $$I(t)= \sum_{s\in S(t)} I_0(s); \quad S(t)=\{s\,|\,s+m(s)=t\}.$$

This simply states that investment expenditures at time t will be equal to the sum of all the past orders which are due to arrive at t. The set of times of past orders which will arrive at t is given by $S(t)$ and the right-hand side of 11.2 is just the sum of the past orders whose time indices lie in this set. This set could be empty or it could consist of an interval containing one or more consecutive past points in time. If the lag $m(s)$ is a constant m, the set $S(t)$ consists of the single element $t-m$ and thus 11.2 reduces to the obvious equation,

11.3 $$I(t)=I_0(t-m).$$

So we have already struck a most serious problem in the construction of investment *expenditure* equations. If there is a variable delivery lag, which in all probability there is, then investment expenditures are going to be a rather complex function of past orders involving a variable lag. Such variable lags can be taken into account by allowing the lag weights to depend on some variable, such as the ratio of the order back log to capacity in the capital goods industry, which is correlated with the delivery lag.[2] Although this is perfectly feasible it tends to make the structure of an investment expenditure equation rather complex and for that reason it is probably a good plan to estimate an equation explaining orders for new capital goods and then to explain actual expenditures by past orders, at least if the primary aim is to investigate the actual structure of the investment decisions of the firm.

There are a number of investment studies which make the lags involved in the actual process of investment an explicit element in their analysis and it is this particular point which we shall now consider. Since these studies typically assume both fixed lags and exponential evaporation of capital stock without scrapping we shall apply these assumptions to the orders equation 11.1 to give

11.4 $\qquad I_0(t) = \bar{K}(t, t+m) - (1-\delta)K(t, t+m-1)$

where δ is the rate of decay. An important point to note is that, with the fixed lag and exponential decay, the future capital stock at time $t+m-1$ is in fact known with certainty at time t. This is because the basic equation of capital accumulation, namely

11.5 $\quad K(t+m-1) = I(t+m-1) + (1-\delta)K(t+m-2),$ $\qquad$ all $t,$

may be extended by backward substitution to give

11.6 $\quad K(t+m-1) = \sum_{i=1}^{m} (1-\delta)^{i-1} I(t+m-i) + (1-\delta)^m K(t-1).$

Since the lag is fixed, $I(s) = I_0(s-m)$ all s, and thus 11.6 may be written as

$$K(t+m-1) = \sum_{i=1}^{m} (1-\delta)^{i-1} I_0(t-i) + (1-\delta)^m K(t-1),$$

where all the variables on the right-hand side are known with certainty at time t. Consequently, $K(t, t+m-1)$ may be replaced by the actual capital stock in 11.4 to give

11.7 $\qquad I_0(t) = \bar{K}(t, t+m) - (1-\delta)K(t+m-1).$

Another point worth noting is that since $I(t+m) = I_0(t)$, the basic equation of capital accumulation implies that in this case the actual level of capital stock attained at time $t+m$ will be equal to the level which the firm thinks at time t it will require at that time, that is,

11.8 $\qquad K(t+m) = \bar{K}(t, t+m) \qquad$ all t.

It should be emphasized that the level of capital stock given by $\bar{K}(t, t+m)$ is not to be confused with the level of 'desired' capital stock as it is often defined. $\bar{K}(t, t+m)$ is the level of capital stock which the firm really wishes to possess taking into account all adjustment costs and the like. We shall return to this in the next section but for the moment it is not the major point at issue.

The type of empirical study which makes the lags in the actual process of investment an integral part of the analysis is epitomized by the work of Jorgenson and his collaborators,[3] where indeed these are the *only* lags in the consequent investment equation. In this kind of work it is assumed that instead of the order for new capital being fulfilled on some fixed date in the future, various proportions of the order are fulfilled at various different dates in the future.[4] Thus it is assumed that a proportion ω_i of an order at time t is delivered at time $t+i$ where the ω_i are fixed through time and sum to unity. The reasons for this assumption have never been made very clear but one in particular that springs to mind is that the capital stock typically considered in empirical work consists of a number of different types of capital good, each of which is likely to have a different delivery time associated with it. To give some idea of the effects of this type of aggregation, suppose there are two types of capital good, labelled 1, 2, with delivery times m_1 and m_2 respectively, where $m_2 > m_1$. Then for each time period there are two equations corresponding to 11.7, namely

11.9 $I_0{}^1(t) = \bar{K}^1(t, t+m_1) - (1-\delta)K^1(t+m_1-1)$ all t,

11.10 $I_0{}^2(t) = \bar{K}^2(t, t+m_2) - (1-\delta)K^2(t+m_2-1)$ all t,

where the superscripts refer to the type of capital and both types are assumed to decay at the same rate. Note also that $\bar{K}^1(t, t+m_1)$ is chosen with a knowledge of $K^2(t+m_1)$ which has already been determined by past orders for capital goods of type 2 which have the longer delivery lag. Suppose first that the two types of capital good must be employed in fixed proportions. Then there exists some fixed number α such that

11.11 $$K^1(t) = \alpha K^2(t) \qquad \text{all } t,$$

and, furthermore, for all t, $\bar{K}^1(t, t+m_1)$ is chosen to satisfy

11.12 $\bar{K}^1(t, t+m_1) = \alpha K^2(t+m_1)$

$$= \alpha \bar{K}^2(t-m_2+m_1, t+m_1) \qquad \text{from 11.8.}$$

Finally the total capital stock in any period and the total investment in any period satisfy

11.13 $$K(t) = K^1(t) + K^2(t) = (1+\alpha)K^2(t) = \frac{1+\alpha}{\alpha} K^1(t),$$

11.14 $$I(t) = I^1(t) + I^2(t) = (1+\alpha)I^2(t) = \frac{1+\alpha}{\alpha} I^1(t).$$

Since the lags are fixed, total investment at time t is given by,

$$I(t) = I^1(t) + I^2(t)$$

$$= I_0^1(t - m_1) + I_0^2(t - m_2)$$

$$= \bar{K}^1(t - m_1, t) + \bar{K}^2(t - m_2, t) - (1 - \delta)K^1(t - 1) - (1 - \delta)K^2(t - 1)$$

$$= (1 + \alpha)\bar{K}^2(t - m_2, t) - (1 - \delta)K(t - 1) \quad \text{from 11.12, 11.13,}$$

$$= \bar{K}(t - m_2, t) - (1 - \delta)K(t - 1) \quad \text{from 11.8, 11.13.}$$

Therefore there are no distributed lags in the investment equation when the different types of capital are used in fixed proportions. The reason for this is clear. Since there are fixed proportions, the type 1 capital requirements are determined when the orders for type 2 capital goods are put in (m_2 periods before delivery) in spite of the fact that they do not have to be ordered for another $m_2 - m_1$ periods. Consequently, investment in period t depends solely on the capital stock requirement predicted in period $t - m_2$ and there is no distributed lag.[5]

Clearly, in order to have some sort of distributed lag we must make the more sensible assumption that there exists at least some degree of substitutability between the two types of capital goods. Again we have

$$I(t) = \bar{K}(t - m_1, t) + \bar{K}^2(t - m_2, t) - (1 - \delta)K(t - 1)$$

but since there is substitution $\bar{K}^1(t - m_1, t)$ does not bear any simple relationship to $\bar{K}^2(t - m_2, t)$. There is also a problem of how to define $\bar{K}(t - m_1, t)$, the total capital stock which the firm thinks at time $t - m_1$ will be required at time t. This can either be defined taking the already ordered quantity of type 2 capital at time t as given or it can be defined as the total quantity of capital which would be required at time t if both types of capital were freely available. The second definition is probably more in accord with the typical way in which these things are dealt with in the empirical literature, in which case we can write $\bar{K}^1(t - m_1, t)$ as some proportion of $\bar{K}(t - m_1, t)$ where the *proportion* depends on the amount of type 2 capital already ordered. Assuming that the relative prices of the two types of capital remain constant, we can write

$$\bar{K}^2(t - m_2, t) = \alpha_2 \bar{K}(t - m_2, t)$$

and

$$\bar{K}^1(t - m_1, t) = \alpha_1 \{\bar{K}^2(t - m_2, t), \bar{K}(t - m_1, t)\} \bar{K}(t - m_1, t)$$

where we might expect α_2 to remain constant over time but α_1 typically to be variable. It would to be equal to $1-\alpha_2$ only if the firm happens to think that the total capital stock wanted at time t is the same at $t-m_1$ as it was at $t-m_2$. On the other hand, if the firm thinks at time $t-m_1$ that it requires more (less) total capital stock at time t than it thought at time $t-m_2$, the proportion α_1 will then be greater (less) than $1-\alpha_2$. In any event the lag structure is likely to be fixed only if the predictions of the capital requirements at any particular date remain constant as that date comes closer to the present. This is typically not the case and therefore we are back to the problem of variable lags without even considering the possibility of changes in the relative prices of the two types of capital goods.

Suppose now that the distribution of future deliveries over time is not due to different capital goods having different delivery times, but simply arises from the fact that for the single capital good in question it just so happens that a proportion α_1 is delivered after m_1 periods and a proportion α_2 after m_2 periods, where $\alpha_1+\alpha_2=1$. This seems rather strange but in the work of Jorgenson and his associates, for example, the aggregated capital stock is assumed to behave in this way. The problem now arises as to how the firm should behave. The reason why there is a problem is that any attempt to order enough capital at time t to close a particular gap between the required capital and actual capital at time $t+m_1$ will also lead to an arbitrary addition of some more capital, which may be quite unwanted, at time $t+m_2$. One possible way around this is for the firm to order enough capital at time t to close the gap between the capital required at time $t+m_2$ and the actual capital at time $t+m_2$. The fact that part of this newly ordered capital will arrive at $t+m_1$ is then simply ignored; it may come in useful or on the other hand it may be entirely useless until $t+m_2$. This possibility would then lead to an orders equation of the form

$$11.15 \qquad I_0(t) = \bar{K}(t,\, t+m_2) - (1-\delta)K(t,\, t+m_2-1)$$

where we cannot write $K(t+m_2-1)$ in the second term on the right-hand side because the firm cannot know at time t exactly how much capital it will have at time $t+m_2-1$, since this will depend on all the orders it makes up until $t+m_2-m_1-1$. A possible predictor of this quantity of capital stock is the capital that the firm thinks at time $t-1$ that it will require at time $t+m_2-1$, namely $\bar{K}(t-1,\, t+m_2-1)$.

Substituting this term into 11.15 gives

11.16 $\qquad I_0(t) = \bar{K}(t, t+m_2) - (1-\delta)\bar{K}(t-1, t+m_2-1)$

which is almost the equation utilized by Jorgenson. The difference between it and the Jorgenson formulation can be clarified as follows. An equation of the type 11.16 will yield an expenditure equation of the type

$$I(t) = \alpha_1\{\bar{K}(t-m_1, t) - (1-\delta)\bar{K}(t-m_1-1, t-1)\}$$
$$+ \alpha_2\{\bar{K}(t-m_2, t) - (1-\delta)\bar{K}(t-m_2-1, t-1)\},$$

whereas the equivalent Jorgenson formulation is

$$I(t) = \alpha_1\{\bar{K}(t-m_1, t) - \bar{K}(t-m_1-1, t-1)\}$$
$$+ \alpha_2\{\bar{K}(t-m_2, t) - \bar{K}(t-m_2-1, t-1)\} + \delta K(t-1).$$

This latter equation implicitly assumes that the replacement capital is ordered when the actual capital stock at time $t-1$ is known with certainty and this means that replacement capital goods for time t do not need to be ordered before $t-m_1$. Thus the Jorgenson formulation assumes that capital goods which are used for replacement purposes never have a delivery delay longer than the shortest delivery lag for expansion capital. Why this should be so is not at all clear since presumably the capital goods are all of the same type and so this would seem to be rather a strong prior assumption to impose on the equation specification.

The vast majority of other empirical studies do not go into this problem in any very explicit detail[6] and although it poses serious difficulties in empirical work, we cannot allow it to detain us further. The only point that seems worth making is that it is probably a good strategy in any micro-economic investigation of investment demand to try to look at the demand for a fairly homogeneous group of capital goods. Then, if one is estimating an orders equation, the delivery lead time is more or less uniform for all capital in the sample and there is no troublesome problem of a distribution of delivery dates.

In order to enable us to focus attention on other matters we shall henceforward assume that the firm is purchasing a single capital good with a fixed delivery lag.[7] This enables the actual lags in the investment process to be very clearly separated from any other lags which may arise due to expectations and adjustment costs. It should perhaps be made clear that there is no suggestion here that in estimating an investment demand equation, where the investment is aggregated over goods with different, possibly variable, delivery lags, one *should* assume a single fixed delivery lag. This is merely an expositional device and examples taken from the empirical literature will simply be reformulated in accord with the single lag assumption. Some of the well-known empirical formulations may, therefore, look a little strange.

2. Period by Period or Pseudo-static Investment Equations

In this section we shall look at investment equations which follow from the assumption that the investment process is basically static. If m is the fixed lag between orders and deliveries and we assume, for the sake of exposition, that orders and the decisions upon which the orders are based occur simultaneously, then, in this type of world, the capital stock which the firm wishes to have at time $t+m$ is determined at time t quite independently of the capital stock which it knows it will possess at time $t+m-1$. Furthermore it is also determined independently of the capital stocks it may think it requires in any period after $t+m$. This kind of model is of the period by period type discussed in Chapters 2 and 5 and is the correct specification so long as there are no strictly convex costs of adjustment and the investment process is completely reversible. Many of the equations which have been tested are *ostensibly* of this type, in the sense that no explicit strictly convex costs of adjustment or irreversibility assumptions are made in the preliminary theoretical analysis, although, as we shall see, the actual equations used turn out to be impossible to derive from a pseudo-static formulation.[8]

The basic equation which we shall consider has the standard form of 11.1 which we repeat again for convenience, that is

11.17 $I_0(t) = \bar{K}(t, t+m) - K(t, t+m-1) + S(t, t+m-1)$

$$+ D(t, t+m-1)$$

where the delivery lag $m(t)$ is now fixed at m. Then we know that if the only capital stock disappearance is via exponential evaporation we have

11.18 $I_0(t) = \bar{K}(t, t+m) - (1-\delta)K(t+m-1)$

where $K(t+m-1)$ is known at time t.

The crucial point about the period by period model is that $\bar{K}(t, t+m)$ may be derived from a simple static maximization problem and is completely independent of the actual capital stock at any time. Any required capital stock which can be derived in this manner is usually called the 'desired' capital stock and this 'desired' capital stock happens, in the period by period model, to correspond both to the stock of capital which the firm thinks at time t that it wants at time $t+m$, and to the stock of capital which it will actually have at time $t+m$ (given exponential decay and a single rather than a distributed delivery lag). Assuming certain expectations for the period $t+m$, we may distinguish three distinct types of 'desired' capital stock, which we shall denote by K^*.

(1) The firm is a price taker in all markets. If $p(t, t+m)$, $w(t, t+m)$, $c(t, t+m)$ are the expected output price, wage and cost of capital, then using standard notation, K^* is chosen to solve:

$$\max_{K, L} \{p(t, t+m)F(K, L) - w(t, t+m)L - c(t, t+m)K\}$$

which gives

11.19 $\bar{K}(t, t+m) = K^*\{w/p(t, t+m), c/p(t, t+m)\}.$

This problem only has a solution if F has diminishing returns.

(2) The firm is a price taker in the factor markets but faces a downward sloping demand curve for its product. Then, if it has an expected demand curve of the type $z(p)\beta(t, t+m)$, K^* is chosen to solve :

$$\max_{K, L} \{pF(K, L) - w(t, t+m)L - c(t, t+m)K\}$$

subject to $z(p)\beta(t, t+m) = F(K, L)$, which gives

11.20 $\bar{K}(t, t+m) = K^*\{w(t, t+m), c(t, t+m), \beta(t, t+m)\}.$

(3) The future output which the firm expects to have to produce, namely $Q(t, t+m)$, is taken as exogenous and the firm chooses K^* to solve :

$$\min_{K, L} \{w(t, t+m)L + c(t, t+m)K\}$$

subject to $Q(t, t+m) = F(K, L)$, which gives

11.21 $\bar{K}(t, t+m) = K^*\{w/c(t, t+m), Q(t, t+m)\}.$

Sometimes an additional assumption is made, namely that the future output price $p(t, t+m)$ is given by

$$p(t, t+m) = (\text{mark up}) \times \frac{w(t, t+m)L^* + c(t, t+m)K^*}{Q(t, t+m)}$$

where K^*, L^* are the solutions to the minimization problem.

This is then used to eliminate $w(t, t+m)$ to give a final form

11.22 $\qquad \bar{K}(t, t+m) = K^* \{p/c(t, t+m), Q(t, t+m)\}.$

In addition to these three possibilities when future expectations are certain, it is very simple to incorporate uncertain expectations into this model and derive the desired capital stock exactly as was done in the analysis of Chapter 5. For example, if we incorporate uncertain expectations into model (2) and suppose the firm to be risk neutral (with the appropriate cost of capital) we have that the firm chooses K to solve

$$\max_{K} E\big(p\{K, \tilde{w}(t,t+m), \tilde{\beta}(t,t+m)\}F[K, L\{K, \tilde{w}(t,t+m), \tilde{\beta}(t,t+m)\}]$$
$$- \tilde{w}(t,t+m)L\{K, \tilde{w}(t,t+m), \tilde{\beta}(t,t+m)\} - \tilde{c}(t,t+m)K\big)$$

where $p\{K, \tilde{w}(t,t+m), \tilde{\beta}(t,t+m)\}$ and $L\{K, \tilde{w}(t,t+m), \tilde{\beta}(t,t+m)\}$ are the solutions to the two equations,

$$M(p)F_L(K, L) = \tilde{w}(t, t+m)$$
$$z(p)\tilde{\beta}(t, t+m) = F(K, L).$$

As usual $M(p)$ is the marginal revenue and the tildes indicate random variables. This formulation, of course, assumes that labour and the output price are fully adjusted in every period. The resulting value of the desired capital stock may then be written as

11.23 $\quad \bar{K}(t, t+m) = K^*[Eg\{\tilde{w}(t, t+m), \tilde{\beta}(t, t+m)\}, E\tilde{c}(t, t+m)].$

Thus there is a very wide range of possible choices for the 'desired' capital stock and this has been reflected in the many different specifications used in empirical work. Interestingly enough, although a number of studies have explicitly assumed price-taking behaviour on the part of firms, not one has ended up with the formulation of model (1). For example, Jorgenson and his associates have ended up with something rather similar to 11.22, the final equation of model (3), except that in their case the expected level of output $Q(t, t+m)$ which is assumed to be exogenous in model (3), is replaced by the current output, $Q(t)$, which is clearly not exogenous. Indeed since $Q(t)$ depends on the current level of capital stock $K(t)$, this formulation clearly cannot follow from a pseudo-static model and must involve an implicit assumption of some kind of adjustment costs. Jorgenson himself recognized this fact and in Jorgenson (1972) actually specifies the type of adjustment cost model which he has in mind to explain his investment equation formulation. We shall consider this point further when we come on to discuss truly dynamic models of investment in a later section.

Gould and Waud (1973), in a critique of the Jorgenson formulation, have explicitly assumed an imperfectly competitive model and use equation 11.20 for their desired capital stock. In a rather interesting extension of this model Chang and Holt (1973) have incorporated uncertainty using an equation of the type shown in 11.23. They then expand the desired capital stock in a Taylor series about the mean values up to the variance terms and approximate these variance terms by a linear function of the delivery lag m on the argument that the variance of the predictions will be larger, the further into the future these predictions must be made.[9]

Coen (1971) argues for a variant of model (3) where future output is exogenous and in fact uses an equation of the type shown in 11.21. He argues that the stickiness of prices implies that even in a fairly competitive industry the firms must look to the future industry demand and derive their future desired output from this. Nerlove (1972) produces a formal derivation of a model of this type (though there are adjustment costs) and shows how industry output will directly affect the investment decisions of competitive firms in a world where prices and demands from individual firms do not change instantaneously, thereby producing temporary elements of monopoly.

Numerous other studies use some kind of variant of models (2) or (3) and almost all are agreed that some index of future output or demand is an important factor in determining current investment decisions. There are two major problems stemming from this. The first is to find a variable which adequately measures demand. The second is to find a specification which takes into account the fact that it is the future demand that is important. We shall look at these in turn.

The problem concerning demand is that it is almost unmeasurable. From equation 11.20 it is obvious that what we are looking for is a measure of the position of the demand curve, which is a variable that is truly exogenous to the firm. It is clear that output will not do since it is not exogenous to the firm and depends on the capital stock, among other things. One possibility is to correct output for unintended inventory changes which will certainly capture some of the influence of exogenous demand, and this is done in the Canadian macro-model RDX2 (see Helliwell *et al.*, 1971). Another possibility is to use orders, which is done in a number of studies, for example Coen (1971). Gould and Waud (1973), on the other hand, make sure of exogeneity by using national income as their index of demand curve position. Other variables such as capacity utilization and sales are quite popular but these are perhaps a little too dependent on current capital stock to be seen as truly exogenous. Of course, as we have mentioned in respect of the Jorgenson formulation, such dependence on existing capital stock may be desirable in a truly dynamic model of investment but cannot be valid in any definition of 'desired' capital stock.

Turning now to the problem of taking into account the fact that the arguments of K^* are all expected variables, there are a number of possible approaches which have been used. The simplest assumption is one of static expectations, that is to say that all variables of the type $x(t, t+m)$ are simply replaced by $x(t)$. The future is assumed to be identical to the present. This approach is to be found in Jorgenson (1965) and Gould and Waud (1973) for example. A second approach is to suppose that the variable will continue to grow or decline as it has been doing in the past. Thus a variable of the type $x(t, t+m)$ is replaced either by $x(t)(1+g)^m$ where g is a trend rate of growth or by $x(t) \prod_{i=0}^{m} (1+g_{t-i})^{\alpha i}$ where g_{t-i} is the rate of growth in period $t-i$ and α_i are exponents to be estimated. Expectational mechanisms of this type have been used by Feldstein and Flemming (1971) and also by Kisselgoff and Modigliani (1957) in a very tightly specified micro-investigation of the determinants of investment in the electricity supply industry.

A rather looser expectational mechanism is simply to assume that $x(t, t+m)$ may be written as $\sum_0^\infty \alpha_i x(t-i)$, that is to say that the expected value of x is some distributed lag of past values of x, an approach used both by Coen (1971) and Bischoff (1971b). A more structured mechanism of the same basic type is used by Helliwell and Glorieux (1970) who start by defining expectations one period in advance using the basic equation

$$x(t, t+1) = \sum_{i=0}^{\infty} \alpha_i (1+g)^i x(t-i)$$

$$+ b \sum_{i=0}^{\infty} [\lambda_i \{ x(t-i) - (1+g)x(t-i-1) \}]$$

where $\Sigma\alpha_i = \Sigma\lambda_i = 1$ and the first summation is an attempt to capture the trend growth of the variable, the second to capture the deviations from this trend.

Writing the equation in more succinct notation gives

$$x(t, t+1) = \sum_{i=0}^{\infty} \beta_i x(t-i)$$

where $\beta_1 = \alpha_1(1+g) + b\lambda_1$, $\beta_2 = \alpha_2(1+g)^2 + b\{\lambda_2 - (1+g)\lambda_1\}$, etc. Assuming that expectations further ahead are formed in a similar manner gives

$$x(t, t+k) = \sum_{i=0}^{k-1} \beta_i x(t, t+k-i)$$
$$+ \sum_{i=k}^{\infty} \beta_i x(t+k-i) \qquad \text{for } k = 1, 2, \ldots, m,$$

and this set of equations can then be solved recursively for $x(t, t+m)$ in terms of the $x(t-i)$, $i \geqslant 0$.

Another interesting procedure is that of Chang and Holt (1973) who use four quarter moving averages of past values in order to derive their expected variables but then go on to estimate an equation to explain desired capital stock and use the fitted values in their actual investment equation. Along similar lines, Craine (1975) uses the basic Gould–Hartman adjustment cost model with uncertainty (see p. 93), making use of explicitly estimated autoregressive-moving average processes to predict the expected future wage and price levels, and Birch and Siebert (1976) utilize an estimated sales equation to form an expected sales series for inclusion in their investment equation.

Other studies have taken a rather different approach, usually in the context of a slightly looser specification, which is to proxy the expected future variable by some other completely different variable which hopefully incorporates some expectational elements. A typical example is current profits, though it is not quite clear why they should provide any more information about future demand than current demand itself. A more likely variable is the level of share prices. This, of course, also affects the cost of capital and hence plays a dual role but it should certainly contain some expectational information. An alternative used by Eckstein (1965) is an index of leading business indicators which will clearly affect the formation of current expectations. Another possibility which does not seem to have been considered is to use published GNP predictors which are now readily available, for example, those produced by the National Institute for the UK. It would seem quite reasonable to include such a variable in an expectations formation mechanism for future levels of demand as an exogenous addition to the purely regressive–extrapolative mechanisms normally used.

This concludes our discussion of the possible specifications of 'desired' capital stock, a concept which arises naturally in the context of pseudo-static models of investment because not only is it the capital stock 'desired' but it is also the capital stock which firms really wish to possess and, in the context of a single delivery lag with exponential evaporation, it is additionally the capital stock which the firms will get. Under these circumstances an orders equation can be written as

$$I_0(t) = K^*(.) - (1 - \delta)K(t + m - 1)$$

where K^* is the desired capital stock which depends solely on expected exogenous variables and *not* on the actual capital stock at any point in time. Many investment studies, though they make no explicit mention of any assumptions which would rule out the period by period formulation, in fact end up with an equation which cannot be written in this form *when a single fixed delivery lag is assumed.* Consequently, it becomes essential to investigate the possible structures which can arise if we assume some form of convex costs of adjustment which will then rule out the pseudo-static approach. There will, however, still be a role for 'desired' capital stock as defined here even though it will no longer be identical to the capital stock which the firm actually wants to achieve when it is sending out orders. Therefore our investigation of the properties of such an animal will not be rendered pointless when we move on to more sophisticated models.

3. Dynamic Models of Investment. (i) Putty-clay

As a first stop on the road towards a truly dynamic formulation we shall consider investment equations which are based on the assumption of a putty-clay technology. That is to say that the capital goods to be purchased may be chosen from a whole range of possibilities which require more or less labour to work with them. These possibilities are typically represented by a production function. After purchase, however, the quantity of labour to be used with any particular unit of capital is fixed henceforward. Intuitively, the effect of such restrictions is to slow down the response of the aggregate capital–labour ratio to relative price changes, since the capital–labour ratio on all existing capital stock is fixed. On the other hand, it would not affect the response rate to changes in demand. In order to clarify this effect we shall formally derive an investment demand function for a model of this type and then go on to discuss some of the studies which have used this type of specification. For our exposition we shall assume that the *ex ante* choices open to the firm may be described by a constant returns to scale production function. Then, if the capital–labour ratio selected for capital purchased at time s is given by $k(s)$, we may write the output per head produced by capital of this vintage as $f\{k(s)\}$. Then, if $I(s)$ is the quantity of capital purchased at time s and δ is the rate of exponential evaporation, we have,

$$I(s)(1-\delta)^{t-s}/k(s) = l(s, t),$$

the labour utilized at time t on capital purchased at time s, and

$$I(s)f\{k(s)\}(1-\delta)^{t-s}/k(s) = Q(s, t),$$

the output produced at time t using capital purchased at time s.

Before setting up the present value formula it is first necessary, as we are working in discrete time, to think rather carefully about the timing of events. Since we have been writing gross investment at time t as $K(t)-(1-\delta)K(t-1)$, we shall assume that the investment goods labelled $I(t)$ are purchased at the beginning of the year stretching from t to $t+1$ and that output labelled $Q(t)$ is produced at the end of this same year. This implies that at the end of the year stretching from t to $t+1$, there is a revenue to the firm from this output of $p(t)Q(t)$, a wage payment $w(t)L(t)$ and also a purchase of investment goods for the next period $q(t+1)I(t+1)$. So if r is the fixed rate of interest, the firm will choose a production plan to maximize.

$$\sum_{t=0}^{\infty} 1/(1+r)^{t+1}\{p(t)Q(t) - w(t)L(t) - q(t+1)I(t+1)\}$$

where in this model

$$Q(t) = \sum_{s=-\infty}^{t} Q(s, t),$$

the total output at time t,

$$L(t) = \sum_{s=-\infty}^{t} l(s, t),$$

the total labour input at time t, and

$$Q(t) = z\{p(t)\}\beta(t),$$

the demand at time t (in standard notation).

Furthermore, given our assumed timing of events, we have that the total output produced at the end of year t, $Q(t)$, is equal to the additional capacity output brought in at the beginning of the year t, $Q(t, t)$, plus $(1 - \delta)$ times the total output at the end of the year $t - 1$. Thus we have

11.24 $$Q(t) = Q(t, t) + (1 - \delta)Q(t - 1).$$

In solving this problem the firm chooses a sequence of capital-labour ratios $k(0)$, $k(1)$ ... and a corresponding sequence of actual investments $I(0)$, $I(1)$ ... Before going on to discuss the necessary conditions, it is worth noting immediately that there will be a serious difficulty if the firm wishes to disinvest, for it is clear that under these circumstances it cannot *choose* unrestrictedly the capital-labour ratio associated with the capital goods which it is selling, since it only possesses a limited quantity of certain types. We shall sidestep this difficulty by simply supposing that the firm is never faced with the circumstances which would lead it to disinvest. There are then two necessary conditions associated with the problem, both of which are rather complex but which can be deduced as follows. Suppose we keep the level of investment fixed but increase by one unit the quantity of labour working on a marginal unit of investment purchased at time t. Since the capital–labour ratio on this unit must be fixed henceforward and since the unit will decay at rate δ, this change will incur a whole sequence of additional wage costs of the form $w(t)$, $w(t+1)(1-\delta)$, $w(t+2)(1-\delta)^2$ ..., with a total present value at time t given by

$$\sum_{s=t}^{\infty} \frac{w(s)}{1+r} \left(\frac{1-\delta}{1+r}\right)^{s-t} = \bar{w}(t) \quad \text{say.}[10]$$

In return for this extra expenditure at time t the firm will receive an additional sum in each subsequent period, s, equal to the marginal revenue product of labour on a machine bought at time t times the proportion of the machine remaining at time s. The present value of this sum will be equal to

$$\sum_{s=t}^{\infty} M\{p(s)\}[f\{k(t)\} - k(t)f'\{k(t)\}] \frac{(1-\delta)^{s-t}}{(1+r)^{s-t+1}}$$

where $M(.)$ is the marginal revenue and $f - kf'$ is the marginal product of labour on a machine of vintage t. By the usual marginal arguments this total return must just balance the cost on the optimal path and thus we have the first necessary condition,

$$11.25 \qquad \sum_{s=t}^{\infty} M\{p(s)\}\,[f\{k(t)\} - k(t)f'\{k(t)\}]\,\frac{(1-\delta)^{s-t}}{(1+r)^{s-t+1}} = \bar{w}(t).$$

The other necessary condition will be concerned with the actual quantity of investment at time t. If this is increased by one unit it will incur a total cost of $q(t)$ plus the present value cost of all the additional labour required to work on it. One unit of capital purchased at t requires $\{1/k(t)\}(1-\delta)^{s-t}$ units of labour to work with it at time s and so the total present value cost is given by

$$11.26 \qquad q(t) + \sum_{s=t}^{\infty} \frac{w(s)}{k(t)}\,\frac{(1-\delta)^{s-t}}{(1+r)^{s-t+1}} = q(t) + \frac{\bar{w}(t)}{k(t)}.$$

In return for this extra expenditure, the firm will receive the present value of the future returns on this additional unit of investment. Since one extra unit of capital purchased at t will provide $[f\{k(t)\}/k(t)]\,(1-\delta)^{s-t}$ extra units of output at time s, the total present value return is given by

$$\sum_{s=t}^{\infty} M\{p(s)\}\,\frac{f\{k(t)\}}{k(t)}\,\frac{(1-\delta)^{s-t}}{(1+r)^{s-t+1}}.$$

On the optimal path, the total return on the marginal unit must be equal to total cost and thus we have the second necessary condition

$$11.27 \qquad f\{k(t)\} \sum_{s=t}^{\infty} M\{p(s)\}\,\frac{(1-\delta)^{s-t}}{(1+r)^{s-t+1}} = q(t)k(t) + \bar{w}(t).$$

By eliminating the sum of the marginal revenues between 11.27 and 11.25 we have, after some manipulation, a simple equation for the optimal capital–labour ratio at time t, namely

$$11.28 \qquad \frac{f'\{k(t)\}}{f\{k(t)\} - k(t)f'\{k(t)\}} = \frac{q(t)}{\bar{w}(t)}.$$

Since the left-hand side is in fact monotone decreasing in $k(t)$, we may solve for $k(t)$ to get

$$11.29 \qquad k(t) = g\{q(t)/\bar{w}(t)\}, \qquad \text{where } g' < 0,$$

and using this we may derive the optimal capital output ratio for capital purchases at time t, which is $k(t)/f\{k(t)\}$, as

11.30 $\qquad k(t)/f\{k(t)\} = g/f(g) = V\{q(t)/\bar{w}(t)\}$ say,

where V' is also negative.

Returning now to equation 11.25, this may be written as

$$\sum_{s=t}^{\infty} M\{p(s)\} \frac{(1-\delta)^{s-t}}{(1+r)^{s-t+1}} = \frac{\bar{w}(t)}{f\{k(t)\} - k(t)f'\{k(t)\}}$$
$$= q(t)/f'\{k(t)\} \qquad \text{from } 11.28,$$
$$= \phi\{q(t), \bar{w}(t)\} \text{ say}, \qquad \text{from } 11.29,$$

where it may be shown that $\phi_q > 0$ and $\phi_{\bar{w}} > 0$ (see Appendix, proposition 1).

Since this above expression holds for all t, we may take the expression at time $t+1$, multiply it by $(1-\delta)/(1+r)$ and subtract it from the expression at t which gives

11.31 $\quad M\{p(t)\} = [\phi\{q(t), \bar{w}(t)\}(1+r) - \phi\{q(t+1), \bar{w}(t+1)\}(1-\delta)].$

The marginal revenue being an increasing function of the price, we may solve for the price at time t to give

$$p(t) = \theta[\phi\{q(t), \bar{w}(t)\}(1+r) - \phi\{q(t+1), \bar{w}(t+1)\}(1-\delta)]$$

where $\theta' > 0$. Then, for the final step, we may use the fact that the total output at time t, $Q(t)$, is equal to the demand, $z\{p(t)\}\beta(t)$, to derive the optimal output at time t as

$$Q(t) = z\{\theta(\,.\,)\}\beta(t)$$

or

11.32 $\qquad Q(t) = \beta(t)\psi[\phi\{q(t), \bar{w}(t)\}(1+r)$
$$-\phi\{q(t+1), \bar{w}(t+1)\}(1-\delta)]$$

where $\psi = z\{\theta(\,.\,)\}$ and $\psi' < 0$ since $z' < 0$ and $\theta' > 0$.

From the definition of total output we can immediately derive the optimal investment equation.

Since

$$Q(t, t) = I(t)f\{k(t)\}/k(t) \qquad \text{by definition}$$
$$= I(t)/V(t) \qquad \text{from } 11.30.$$

we have, using 11.24, that

11.33 $\qquad Q(t) = I(t)/V(t) + (1-\delta)Q(t-1)$

and thus the optimal investment at time t is given by

11.34 $$I(t) = V(t)\{Q(t) - (1-\delta)Q(t-1)\}$$

or writing it in full using 11.30 and 11.32

11.35 $$I(t) = V\{q(t)/\bar{w}(t)\}$$
$$\times \left(\beta(t)\psi[\phi\{q(t), \bar{w}(t)\}(1+r) - \phi\{q(t+1), \bar{w}(t+1)\}(1-\delta)]\right.$$
$$- (1-\delta)\beta(t-1)\psi[\phi\{q(t-1), \bar{w}(t-1)\}(1+r)$$
$$\left. - \phi\{q(t), \bar{w}(t)\}(1-\delta)]\right).$$

There are several interesting points to notice about this equation. First, the structure which is clear in 11.34 is typical of putty-clay investment equations. The optimal investment at time t is equal to the product of the optimal capital output ratio to be chosen at t and the total additions to output required in period t. Second, the cost of capital as it is normally derived, namely $q(r + \delta - \dot{q}/q)$, does not appear. On the other hand, if we assume a constant wage, then $q(t)/\bar{w}(t)$ reduces to $q(t)(r+\delta)/w$ and, under these circumstances, the optimal capital–output ratio depends on the normal cost of capital *without* the capital gains term. Changes in the price of capital goods do affect the optimal level of output, as can be seen from 11.32, but not in a simple way. Finally, the optimal output depends linearly on the demand index, $\beta(t)$, and both the optimal output and the capital–output ratio depend on current and future wage rates.

To move from this analysis to an investment orders equation with a single delivery lag is very straightforward. The first point to notice is that, at time t, all the orders for new investment up until time $t + m - 1$ will have been made and the capital output ratios for these orders will have been specified. Consequently, if we assume exponential decay, the output at time $t + m - 1$ will be known with certainty at time t. On the other hand, the optimal capital output ratio to be ordered for $t + m$ and the optimal output required at $t + m$ must both be predicted. This will require predictions to be made of the rate of interest and the level of demand at time $t + m$, the price of capital goods at $t + m$ and at $t + m + 1$ and the wage rate in all periods from $t + m$ onwards. Using these predictions it is then possible to compute the required values of V and Q which will be written as $V^*(t, t+m)$, $Q^*(t, t+m)$. The orders equation then becomes

11.36 $$I_0(t) = V^*(t, t+m)\{Q^*(t, t+m) - Q(t+m-1)(1-\delta)\}$$

and, since there is a single delivery lag, the actual expenditure equation is simply

11.37 $\quad I(t+m) = V^*(t, t+m)\{Q^*(t, t+m) - Q(t+m-1)(1-\delta)\}.$

It is worth noting that, as in the pseudo-static model of the last section, the level of capacity output $Q^*(t, t+m)$ predicted at time t will be that capacity which is actually achieved at $t+m$. This follows from the fact that the actual capacity at $t+m$ satisfies

$$Q(t+m) = I(t+m)/V^*(t, t+m) + (1-\delta)\{Q(t+m-1)\}$$

from 11.33 and substituting for $I(t+m)$ from 11.37 gives

$$Q(t+m) = Q^*(t, t+m).$$

Since this holds for all t it is possible to write 11.37 in an alternative form as

11.38 $\quad I(t+m) = V^*(t, t+m)$
$$\times \{Q^*(t, t+m) - (1-\delta)Q^*(t-1, t+m-1)\}$$

which has essentially the same *structure* as the equations derived by Bischoff (1971b), Hausman (1972) and Ando *et al.* (1974).[11]

The question now arises as to the best way of actually specifying $V^*(t, t+m)$ and $Q^*(t, t+m)$. A crude but simple technique would be to define two new variables $\bar{V}(s)$, $\bar{Q}(s)$ where these are derived from 11.30 and 11.32 using known current values for the cost of capital variable q and the demand variable β and estimating $\bar{w}(t)$ by assuming some constant rate of inflation. Of course, it is also necessary to parametrize the production and demand functions in order to produce a form which can be estimated and, furthermore, the problems of measuring β remain as before. As an illustration we show in proposition 2 of the Appendix that if the production function is Cobb–Douglas, that is $f(k) = k^\alpha$ and the demand function is $z(p) = Ap^{-\epsilon}$, $\epsilon > 1$, then the variables $\bar{V}(s)$ and $\bar{Q}(s)$ are given by

$$\bar{V}(s) = \left\{\frac{\alpha}{1-\alpha} \frac{\bar{w}(s)}{q(s)}\right\}^{1-\alpha}$$

$$\bar{Q}(s) = B\left(\left[\frac{q(s)^\alpha \bar{w}(s)^{1-\alpha}\{1+r(s)\} - q(s+1)^\alpha \bar{w}(s+1)^{1-\alpha}(1-\delta)}{(\epsilon-1)}\right]\epsilon\right)^{-\epsilon}\beta(s)$$

where

$$\bar{w}(s) \simeq \frac{w(s)}{\{r+\delta-i_w(s)\}},$$

$i_w(s)$ being the current rate of wage inflation and B is a constant. An interesting point to note is that the denominator of $\bar{w}(s)$ now contains a term very close to the cost of capital except that the rate of capital goods inflation is replaced by the rate of wage inflation. This is very akin to some of the results derived by Ando and his associates where they explicitly take account of inflation and technical progress in defining V.

In order to go from the definitions of $\bar{V}$ and $\bar{Q}$ to an expectation estimate one can define $V^*(t, t+m)$, $Q^*(t, t+m)$ simply as

$$V^*(t, t+m) = \sum_{i=0}^{\infty} \chi_i \bar{V}(t-i), \quad \bar{Q}^*(t, t+m) = \sum_{i=0}^{\infty} \xi_i \bar{Q}(t-i).$$

This closely follows the Bischoff (1971b) approach except that he has defined $Q^*(t, t+m)$ in terms of lagged values of the actual output. This clearly will not do in the context of the current model because current output, being constrained by current capital stock, may well bear no relationship to what will be wanted in the future. For example, if factor prices have remained constant for ever and hence presumably V^* remains fixed at the true value then, if Q^* is determined by past values of the output Q itself, the investment equation will be

$$I(t) = V^* \left\{ \sum_{0}^{\infty} \xi_i Q(t-m-i) - (1-\delta) \sum_{0}^{\infty} \xi_i Q(t-m-i-1) \right\}.$$

But since $Q(t+m) = I/V^* + (1-\delta)Q(t-m-1)$ by definition, combining the two equations gives

$$Q(t+m) = (1-\delta)Q(t-m-1)$$

$$+ \left\{ \sum_{0}^{\infty} \xi_i Q(t-m-i) - (1-\delta) \sum_{0}^{\infty} \xi_i Q(t-m-1) \right\}$$

which holds for all t. The consequence of this is that output is determined by this equation for all time independently of demand, so long as factor prices remain fixed. This is clearly absurd but it follows from the assumption that only past output determines expected future capacity needs.[12]

Returning finally to the investment equation 11.38 we have, by substituting the expectations formation mechanisms and transposing back to time t,

$$I(t) = \sum_{i=0}^{\infty} \chi_i \bar{V}(t-m-i)$$
$$\times \left\{ \sum_{i=0}^{\infty} \xi_i \bar{Q}(t-m-i) - (1-\delta) \sum_{i=0}^{\infty} \xi_i \bar{Q}(t-m-i-1) \right\}$$

or, more succinctly

11.39 $$I(t) = \sum_{i=0}^{\infty} \sum_{j=0}^{\infty} \beta_{ij} \bar{V}(t-m-i) \bar{Q}(t-m-j)$$

where $\beta_{ij} = \chi_i \xi_j - (1-\delta)\chi_i \xi_{j-1}$ with $\xi_{-1} = 0$.

It is worth noting that with a model which allows substitution *ex post* it is possible to write the investment equation as

$$I(t) = V^*(t-m, t)Q^*(t-m, t)$$
$$- (1-\delta)V^*(t-m-1, t-1)Q^*(t-m-1, t-1)$$

since it is obviously possible to write the desired capital as the product of the desired output and the desired capital–output ratio. Using the same expectations formation equations this will give

11.40 $$I(t) = \sum_{i=0}^{\infty} \sum_{j=0}^{\infty} \bar{\beta}_{ij} \bar{V}(t-m-i) \bar{Q}(t-m-j)$$

where $\bar{\beta}_{ij} = \chi_i \xi_j - (1-\delta)\chi_{i-1}\xi_{j-1}$ with $\chi_{-1} = \xi_{-1} = 0$. One of the crucial differences between the putty-clay formulation and the free substitution formulation may be brought out by comparing the sums of the two sets of coefficients over j. Thus we have,

$$\sum_j \beta_{ij} = \left(\sum_j \xi_j \right)(\delta\chi_i) \text{ and } \sum_j \bar{\beta}_{ij} = \left(\sum_j \xi_i \right)\{\chi_i - (1-\delta)\chi_{i-1}\}$$

Typically we would expect the χ_i to be a declining positive series, which is almost certainly declining fast enough for $\chi_i/\chi_{i-1} \lessdot (1-\delta)$ for at least some i. Thus, while the $\sum_j \beta_{ij}$ would be expected to be positive, we would expect some, at least, of the $\sum_j \bar{\beta}_{ij}$ to be negative. Therefore, if we estimate the β_{ij} from an equation such as 11.39 (restricting the number of parameters to be estimated by some suitable technique), we can compute the sums over j and use the results as an indicative test of the putty-clay hypothesis as against the full substitution hypothesis, and this has indeed been done in Bischoff (1971b). It is, however, a very crude procedure and it is possible to go a little further by looking at the structure of the desired output and desired capital–output ratio themselves in the case where *ex post* substitution is allowed. In the Cobb–Douglas case with a constant elasticity demand function, suitably specializing the derivation of 11.20 gives the desired capital output ratio, $\bar{V}(s)$, and the desired output, $\bar{Q}(s)$, as

$$\bar{V}(s) = \left[\frac{\alpha}{1-\alpha} \frac{w(s)}{q(s)\{r + \delta - i_q(s)\}} \right]^{1-\alpha}$$

$$\bar{Q}(s) = B\left(\left[\frac{w(s)^{1-\alpha}\{q(s)(1+r) - q(s+1)(1-\delta)\}^{\alpha}}{(\epsilon-1)} \right] \epsilon \right)^{-\epsilon} \beta(s)$$

where $i_q(s)$ is the current rate of inflation of capital goods prices. Comparison with the equivalent putty-clay formulae reveals some significant structural differences which could perhaps be tested by imbedding both formulations in some suitably general specification, although it does not seem possible for one of the structures to be formulated as a special case of the other. A final possible method of discriminating between the two formulations is to compare their predictive powers outside the sample period, a procedure which has been used to some effect by Hausman (1972).

4. Dynamic Models of Investment. (ii) Adjustment Costs

As we have seen there are a large number of investment studies which, either implicitly or explicitly, assume the existence of some form of increasing marginal (strictly convex) costs of adjustment, for only by making an assumption of this type does the actual capital stock which the firm thinks at time t that it would like to possess at time $t+m$ depend on existing levels of capital stock. A typical example of this dependence is provided by the equation which follows from the simple adjustment costs assumption, if it is assumed that the values of all the exogenous variables are expected to remain constant from $t+m$ onwards. In these circumstances proposition 3 of the appendix to Chapter 3 shows that enough capital stock will be ordered at time t to satisfy

11.41 $I_0(t) = \lambda_1\{K^*(t, t+m) - K(t+m-1)\} + \delta K(t+m-1)$

$K^*(t, t+m)$ is the level of 'desired' capital stock which is expected to remain constant from $t+m$ onwards and λ_1 is some positive constant less than unity. This is the so-called flexible accelerator model and comparison with 11.7 reveals that the capital stock which the firm really wishes to own at time $t+m$, when adjustment costs are taken into account, is given by

11.42 $\quad \bar{K}(t, t+m) = \lambda_1 K^*(t, t+m) + (1-\lambda_1)K(t+m-1).$

So $\bar{K}(t, t+m)$ is simply a convex combination of the 'desired' capital stock and the actual capital stock which the firm knows it will possess at time $t+m-1$. $\bar{K}$ thus depends on the existing capital stock at time $t+m-1$ for all values of λ_1 less than unity and, of course, if λ_1 is equal to unity there can be no adjustment costs.

This type of model has its uses but it is very badly limited by the assumption of entirely static expectations after time $t+m$. The implication of these static expectations is that the firm always moves towards the 'desired' capital stock so, even if the firm does not want it just yet,[13] it remains desirable enough to aim at. However, with non-static expectations there is a different 'desired' capital stock corresponding to each future period after $t+m$ and the problem of precisely what the firm should aim at is rather tricky. It is clear from the analysis of Chapter 3, section 3, that the firm should be aiming at some sort of average of all the different future 'desired' capital stocks, but we have not discussed any form of analytical solution to this problem. At this point, however, this is exactly what is needed, if only in approximate terms, and so this will be the concern of the next part of this section.

Consider the following model. We have an imperfectly competitive firm facing a demand curve of the usual type, namely $z(p)\beta(t)$ in current standard notation. It faces adjustment costs of the form $bI(t)^2$ and maximizes present value

$$\sum_{t=0}^{\infty} \frac{1}{(1+r)^{t+1}}$$
$$\times [p(t)F\{K(t), L(t)\} - w(t)L(t) - q(t+1)I(t+1) - bI(t+1)^2]$$

subject to the usual constraints. Note that we are sticking to the same timing of events as in the previous section.

As usual we assume, as a first approximation, that the output price is adjusted to equate demand to the output being produced and also that labour will be employed up to the point where the marginal revenue product of labour is equal to the wage. Thus we have,

$$z(p)\beta(t) = F(K, L), \quad M(p)F_L = w$$

in standard notation. These equations may be solved to give

$L(K, \beta, w)$, $p(K, \beta, w)$ at each point in time and the solutions used to construct the marginal revenue product of capital in terms of the capital stock, the demand parameter and the wage. Thus we have

$$M\{(p(K, \beta, w)\}F_K\{K, L(K, \beta, w)\} = G\{K(t), \beta(t), w(t)\} \text{ say,}$$

where $G_K < 0$ from proposition 4 in the Appendix to Chapter 3. To determine the optimal capital stock we simply equate the costs and returns of adding an extra unit of capital stock at time t. This gives

$$\frac{d}{dI(t)}\{bI(t)^2\} + q(t) = \sum_{s=t}^{\infty} G(s)\frac{(1-\delta)^{s-t}}{(1+r)^{s-t+1}}$$

which is the discrete time version of equation A.17 in the Appendix to Chapter 3, and holds for all t. If we then take this equation at $t+1$, multiply it by $(1-\delta)/(1+r)$ and subtract it from the equation at t, we have, after some manipulation,

11.43 $$2bI(t+1)(1-\delta) - 2bI(t)(1+r) + G\{K(t), \beta(t), w(t)\}$$

$$= q(t)r + q(t+1)\delta - \{q(t+1) - q(t)\}.$$

Writing the right-hand side, which is the cost of capital, as $c(t)$, and substituting $K(t) - (1-\delta)K(t-1)$ for $I(t)$, we have that the optimal capital stock satisfies the second order difference equation

11.44 $$2b(1-\delta)K(t+1) - 2b\{(1-\delta)^2 + (1+r)\}K(t)$$

$$+ G\{K(t), .\} + 2b(1+r)(1-\delta)K(t-1)$$

$$= c(t).$$

Using this equation we may now define the 'desired' capital stock at time t as that capital stock which is the stationary solution to 11.44 assuming that $w(t)$, $\beta(t)$, $c(t)$ remain constant at their current values. Thus $K^*\{w(t), \beta(t), c(t)\}$ is defined by

$$2b(1-\delta)K^* - 2b\{(1-\delta)^2 + (1+r)\}K^*$$

$$+ G\{K^*, \beta(t), w(t) + 2b(1+r)(1-\delta)K^*$$

$$= c(t)$$

or

11.45 $$G\{K^*, \beta(t), w(t)\} = c(t) + 2b(r+\delta)\delta K^*.$$

This is the standard definition of desired capital stock in the case of quadratic adjustment costs, for 11.45 simply states that the marginal revenue product of capital is equal to the cost of capital plus the marginal adjustment costs of installing the annual replacement needed to maintain the desired capital.[14] In fact, this is the capital stock at which the firm would aim if $\beta(t)$, $w(t)$ and $c(t)$ were all to remain constant.

We are now in a position to prove the following result, which is discussed at some length in the Appendix, proposition 3. This result shows that the optimal level of investment at time t is given approximately by

$$11.46 \quad I(t) \simeq \lambda_1 \left[K^*(t) + \frac{\lambda_1 + r}{1 + r} \sum_{s=t+1}^{\infty} \left(\frac{1 - \lambda_1}{1 + r} \right)^{s-t} \right.$$
$$\left. \times \{ K^*(s) - K^*(t) \} - K(t-1) \right] + \delta K(t-1)$$

where $K^*(s)$ is the 'desired' capital stock defined for prices and demand levels ruling at time s and $0 < \lambda_1 < 1$.

Equation 11.46 gives us precisely what we are looking for. Instead of the firm aiming at a simple 'desired' capital stock, K^*, it aims at the desired capital stock for the next period plus an exponential weighted sum of the differences between the desired capital stock next period and the different desired capital stocks for all the future periods. With stationary expectations, of course, all these differences are zero and we are back to the standard flexible accelerator model. In addition, we are also able to show that $\partial \lambda_1 / \partial b < 0$. Thus, as might be expected, as adjustment costs become more important, the speed of adjustment becomes slower and, furthermore, greater weight is given to future values of the desired capital stock compared with the current value in determining the stock towards which the firm is adjusting.

In order to use this model in the context of the single delivery lag specification it is simply a matter of replacing the future values of demand and prices by their expectations. Thus we have the orders equation

$$11.47 \quad I_0(t) = \lambda_1 \left[K^*(t, t+m) + \frac{\lambda_1 + r}{1 + r} \sum_{s=t+m+1}^{\infty} \left(\frac{1 - \lambda_1}{1 + r} \right)^{s-t-m} \right.$$
$$\left. \times \{ K^*(t, s) - K^*(t, t+m) \} - K(t+m-1) \right]$$
$$+ \delta K(t+m-1)$$

where $K^*(t, s) = K^*\{c(t, s), w(t, s), \beta(t, s)\}$, and one can specify these expectations using one of the techniques described in section 2, p. 254.[15]

The only serious problems with this specification are, first that it does not provide for future expected variations in the rate of interest and so one must define r as fixed at $r(t, t+m)$ and, second that one may wish to consider the variations in the value of λ_1 which follow both from variations in the value of r and of b. This suggests replacing λ_1 by some function to be estimated such as $\alpha_0 + \alpha_1 r(t, t+m) + \alpha_2 b(t, t+m)$ where expectations about b are also assumed stationary. On the other hand, the equation to be estimated would then become overburdened with parameters and it would probably be necessary to make some further simplifying assumptions to knock it into some reasonable shape.

Turning now to some of the equations of this type which have been estimated, the first point to note is that equation 11.47 gives a fairly good idea as to where the existing levels of capital stock should enter the specification in adjustment cost models. None of the starred variables in 11.47 should contain any actual capital stock levels because, being 'desired' variables, they should not be constrained by what actually exists. The constraining effect of the existing stock comes through from the $K(t+m-1)$ term in the large parentheses combined with the fact that λ_1 is less than unity. Compare this with a Jorgenson type specification which may be written as

$$11.48 \quad I_0(t) = [K^*\{Q(t),\, p(t)/c(t)\} - K^*\{Q(t-1),\, p(t-1)/c(t-1)\}]$$
$$+ \delta K(t+m-1).$$

Here the expectations are completely static and therefore the future expected levels of output and prices are simply replaced by their current values. The specification of 11.48 is clearly a far cry from the structure of 11.47. The capital stock at which the firm is aiming is entirely dependent on the current stock via current output, whereas we know from 11.42 that the capital stock which the firm actually wishes to possess at time $t+m$ will be some convex combination of actual capital stock (the constraining element) and some average of 'desired' capital stocks which must be independent of any existing capital stock values, in fact must be exogenously determined.

On this matter we must go a little further because in Jorgenson (1972) there is an actual specification of the type of adjustment cost model which he had in mind as the basis of the type of investment equation illustrated by 11.48. This particular model, which we have not discussed in this book, is one that has been analysed in Lucas (1967). It is rather a strange model in the sense that the firm is both perfectly competitive and has constant returns to scale. In fact the production function can be written as $F(K, L) - C(I, K)$ where adjustment costs are now incorporated into the production function, that is to say they are measured in terms of output. Both F and C are homogeneous of degree 1 but C is strictly convex in I as usual. The result of this formulation is that, given constant prices, the firm will grow or contract indefinitely but at a finite rate because of the strict convexity of costs with respect to I. There is no point in analysing this model in detail and we shall simply quote the required results from the Lucas paper. The basic result is that in each period gross investment is given by

$$I(t) = K(t-1)h(w/p, q/p, r, \delta)$$

where all prices are assumed constant. This implies that current investment is completely determined by existing capital stock and relative prices. So in a sense this model is rather close to the Jorgenson structure, but very much simpler. The sort of orders equation which it would produce would be

$$I_0(t) = K(t+m-1)h\{w/p(t, t+m), q/p(t, t+m), r(t, t+m), \delta\}$$

and there seems no need to consider output at all. Indeed, since output in fact depends on investment via the production function, there seems little sense in trying to turn things the other way round and make investment depend on output. So it is not really absolutely clear how any formulation which uses current output entirely to determine the target capital stock can be considered as having been derived from value maximizing behaviour on the part of the firm. On the other hand, it is only fair to add that it might be possible to construct some variation of the Lucas model which does indeed lead to this formulation. All one can say at the moment is that, so far, it has not been done.

Many other empirical studies have either implicitly or explicitly used the type of adjustment cost formulation shown in 11.47. Note, for example, that, if the prices c and w are assumed to have negligible influence either because of lack of substitutability or for some other reason, the equation reduces to an accelerator model based entirely on demand. Eisner in particular favours this kind of specification, usually proxying demand by sales. Indeed in Eisner (1967) he puts forward a 'permanent income' theory of investment where, essentially because of adjustment costs and presumably irreversibility, firms like to feel fairly certain about the permanency of demand changes before embarking on investment programmes to provide new capacity. This type of behaviour follows naturally from the sort of assumptions that lead to equation 11.47. It is clear from 11.47 that if, for example, demand at time $t+m$ is expected to be high for only a short time, then, even though $K^*(t, t+m)$ is high, the more distant values of K^* would be lower and this would imply a lower level of capital stock for the firm to aim at compared with the situation where demand is expected to remain high.

A number of papers have extended the adjustment cost formulation to include the costs of adjusting factors of production other than the capital stock, notably labour. Since it is undoubtedly true that the labour input is not freely adjustable, it is natural to suppose that the costs of labour adjustment may enter the demand for investment. The theoretical structure of such models has been investigated by Treadway (1970) and Mortenson (1973) and these models have been applied in empirical work by Nadiri and Rosen (1969), Schramm (1970) and Brechling (1975).

Unfortunately, as we noted in Chapter 3, there does not seem to be a very strong case for strict convexity of adjustment costs internal to the firm and without such strict convexity the structure of the cost of adjustment model falls to the ground. It is true that the irreversibility of investment, which seems likely to be at least partially valid, does yield effects which are somewhat similar to strictly convex adjustment costs, especially in the sense that the firm would probably wish to be fairly sure that upward movements in demand or downward movements in capital cost were likely to be permanent before embarking on new capital programmes. But, unfortunately, irreversibility does not yield the tightly specified equation structure which flows naturally from the adjustment cost approach.

On the other hand, as we have already mentioned, there is one particular type of cost which could well save the day for this type of specification. In Chapter 8 on finance we noted that there are good *a priori* grounds for thinking that the cost of capital is upward sloping in the level of investment and at an ever increasing rate. In particular, the position of this cost of capital schedule is sensitive to the flow of internally generated funds and, possibly, to the initial quantity of debt outstanding in comparison to the value of the firm (remember that internal funds can be used either for real investment or for reducing the level of debt). Then it would be reasonable to suppose that one of the effects of this type of capital cost structure is akin to that of a strictly convex adjustment cost where the importance of the adjustment cost depends on the flow of funds relative to the initial debt–valuation ratio and the desired quantity of investment. So, for example, in the stationary expectations equation 11.41 we would have

$$I_0(t) = \lambda_1\{K^*(t, t+m) - K(t+m-1)\} + \delta K(t+m-1)$$

where λ_1 might perhaps be written as

11.49 $$\lambda_1 = \alpha_0 + (1-\alpha_0)\{1 - \exp(-x)\}$$

where x is specified as

$$x = \frac{\alpha_1 F(t, t+m)}{K^*(t, t+m) - K(t+m-1)(1-\delta)} + \frac{\alpha_2\{F(t, t+m) - B(t, t+m-1)\}}{VA(t, t+m)}.$$

F is the expected flow of funds which is the sum of expected after-tax profits and depreciation charges, B is the expected outstanding debt and VA is the expected total valuation of the firm.[16] Then, given

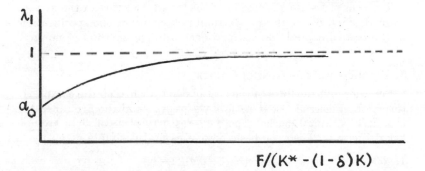

Figure 11.1

that we know that an increase in the importance of adjustment costs slows the rate of adjustment ($\partial \lambda_i / \partial b < 0$ if adjustment costs are bI^2), we would expect both α_1 and α_2 to have positive signs. The rather complex structure of this specification ensures that λ_1 is bounded above by unity and has the appropriate shape as a function of available funds. The function is illustrated in Figure 11.1 and, as can be seen, the speed of adjustment increases rapidly at low levels of availability with the rate of increase slowing down as funds become more plentiful.

Adjustment cost structures of this type have been tried by Greenberg (1964), Coen (1971) and Prior (1976), although none of the specifications used is particularly satisfactory. Greenberg uses the absolute level of profits rather than their level relative to desired expansion. Coen and Prior, on the other hand, use a linear specification that is clearly the wrong shape for the relationship which must obviously have an upper bound of unity.

As a final example of the use of the adjustment cost notion it is worth mentioning again the work of Chang and Holt (1973) who assume that there are quadratic costs involved in changing the level of investment orders. This type of cost is of a higher order than the others we have considered since it is a convex function of dI_0/dt rather than of I or I_0. The rationale for this is that too much variability in orders will impose great strains on the planning organization within the company and it is therefore desirable that they be smoothed. Chang and Holt work out an explicit equation based on this particular formulation.

This completes the discussion of the broad structure of the investment demand equation and we shall now consider the specification of the cost of capital and its relationship to the method of finance.

5. Finance and the Cost of Capital

Consider first the form of the cost of capital when all the complexities of the financial tax structure are ignored and the firm operates in a perfect capital market where interest payments on debt are not tax deductible. Then the basic cost of capital is simply given by

$$11.50 \qquad c(t) = \hat{q}(r + \delta - \dot{q}/q)/(1 - \tau_c)$$

from equation 9.3 putting $\bar{\theta}$ equal to zero. Remember that $\hat{q}$ is the effective cost of capital when all the depreciation allowances are taken into account and τ_c is the rate of tax on corporate profits. The first point to note is that this formula depends crucially on the assumption of exponential decay. For example we know from the chapter on replacement, equation 7.9, that, if capital goods are certain to disintegrate after T years of fully productive life, δ must be replaced by $r \exp(-rT)$ and, for general forms of mechanistic decay with constant prices, δ takes the form $\{1 - r \int_0^\infty \exp(-rt) \, \delta(t) dt\}/\int_0^\infty \exp(-rt)\delta(t)dt$ where $\delta(t)$ is the proportion of the capital good remaining in operation after t years of life (see Chapter 7, footnote 6). Second, the effective price of capital goods depends on both the current and the expected future structure of depreciation allowances, corporate tax levels and rates of discount. Most investment studies whose equation structure gives important weight to the cost of capital have been rather careful to take these matters into account, good examples being Coen (1971) and Hall and Jorgenson (1967).

Typically, however, most studies have ignored the capital gains term with the notable exception of Jorgenson and Stephenson (1967). Care must be taken with this particular term because it may lead to levels of desired capital stock which are rather high in a period of rapidly increasing prices solely because the firm wishes to *realize* capital gains after the price has finished rising. Such behaviour may be ruled out in the case of fixed capital and therefore the weight that is attached to the capital gains term may in fact be rather lower than is directly suggested by equation 11.50. This is not, however, to suggest that it be entirely ignored, for clearly in a period of rising (or falling) prices the firm will have an incentive to bring forward (or postpone) capital expenditures.

The really interesting term in the cost of capital is of course the rate of interest, r, and it is this term which causes the most problems and gives rise to the greatest controversy. We shall begin by discussing the standard Modigliani–Miller approach of which a good example is to be found in the previously mentioned work by Ando *et al.* Assume that the rate at which the market would discount the after-tax flow of earnings from the firm if it was unlevered is given by ρ and further that interest payments are now tax deductible. Suppose that the expected earnings from *existing* assets form a sequence $\hat{z}(K)$, $\hat{z}(K)(1+g)$, $\hat{z}(K)(1+g)^2, \ldots$, where g is the expected growth rate and K is the current capital stock. Then, if B is the existing stock of debt, it seems not unreasonable to suppose that this stock will grow in line with future earnings and that, in the firm's valuation, the future tax savings due to the tax deductibility of interest payments on debt will be discounted at ρ' which is some discount rate between ρ and the rate of interest on debt, r. The reason why ρ' is greater than r is that the future level of debt which can be supported by the earnings stream is uncertain because the growth rate is a random variable. However, the degree of uncertainty cannot be greater than that inherent in the earnings stream itself so ρ' cannot be greater than ρ.

So, if S is the stock of equity, the total value of the firm is given, in the Modigliani–Miller formulation, by the expression

$$11.51 \qquad VA = S + B = \sum_{t=1}^{\infty} \hat{z}(K) \frac{(1+g)^{t-1}}{(1+\rho)^t} (1 - \tau_c)$$

$$+ \tau_c r \sum_{t=1}^{\infty} \frac{B(1+g)^{t-1}}{(1+\rho')^t}$$

$$= \frac{\hat{z}(K)(1-\tau_c)}{\rho - g} + \frac{\tau_c r B}{\rho' - g},$$

where note that the term $\tau_c r B / (\rho' - g)$ is the present value of all future tax savings due to the tax deductibility of debt interest payments. If the firm purchases an increment of capital stock dK which it finances partly by new equity dS_n and partly by new bonds dB, where

$$11.52 \qquad\qquad dK = dS_n + dB,$$

then if S_0 is the value of the old equity we have, by differentiating 11.51,

$$\frac{dS_0}{dK} + \frac{dS_n}{dK} + \frac{dB}{dK} = \frac{1 - \tau_c}{\rho - g} \frac{d\hat{z}}{dK} + \frac{\tau_c r}{\rho' - g} \frac{dB}{dK}$$

or from 11.52

$$\frac{dS_0}{dK} = \frac{1 - \tau_c}{\rho - g} \frac{d\hat{z}}{dK} + \frac{\tau_c r}{\rho' - g} \frac{dB}{dK} - 1.$$

This can be expressed in summation form as

$$\frac{(\rho' - g)}{(\rho' - g - \tau_c r \, dB/dK)} \frac{dS_0}{dK} = \sum_{t=1}^{\infty} \frac{(d\hat{z}/dK)(1-\tau_c)(1+g)^{t-1}}{\left\{ 1 + \rho - \dfrac{(\rho - g)\tau_c r \, dB/dK}{(\rho' - g)} \right\}^t} - 1$$

The unit marginal investment yields a sequence of expected returns $(d\hat{z}/dK)(1-\tau_c)$, $(d\hat{z}/dK)(1-\tau_c)(1+g)$, ... If the expected present value of these future returns covers the cost of the investment when they are discounted at a rate

$$\rho - \frac{(\rho - g)\tau_c r \, dB/dK}{(\rho' - g)},$$

the above equation immediately reveals that this investment should be undertaken, for it increases the value of the original shares. So the cut-off discount rate for new capital purchases, which is the rate of interest term in the cost of capital,[17] is given by

$$\rho - \frac{(\rho - g)}{\rho' - g} \tau_c r \, dB/dK.$$

Assuming that dB/dK is equal to the long run 'optimal' proportion of debt finance, which is termed L, we have the effective rate of discount

$$\rho - \frac{(\rho-g)\tau_c rL}{\rho'-g}$$

or in a different form

11.53 $$\rho(1-\tau_c L) + \frac{\tau_c L}{\rho'-g}\{(\rho'-r)\rho-(\rho-r)g\}$$

If g is zero, then the future tax savings on debt are certain and $\rho'=r$. The discount rate then reduces to $\rho(1-\tau_c L)$, the standard Modigliani–Miller result on the cost of capital. Otherwise the cost of capital differs from $\rho(1-\tau_c L)$ by the final term of 11.53, which is almost certainly very small and can probably be safely ignored so long as the expected growth rate is not enormous.

The usual procedure is to estimate the unobservable ρ by using 11.51 and assuming that ρ' is either equal to r or to ρ. If $\rho'=r$ we have

$$\rho = g + \frac{\hat{z}(1-\tau_c)}{S+B\{1-\tau_c r/(r-g)\}}$$

and if $\rho'=\rho$ then

$$\rho = g + \frac{\hat{z}(1-\tau_c)+\tau_c rB}{S+B}.$$

If $\hat{\Pi}$ is the firm's expected net earnings excluding any growth factor then $\hat{z}(1-\tau_c) = \hat{\Pi} + (1-\tau_c)rB$ and thus ρ can be estimated either from 11.54(i)

$$\rho = \frac{S}{S+B\{1-\tau_c r/(r-g)\}}\left(\frac{\hat{\Pi}}{S}\right) + \frac{(1-\tau_c)Br}{S+B\{1-\tau_c r/(r-g)\}} + g$$

or from

11.54(ii) $$\rho = \left(\frac{S}{S+B}\right)\left(\frac{\hat{\Pi}}{S}\right) + \left(\frac{B}{S+B}\right)r + g.$$

These kinds of weighted average formulae are rather popular and Π is often approximated by current earnings (Jorgenson and Stephenson, 1967) or by current dividends divided by a target pay-out ratio (Bischoff, 1972). Explicit correction for growth is rather rare although it is done in the Canadian macro-model RDX2 (Helliwell *et al.*, 1971) and in Jorgenson and Siebert (1968b).

Unfortunately there are severe problems with this kind of simple formulation of the cost of capital and these may be revealed by simply extending the model to take account of more of the details of the corporate tax structure. Let $\bar{\rho}$ be the rate at which the *after-tax dividend* flow from an unlevered firm is discounted, let τ_p be the (uniform) personal tax rate and let θ be the opportunity cost of retained earnings in terms of forgone dividends. These latter two definitions are the same as in the previous chapters. Suppose, for simplicity that there is no capital gains tax. Then, if $\bar{r}$ is the rate of discount to be applied to a safe *after-tax* stream, the firm must pay a rate $r = \bar{r}/(1-\tau_p)$ on its (safe) debt. So, if there is zero expected growth and if R is the level of retentions in the current period, the firm valuation equation is given by

$$11.55 \quad VA = S + B = \frac{\hat{z}(1-\tau_c)\theta}{\bar{\rho}} - \frac{(1-\tau_c)Br\theta}{\bar{r}} - R\theta + \frac{Br(1-\tau_p)}{\bar{r}}$$

This equation looks a little forbidding but it is really quite simple to explain. The first term on the right-hand side is the present value of what would have been the dividend stream of the firm if it were unlevered, which is why it is discounted at $\bar{\rho}$. Each year a quantity $(1-\tau_c)Br$ is subtracted to pay the interest on the debt and this is discounted at the safe rate. Also, in the first year R is removed from current earnings to finance investment. Finally, the last term is the present value of the debt which, of course, reduces to B since $r = \bar{r}/1-\tau_p$. Making this substitution throughout then gives

$$11.56 \quad VA = S + B = \frac{\hat{z}(1-\tau_c)\theta}{\bar{\rho}} - \frac{(1-\tau_c)\theta B}{(1-\tau_p)} - R\theta + B.$$

Again if we add a marginal unit of capital, dK, where now

$$11.57 \qquad dK = dS_n + dB + dR$$

since we explicitly allow retentions, differentiating with respect to K and using 11.57 gives

$$\frac{\bar{\rho}}{\theta}\frac{dS_0}{dK} = \frac{d\hat{z}(1-\tau_c)}{dK} - \frac{\bar{\rho}}{\theta}\left[1 - \frac{dB}{dK}\left\{1 - \frac{(1-\tau_c)\theta}{(1-\tau_p)}\right\} - \frac{dR}{dK}(1-\theta)\right]$$

where the last term on the right is now the interest element of the cost of capital. This may be written as

$$11.58 \qquad \frac{\bar{\rho}}{\theta}(1-L-\lambda) + \bar{\rho}\frac{(1-\tau_c)L}{(1-\tau_p)} + \bar{\rho}\lambda$$

where $L = dB/dK$ and $\lambda = dR/dK$, the proportions of the marginal investment unit financed by debt and retentions respectively. This is very much what our analysis of the last chapter would lead us to expect. The cost of debt is $\bar{\rho} (1-\tau_c)/(1-\tau_p)$, the cost of retentions is $\bar{\rho}$ and the cost of equity is $\bar{\rho}/\theta$. In the standard Modigliani–Miller formulation it is argued that L may be taken as the exogenous 'optimal' proportion of debt. But when we extend the Modigliani–Miller formulation to take proper account of the personal and corporate tax structure we see that there is another parameter to be included, namely λ. And with this parameter there seems no possibility of arguing that it should take on some exogenous optimal value. Clearly, since θ is typically less than unity, it would be desirable for the firm to make $\lambda = 1 - L$. But this may not be possible because the requisite quantity of retained earnings may just not be available. So, even starting from Modigliani–Miller assumptions, the tax system ensures that the quantity of current earnings is going to be important and that the cost of capital which actually operates in any period cannot be taken as given independent of the level of investment. Thus we are confronted with a serious, and as yet unsolved problem, which is compounded if we suppose, as the analysis of Chapter 8 indicates, that the existence of bankruptcy effectively negates the Modigliani–Miller theorem.

There is a possible way out of this difficulty for, in the specification of our investment equation, the cost of capital is used to determine the 'desired' capital stock, that is to say, that capital stock which the firm would eventually achieve in a world of constant demand and factor prices. It seems reasonable to presume that the firm will, in the long run, have enough retentions to finance the purchase of this entire capital stock and also to reduce the level of debt to the point where it is operating at the minimum point of the U-shaped relationship between the cost of capital and the debt–equity ratio. So the most sensible strategy would seem to be the following.[18] In order to formulate a cost of capital for use in the computation of the 'desired' capital stock, first specify $\bar{\rho}$ using 11.56 which gives

$$\bar{\rho} = \frac{\hat{z}(1-\tau_c)}{S/\theta + B(1-\tau_c)/(1-\tau_p) + R}$$

Then use the same kind of method as illustrated in 11.54(i) or (ii) to estimate $\bar{\rho}$, being careful not to omit the growth correction which we have omitted in this last exposition for the sake of simplicity.[19] Finally using this estimate of $\bar{\rho}$, which takes account of the level of both the risk premium and the safe rate of interest,[20] assume a specification of the form

11.59 $$\left[1 - \beta_1 \left\{1 - \frac{(1-\tau_c)}{(1-\tau_p)}\theta\right\} - \beta_2(1-\theta)\right]\frac{\bar{\rho}}{\theta}$$

as the interest rate term in the cost of capital where β_1 and β_2 are to be estimated. Following on from the previous discussion, if it is true that in order to specify a long-run cost of capital we should assume that the firm can always generate the requisite quantity of internal funds,[21] then we should expect β_1 and β_2 to sum to unity.

This type of specification then allows us to incorporate short run flow of funds effects, due to the cost of capital rising at the investment margin, in the speed of adjustment mechanism which we described in the previous section (equation 11.49). This seems a very natural method of capturing the effects of various aspects of financial policy, for it is clear that there are no sound theoretical reasons for believing that the availability of internal funds is going to have any effect on the final equilibrium capital stock of a firm facing a static environment.

This formulation is, of course, one of massive complexity and probably has too many free variables to be estimated. On the other hand, it does take into account all the exogenous influences on the cost of capital schedule which were discussed in the final section of Chapter 9 (except that it ignores capital gains taxation) and furthermore it incorporates the fact that the schedule is upward sloping. Turning now to the formulations that have actually been used, Greenberg (1964), Coen (1971) and Prior (1976) are the only ones to incorporate explicitly the flow of funds as an adjustment cost variable. Feldstein and Flemming (1971) have used this variable in the desired capital stock but other studies which make use of variables of this type have simply added it into the equation as a separate regressor. The problems with this are twofold. First, it will signally fail to capture the notion that internal funds are only significant in relation to desired expansion. If the firm does not wish to expand because of a poor demand outlook, for example, the availability of internal funds can hardly be relevant to its investment decision. Simple inclusion of a flow of funds variable will thus produce a rather patchy showing which will be exacerbated by the second problem, that of the well-known collinearity of such variables with those of the accelerator type. This is a problem which the adjustment cost formulation appears to avoid.[22]

Looking now at the use of alternative financial variables, Lintner (1967) uses the difference between retained earnings and long-term debt as a proportion of total value, in order to capture the fact that retentions can also be used to retire debt.[23] They are more likely to be so used if initial debt is a high proportion of total value because such debt will then be very expensive at the margin, implying a higher opportunity cost of real investment. Other studies such as Anderson (1964) and Resek (1966) have used both the cash flow and the debt–asset ratio as separate variables and Anderson also investigates the effect of short-term liquidity. A very interesting approach to the whole problem of finance is that of Dhrymes and Kurz (1967) who, instead of trying to restrict the specification of the investment demand equation to exogenous variables, explicitly recognize the simultaneity of the finance and investment decisions by specifying three simultaneous equations explaining dividends, investment and external finance. The separation of investment and external finance into different equations is a first step on the road to a simultaneous equation treatment of the problems arising from the endogeneity of the proportions of debt and retention finance in the cost of capital expression 11.58. Clearly this is ultimately the direction in which empirical studies of the investment decision must go.

6. Depreciation and Replacement

If we return now to our original specification of an orders equation with a fixed lag m, namely

11.60

$$I_0 = \bar{K}(t, t+m) - K(t, t+m-1) + S(t, t+m-1) + D(t, t+m-1)$$

we see that it is necessary to specify both the expected quantity of capital which will be scrapped, S, and the expected quantity of capital which will evaporate, D. As we have seen, by far the simplest specification is to assume that $S + D$ may be entirely represented by exponential evaporation at a constant rate δ. In this case the equation reduces to

11.61 $$I_0(t) = \bar{K}(t, t+m) - (1 - \delta)K(t+m-1)$$

where $K(t+m-1)$ is known at time t. Alternatively, some other form of mechanistic decay may be incorporated and, in its most general form, $S + D$ can be replaced by the expression

$$\sum_{\nu=0}^{\infty} \{\delta(\nu) - \delta(\nu+1)\} I(t+m-\nu-1)$$

where $\delta(\nu)$ is the proportion of new capital goods which remain operational after ν periods. This may then be transformed into investment orders giving an equation of the form

$$I_0(t) = \bar{K}(t, t+m) - k(t, t+m-1) + \sum_{\nu=0}^{\infty} \{\delta(\nu) - \delta(\nu+1)\} I_0(t-\nu-1)$$

where the cost of capital used to compute $\bar{K}$ must be suitably adjusted to be compatible with the assumed form of mechanistic decay. Furthermore, if the measured capital stock is a necessary part of $\bar{K}$ and if it is computed by the declining balance method, using a series for gross investment plus some benchmark capital stock, then it should be generated using the same mechanistic decay assumption as that incorporated into the rest of the model.

In Chapter 7 on replacement our analysis indicated that the assumption of mechanistic evaporation was somewhat unappealing and that it was much more natural to suppose that scrapping and the rate of evaporation were both economically rather than mechanistically determined. This would not necessarily rule out even the exponential decay specification for an actual investment equation, for one might argue that the firm will *predict* its replacement needs as some proportion of its capital stock in each period. When the period actually arrives it will adjust its actual level of scrapping and evaporation (via changes in maintenance expenditure) in the light of the differences between its actual and predicted needs for capital stock. The crucial point is that scrapping and evaporation decisions enable the firm to adjust instantaneously its current capital stock to current circumstances. So the simple observation that scrapping and evaporation are economic decisions which do not fit into the exponential decay pattern does not necessarily rule out the specification of investment equations including an exponential decay term. Thus, for example, one could have

$$S(t, t+m-1) + D(t, t+m-1) = \delta K(t, t+m-1),$$

that is to say, expected scrapping plus expected decay is equal to $1 - \delta$ times expected capital stock. It is no longer possible to know the capital stock at time $t+m-1$ precisely because the actual rates of scrapping and evaporation in the intervening periods cannot be known. Consequently, this assumption does not lead to the same equation specification as true mechanical exponential decay and in this case 11.60 becomes

11.62 $I_0(t) = \bar{K}(t, t+m) - (1-\delta)K(t, t+m-1).$

There are two natural possibilities for specifying $K(t, t+m-1)$. The first is simply to replace it by $\bar{K}(t-1, t+m-1)$. In a period by period model this would be quite simple but in a dynamic model, even of the simple type, $\bar{K}$ itself is a function of the actual capital stock (see equation 11.42) and this involves continual backward substitution until $I_0(t)$ is expressed entirely in terms of desired capital stocks and current actual capital stock. The other alternative is to suppose that the firm predicts that exponential decay will hold all the way up to $t+m-1$ and we have,

$$K(t, t+m-1) = K(t-1)(1-\delta)^m + \sum_{i=1}^{m} (1-\delta)^{i-1} I_0(t-i)$$

$$= K(t-1)(1-\delta)^m + \sum_{i=1}^{m} (1-\delta)^{i-1} I(t+m-i).$$

The expenditures equation would then be specified as

$$I(t) = \bar{K}(t-m, t) - (1-\delta) \left\{ K(t-m-1)(1-\delta)^m + \sum_{i=1}^{m} (1-\delta)^{i-1} I(t-i) \right\}$$

where the term in parentheses will be different from, and cannot be replaced by, $K(t-1)$.[24]

This kind of strategy is a bit feeble because, if the firm knows that scrapping and evaporation are economic decisions, the least one might expect is that it will try to predict what sort of economic decisions it is going to make. From section 4 of Chapter 7 we know that the rate of scrapping is likely to decrease during booms in demand but is likely to increase during capital expansions caused by a fall in costs, at least in the presence of adjustment costs. A possible measure of the expectations of such events would be some weighted average of expected demand and cost changes. For example, one might specify the size of the expected change in demand $\Delta\beta(t, t+m)$ and the size of the expected change in capital costs $\Delta c(t, t+m)$ as follows

$$\Delta\beta(t, t+m) = \sum_{i=-k}^{k} \gamma_i\{\beta(t, t+m+i) - \beta(t, t+m+i-1)\}$$

$$\Delta c(t, t+m) = \sum_{i=-l}^{l} \omega_i\{c(t, t+m+i) - c(t, t+m+i-1)\}$$

where $\sum\gamma_i = \sum\omega_i = 1$. The simplest possible formulation would be to put $k=l=0$. Then instead of having the simple exponential formulation, one would define $S + D$ as

$$S(t, t+m-1) + D(t, t+m-1)$$
$$= \delta\{\Delta\beta(t, t+m-1), \Delta c(t, t+m-1)\}K(t, t+m-1)$$

where $\partial\delta/\partial\Delta\beta < 0$ and $\partial\delta/\partial\Delta c > 0$. An even more sophisticated possibility would be to try to pick up echo effects by including a third argument in the function δ which would be the quantity of investment in period $t+m-T$ as a proportion of the expected capital stock at $t+m-1$ where T is the known average life of capital, or, perhaps even better, to have some average of the form $\sum_{i=-j}^{j} \xi_i I(t+m-T+i)/K(t, t+m-i)$ with $\sum \xi_i = 1$. δ would, of course, be increasing in this variable and if δ were linear this would simply mean the inclusion of the investment around time $t+m-T$ as an additional explanatory variable.

As far as actual investment studies are concerned, many have assumed exponential decay, though Bischoff (1971b) for example, uses an equation of the type 11.62 whereas Jorgenson uses the type 11.61. Coen (1975) on the other hand has had some considerable success in testing many different forms of mechanistic decay using the type of methodology which we described at the beginning of this section. Studies which do not assume mechanistic decay tend to ignore scrapping and evaporation completely, simply supposing that the determinants of net investment are the same as the determinants of gross investment. For example, Eisner (1972) has two separate equations for expansion investment and replacement investment with precisely the same variables in both. He does, however, include a variable representing the total depreciation reserves as some kind of proxy for the age structure of the capital stock. One notable exception to this trend, however, is contained in a paper by Bitros (1975) on the demand for locomotives, where the investment demand function specifically includes scrapping rates and maintenance expenditures, both of which are treated as endogenous.

This concludes the analysis of the specification of investment demand functions and now it simply remains to discuss what we actually know about investment decisions. This will be the subject of the last chapter.

Appendix

Proposition 1 (p. 251). If, in standard notation, $k(t)$ is defined by $f'(k(t)/[f\{k(t)\} - k(t)f'\{k(t)\}]) = q(t)/\bar{w}(t))$ and if the function ϕ is defined by $\phi\{q(t), \bar{w}(t)\} = q(t)/f'\{k(t)\}$, then $\phi_q > 0$ and $\phi_{\bar{w}} > 0$.

Proof. Straightforward differentiation reveals that

$$\frac{\partial k}{\partial q}=\frac{(f-kf')^2}{\bar{w}ff''} \text{ and } \frac{\partial k}{\partial \bar{w}}=\frac{-q}{\bar{w}^2}\frac{(f-kf')^2}{ff''}.$$

Then

$$\frac{\partial \phi}{\partial q}=\frac{f'-qf''\partial k/\partial q}{f'^2}=k/f>0,$$

$$\frac{\partial \phi}{\partial w}=\frac{-q}{f'^2}f''\frac{\partial k}{\partial \bar{w}}=\frac{q^2}{\bar{w}^2}\frac{(f-kf')^2}{ff'^2}>0.$$

Proposition 2 (p. 253). Suppose $k(t)$ and ϕ are defined as in proposition 1 and $\bar{V}(t)$ and $\bar{Q}(t)$ are defined as,

$\bar{V}(t)=k(t)/f\{k(t)\}$

$\bar{Q}(t)=\beta(t)\psi[\phi\{q(t),\bar{w}(t)\}(1+r)-\phi\{q(t+1),\bar{w}(t+1)\}(1-\delta)]$

where $\psi=z\{M^{-1}(.)\}$, z being the demand function and M the marginal revenue function. Then, if $f\{k(t)\}=k^\alpha$ and $z\{p(t)\}=Ap(t)^{-\epsilon}$, $\epsilon>1$, we have

$$\bar{V}(t)=\left\{\frac{\alpha}{1-\alpha}\frac{\bar{w}(t)}{q(t)}\right\}^{1-\alpha}$$

$$\bar{Q}(t)=\beta(t)B\left(\frac{[q(t)^\alpha\bar{w}(t)^{1-\alpha}\{1+r(t)\}-q(t+1)^\alpha\bar{w}(t+1)^{1-\alpha}(1-\delta)]\epsilon}{(\epsilon-1)}\right)^{-\epsilon}.$$

Also if there is a constant rate of wage inflation i_w, $\bar{w}(t)$ satisfies

$$\bar{w}(t)\simeq\frac{w(t)}{(r+\delta-i_w)}.$$

Proof. If $f=k^\alpha$, then $f'/(f-kf')=\alpha/(1-\alpha)k$. Hence $k=\bar{w}\alpha/q(1-\alpha)$.
Thus

$$V=k/f=k^{1-\alpha}=\{\bar{w}\alpha/q(1-\alpha)\}^{1-\alpha}$$

$$\phi=q/f'=qk^{1-\alpha}/\alpha=\frac{q}{\alpha}(\bar{w}\alpha)^{1-\alpha}\{q(1-\alpha)\}^{\alpha-1}$$

$$=B_1q^\alpha\bar{w}^{1-\alpha}$$

where B_1 is a constant.
Since $z=Ap^{-\epsilon}$, $M^{-1}=1/(1-1/\epsilon)=\epsilon/(\epsilon-1)$.

Thus

$$Q = \beta(t)B \left[\frac{\{q(t)^\alpha \bar{w}(t)^{1-\alpha}(1+r) - q(t+1)^\alpha \bar{w}(t+1)^{1-\alpha}(1-\delta)\}\epsilon}{1-\epsilon} \right]^{-\epsilon}.$$

By definition

$$\bar{w}(t) = \sum_{s=t}^\infty w(s) \frac{(1-\delta)^{s-t}}{(1+r)^{s-t+1}}.$$

If there is a constant rate of wage inflation i_w, then $w(s) = w(t) \times (1+i_w)^{s-t}$.

So

$$\bar{w}(t) = \sum_{s=t}^\infty w(t) \frac{\{(1+i_w)(1-\delta)\}^{s-t}}{(1+r)^{s-t+1}}$$

$$= \frac{w(t)}{r+\delta-i_w+i_w\delta}$$

$$\simeq \frac{w(t)}{r+\delta-i_w}$$

if both δ and i_w are small.

Proposition 3 (p. 259). If, in standard notation, the optimal level of capital stock satisfies the necessary condition

$$2b(1-\delta)K(s+1) - 2b\{(1-\delta)^2 + (1+r)\}K(s) + G\{K(s),\, \beta(s),\, w(s)\}$$

$$+ 2b(1+r)(1-\delta)K(s-1) = c(s) \qquad \text{for all } s,$$

and the 'desired' capital stock at time s is defined by

$$G\{K^*(s),\, \beta(s),\, w(s)\} = c(s) + 2b(r+\delta)\delta K^*(s)$$

where $K^*(s) \leqslant \hat{K}$ for all s, then the optimal investment at any time t is given approximately by

$$I(t) = \lambda_1 \left[K^*(t) + \frac{\lambda_1+r}{1+r} \sum_{s=t+1}^\infty \left(\frac{1-\lambda_1}{1+r} \right)^{s-t} \{K^*(s) - K^*(t)\} - K(t-1) \right]$$

$$+ \delta K(t-1)$$

where $0 < \lambda_1 < 1$ and $\partial \lambda_1/\partial b < 0$.

Proof. Substitute for $c(s)$ in the difference equation using the definitions of $K^*(s)$. This gives

$$2b(1-\delta)K(s+1) - 2b\{(1-\delta)^2 + (1-r)\}K(s) + G\{K(s), \beta(s), w(s)\}$$
$$+ 2b(1+r)(1-\delta)K(s-1)$$
$$= G\{K^*(s), \beta(s), w(s)\} - 2b(r+\delta)\delta K^*(s), \text{ all } s.$$

Define $\bar{K}^*$, $\bar{\beta}$, $\bar{w}$ as the average values of $K^*(s)$, $\beta(s)$, $w(s)$ and expand G about this point. Thus

$$G\{K(s), \beta(s), w(s)\} \simeq G(\bar{K}^*, \bar{\beta}, \bar{w}) + G_K(\bar{K}^*, \bar{\beta}, \bar{w})\{K(s) - \bar{K}^*\}$$
$$+ G_\beta(\bar{K}^*, \bar{\beta}, \bar{w})\{\beta(s) - \bar{\beta}\}$$
$$+ G_w(\bar{K}^*, \bar{\beta}, \bar{w})\{w(s) - \bar{w}\}$$

and

$$G\{K^*(s), \beta(s), w(s)\} \simeq G(\bar{K}^*, \bar{\beta}, \bar{w}) + G_K(\bar{K}^*, \bar{\beta}, \bar{w})\{K^*(s) - \bar{K}^*\}$$
$$+ G_\beta(\bar{K}^*, \bar{\beta}, \bar{w})\{\beta(s) - \bar{\beta}\}$$
$$+ G_w(\bar{K}^*, \bar{\beta}, \bar{w})\{w(s) - \bar{w}\}.$$

Substituting this into the difference equation gives

$$2b(1-\delta)K(s+1) - [2b\{(1-\delta)^2 + (1+r)\} - G_K(\bar{K}^*, \bar{\beta}, \bar{w})]K(s)$$
$$+ 2b(1+r)(1-\delta)K(s-1)$$
$$\simeq \{G_K(\bar{K}^*, \bar{\beta}, \bar{w}) - 2b(r+\delta)\delta\}K^*(s)$$

or in more compact notation

$$a_1 K(s+1) + a_2 K(s) + a_3 K(s-1) = (a_1 + a_2 + a_3)K^*(s),$$

where $a_1 = 2b(1-\delta) > 0$, $a_2 = -2b\{(1-\delta)^2 + (1+r)\} + G_K(\bar{K}^*, \bar{\beta}, \bar{w}) < 0$, $a_3 = 2b(1+r)(1-\delta) > 0$, where note that $G_K < 0$.

Writing the difference equation using the lag operator L and the lead operator L^{-1} gives

$$(a_1 L^{-1} + a_2 + a_3 L)K(s) \simeq (a_1 + a_2 + a_3)\bar{K}^*(s).$$

Now factorize the lag polynomial as

$$\alpha_1(1 - \alpha_2 \lambda L^{-1})(1 - \lambda L)$$

where, by comparing coefficients, we have

$$\alpha_1(1 + \alpha_2 \lambda^2) = a_2, \ \alpha_1 \alpha_2 \lambda = -a_1, \ \alpha_1 \lambda = -a_3,$$

which implies that λ must be a root of the quadratic

$$a_1 \lambda^2 + a_2 \lambda + a_3 = 0.$$

Since

$$a_2{}^2 - 4a_1a_3 = \{(1-\delta)^2 - (1+r)\}^2 4b^2 + G_K{}^2 - 4b\{(1-\delta)^2 + (1+r)\}G_K$$
$$= [2b\{(1-\delta)^2 - (1+r)\} - G_K]^2 - 8b(1+r)G_K > 0,$$

the roots are real. Since both the product and the sum of the roots are positive, both roots are positive. Finally, since $a_1 + a_2 + a_3 < 0$, the quadratic expression is negative when $\lambda = 1$, but is positive for $\lambda = 0$ and λ large ($a_1 > 0$, $a_3 > 0$), and consequently the two roots must lie on either side of unity. Let μ_1 be the root such that $0 < \mu_1 < 1$. Then we may write the difference equation as

$$\alpha_1(1 - \alpha_2\mu_1 L^{-1})(1 - \mu_1 L)K(s) \simeq (a_1 + a_2 + a_3)K^*(s).$$

and since μ_1 is the stable root we can invert to give

$$(1 - \mu_1 L)K(s) \simeq \frac{(a_1 + a_2 + a_3)K^*(s)}{\alpha_1(1 - \alpha_2\mu_1 L^{-1})}.$$

Clearly this will yield the appropriate optimal path because the other root will yield a path which is unbounded. So if we start from some time t with $K(t-1)$ given, then the optimal $K(t)$ will satisfy

$$(1 - \mu_1 L)K(t) \simeq \frac{(a_1 + a_2 + a_3)K^*(t)}{\alpha_1(1 - \alpha_2\mu_1 L^{-1})}$$

or

$$K(t) - \mu_1 K(t-1) \simeq \frac{a_1 + a_2 + a_3}{\alpha_1} \sum_{s=t}^{\infty} (\alpha_2\mu_1)^{s-t} L^{-(s-t)}K^*(t)$$

where note that

$$\alpha_2\mu_1 = \frac{a_1}{a_3}\mu_1 = \frac{\mu_1}{1+r} < 1$$

from the definition of α_1, α_2.

Furthermore

$$\frac{a_1 + a_2 + a_3}{\alpha_1} = \frac{a_1 + a_2 + a_3}{\alpha_1(1 - \mu_1\alpha_2)(1 - \mu_1)}(1 - \mu_1\alpha_2)(1 - \mu_1)$$

$$= \frac{(a_1 + a_2 + a_3)(1 - \mu_1\alpha_2)(1 - \mu_1)}{\alpha_1(1 + \alpha_2\mu_1{}^2) - \alpha_1\alpha_2\mu_1 - \alpha_1\mu_1}$$

$$= \frac{(a_1 + a_2 + a_3)(1 - \mu_1/1+r)(1 - \mu_1)}{(a_1 + a_2 + a_3)} \qquad \text{by definition}$$

$$= \left(1 - \frac{\mu_1}{(1+r)}\right)(1 - \mu_1).$$

Consequently

$$K(t) \simeq (1-\mu_1)\left(1-\frac{\mu_1}{1+r}\right)\sum_{s=t}^{\infty}\left(\frac{\mu_1}{1+r}\right)^{s-t}K^*(s)+\mu_1 K(t-1)$$

and hence

$$I(t)=K(t)-(1-\delta)K(t-1)$$

$$\simeq (1-\mu_1)\left\{\left(1-\frac{\mu_1}{1+r}\right)\sum_{s=t}^{\infty}\left(\frac{\mu_1}{1+r}\right)^{s-t}K^*(s)-K(t-1)\right\}+\delta K(t-1).$$

Letting $\lambda_1 = 1-\mu_1$ and noting that

$$\left(1-\frac{\mu_1}{1+r}\right)\sum_{s=t}^{\infty}\left(\frac{\mu_1}{1+r}\right)^{s-t}=1,$$

enables us to rewrite the expression as

$$I(t)=\lambda_1\left[K^*(t)+\left(\frac{\lambda_1+r}{1+r}\right)\sum_{s=t+1}^{\infty}\left(\frac{1-\lambda_1}{1+r}\right)^{s-t}\right.$$

$$\left. \times\{K^*(s)-K^*(t)\}-K(t-1)\right]+\delta K(t-1)$$

where $0<\lambda_1<1$.

Finally, suppose that the parameter b is increased from b_1 to b_2. If the two roots corresponding to b_i are $\mu_1{}^i$, $\mu_2{}^i$ respectively, then from the definitions of a_1, a_2, a_3 we have

$$\frac{a_3{}^i}{a_1{}^i}=1+r=\mu_1{}^1\mu_2{}^1=\mu_1{}^2\mu_2{}^2$$

and

$$\mu_1{}^1+\mu_2{}^1=(2b_1\{(1-\delta)^2+(1+r)\}-G_K)/2b_1(1-\delta)$$

$$>(2b_2\{(1-\delta)^2+(1+r)\}-G_K)/2b_2(1-\delta)$$

$$=\mu_1{}^2+\mu_2{}^2.$$

So let $\mu_1{}^2=k\mu_1{}^1$, $\mu_2{}^2=(1/k)\mu_2{}^1$.

Then, from above

$$k\mu_1{}^1+(1/k)\mu_2{}^1<\mu_1{}^1+\mu_2{}^1,$$

i.e.

$$(k-1)\{\mu_1{}^1-(1/k)\mu_2{}^1\}<0.$$

If $k\leqslant 1$, $(1/k)\mu_2{}^1\geqslant\mu_2{}^1>\mu_1{}^1$ and the left-hand side of the inequality is positive. Hence $k>1$ and this implies that $\mu_1{}^2>\mu_1{}^1$. Hence $\partial\mu_1/\partial b>0$ and thus $\partial\lambda_1/\partial b<0$.

Footnotes

[1] There may not be any great merit in deriving explicit expressions for investment demand when dealing with very aggregate data but in this chapter the investment demand equations are constructed with micro-data in mind.

[2] An interesting example of the use of this technique in just this sort of problem is to be found in Almon (1968). Of course, things can be made even more complicated if one assumes that delivery delays can be reduced by making additional payments or that orders can be cancelled at some extra cost. How such factors could be incorporated into a distributed lag structure is not at all clear.

[3] For example, Jorgenson (1965), Jorgenson and Siebert (1968b), Jorgenson and Stephenson (1967), and Hall and Jorgenson (1967).

[4] In fact Jorgenson assumes that corresponding to a particular level of 'starts' of investment projects is some distribution of future 'completions'. In his models, 'starts' are not the same thing as orders. However, the subsequent analysis holds equally well for 'starts' as for orders and the latter is used simply for convenience.

[5] It is, of course, possible for the firm to order capital goods of type 1 such that $K^1(t) \neq \alpha K^2(t)$ in some periods although this has been implicitly ruled out in the text. This may well be desirable if the total capital stock which the firm expects to require is declining over time, for then it may be worth the firm having some excess of type 2 capital since it has been ordered earlier than type 1. It is clear, however, that if we allow this type of behaviour, the resulting investment equation will certainly not take the form of a simple fixed distributed lag.

[6] For an interesting attack on this problem see Helliwell and Glorieux (1970).

[7] The fixity of the delivery lag is unrealistic but when one is estimating orders equations for a homogeneous good, variability of the lag is no problem if one has separate estimates of it.

[8] The period by period model is sometimes referred to as pseudo-static because the delivery lag is the only dynamic element and this has no effect on the basic structure of the investment demand equation.

[9] Not all the studies mentioned in this section in fact use the pseudo-static model. We are commenting only on their specification of 'desired' capital stock.

[10] Note that, because of the timing of events, the first wage costs on a new unit of capital are incurred one year after it is purchased. On the other hand, it does not decay until *after* it has produced its first output. Hence the additional factor $1/1 + r$ in this expression.

[11] The reason why they *have* to use this structure is because they have a spread of delivery times. Under these circumstances it is not possible for the firm to know with certainty the future levels of capital stock.

[12] It is never made very explicit in the Bischoff model what sort of conditions the firm faces in the product market. The strongest clue is provided by his assumption of a cost plus pricing system for output which seems to imply an imperfectly competitive world. On the other hand no mention is made of the firm facing exogenously varying demand conditions.

[13] Of course, the strict convexity of adjustment costs ensures that the firm will *never* achieve it!

[14] Note that equation 11.45 differs from the equation derived from a purely static model because of the inclusion of *gross* investment adjustment costs. Such costs are incurred even in static equilibrium because of replacement, thus leading to an additional term in the standard static formulation which would obviously be absent if there were only net investment adjustment costs. Treadway (1970) discussed this point at some length.

[15] One might, of course, use a different specification of 'desired' capital stock depending on what sort of model one has in mind.

[16] It is often argued that firms base their ordering decisions on the current financial position of the firm rather than the expected future financial position when the orders have to be paid for. For example, in our description of the investment process in section 1, we supposed, following Lund (1971), that finance was 'arranged' when investment was planned. If this is in fact the case then the future expectations in 11.49 can simply be replaced by current values.

[17] Note that this formulation explicitly excludes depreciation and capital gains, so in order that this term can be added to the standard formula for the cost of capital, capital gains on capital goods must be excluded from the future returns sequence $\hat{z}(1+g)^i$.

[18] This is for a single equation approach. An even more sensible strategy might be to explain investment and the elements of financing simultaneously.

[19] Such growth corrections are very difficult to estimate properly since they are probably rather volatile. The usual method is to take some current and past average of earnings growth rates.

[20] This specification of $\bar{p}$ will be almost bound to underestimate the true *marginal* cost of capital because it uses the average cost of debt finance which may be far below the marginal cost. Obviously, however, we could not use the true marginal cost because it is not exogenous.

[21] Or, putting it another way, if we should view the 'desired' capital stock as that which the firm would like to possess in steady state if it could generate the necessary internal funds.

[22] See Coen (1971, p. 171, footnote 31).

[23] The use of retentions instead of earnings may be criticized because retentions and dividends are the two elements of earnings and the split between the two may be influenced by investment opportunities. However, Lintner would argue that, empirically, it is possible to explain dividends as a function of earnings and past dividends quite independently of investment (see Lintner, 1956).

[24] In fact, for many studies, this would come down to the same thing as specifying replacement as $(1-\delta)K(t-1)$ since the measured capital stock is often defined by assuming some rate of depreciation and then using gross investment, plus a measure of capital stock for *one* year, to compute the rest of the capital stock data recursively.

Bibliographical Notes—Chapter 11

Some general surveys of the specification of investment demand equations may be found in Evans (1969), Jorgenson (1971), Lund (1971), Junankar (1972), Helliwell (1972), Klein (1974), Eisner (1974) and Rowley and Trivedi (1975). As far as particular topics are concerned, the question of lag structures is considered in some detail in Griliches (1967), Lund (1971), Nerlove (1972) and Rowley and Trivedi (1975). The problem of the specification of desired capital stock, particularly with reference to the use of endogenous variables, is treated in a succession of papers of which a few of the more interesting are Mundlak (1966, 1967), Gould (1969), Coen (1969) and Jorgenson (1972).

For general information we now list a selection of applied papers which use particular types of equation structure.

1. Some studies that use a desired capital stock formulation: Jorgenson (1965), Coen and Hickman (1970), Coen (1971), Feldstein and Flemming (1971), Gould and Waud (1973), Chang and Holt (1973).
2. Some studies which do not use the desired capital stock formulation: de Leeuw (1962), Eckstein (1965), Eisner (1967), Klein and Taubman (1971).

3. Some studies which *explicitly* use an adjustment cost formulation: Nadiri and Rosen (1969), Schramm (1970), Coen (1971), Chang and Holt (1973), Brechling (1975), Nadiri (1972).
4. Some studies which *explicitly* utilize a putty-clay formulation: Bischoff (1971b), Hausman (1972), Ando *et al.* (1974).
5. Some studies which specify an explicit expectations formation mechanism either for output sales or prices: Helliwell and Glorieux (1970), Ando *et al.* (1974), Craine (1975), Birch and Siebert (1976).
6. Some studies which explicitly use Modigliani–Miller theory in formulating the cost of capital: Jorgenson and Stephenson (1967), Jorgenson and Siebert (1968b), Bischoff (1971b), Ando *et al.* (1974).
7. Some studies which explicitly include flow of funds and related financial variables: Anderson (1964), Resek (1966), Lintner (1967), Schramm (1970), Feldstein and Flemming (1971), Coen (1971), Prior (1976).
8. Some studies which explicitly assume exponential decay: Jorgenson (1965), Coen (1971), Bischoff (1971), Feldstein and Flemming (1971), Hausman (1972), (This last paper, however, assumes only a finite lifetime.)
9. Some studies which assume a non-mechanistic form of decay: Eisner (1967), Evans (1967).
10. A study which assumes non-exponential mechanistic decay: Coen (1975).

CHAPTER 12

SOME EMPIRICAL EVIDENCE

1. The Effects of Demand in the Long Run

In this final chapter we shall consider some of the evidence on the investment behaviour of firms which emerges from the enormous number of econometric and other studies in this field. Our choice of results is, of necessity, somewhat selective, although it is fairly representative, and concentrates on more recent investigations to avoid too much overlap with existing surveys such as those appearing in Eisner and Strotz (1963), Lund (1971) or Jorgenson (1971).

We shall more or less ignore the purely statistical problems which arise in connection with most investment studies and generally accept them at face value, although we shall comment from time to time on the degree of faith one can have in the results. This whole subject is, of course, one of vital importance and it is fair to say that the attention which is paid to such matters as the dynamic and stochastic specification of investment equations and the sequential testing of properly specified hypothesis is, in the majority of studies, rather limited, to say the least. However, any worthwhile investigation of these matters would be necessarily somewhat lengthy and so such considerations will generally be omitted.[1]

The theoretical analysis of the firm's decision to invest in fixed capital reveals that perhaps the single most crucial influence on this decision is the current or expected future level of demand for the firm's output and its relationship to existing capacity. This is borne out by the company planners consulted in a study of sixty-nine UK companies described in Rockley (1973), for as Rockley himself says:

> The writer sought to elucidate information about those factors which had been of importance to company planners when they had formulated past investment programmes. The existence or expectation of a continuing demand for a firm's products and the need to replace worn-out equipment were most frequently cited to be principal determinants of corporate capital spending.[2]

283

The importance of demand for the firm's output is thus agreed upon by economic theorists and businessmen alike but unfortunately it is a variable whose effect is rather difficult to quantify. We saw in the previous chapter that the variable which correctly isolates the effect of demand is an index which measures the position of the demand curve, and this is more or less unobservable. Variables such as output or sales may not be particularly good measures of this index because they are constrained by existing capacity limitations and may be varied by the firm almost at will by changing the output price, even when the level of 'demand' remains fixed. The question then arises as to which variables provide the best proxies for this demand index and what influence they have on the capital stock utilized by the firm in the long run. Short-run effects will be discussed in a later section.

Demand proxies fall into two major groups, namely direct proxies such as sales, output, output corrected for unintended inventory changes, gross national product and orders, and indirect proxies such as profits or cash flow. It has been argued that profits or cash flow will provide a better explanation of investment than direct demand proxies because, in addition to their obvious correlation with current demand levels, they also include important information about the current availability of internal funds which is, in the opinion of some, a vital factor in determining the level of investment. The question as to whether or not investment is best explained by omitting all reference to direct demand proxies has been extensively studied ever since Tinbergen (1939) announced:

> There is fairly good evidence that the fluctuations in investment activity are in the main determined by the fluctuations in profits earned in industry as a whole some months earlier.[3]

On balance, one may conclude from various investigations that the omission of direct demand proxies is not a valid restriction on an equation purporting to explain the level of investment demand.[4] Kisselgoff and Modigliani (1957), for example, conclude that profits and interest rates alone completely fail to explain investment behaviour in electric utilities and that the explanation is greatly improved by considering expected demand relative to capacity. It may, of course, be argued that a regulated industry is somewhat exceptional but the conclusion is reinforced by Kuh (1971) in a massive study using panel data on sixty US firms. He demonstrates that sales are superior to profits in time series regressions on the basis of both significant coefficients and goodness of fit criteria, though lagged profits do show up well *in addition* to sales in cross-sections. We shall refer to this again in our discussion of finance. Jorgenson and Siebert (1968a) compare five different specifications of an investment equation among which are the Jorgenson specification based on the assumption of a Cobb–Douglas technology and including output among the independent variables and two specifications which entirely omit any direct proxies for demand, one based on a liquidity variable and one on a stock-market valuation variable. They demonstrate that the Jorgenson specification is superior on the basis of minimal residual variance, significant coefficients and turning point prediction criteria. This is a study based on time series data for fifteen individual firms but, unfortunately, when its scope was extended by Elliott (1973) to 184 individual firms he discovered that there was no clear-cut superiority for the Jorgenson specification over the liquidity specification, though both were superior to the valuation model. However, Bischoff (1971a), using aggregate data on equipment expenditures, compares a putty-clay specification and a Jorgenson type specification,[5] both based on output, with a liquidity type specification and, using goodness of fit and prediction tests, it appears that the putty-clay specification is very much superior and that there is no clear-cut ranking of the other two.[6] So, again, the conclusion must be that omission of any direct demand proxy is a mis-specification and the Elliott results arose because of the specific weakness of the Jorgenson type of equation structure.

Since the evidence suggests that some direct demand proxy should be included in any statistical attempt to explain investment decisions, the question now arises as to which. On this particular point there is very little to be said. There is some evidence in Gould and Waud (1973) that using a truly exogenous demand proxy such as GNP at the industry level provides better predictive power than using a proxy such as output which is constrained by current capital stock. This is not very conclusive, however, since the comparison model has a Jorgenson-type equation structure which, as we have seen above, seems to be inferior to the putty-clay model in predictive power.

Turning now to some actual estimates of the elasticity of desired capital stock with respect to demand proxies the picture is one of fairly uniform results as can be seen from Table 12.1.

Under constant returns to scale one would expect the elasticity to be insignificantly different from unity and this is indeed the case for all the results except that which arises when Eisner uses a cost of

Table 12.1

Study	Data	Elasticity of desired capital stock with respect to output/sales orders[7]
Bischoff (1969)	US manufacturing, equipment	1·033
Eisner (1970)	US manufacturing, equipment	0·988 (using bond yield in cost of capital) 0·524 (using earnings yield in cost of capital)
Coen (1971)	US manufacturing, structures and equipment	0·90–0·99

capital which contains the earnings–equity value ratio as the rate of interest term. In this case the elasticity is significantly lower than one but, as we shall see in section 5, there are strong reasons for believing that such a definition of the cost of capital is a misspecification which is liable to bias this particular elasticity downwards. It is worth adding that Bischoff (1971a) finds a long run elasticity of 0·9 for aggregate equipment expenditures with respect to output, using a putty-clay specification.[8]

2. Substitutability and the Long-run Effects of Price Changes

Much ink has been spilt over the size of the long-run effects of relative price changes on investment and there is a considerable morass of conflicting evidence to wade through. Before we start, however, one or two theoretical remarks are in order. It is clear that the effect of a change in the cost of capital relative to the wage will depend on the elasticity of substitution of the production function. If the firm is not a price taker in the product market then its desired capital stock is determined as in equation 11.20 and this desired capital stock is *not* homogeneous of degree zero in factor prices nor is its elasticity with respect to either the cost of capital or the wage equal to the elasticity of substitution. In both cases these elasticities depend on the elasticity of demand in the product market and a number of other parameters as specified in the Marshall–Hicks rules for factor demand elasticities.[9] However, if future expected output is taken as exogenous and mark-up pricing is assumed then desired capital stock is derived as in equation 11.22 and only in this case is it a function of *relative* prices with a relative price elasticity equal to the elasticity of substitution. Another point to remember is that, if a firm thinks that relative price changes are not going to be permanent (for example, when the government introduces some new form of depreciation allowance, the firm may continually assign some positive probability to this allowance being removed, at least over the sample period) then the *observed* long-run relative price response may not fully reflect the response which would occur if the firm were certain that the relative price change was here to stay. So, even in the case where the true elasticity of substitution is unity and the true elasticity of desired capital stock with respect to relative prices is equal to this elasticity of substitution, it does not follow that the *observed* long-run elasticity of capital stock with respect to relative prices either will be or should be equal to unity.

The consequence of these two comments is to indicate that it is quite possible for the elasticity of substitution to differ considerably from the correct estimate of the long run elasticity of capital stock with respect to relative prices. This implies that even if the investigator is *certain* that the underlying production function is Cobb Douglas, it is nevertheless incorrect to constrain this long-run elasticity to be unity.

The arguments about the size of the elasticity of desired capital stock with respect to relative prices are typically concerned with the two hypotheses as to whether it is equal to unity or equal to zero. In the light of our previous remarks there seems little natural reason for us to be very interested in whether or not this elasticity is unity and indeed the only reason why the number 'one' has obsessed researchers seems to be that Jorgenson's model actually constrains the relevant elasticity to be equal to one. Bischoff (1969), using Jorgenson and Stephenson's data on US aggregate manufacturing structures and equipment, finds himself unable to reject the hypothesis that the elasticity is equal to unity[10] although, since the point estimate is only 0·358, one might imagine that it would be hard to reject the hypothesis that it takes any value from zero to one inclusive. Perhaps more interestingly, however, by using data simply on manufacturing equipment, he is able to reject the hypothesis that the elasticity is zero and, further, to reject, in the context of a putty–putty model, the joint restriction that the elasticities of desired capital stock with respect to output *and* relative prices are both unity[11] (note these are the prior restrictions of the Jorgenson-type model). This second result is confirmed in Eisner (1970) using the same basic data,[12] although all his results on the relative price elasticity are highly susceptible to the definition of the interest rate term in the cost of capital. This may be one of the reasons for the

Table 12.2

Study	Data	Elasticity of desired capital stock with respect to relative prices[14]
Bischoff (1969)	US manufacturing, equipment	0·828
Eisner (1970)	US manufacturing, equipment	0·876 (using Bischoff's cost of capital) 0·283 (using Jorgenson's cost of capital based on the bond yield) 0·193 (using Jorgenson's cost of capital based on earnings–equity value ratio)
Rowley (1970)	UK fixed capital	0·85
Coen (1971)	US manufacturing, structures and equipment	0·55–0·57 (without financial variables) 0·29 (with financial variables)
Feldstein and Flemming (1971)	UK fixed capital	0·38–0·49
Boatwright and Eaton (1972)	UK manufacturing plant and machinery	0·47–0·65

considerable variation in the point estimates of the relative price elasticity[13] which can be seen in Table 12.2.

Interestingly enough some of the lowest results occur when explicit account is taken of financial variables for both Coen's value of 0·29 and Feldstein and Flemming's value of about 0·4 appear in these circumstances. Thus it seems possible that the long-run effects of relative prices are reduced when the cost of capital effects of the availability of funds are properly accounted for. On the other hand, any such conclusion must be treated with caution because of the considerable variation from study to study both in the investment variables being explained and in the general specification of the model.

All the results discussed so far in the section have emerged from models which allow both *ex ante* and *ex post* substitution. However, Bischoff (1971b) provides some evidence that ruling out *ex post* substitutability provides a preferable investment demand specification. The test described in Chapter 11, p. 255, comes out very much in favour of the putty-clay model and in addition Bischoff (1971a, b) and Hausman (1972) show the putty-clay model to be superior in terms of both goodness of fit and predictive power to alternatives of both the Jorgenson type and the simple accelerator type. In both the putty-clay models described by Bischoff he estimates a long-run elasticity of *capital equipment expenditure* with respect to relative prices which is close to unity.[15]

3. The Time Structure of the Investment Response

Having dealt with the long-run response of investment to changes in demand and relative prices it is time to turn our attention to the short-run effects. Some idea of the time structure of the actual investment process, at least for the construction of new plant, is provided by Mayer (1958) and is based on a survey of 276 companies building new industrial plant in the US. The figures are shown in the following Table 12.3.[16]

Table 12.3

Time from	Number of months
Start of consideration to start of construction	23
Start of drawing of plans to start of construction	7
Final decision to build to start of construction	6
Placing of first significant orders to start of construction	2
Start of financing to start of construction[a]	4
Completion of financing to start of construction[a]	3
Start of construction to completion	15

[a] Some firms had either not started or not completed financing before the start of construction.

Important points to note are that for this form of investment good the lag between the final decision to invest and the completion of investment is about twenty-one months on the average and, secondly, that financing arrangements are made just before the start of construction and about fifteen months before completion. Mayer also concludes that, for equipment purchases *only*, there is a lag of about two months between the time when the need for the new equipment is recognized and the time when an order is placed, and a lag of four or five months between ordering and delivery.[17] Almon (1968) provides some interesting information on the lag between appropriations and investment expenditures for both plant and equipment combined. The lag distributions which she derives are shown in Figure 12.1, the dashed line being for 1953–54 when the order backlogs were low and the continuous line for 1965–66 when the backlogs were high.[18] These

lag distributions seem very much in accord with Mayer's results with
a median lag of between nine months and a year depending on the
degree of pressure in the market for capital goods.

Because of these relatively long lags firms clearly have to predict
some considerable distance into the future when making their
investment plans. On the other hand, there is some evidence to
suggest that firms are able to adjust the final level of capital acquisitions at a fairly late stage in the process, especially in response to
changing demand conditions.[19] For example, Modigliani and
Weingartner (1968) using US data on investment anticipations, find
that about 60% of the average discrepancy between actual invest-

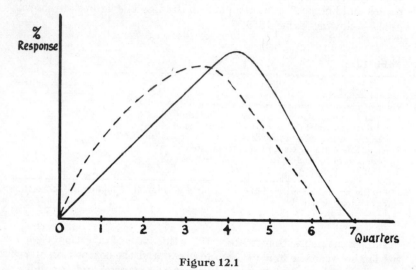

Figure 12.1

ment and anticipated investment can be explained by the difference
between expected and actual sales. Similar results are obtained by
Eisner (1965) and Evans and Green (1966).

Turning now to some actual examples of the timing of the investment response to exogenous changes in demand and relative prices,
we can first look at a typical example of a Jorgenson-type model
where the time response to both these exogenous factors is constrained
to be the same. A good example is provided by Jorgenson and
Stephenson (1967) where they present the following equation for US
manufacturing.[20]

$$NI_t = 0 \cdot 003 \Delta \left(\frac{pQ}{c}\right)_{t-4} + 0 \cdot 002 \Delta \left(\frac{pQ}{c}\right)_{t-5} + 0 \cdot 0027 \Delta \left(\frac{pQ}{c}\right)_{t-6}$$

$$+ 0 \cdot 0037 \Delta \left(\frac{pQ}{c}\right)_{t-7} + 1 \cdot 2 \, NI_{t-1} - 0 \cdot 48 \, NI_{t-2}$$

where NI is net investment, Q is output, p is output price, c is the cost of capital, t refers to quarters and Δ refers to a one-quarter change. Note that the investment response is constrained to be zero for four quarters after an exogenous change in spite of the evidence discussed above concerning the ability of firms to make late adjustments in their plans. It should, however, be pointed out that this particular constraint is not arbitrary but does follow from some statistical analysis. In Figure 12.2 we trace out the time path of the response in net investment to a permanent increase of 10^3 in pQ/c occurring at time -4. This time path is the continuous line; the two dotted lines refer to the time paths which occur if the coefficient of NI_{t-2} is moved up and down by two standard errors. These illustrate how difficult it is to pinpoint a lag distribution of this type and the general lack of robustness in the econometric estimation of investment response patterns.

To bring this point home, if we compute the implied bounds for net investment in each of the first three years following the rise in desired capital stock, we have upper bounds of 0, 29·3, 39·1, and lower bounds of 0, 24·4, $-2·6$. Notice that the bounds are close for the first two years but subsequently diverge very rapidly, making it more or less impossible to make accurate predictions of the investment response to current changes more than two years in the future.

As can be seen from the figure, the peak response of investment to a sustained increase in either output or relative prices occurs some twenty-one months after the exogenous change. This would tie in rather well with Mayer's study (Table 12.3) if the investment referred to was only investment in new plant. But the Jorgenson–Stephenson equation is based on investment in both plant and equipment and therefore the implicit length of response seems to be rather long given that Mayer estimates only a seven or eight month delay between decision and delivery for equipment. One explanation may be that the decision to invest is made on the basis of information which is rather out of date but a more likely possibility is that the restriction implied by imposing the same pattern of response to changes in both output and relative prices is a mis-specification. As we have seen, there is some telling evidence in favour of assuming a

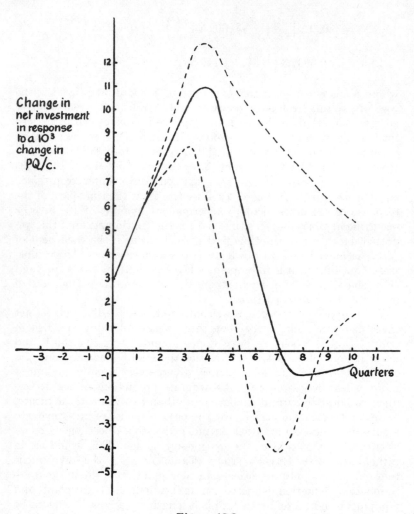

Change in
net investment
in response
to a 10³
change in
PQ/c.

Figure 12.2

putty-clay technology which would imply a much quicker investment response to output changes than to relative price changes. This
is confirmed by both Eisner and Nadiri (1968) and Bischoff (1969)
and in Figure 12.3 we illustrate the two responses derived by
Bischoff for investment in equipment only,[21] where the long-run

elasticities are very much in accord with their constrained values in the Jorgenson–Stephenson equation.

Here we can clearly see the completely different response pattern with the output response peaking after about six months, very much

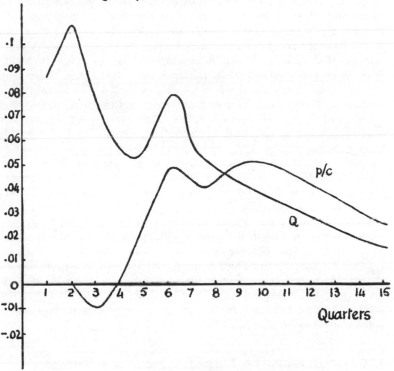

Figure 12.3

in accord with Mayer's results, and the relative price response peaking after about two years with a much flatter profile, much as one would expect in a world where there is little *ex post* substitutability. One can easily see how constraining these two responses to be the same would make the output response appear to peak much later and the relative price response appear to peak much earlier than they do in reality.

There are several other interesting points which emerge from the various estimated lag distributions. First, as one might expect, equipment expenditures respond very much more rapidly than do construction expenditures to any exogenous change. For example, Bischoff (1971a) reveals that in a putty-clay model the peak response to an output change occurs after about one year in the case of equipment and after at least two years in the case of construction.[22] Second, the work of Eisner and Nadiri (1968) consistently reveals a much stronger and more rapid investment response to relative price changes if the cost of capital is measured by an earnings–valuation ratio than if it is measured by a long–term bond rate.[23] The reason for this will be explained when we deal with the cost of capital in section 5, though one can say at this juncture that the former measure of the cost of capital involves a basic mis-specification if the share prices are uncorrected for expected growth. Third, the double peak which shows up in Figure 12.3 in the response of investment to output is considered by some researchers, in particular Evans, to be no statistical accident, but to reflect the fact that firms initiate investment projects, say, two years in advance and then adjust them much closer to completion date in the light of the current output and sales situation.[24] This is precisely the process which we have discussed earlier (p. 290) in connection with the work of Modigliani and Weingartner (1958), Eisner (1965) and Evans and Green (1966) on investment anticipations and it would indeed lead to a double peak so long as aggregation over a lot of capital goods with different gestation periods did not wash it away. It might be added that the solid statistical evidence in favour of the two-peaked response is somewhat slender.

4. Expectations Formation and Expectational Variables

In the studies which were discussed in the last section the derived distributed lags are a mixture of the lags inherent in the investment process, which are themselves rather a *melange* because of aggregation over goods with different gestation periods, and the lags involved in the process of expectations formation. Some other studies try to separate out the expectations formation mechanism and one of the more sophisticated examples of this is provided by Helliwell and Glorieux (1970). For the formation of expectations about real domestic product in Canada they derive as their best equation,

$$Y^*_{t,\ t-1} = 0 \cdot 1\{(1 \cdot 0151)\,Y_{t-1} + (0 \cdot 9)\,(1 \cdot 0151)^2\,Y_{t-2}$$

$$+ (0 \cdot 9)^2 (1 \cdot 0151)^3\,Y_{t-3} + \ldots\}$$

$$+ 0 \cdot 6\,[\{Y_{t-1} - (1 \cdot 0151)\,Y_{t-2}\} + (0 \cdot 6)\{Y_{t-2} - (1 \cdot 0151)\,Y_{t-3}\}$$

$$+ (0 \cdot 6)^2 \{Y_{t-3} - (1 \cdot 0151)\,Y_{t-4}\} + \ldots]$$

where $Y^*_{t,\ t-1}$ is the level of output expected at $t-1$ to occur at time t.[25] The expectations formation mechanism has two parts. The first part, which is the regressive element, consists of a very slowly declining weighted average of past outputs with a trend growth rate of $0 \cdot 0151$. The second part, which is the extrapolative element, consists of a rapidly declining sequence of successive deviations from the trend growth rate and has rather a high weighting. This would tend to indicate that firms take rather a lot of notice of recent fluctuations in the level of output in forming their expectations. It should also be noticed that the coefficients on all the lagged Y's do not sum to unity which is probably quite sensible in the context of a growing economy.

Concerning the effects of recent fluctuations about the trend, Feldstein and Flemming (1971) come to a conclusion opposite to that implied in the work of Helliwell and Glorieux when they assert that their results for the UK imply that recent deviations of output from long-run trends tend to be considered by producers as primarily cyclical and have little effect on investment.[26] Coen (1971) also defines separate expectational lags but in his case it is not quite clear what they mean since he assumes that the orders variable which appears in desired capital stock is simply a distributed lag of past orders. Quite what is being expected, and when, is not really made very clear. However, it does emerge very strongly from his results that too much current weight on the relative price variable leads to perverse signs, thus confirming the very slow response of investment to relative price changes.[27]

A slightly more eclectic approach to expectations formation is taken by Birch and Siebert (1976) who use as their measure of expected 'permanent' sales, the fitted values derived from the sales prediction equation,

$$S_t = 96 + 0 \cdot 91\{\tfrac{1}{3}(S_{t-1} + S_{t-2} + S_{t-3})\} + 0 \cdot 05 M V F_{t-1} + 0 \cdot 73 P_{t-1}$$
$$(0 \cdot 42)\phantom{\{\tfrac{1}{3}(S_{t-1}}(0 \cdot 019)\phantom{M V F_{t-1} + }(0 \cdot 20)$$

where S_t is firm sales at time t, MVF_t is the market value of the firm. P_t is firm profits and the figures in brackets are standard errors.[28] It may be noted that both current profits and current market value are useful predictors of future activity, *independently* of current demand, quite a surprising result in the case of the former variable. The use of the expected 'permanent' sales variable in the investment equation is relatively successful and it turns out to be a more satisfactory explanatory variable than actual sales in a fairly standard accelerator type model.

On a rather different track it may be recalled from the section on putty-clay models in Chapter 11, section 3, that the optimal capital output ratio at time t is a function of the expected rate of inflation (see p. 253). In their analysis of US demand for machinery and equipment, Ando *et al.* (1974) investigate the role of inflationary expectations in a putty-clay model and conclude that decision-makers do take account of inflation, at least when it is serious. So, for example, in the US it was more or less ignored before 1964 but figured in investment decision making after 1964 as firms became conscious of the effect of high rates of inflation on the real rate of interest. Bischoff (1971a) derives a long-run equipment expenditures elasticity of 0·161 with respect to the expected rate of inflation, this figure being derived from the model described in the paper by Ando *et al.* (1974) mentioned above.[29]

Some other studies have not tried to estimate an expectations formation mechanism explicitly but have used specific variables which incorporate elements of expectations. The most obvious variable of this type, which has been used by Eisner (1967), is an actual measure of expected sales changes up to four years in advance which is derived from survey data. This variable shows up very significantly as one might expect and indeed incorporates a considerable amount of additional information over and above the series of lagged sales changes already included in the model. This is probably the most clear-cut evidence from statistical work of how important future expectations are in determining current levels of investment. Another variable of this type which has been frequently utilized is the stock-market price. Evans (1969), for example, reports that, for some industries, stock prices show up with rather a short lag and he suggests that they contain additional information on expectations which is not contained in current or lagged values of other variables.[30] He also hypothesizes that the significant showing of stock prices is not due to any cost of capital effects, claiming that these effects only show up with a long lag because all financial decisions concerning investment projects are made when the project is initiated. Mayer's results in Table 12.3 would tend to confirm this although it should be borne in mind that Mayer also presents the average lag between decision and delivery for capital equipment as only about two or three quarters. The only true test of the Evans hypothesis would be to see whether stock prices showed up as significant when they were also included as an element of the cost of capital in a reasonably specified 'desired' capital stock. Another variant of this same idea was tried by Lund and Holden (1968) who found that the difference between the actual level of share prices and the 'normal' level associated with the current level of gross domestic product was a significant explanatory variable in the demand for gross fixed capital stock in the UK. The confusion between the expectational effects and the cost of capital effects of changes in share prices makes it a difficult variable to use in investment demand equations because the firm's investment decision is influenced in very different ways by expectational changes and changes in the cost of capital. Some results which bear on this point will be discussed in relation to the cost of capital and it is to the evidence on this matter which we now turn.

5. Financial Decisions and the Cost of Capital

A large number of investment studies have incorporated a cost of capital term explicitly into their definition of desired capital stock and nearly all these have suitably adjusted the price of capital goods for depreciation allowances in the manner described in Chapter 9, section 1. Most of the studies ignore the capital gains element of the cost of capital, although there is some evidence provided in Jorgenson and Siebert (1968b) to the effect that any such omission is a mis-specification.[31] In all these studies, however, there are considerable variations in the specification of the rate of interest term in the cost of capital. Consider first those studies that base their analysis on the Modigliani–Miller theory of corporate finance and consequently completely ignore the effect of current earnings on the level of investment demand. Two examples of this approach are provided by Jorgenson and Stephenson (1967) and Bischoff (1971b), and both studies use as a basis the Modigliani–Miller formula $\rho(1 - \tau_c L)$ where ρ is the market discount rate for the after-tax returns of the un-levered firm, τ_c is the corporate tax rate and L is the optimal proportion of debt to total valuation. Jorgenson and Stephenson use the

ratio of after-tax profits plus interest payments to the sum of equity
and bond values as a proxy for ρ and for the same parameter
Bischoff uses a weighted sum of the bond yield and the equity yield
with the weights to be estimated. In neither case is there a correction
for expected growth of earnings which should be added as shown in
equation 11.54. Miller and Modigliani (1966) present a considerable
body of evidence to show that the omission of the growth factor is a
serious mis-specification of the cost of capital and leads to very much
the wrong answer.[32] The basic problem is the following. Suppose that
the current level of demand and hence sales and output falls. This
will probably lead to a decline in expected earnings, and a drop in
share value. In a proper growth corrected specification of the cost of
capital, this will not imply any change in the measured capital cost
and this is indeed correct. There is no change in the true cost of
capital.[33] On the other hand, the decline in current sales or output
will lead to a fall in desired capital stock, a fall in current orders and
a change in the future level of investment. This will appear in the
estimates as a change in investment in response to a change in output
with the lag associated with the change in output. Now consider what
will happen if there is no growth correction. The decline in current
output and consequent decline in expectations will cause a fall in
share price with no offsetting change in the growth correction. There
is a spurious rise in the cost of capital as well as a fall in desired
capital stock. The subsequent drop in investment will appear to have
been caused not only by the drop in output but also by the rise in the
cost of capital. Some of the effect of the drop in output on subsequent
investment will be taken over by the change in the cost of capital
and this will show up as investment having been influenced by the
cost of capital at a lag appropriate to changes in output. This is
likely to have two effects. First, it will cause a spurious reduction in
the long-run effects of output changes on investment and a spurious
rise in the long-run effects of relative price changes in so far as
relative prices include the cost of capital. Second, it will cause a
spurious reduction in the lag associated with relative price changes.
Both these effects have been mentioned already in this chapter in the
discussion of Eisner and Nadiri's results on lag structures on p. 294
and Eisner's results on the long-run elasticity of desired capital
stock with respect to output shown in Table 12.1. Another good
example of these effects is provided in Eisner (1970) in Table 1 where,
using Jorgenson and Stephenson's data, it appears that the long-run
elasticity of desired capital stock with respect to output is always

larger when the cost of capital excludes the earnings–valuation ratio and the elasticity with respect to relative prices is almost always smaller in the same circumstances.

Interestingly enough, when Bischoff estimates the weights to be accorded to the bond yield and the dividend yield in his cost of capital he finds the estimates to be quite unstable when small changes are made in the sample or the model. In addition, the coefficient on the dividend yield is very much lower relative to that on the bond yield than might have been expected *a priori*, indicating that dividend yield changes were having a much smaller effect on the cost of capital than the Bischoff cost of capital construct would indicate. In all probability the reason is that most of the variation in the dividend yield is caused by variations in share prices in response to changes in earnings expectations which have no effect at all on the true cost of capital and would be cancelled out by an expected growth correction.[34]

The real problem here is that it is rather difficult to make a very accurate expected growth correction although both Jorgenson and Siebert (1968b) and Helliwell *et al.* (1971) do make the attempt. The alternative is to omit equity values from the cost of capital entirely but then, of course, one risks losing altogether the very real changes in the cost of capital due to changes in market risk aversion or changes in the market view as to the firm's riskiness. It should be added, however, that in Miller and Modigliani's (1966) study of the cost of capital to electric utilities, the best approximation to the correctly computed cost of capital series was provided by the yield on AAA public utility bonds which was very much closer to the truth than any form of weighted average cost of capital based on dividend yields. Coen (1971) uses this information as justification for his use of the AAA bond yield in the cost of capital thereby avoiding all the problems which occur when share values are included.

Some results on the long-run elasticity of capital expenditures with respect to interest rates and other cost of capital measures are presented in Table 12.4. These results on interest rates are all of roughly the same order of magnitude and indicate that a 1% change in the bond yield will change investment between $\frac{1}{4}$ and $\frac{1}{2}$%. The elasticity with respect to the dividend yield is somewhat lower for reasons which we have already explained.

Turning now to some results from studies which have also included financial variables, we can present some elasticities of investment expenditures with respect to changes in the flow of internally generated funds. Considering first those studies which have simply included some kind of flow of funds variable as a separate term in the regression, Evans (1969) computes two-year elasticities of 0·54 based on the equation of Meyer and Glauber (1964) and of 0·10 based on his own work.[36] This straightforward inclusion of the variable in the regression effectively implies a direct impact of the flow of funds on desired capital stock rather than simply on the timing of investment decisions and there is some evidence that this is a mis-specification, as we shall see.

Table 12.4[35]

	Bond yield	Dividend yield
Meyer and Glauber (1964) Gross manufacturing Two-year elasticity	−0·24	
Griliches and Wallace (1965) Gross manufacturing Two-year elasticity	−0·59	
Evans (1969) Gross investment Two-year elasticity	−0·22	
Bischoff (1971b) Manufacturing equipment Long-run elasticity	−0·21	−0·05
Bischoff (1971a) Manufacturing equipment Long-run elasticity	−0·36	−0·164

Feldstein and Flemming (1971) include the ratio of retained earnings plus depreciation allowances to trend output as a term in the cost of capital with its own separate elasticity and this is part of the measure of desired capital stock. In this form the variable is completely insignificant, which implies that the long-run effects of this variable are negligible.[37] That is to say that if the flow of funds does have an effect on the level of investment it operates on the timing of investment expenditures rather than on the long-run level of desired capital stock, which is indeed the role which we would expect it to play on the basis of our theoretical considerations (see Chapter 8, p. 185, Chapter 9, p. 212, and Chapter 11, p. 262). Eisner (1967) provides some direct evidence to this effect, for he finds that firms tend to make higher capital expenditures in the periods following higher profits but that over the long run firms earning higher profits do not make markedly greater capital expenditures than firms earning lower profits.[38]

Coen (1971) and Prior (1976) are the only studies which incorporate the flow of funds relative to desired expansion into the adjustment cost mechanism, which is where our theory indicates that it belongs, and they both conclude that it has a very significant effect on the speed of adjustment. For example, Coen's results indicate that if the cash flow available for expansion in the current period is small relative to the gap between desired and actual capital stock, then only about 10–12% of this gap is closed in one quarter whereas between 28 and 33% of the gap is closed if the quantity of cash flow is equal to this gap.[39] In general he concludes that the variable speed of adjustment model is superior in every respect to the fixed speed of adjustment model and his study certainly indicates that any omission of cash flow considerations from investment demand functions is an unacceptable prior restriction. Prior, who analyses UK machine-tool orders, finds, at least on the face of it, a far smaller cash flow effect than Coen, though it is nevertheless strongly significant. However, the small size of his effect arises simply from the fact that machine-tool orders are a very small proportion of total new investment orders whereas the cash flow term he uses is based on the aggregate cash flow of all UK companies. It is then very simple to check that in order to put the two studies on the same footing, the appropriate coefficient in the Prior study should be divided by the proportion of machine tools in total investment, the result of which is to indicate that cash flow effects on investment in the UK are very similar to those found by Coen for the US. Lintner (1967) directly includes a leverage variable (long-term debt less retentions as a proportion of the market value of equity) as a measure of the cost of funds at the debt margin and finds a strongly significant negative effect, even when the rate of interest and a Jorgenson-type desired capital stock are included. This again conforms to our prior theorizing as set out in Chapter 9, section 3, and Chapter 11, section 4, especially equation 11.49 and thereabouts. Interestingly enough, both Lintner and Coen discover that the financial constraints on investment seem to apply with rather a short lag which at first sight is completely opposed to the conclusion of Kuh (1971), that the liquidity flow is only an active constraint on investment during the planning period rather than when expenditures are actually made.[40] On the other hand, remembering again that Mayer's lag between decision and delivery for equipment is only two or three quarters combined with the fact that expenditures on plant are not necessarily coincident with final deliveries but can easily be made throughout the construction period, one would not necessarily expect any very lengthy lag between changes in the financial position and effects on investment expenditures. Admittedly, however, neither Coen (1971) nor Lintner (1967) appear to have tested the hypothesis of a short lag for financial effects against the alternative of a longer lag, so the question remains open.

A rather different matter concerning the interplay between financial and capital investment decisions is the relationship between the level of investment and the dividend pay-out. Since it appears that cash flow is important in the investment decision it is possible that the dividend pay-out decision will affect the level of investment. Using cross-section data on different industries in the US, Dhrymes and Kurz (1967) conclude that this is indeed the case on the basis of their simultaneous equation model discussed on p. 271. The implication of this is that the level of retentions is not an exogenous variable as far as the investment decision is concerned and that in single equation models of investment demand one should use the level of after-tax profits plus depreciation allowances as the appropriate measure of cash flow (as was done by Coen but not by Lintner). However, Fama (1974) in a fairly exhaustive study using individual firm time-series data comes to completely the opposite conclusion to Dhrymes and Kurz, finding that the level of dividend pay-outs has no influence whatever on the level of investment and seems to be determined quite independently. Since we have some evidence that cash flow is very influential in investment decisions this appears to indicate that firms look at the quantity of cash available at the beginning of the period, decide on a dividend and then start making investment decisions on the basis of what is left. This appears, at least superficially, to be a sub-optimal way of going about things; on the other hand, as we remarked in Chapter 9, p. 207, our theoretical understanding of the role of dividend pay-outs especially as a form of signal to shareholders concerning current and future prospects in an uncertain world does not seem to be completely satisfactory. This 'independence' of dividend pay-outs from investment decisions is brought home by the fact that all the studies of dividend behaviour find a satisfactory explanation in terms of a lagged adjustment towards a 'target' dividend pay-out which is a function of current earnings and of the opportunity cost of retentions in terms of forgone dividends, the tax parameter, θ.[41] The dividend pay-out is directly related to θ with a typical long-run elasticity of somewhere between 0·4 (King, 1971) and 1·0 (Feldstein, 1970) depending on which data set is used.[42] Since the dividend pay-out referred to is that *after all taxes*, this implies that the quantity of retentions available after dividends is itself *positively* related to θ.[43] Consequently, it is somewhat surprising that Feldstein and Flemming (1971) find that the long-run elasticity of investment expenditures with respect to this parameter is $-0·14$, with the implication that investment is inversely related to long-run retentions. It is explained in their paper by reference to the results of Feldstein (1970) but the discussion is couched as if the dividend pay-out referred to in the earlier paper is necessarily inversely related to the level of retentions.[44] However, with the estimates provided in Feldstein (1970) quite the reverse is true and both long-run retentions and long-run net dividends move in the same direction in response to *ceteris paribus* changes in θ. The result, therefore, remains something of a riddle.

Some interesting further information on financial behaviour and its relationship to investment is provided by Baumol *et al.* (1970). Using regressions of earnings on the amounts of various forms of finance used in the years 1956–59, they conclude that the rates of return on retentions, debt and equity capital are in the ranges of 3·0–4·6%, 4·2–14% and 14·5–20·8% respectively.[45] This is very much in accord with what one would expect from our discussion in sections 2 and 3 of Chapter 9, bearing in mind that with the US tax system *initial* debt is cheaper than retentions which in their turn are cheaper than equity. If retentions are adequate to finance the amount of investment required to push its marginal return down to the marginal cost of debt, debt is simply maintained at a level where its marginal cost is equal to that of retentions. We would never expect the marginal return on debt to be lower than that on retentions, because then it would be worth increasing the debt and using the retentions to pay more dividends. On the other hand, if retentions are not adequate to finance all investment then new debt will be issued raising its marginal cost up to the point where this equals the marginal return on new investment. If, however, the marginal return on new investment is so high that the marginal cost of debt reaches the marginal cost of new equity before investment opportunities yielding more than this return are exhausted, then new equity is issued. This process leads to just the type of rate of return figures shown above. Unfortunately, however, the econometric methodology of this study includes a number of somewhat arbitrary assumptions as has been noted by Brealey *et al.* (1976) and a similar study for the UK by Whittington (1972) provides little in the way of confirmation of these results.

Finally, in this section it is briefly worth mentioning some recent investigations into the Modigliani–Miller view of the world. Glyn (1973) in a very interesting analysis of UK company stock market valuations, concludes that bank borrowing makes additional contributions to earnings roughly in line with tax savings, which is in accord with the Modigliani–Miller theorem. On the other hand, in a paper which again uses UK company data, Davenport (1971) detects a cost of capital curve which is significantly U-shaped with respect to leverage and hence concludes rather forcefully that the existence of bankruptcy negates the Modigliani–Miller theorem in practice as well as in theory. Thus the evidence on the Modigliani–Miller theorem is still somewhat inconclusive. However, as far as investment decisions are concerned, the weight of the evidence now suggests a significant role for cash flow, at least in the timing of investment expenditures. Simply including a cost of capital of the Modigliani–Miller type in the definition of desired capital stock does not adequately capture the influence of financial variables on investment decisions.[46]

6. Replacement and Capacity Utilization

In a large number of investment studies it is assumed *a priori* that the ratio of potential replacement investment to current capital stock is constant, where potential replacement is defined to be the quantity of gross investment required in any period to maintain existing capital stock at a constant level. In our chapter on replacement and decay (Chapter 7) we showed that for *non-exponential* decay, the potential replacement–capital stock ratio is constant if, and only if, the age structure remains constant over time. Feldstein and Rothschild (1974), quoting from the US Department of Commerce study of fixed non-residential business capital (1971), give the following figures on the percentage of gross capital stock less than nine years old. These are, 34·4% in 1925, 23·1% in 1938, 52·5% in 1958, 50·7% in 1963 and 54·4% in 1968.[47] This demonstrates really wide-ranging fluctuations in age structure which consequently implies that the prior assumption of a fixed potential replacement–capital stock ratio is effectively equivalent to a prior assumption of exponential evaporation of capital stock. This is confirmed by the use of a constant depreciation term in the cost of capital in these same studies.

A number of studies have directly attempted to measure the rate of decay for some capital goods, specifically motor cars and pick-up trucks, using price data from the well-developed second-hand market. Three studies, namely Cagan (1965), Griliches (1970) and Hall (1971) conclude that exponential decay is not a bad approximation to reality after the first year (none of these studies includes the first year). It should be added, however, that Hall's specific test of a constant rate of decay reveals that this hypothesis must be rejected even at the 1% level.[48] In addition, Wykoff (1970) shows that, while the pattern of decay for vehicles is close to exponential after the first year, the rate of decay within the first year is almost twice as large as the average rate in subsequent years for all vehicle types.[49] Wykoff concludes from his study that 'Depreciation rates for automobiles are not exponential; . . . and the assumption that depreciation patterns remain fixed over time is in doubt.[50] Taubman and Rasche (1969) have made a similar study of office buildings and their work shows that for this type of capital good even straight line depreciation is far too fast in the initial stages.[51]

More direct evidence on these matters has been collected by Winfrey (1935) on the service life distribution of failing goods. Remember that the equivalent to the exponential decay assumption for goods which fail at an uncertain point in their lives is that the lifetime of the good should have an exponential distribution (see Chapter 7, footnote 5). According to Feldstein and Rothschild (1974) only one out of 176 of Winfrey's empirical frequency curves looks remotely like an exponential distribution.[52] In general then we can safely conclude that any prior assumption that capital goods decay exponentially is unacceptable.

Both Feldstein and Foot (1971) and Eisner (1972) have made use of data on the actual level of replacement investment to investigate how this level varies in response to changes in demand and capital costs. They both conclude that replacement demand varies in response to economic factors rather than being simply determined mechanistically as would be the case with exponential decay so long as gross investment exceeded potential replacement. Feldstein and Foot also detect a significant inverse relationship between replacement and expansion which is theoretically predicted by our maintenance cost model in the presence of gross investment adjustment costs (see Chapter 7, p. 136). On the other hand, this result is not confirmed by Eisner and neither is it confirmed by Bitros and

Kelejian (1974) in their study of scrapping rates. Eisner does produce one particularly interesting result which is that sales changes have a strongly significant effect on expansion investment but do not influence replacement demand. This would follow from the maintenance cost model of Chapter 7, section 3, so long as sales changes and demand were predominantly *increasing*. There are, however, a number of drawbacks to the Feldstein and Foot, and Eisner studies, one being that the capital stock measures used in these studies are derived by the perpetual inventory method which assumes a constant rate of decay. Another drawback is that the level of replacement is an extremely unnatural variable to explain because it is a residual of the true decision variables of the firm, which are the level of gross investment, the level of maintenance expenditures and the rate of scrapping. This has led Bitros and Kelejian (1974) to study the rate of scrapping in the electric utilities industry and they come up with some results very much in accord with the maintenance cost models discussed in sections 3 and 4 of Chapter 7. Specifically, they conclude, using the correct simultaneous equation techniques, that scrapping is inversely related to the level of maintenance expenditure and the cost of capital as represented by the rate of interest. They also find that scrapping is not significantly affected by the level of capacity utilization which may well reflect the two opposing forces discussed in Chapter 7, p. 139, namely that increased capacity utilization tends to accompany increases in demand which would reduce the rate of scrapping but would also reduce the productivity of the oldest capital goods because of the increasing intensity of use. The one result which does not follow directly from the maintenance cost model is that the scrapping rate is positively affected by increases in gross investment. This runs counter to the expectation that scrapping rates will fall in response to demand increases. However, on p. 130 we show that the optimal lifetime of capital goods is inversely related to the rate of technical progress which indicates that if technical progess is related to the level of gross investment in the the sense that more advanced techniques are embodied in new capital goods, then this would tend to increase the rate at which old ones are scrapped. This may go some way towards explaining the above-mentioned result and it is indeed the explanation provided by Bitros and Kelejian themselves.[53] A further paper by Bitros (1975) on the investment and scrapping rates of US class I railway locomotives tends to confirm all the conclusions of his earlier paper with Kelejian, with the additional result that scrapping rates are inversely related to output changes, again as we would expect from our maintenance cost model.[54]

These last-mentioned empirical studies are the only ones which directly attempt to relate the rate of capacity utilization to the rate of decay, and hence to the rate of scrapping, although a number of other studies use capacity utilization measures to explain gross investment.[55] In these, however, capacity utilization is simply used as a measure of demand relative to existing capacity and they are not specifically concerned with the direct effects of capacity utilization on the rate of decay of capital goods.

As a general point, it is clear enough from the evidence that scrapping and replacement rates are not simply determined by the mechanical decay of capital goods but are based on economic decisions and vary in response to economic forces. On the other hand, as we emphasized in section 6 of the previous chapter, this does not necessarily mean that firms do not *predict* replacement requirements on some fairly mechanistic basis. Since it is these predictions which should occur in investment equations, it may still be correct to specify replacement demand using some mechanical decay assumption. Variations in the scrapping rate are then simply explained by the firm adjusting its *current* capital stock in response to *unforeseen* changes in its economic environment. A rather crude test of this idea has been provided in the attempts by Meyer and Kuh (1957) to detect echo effects by seeing whether the mean age of capital goods, as proxied by accumulated depreciation reserves divided by fixed assets, had any positive effect on the level of investment. Similar attempts have also been made by Eisner (1972) and in neither case have they met with much success, with the variable often insignificant and of the wrong sign. However, as we have shown in Chapter 7, p. 122, the existence of echo effects is neither confirmed nor refuted by the discovery of no systematic relationship between mean age of capital stock and investment, and consequently no conclusions at all can be derived from these results.

A far more sophisticated attempt to incorporate and test alternative forms of decay in investment equations has been provided by Coen (1975) who tested five different forms of decay assumption in net investment equations for structures and for equipment in each of twenty-one industries in the US. The five different types of decay considered were exponential decay (ED), exponential decay but with a finite life (EDF), sum of years digits decay where the fraction of the original capacity lost in the ith period $= (n+1-i)/\sum_1^n i$, where n is the service life (SYD), 'one hoss shay' where the capital good simply disappears after n periods of zero decay (OHS) and straight line decay where $1/n$ of the good is lost each period if n is the service life (SL). Coen also adjusted the cost of capital to correspond to the assumed form of decay and came up with the following conclusions using the standard error of the net investment equation as a basis for testing. For equipment investment, out of twenty-one industries the best decay assumptions were 1 ED, 8 EDF, 2 SYD, 2 OHS, 8 SL. For structures investment the best were 0 ED, 4 EDF, 1 SYD, 11 OHS, 5 SL. The first conclusion stands out clearly, in only one out of the forty-two equations does the standard exponential decay assumption emerge as the best. For structures where 'one hoss shay' and straight line dominate, exponential decay is clearly far too fast at the beginning which confirms the results of Taubman and Rasche (1969). For equipment, exponential decay is again either too fast initially in the cases where straight line dominates or it should be cut off after some point indicating the importance of scrapping. On the basis of Coen's study it seems that the exponential decay assumption generally leads to a mis-specification of the investment demand function and that alternatives should be investigated.

7. Final Remarks

This concludes our survey of the evidence on fixed capital investment decisions and, indeed, completes our study. It is clear from what has gone before that there is a great deal which remains to be done, both in the way of difficulties to be resolved and facts to be brought to light. It only remains to hope that the reader has been provided with sufficient enlightenment and encouragement to help with these tasks.

Footnotes

[1] For a very detailed analysis of these points the reader should consult Rowley and Trivedi (1975).

[2] Rockley (1973, p. 247).

[3] Tinbergen (1939, p. 49).

[4] There is, however, some recent evidence to suggest that aggregate investment expenditures can be very well explained by the asset price of capital. Engle and Foley (1975), for example, successfully explain aggregate investment as a function of GNP (or potential GNP) and lagged values of (adjusted) stock prices, the idea being that these adjusted stock prices represent the asset price of capital with the estimated equation being looked upon as essentially a supply response. However, there seems no particular reason why such an equation could not be re-interpreted as a demand equation with GNP perform-

ing as a demand proxy and lagged stock prices incorporating both expected demand and cost of capital elements.

[5] The specification tested is not exactly the same as that used by Jorgenson and his associates since it does not assume completely static expectations.

[6] It might also be noted that in this work Bischoff takes some account of possible autocorrelation in his specification of the error structure.

[7] These elasticities are taken respectively from Bischoff (1969, p. 366, Table 5); Eisner (1970, p. 750, Table 2, C and B); Coen (1971, pp. 172–173, Tables 4.8, 4.9).

[8] This elasticity is taken from Bischoff (1971a, p. 28, Table 4).

[9] See Hicks (1932).

[10] Bischoff (1969, Tables 1 and 2).

[11] Bischoff (1969, Table 4).

[12] Eisner (1970, Table 2).

[13] We shall discuss this point in greater detail when we consider the cost of capital in section 5.

[14] The elasticities are taken respectively from Bischoff (1969, p. 366, Table 5); Eisner (1970, p. 750, Table 2, A, C, B); Rowley (1960, p. 1011, Table 2); Coen (1971, pp. 172–173, Tables 4.7, 4.8, 4.9); Feldstein and Flemming (1971, Table 2 and text); Boatwright and Eaton (1972, pp. 409 and 412).

[15] See Bischoff (1971a, p. 28, Table 4).

[16] See Mayer (1958, p. 364, Table 4).

[17] See Mayer (1958, p. 364, Section VIII).

[18] See Almon (1968, p. 204, Figure 6).

[19] This may be done by cancelling existing orders, ordering more short delay equipment, etc.

[20] See Jorgenson and Stephenson (1967, p. 189). The equation has been slightly adjusted by assuming that the lagged capital stock term on the right-hand side correctly represents capital decay.

[21] See Bischoff (1969, Table 5).

[22] See Bischoff (1971a, Table 3).

[23] Compare for example the response patterns given in Eisner and Nadiri (1968, Tables 5 and 6).

[24] See the discussion in Evans (1969, Chapter 4, pp. 102–105).

[25] See Helliwell and Glorieux (1970, pp. 506–509).

[26] See Feldstein and Flemming (1971, p. 422).

[27] Note the discussion in Coen (1971, p. 167).

[28] Birch and Siebert (1976, equation (11), p. 23).

[29] See Bischoff (1971a, Table 5).

[30] See Evans (1969, pp. 108–112).

[31] See the discussion in Jorgenson and Siebert (1968, p. 1143).

[32] The discussion on pp. 373–379 in Miller and Modigliani (1966) is very revealing, especially Table 5.

[33] This is not quite true because the possible increased risk of bankruptcy may lead to a rise in the marginal cost of debt. This is probably a rather minor effect and is not germane to the main point at issue.

[34] It is only fair to add that Bischoff was fully aware of this possibility which is discussed at some length in Bischoff (1971b, p. 95).

[35] The first three elasticities are lifted directly from Evans (1969, p. 136, Table 3.9) (using 1958 : 1 prices) and from Bischoff (1971b, Table 5, p. 30) (using 1970 : 4 prices).

[36] See Evans (1969, p. 136, Table 5.8).

[37] See Feldstein and Flemming (1971, p. 427 and Table 1, equation 1.6).

[38] See Eisner (1967, p. 386).

[39] See Coen (1971, p. 173) for details.

[40] See Kuh (1971, p. 242).

[41] See, for example, Lintner (1956) for the US and Feldstein (1970) for the UK.

[42] See, for example, King (1971) and Feldstein (1970, Tables II, III, IV).

[43] If τ_c is the corporate profits tax if no profits are distributed and Π, R, D, A are gross profits, retentions, dividends and allowances respectively then $R = \Pi(1 - \tau_c) + A\tau_c - D/\theta$. So, if the long-run elasticity of D with respect to θ is less than unity, retentions are positively related θ in the long run.

[44] See Feldstein and Flemming (1971, p. 426).

[45] See Baumol et al. (1970, p. 353 in the text).

[46] It is worth noting yet again that the influence of cash flow on investment decisions is not incompatible with the Modigliani–Miller theorem holding good. See Chapter 8, p. 188, for a full disucssion.

[47] See Feldstein and Rothschild (1974, p. 402).

[48] See Hall (1971, p. 257).

[49] See Wykoff (1970, p. 172, Table 7).

[50] See Wykoff (1970, p. 172, section V).

[51] Of course, straight line decay is much slower than exponential in the initial stages for goods of the same useful life. For interesting further discussion on these matters, see Denison (1972, pp. 101–109).

[52] See Feldstein and Rothschild (1974, p. 404).

[53] Another interesting confirmation of the maintenance cost model of section 3, Chapter 7, is provided by Barna (1962) who finds that the typical maintenance pattern for plant and equipment used in British manufacturing is for the capital goods to be well maintained until some time shortly before retirement after which point maintenance is drastically cut back.

[54] Bitros (1975, Table 4).

[55] See, for example, Junankar (1970) and works cited therein.

Bibliographical Notes—Chapter 12

Surveys of the actual results obtained in empirical work are quite rare, although a lot of information may be found in Evans (1969, Chapters 4 and 5), Lund (1971), Bridge (1971), Rowley and Trivedi (1975), and Greenberg (1976). On the other hand, there are a large number of papers devoted to statistical comparisons of small numbers of investment equations. Unfortunately, few of these are very careful in specifying the alternative hypotheses which are being tested—more often they simply look at, say, the predictive power of completely different equation specifications. Among the papers in this category are Jorgenson and Siebert (1968a), Jorgenson, Hunter and Nadiri (1970), Bischoff (1969, 1971a), Hausman (1972), Elliott (1973), Gould and Waud (1973), Engle and Foley (1975). Of these papers, only Bischoff (1969) indulges in really careful hypothesis testing, although it must be admitted that many of the other papers are interested in comparing alternatives which cannot easily be couched in terms of a nested sequence of hypotheses (i.e. typically one theory is not a special case of another). Furthermore, caution must be exercised in interpreting many of the results of the comparison tests, for they frequently reflect differences in the care taken over the stochastic specification of the different equations and shed little or no light on the validity of the underlying theories. Jorgenson, Hunter and Nadiri (1970) is replete with examples of this type.

BIBLIOGRAPHY

Almon, S. (1968) 'Lags between investment decisions and their causes', *Review of Economics and Statistics*, **50** (May), 193–206.

Anderson, W. H. L. (1964) *Corporate Finance and Fixed Investment, an Econometric Study*. Boston: Division of Research, Graduate School of Business Administration, Harvard University.

Ando, A. K., Modigliani, F., Rasche, R. and Turnovsky, S. J. (1974) 'On the role of expectations of price and technological change in an investment function', *International Economic Review*, **15** (June), 384–414.

Arrow, K. J. (1962) 'Optimal capital adjustment', in *Studies in the Mathematical Theory of Investment and Production*, edited by K. J. Arrow, S. Karlin and H. Scarf. Stanford: Stanford University Press, pp. 1–17.

Arrow, K. J. (1963) 'Comment', *Review of Economics and Statistics*, **45** (February), 25–27.

Arrow, K. J. (1964a) 'The role of securities in the optimal allocation of risk-bearing', *Review of Economic Studies*, **31** (April), 91–96.

Arrow, K. J. (1964b) 'Optimal capital policy, the cost of capital and myopic decision rules', *Annals of the Institute of Statistics and Mathematics, Tokyo*, **16**, 21–30.

Arrow, K. J. (1968) 'Optimal capital policy with irreversible investment', in *Value, Capital and Growth, Papers in Honour of Sir John Hicks*, edited by J. N. Wolfe. Edinburgh University Press, pp. 1–19.

Barna, T. (1962) *Investment and Growth Policies in British Industrial Firms*, Occasional Paper 20. Cambridge, England: Cambridge University Press for National Institute of Economic and Social Research.

Baron, D. P. (1970) 'Price uncertainty, utility and industry equilibrium in pure competition', *International Economic Review*, **11** (October), 463–480.

Baron, D. P. (1974) 'Default risk, homemade leverage and the Modigliani–Miller theorem', *American Economic Review*, **64** (March), 176–182.

Baron, D. P. (1976) 'Default risk and the Modigliani–Miller theorem: a synthesis', *American Economic Review*, **66** (March), 204–212.

Batra, R. N. and Ullah, A. (1974) 'The competitive firm and the theory of input demand under price uncertainty', *Journal of Political Economy*, **82** (May/June), 537–548.

Baumol, W. J. and Malkiel, B. (1967) 'The firm's optimal debt–equity combination and the cost of capital', *Quarterly Journal of Economics*, **18** (November), 547–578.

Baumol, W. J., Heim, P., Malkiel, B. G. and Quandt, R. E. (1970) 'Earnings retention, new capital and the growth of the firm', *Review of Economics and Statistics*, **52** (November), 345–355.

Birch, E. M. and Siebert, C. D. (1976) 'Uncertainty, permanent demand and investment behaviour', *American Economic Review*, **66** (March) 15–27.

Bischoff, C. W. (1969) 'Hypothesis testing and the demand for capital goods', *Review of Economics and Statistics*, **51** (August), 354–368.

Bischoff, C. W. (1971a) 'Business investment in the 1970s: a comparison of models', *Brookings Papers on Economic Activity*, **1**, 13–63.

Bischoff, C. W. (1971b) 'The effect of alternative lag distributions', in *Tax Incentives and Capital Spending*, edited by G. Fromm. Washington: Brookings Institution, pp. 61–130.

Bitros, G. C. (1975) 'A model of and some evidence on the interrelatedness of decisions underlying the demand for capital services'. Paper presented at the *World Econometric Congress*, Toronto.

Bitros, G. C. and Kelejian, H. H. (1974) 'On the variability of the replacement investment capital stock ratio: some evidence from capital scrappage', *Review of Economics and Statistics*, **56** (August), 270–278.

Bliss, C. J. (1975) *Capital Theory and the Distribution of Income*. Amsterdam: North-Holland Publishing Co.

Boddy, R. and Gort, M. (1971) 'The substitution of capital for capital', *Review of Economics and Statistics*, **53** (May), 179–188.

Boddy, R. and Gort, M. (1973) 'Capital expenditures and capital stocks', *Annals of Economic and Social Measurement*, **2** (July), 245–261.

Borch, K. (1963) 'Topics in economic theory: Discussion', *American Economic Review*, **53** (May), 272–274.

Borch, K. (1968) *The Economics of Uncertainty*. Princeton, NJ: Princeton University Press.

Borch, K. (1969) 'A note on uncertainty and indifference curves', *Review of Economic Studies*, **36** (January), 1–4.

Brechling, F. (1975) *Investment and Employment Decisions*. Manchester University Press.

Brealey, R. A., Hodges, S. D. and Capron, D. (1976) 'The return on alternative sources of finance', *Review of Economics and Statistics*, **58** (November), 469–477.

Bridge, J. L. (1971) *Applied Econometrics*. Amsterdam: North-Holland Publishing Co.

Cagan, P. (1965) 'Measuring quality changes and the purchasing power of money: an exploratory study of automobiles', *National Banking Review* (December), 217–236.

Chang, J. C. and Holt, C. C. (1973) 'Optimal investment orders under uncertainty and dynamic costs: theory and estimates', *Southern Economic Journal*, **39** (April), 508–525.

Chenery, H. B. (1952) 'Overcapacity and the acceleration principle', *Econometrica*, **20** (January), 1–28.

Christensen, L. R. and Jorgenson, D. W. (1969) 'The measurement of U.S. real capital input, 1929–1967', *Review of Income and Wealth*, Series 15 (December). 293–320.

Clark, J. M. (1917) 'Business acceleration and the law of demand: a technical factor in economic cycles', *Journal of Political Economy*, **25**, 217–235.

Coen, R. M. (1969) 'Tax policy and investment behaviour: comment', *American Economic Review*, **59** (June) 370–379.

Coen, R. M. (1971) 'The effect of cash flow on the speed of adjustment', in *Tax Incentives and Capital Spending*, edited by G. Fromm. Washington: Brookings Institution, pp. 131–196.

Coen, R. M. (1975) 'Investment behaviour, the measurement of depreciation and tax policy', *American Economic Review*, **65** (March), 59–74.

Coen, R. M. and Hickman, B. G. (1970) 'Constrained joint estimation of factor demand and production functions', *Review of Economics and Statistics*, **52** (August), 287–300.

Craine, R. (1975) 'Investment, adjustment costs and uncertainty', *International Economic Review*, **16** (October), 648–661.

Davenport, M. (1971) 'Leverage and the cost of capital: some tests using British data', *Economica*, **138** (May), 136–162.

Leeuw, F. de (1962) 'The demand for capital goods by manufacturers: a study of quarterly time series', *Econometrica*, **30** (July), 407–423.

Denison, E. F. (1967) *Why Growth Rates Differ, Postwar Experiences in Nine Western Countries*, assisted by J. P. Poullier. Washington, DC: Brookings Institution.

Denison, E. F. (1972) 'Final comments', *Survey of Current Business*, **52** (May, Part II), 95–110.

Dhrymes, P. J. and Kurz, M. (1967) 'Investment, dividends and external finance behaviour of firms', in *Determinants of Investment Behaviour*, edited by F. Ferber, Universities–National Bureau Conference Series, No. 18. New York: Columbia University Press for NBER.

Diamond, P. (1967) 'The role of a stock market in a general equilibrium model with technological uncertainty', *American Economic Review*, **57** (September), 759–776.

Dreze, J. H. (1974) 'Investment under private ownership: optimality, equilibrium and stability', in *Allocation Under Uncertainty, Equilibrium and Optimality*, edited by J. H. Dreze. London: Macmillan Press Ltd., pp. 129–166.

Eckstein, O. (1965) 'Manufacturing investment and business expectations, extensions of de Leeuw's results', *Econometrica*, **38** (April), 410–421.

Eisner, R. (1965) 'Realization of investment anticipations', in *Brookings Quarterly Econometric Model of the United States*, edited by J. S. Ducsenberry, G. Fromm, L. R. Klein and E. Kuh. Amsterdam: North-Holland Publishing Co., pp. 92–128.

Eisner, R. (1967) 'A permanent income theory for investment: some empirical explorations', *American Economic Review*, **57** (June), 363–390.

Eisner, R. (1970) 'Tax policy and investment behaviour: further comment', *American Economic Review*, **60** (September), 746–752.

Eisner, R. (1972) 'Components of capital expenditures: replacement and modernization versus expansion', *Review of Economics and Statistics*, **54**, 297–305.

Eisner, R. (1974) 'Comment', *Journal of Economic Literature*, **12** (March), 49–50.

Eisner, R. and Strotz, R. H. (1963) 'Determinants of business investment', in *Commission on Money and Credit: Impacts of Monetary Policy*. Englewood Cliffs, NJ: Prentice-Hall, pp. 60–138.

Eisner, R. and Nadiri, M. I. (1968) 'Investment behaviour and the neoclassical theory', *Review of Economics and Statistics*, **50** (August), 369–382.

Elliott, J. W. (1973) 'Theories of corporate investment behaviour revisited', *American Economic Review*, **63** (March), 195–207.

Engle, R. F. and Foley, D. K. (1975) 'An asset price model of aggregate investment', *International Economic Review*, **16** (October), 625–647.

Evans, M. K. (1967) 'A study of industry investment decisions', *Review of Economics and Statistics*, **49** (May), 151–164.

Evans, M. K. (1969) *Macroeconomic Activity, Theory, Forecasting and Control*. New York: Harper and Row.

Evans, M. K. and Green, E. W. (1966) 'The relative efficiency of investment anticipation', *Journal of the American Statistical Association*, **61** (March), 104–116.

Fama, E. F. (1974) 'The empirical relationships between the dividend and investment decisions of firms', *American Economic Review*, **64** (June), 304–317.

Fama, E. F. and Miller, M. H. (1972) *The Theory of Finance*. New York· Holt, Rinehart and Winston.

Feinstein, C. H. (1972) *National Income, Expenditure and Output of the United Kingdom* 1855–1965. Cambridge: Cambridge University Press.

Feldstein, M. S. (1969) 'Mean-variance analysis in the theory of liquidity preference and portfolio selection', *Review of Economic Studies*, **36** (January), 5–12.

Feldstein, M. S. (1970) 'Corporate taxation and dividend behaviour', *Review of Economic Studies*, **37** (January), 57–72.

Feldstein, M. S. and Foot, D. (1971) 'The other half of gross investment: replacement and modernization expenditures', *Review of Economics and Statistics*, **53** (February), 49–58.

Feldstein, M. S. and Flemming, J. S. (1971) 'Tax policy, corporate saving and investment behaviour in Britain', *Review of Economic Studies*, **38** (October), 415–434.

Feldstein, M. S. and Rothschild, M. (1974) 'Towards an economic theory of replacement investment', *Econometrica*, **42** (May), 393–424.

Fisher, F. M. (1969) 'The existence of aggregate production functions', *Econometrica*, **37** (October), 553–577.

Fisher, I. (1930) *Theory of Interest*. London: Macmillan and Co.

Friedman, M. and Savage, L. J. (1948) 'The utility analysis of choices involving risk', *Journal of Political Economy*, **56** (August), 279–304.

Galbraith, J. K. (1967) *The New Industrial State*, André Deutsch Ltd.

Glaister, S. (1974) 'Advertising policy and returns to scale in markets where information is passed between individuals', *Economica*, **41** (May), 139–156.

Glyn, A. (1973) 'The stock market valuation of British companies and the cost of capital 1955–69', *Oxford Economic Papers* (July), 213–240.

Goodwin, R. M. (1948) 'Secular and cyclical aspects of the multiplier and the accelerator', in *Essays in Honor of A. H. Hansen, Income, Employment and Public Policy*. New York: W. W. Norton, pp. 108–132.

Gorman, W. M. (1968) 'Measuring the quantities of fixed factors', in *Value, Capital and Growth*, edited by J. N. Wolfe. Edinburgh: Edinburgh University Press.

Gould, J. P. (1968) 'Adjustment costs in the theory of investment of the firm', *Review of Economic Studies*, **35** (January), 47–55.

Gould, J. P. (1969) 'The use of endogenous variables in dynamic models of investment', *Quarterly Journal of Economics*, **83** (November), 580–599.

Gould, J. P. and Waud, R. N. (1973) 'The neoclassical model of investment behaviour; another view', *International Economic Review*, **14** (February), 33–48.

Green, H. A. J. (1964) *Aggregation in Economic Analysis: An Introductory Survey*. Princeton: Princeton University Press.

Greenberg, E. (1964) 'A stock adjustment investment model', *Econometrica*, **32** (July), 339–357.

Greenberg, E. (1976) 'Fixed investment', Chapter 4 of *Topics in Applied Macroeconomics*, edited by D. Heathfield. London: Macmillan.

Griliches, Z. (1967) 'Distributed lags: a survey', *Econometrica*, **35** (January), 16–49.

Griliches, Z. (1970) 'The demand for a durable input: U.S. farm tractors, 1921–57', in *The Demand for Durable Goods*, edited by A. C. Harberger. Chicago: Chicago University Press.

Griliches, Z. and Wallace, N. (1965) 'The determinants of investment revisited', *International Economic Review*, **6** (September), 311–329.

Grossman, S. J. and Hart, O. D. (1976) 'A theory of competitive equilibrium in stock market economies', Stanford Institute for Mathematical Studies in the Social Sciences (mimeo).

Grossman, S. J. and Stiglitz, J. E. (1976) 'On stockholder unanimity in making production and financial decisions', Stanford Institute for Mathematical Studies in the Social Sciences, Report no. 224.

Haavelmo, T. (1960) *A Study in the Theory of Investment*. Chicago: University of Chicago Press.

Hagen, K. P. (1976) 'Default risk, homemade leverage and the Modigliani–Miller theorem: note', *American Economic Review*, **66** (March), 199–203.

Hall, R. E. (1971) 'The measurement of quality change from vintage price data', in *Price Indexes and Quality Change*, edited by Z. Griliches. Cambridge: Harvard University Press.

Hall, R. E. and Jorgenson, D. W. (1967) 'Tax policy and investment behaviour', *American Economic Review*, **53** (May), 247–259.

Hart, O. D. (1976) 'Takeover bids and stock market equilibria'. Cambridge: Churchill College (mimeo).

Hart, O. D. (1977) 'Monopolistic competition in a large economy with differentiated commodities'. Cambridge: Churchill College (mimeo).

Hartman, R. (1972) 'The effect of price and cost uncertainty on investment', *Journal of Economic Theory*, **5** (October), 258–266.

Hartman, R. (1973) 'Adjustment costs, price and wage uncertainty and investment', *Review of Economic Studies*, **40** (April), 259–268.

Hausman, J. A. (1972) 'A theoretical and empirical study of the investment function: vintage and non-vintage models', B.Phil. Thesis, Nuffield College, Oxford.

Helliwell, J. (1972) 'Aggregate investment equations: a survey of issues', *Discussion Paper No. 73*, Dept. of Economics, University of British Columbia.

Helliwell, J. and Glorieux, G. (1970) 'Forward-looking investment behaviour', *Review of Economic Studies*, **37** (October), 499–516.

Helliwell, J. R., Shapiro, H. T., Sparks, G. R., Stewart, I. A., Gorbet, F. W. and Stephenson, D. R. (1971) *The Structure of RDX2 : Part 1 and Part 2*, Bank of Canada Staff Research Studies, No. 7. Ottawa: Bank of Canada.

Hicks, J. R. (1932) *Theory of Wages*. London: Macmillan and Co.

Hirshleifer, J. (1965) 'Investment decision under uncertainty: choice theoretic approaches', *Quarterly Journal of Economics*, **79** (November), 509–536.

Hirshleifer, J. (1970) *'Investment, Interest and Capital'*. Englewood Cliffs, NJ: Prentice-Hall.

Hochman, E., Hochman, O. and Razin, A. (1973) 'Demand for investment in productive and financial capital', *European Economic Review*, **4** (April), 67–83.

Hotelling, H. (1925) 'A general mathematical theory of depreciation', *Journal of American Statistical Association*, **20**, 340–353.

Jaffee, D. M. (1972) 'A theory and test of credit rationing; further notes', *American Economic Review*, **62**, 484–488.

Jaffee, D. M. and Modigliani, F. (1969) 'A theory and test of credit rationing', *American Economic Review*, **59** (December), 850–872.

Jensen, M. C. (1972) 'Capital markets: theory and evidence', *Bell Journal of Economics and Management Science*, **3** (Autumn), 357–398.

Jorgenson, D. W. (1965) 'Anticipations and investment behaviour', in *Brookings Quarterly Model of the United States*, edited by J. Duesenberry, G. Fromm, L. Klein and E. Kuh. Chicago: Rand McNally and Co., pp. 35–92.

Jorgenson, D. W. (1967) 'The theory of investment behaviour', in *Determinants of Investment Behaviour*, edited by R. Ferber, Universities–National Bureau Conference Series, No. 18. New York: Columbia University Press for NBER.

Jorgenson, D. W. (1971) 'Econometric studies of investment behaviour; a survey', *Journal of Economic Literature*, **9** (December), 1111–1147.

Jorgenson, D. W. (1972) 'Investment behaviour and the production function', *Bell Journal of Economics and Management Science*, **3** (Spring), 220–251.

Jorgenson, D. W. (1974) 'The economic theory of replacement and depreciation', in *Econometrics and Economic Theory; Essays in Honour of Jan Tinbergen*, edited by Willy Sellakaerts. London: Macmillan, pp. 189–222.

Jorgenson, D. W., McCall, J. J. and Radner, R. (1967) *Optimal Replacement Policy*. Chicago: Rand McNally and Co.

Jorgenson, D. W. and Stephenson, J. A. (1967) 'Investment behaviour in U.S. manufacturing, 1947–1960', *Econometrica*, **35** (April), 169–220.

Jorgenson, D. W. and Siebert, C. D. (1968a) 'A comparison of alternative theories of corporate investment behaviour', *American Economic Review*, **58** (September), 681–712

Jorgenson, D. W. and Siebert, C. D. (1968b) 'Optimal capital accumulation and corporate investment behaviour', *Journal of Political Economy*, **76** (November–December), 1123–1151.

Jorgenson, D. W., Hunter, J. and Nadiri, M. I. (1970) 'A comparison of alternative models of quarterly investment behaviour', *Econometrica*, **38** (March), 187–212.

Junankar, P. N. (1970) 'The Relationship between investment and spare capacity in the United Kingdom, 1957–66', *Economica*, **37** (August), 277–292.

Junankar, P. N. (1972) *Investment: Theories and Evidence*. London: Macmillan Press Ltd.

Kalecki, M. (1937) 'The principle of increasing risk', *Economica*, **4** (November), 440–447.

Kamien, M. I. and Schwartz, N. L. (1975) 'Market structure and innovation: a survey', *Journal of Economic Literature*, **13** (March), 1 37.

Keynes, J. M. (1936) *The General Theory of Employment, Interest and Money*. London: Macmillan and Co.

King, M. A. (1971) 'Corporate taxation and dividend behaviour', *Review of Economic Studies*, **38**, 377–380.

King, M. A. (1972) 'Taxation and investment incentives in a vintage investment model', *Journal of Public Economics*, **1**, 121–148.

King, M. A. (1974a) 'Taxation and the cost of capital', *Review of Economic Studies*, **41** (January), 21–36.

King, M. A. (1974b) 'Dividend behaviour and the theory of the firm', *Economica*, **41** (February), 25–34.

King, M. A. (1974c) 'Corporate policy, uncertainty and the stock market', St. John's College, Cambridge (mimeo).

King, M. A. (1975) 'Taxation, corporate financial policy and the cost of capital—a comment', *Journal of Public Economics*, **4** (August), 271–280.

King, M. A. (1977) *Public Policy and the Corporation*. London: Chapman and Hall.

Kisselgoff, A. and Modigliani, F. (1957) 'Private investment in electric power and the acceleration principle', *Review of Economics and Statistics*, **39**, 363–379.

Klein, L. (1974) 'Issues in econometric studies of investment behaviour', *Journal of Economic Literature*, **12** (March), 43–49.

Klein, L. R. and Taubman, P. (1971) 'Estimating effects within a complete econometric model', in *Tax Incentives and Capital Spending*, edited by G. Fromm. Washington: Brookings Institution, pp. 197–242.

Koyck, L. M. (1954) *'Distributed Lags and Investment Analysis'*. Amsterdam: North-Holland Publishing Co.

Kuh, E. (1971) *'Capital Stock Growth: A Micro-Econometric Approach'*. Amsterdam: North-Holland Publishing Co.

318 THE INVESTMENT DECISIONS OF FIRMS

Leijonhufvud, A. (1968) *On Keynesian Economics and the Economics of Keynes*. Oxford: Oxford University Press.
Leland, H. (1972) 'Theory of the firm facing random demand', *American Economic Review*, **62** (June), 278–291.
Leland, H. (1974) 'Production theory and the stock market', *Bell Journal of Economics and Management Science*, **5** (Spring), 125–144.
Leontief, W. W. (1947) 'Introduction to a theory of the internal structure of functional relationships', *Econometrica*, **15** (October), 361–373.
Lerner, A. P. (1944) *The Economics of Control*. New York: Macmillan and Co.
Liesner, T. (1975) *Statistical Sources: Investment*. Milton Keynes: The Open University Press.
Lintner, J. (1956) 'Distribution of incomes of corporations among dividends, retained earnings and taxes', *American Economic Review*, **46** (May) 97–113.
Lintner, J. (1962) 'Dividends, earnings, leverage, stock prices and the supply of capital to corporations', *Review of Economics and Statistics* (August), 243–269.
Lintner, J. (1964) 'Optimal dividends and corporate growth under uncertainty', *Quarterly Journal of Economics*, **78** (February), 49–95.
Lintner, J. (1965) 'The valuation of risk assets and the selection of risky investments in stock portfolios and capital budgets', *Review of Economics and Statistics*, **47** (February), 13–37.
Lintner, J. (1967) 'Corporation finance, risk and investment', in *Determinants of Investment Behaviour*, edited by R. Ferber, Universities–National Bureau Conference Series, No. 18. New York: Columbia University Press for NBER.
Lucas, R. E. (1967a) 'Optimal investment policy and the flexible accelerator', *International Economic Review*, **8** (February), 78–85.
Lucas, R. E. (1967b) 'Adjustment costs and the theory of supply', *Journal of Political Economy*, **75** (August), 321–334.
Luce, R. D. and Raiffa, H. (1957) *Games and Decisions*. New York: Wiley.
Lund, P. J. (1971) *Investment, the Study of an Economic Aggregate*. Edinburgh: Oliver and Boyd.
Lund, P. J. and Holden, K. (1968) 'An econometric study of private sector gross fixed capital formation in the United Kingdom, 1923–38', *Oxford Economic Papers*, **20** (March), 56–73.
Lydall, H. F. (1968) *The Structure of Earnings*. Oxford: Oxford University Press.
Maccini, L. J. (1973) 'Delivery lags and the demand for investment', *Review of Economic Studies*, **40** (April), 269–281.
Malcomson, J. M. (1975) 'Replacement and the rental value of capital equipment subject to obsolescence', *Journal of Economic Theory*, **10** (February), 24–41.
Malinvaud, E. (1973) 'The allocation of individual risks in large markets', *Journal of Economic Theory*, **4** (April), 312–328.
Manne, A. D. (1961) 'Capital expansion and probabilistic growth', *Econometrica*, **29** (October), 632–649.
Marglin, S. (1970) 'Investment and interest: a reformulation and extension of Keynesian theory', *Economic Journal*, **80** (December), 910–931.

Marris, R. (1964a) *The Economics of Capital Utilization: A Report on Multiple Shift Working.* Cambridge: Cambridge University Press.

Marris, R. (1964b) *The Economic Theory of Managerial Capitalism.* London: Macmillan.

Marris, R. and Wood, A. (eds.) (1971) *The Corporate Economy.* London: Macmillan Press Ltd.

Marschak, T. and Nelson, R. (1962) 'Flexibility, uncertainty and economic theory', *Metroeconomica*, **14**, 42.

Martirena-Martel, A. M. (1971) 'Optimal inventory and capital policy under certainty', *Journal of Economic Theory*, **3** (September), 241–253.

Maurice, R. (ed.) (1968) *National Accounts Statistics, Sources and Methods.* London: Central Statistical Office, HMSO.

Mayer, T. (1958) 'The inflexibility of monetary policy', *Review of Economics and Statistics*, **40** (November), 358–374.

Meeks, G. and Whittington, G. (1975) 'Directors' pay, growth and profitability', *Journal of Industrial Economics*, **24** (September), 1–14.

Meyer, J. R. and Kuh, E. (1957) *The Investment Decision.* Cambridge: Harvard University Press.

Meyer, J. R. and Glauber, R. R. (1964) *Investment Decisions, Economic Forecasting and Public Policy.* Boston: Harvard University Press.

Miller, M. H. and Modigliani, F. (1966) 'Some estimates of the cost of capital to the electric utility industry, 1954–57', *American Economic Review*, **56** (June), 333–391.

Modigliani, F. and Miller, M. H. (1958) 'Cost of capital, corporation finance and the theory of investment', *American Economic Review*, **48** (June), 261–297.

Modigliani, F. and Weingartner, H. M. (1958) 'Forecasting uses of anticipatory data on investment and sales', *Quarterly Journal of Economics*, **72** (February), 23–54.

Modigliani, F. and Miller, M. H. (1963) 'Corporate income taxes and the cost of capital: a correction', *American Economic Review*, **53** (June), 433–443.

Mortenson, D. T. (1973) 'Generalized costs of adjustment and dynamic factor demand theory', *Econometrica*, **41** (July), 657–667.

Mossin, J. (1966) 'Equilibrium in a capital asset market', *Econometrica*, **34** (October), 768–783.

Mundlak, Y. (1966) 'On the microeconomic theory of distributed lags', *Review of Economics and Statistics*, **48** (February), 51–60.

Mundlak, Y. (1967) 'Long-run coefficients and distributed lag analysis', *Econometrica*, **35** (April), 278–293.

Myers, S. C. (1974) 'Interactions of corporate financing and investment decisions—implications for capital budgeting', *Journal of Finance*, **29** (March), 1–26.

Nadiri, M. I. (1972) 'An alternative model of business investment spending', *Brookings Papers on Economic Activity*, **3**, 547–578.

Nadiri, M. I. and Rosen, S. (1969) 'Interrelated factor demand functions', *American Economic Review*, **59** (September), 457–471.

Nerlove, M. (1972) 'Lags in economic behaviour', *Econometrica*, **40** (March), 221–252.

Nickell, S. J. (1974a) 'On the role of expectations in the pure theory of investment', *Review of Economic Studies*, **41** (January), 1–20.

Nickell, S. J. (1974b) 'On expectations, government policy and the rate of investment', *Economica*, **41** (August), 241–255.

Nickell, S. J. (1975) 'A closer look at replacement investment', *Journal of Economic Theory*, **10** (February), 54–88.

Nickell, S. J. (1977a) 'The influence of uncertainty on investment', *Economic Journal*, **87** (March), 47–70.

Nickell, S. J. (1977b) 'Uncertainty and lags in the investment decisions of firms', *Review of Economic Studies*, **44** (June), 249–263.

Norstrom, C. J. (1974) 'Optimal capital adjustment under uncertainty', *Journal of Economic Theory*, **8**, 139–148.

Orr, D. (1966) 'Capital flexibility and long-run cost under stationary uncertainty', in *Essays in Mathematical Economics in Honour of Oskar Morgenstern*, edited by M. Shubik. Princeton: Princeton University Press, pp. 171–187.

Pratt, J. W. (1964) 'Risk aversion in the small and in the large', *Econometrica*, **32** (January–April), 122–136.

Prior, M. J. (1976) 'The effect of distinguishing between new orders and deliveries on the rate of adjustment in investment demand functions', *Discussion Paper No. 80*, University of Essex.

Pye, G. (1972) 'Capital gains taxation, dividends and capital budgeting', *Quarterly Journal of Economics*, **86** (May), 226–242.

Quirk, J. P. (1961) 'The capital structure of firms and the risk of failure', *International Economic Review*, **2** (May), 210–228.

Resek, R. W. (1966) 'Investment by manufacturing firms: a quarterly time series analysis of industry data', *Review of Economics and Statistics*, **48** (August), 322–333.

Robichek, A. A. and Myers, S. C. (1965) *Optimal Financing Decisions*. Englewood Cliffs, New Jersey: Prentice Hall Inc.

Rockley, L. E. (1973) *Investment for Profitability*. London: Business Books Ltd.

Rothschild, M. (1971) 'On the cost of adjustment', *Quarterly Journal of Economics*, **85** (November), 605–622.

Rothschild, M. and Stiglitz, J. E. (1970) 'Increasing risk: I. A definition', *Journal of Economic Theory*, **2** (September), 225–243.

Rothschild, M. and Stiglitz, J. E. (1971) 'Increasing risk: II. Its economic consequences', *Journal of Economic Theory*, **3** (March), 66–84.

Rowley, J. C. R. (1970) 'Investment functions: which production function?', *American Economic Review*, **60** (December), 1008–1012.

Rowley, J. R. C. and Trivedi, P. K. (1975) *The Econometrics of Investment*. London: Wiley and Sons.

Samuelson, P. A. (1971) 'The fundamental approximation theorem of portfolio analysis in terms of means, variances and higher moments', *Review of Economic Studies*, **38** (October), 537–542.

Sandmo, A. (1971) 'On the theory of the competitive firm under price uncertainty', *American Economic Review*, **61** (March), 65–73.

Schmalensee, R. (1972) *The Economics of Advertising*. Amsterdam: North-Holland Publishing Co.

Schramm, R. (1970) 'The influence of relative prices, production conditions and adjustment costs on investment behaviour', *Review of
Economic Studies*, **37** (July), 361–376.

Sharpe, W. (1964) 'Capital asset prices: a theory of market equilibrium
under conditions of risk', *Journal of Finance*, **19** (September), 425–442.

Shell, K. and Stiglitz, J. E. (1967) 'The allocation of investment in a
dynamic economy', *Quarterly Journal of Economics*, **81** (November),
592–609.

Smith, K. R. (1969) 'The effects of uncertainty on monopoly price,
capital stock and utilization of capital', *Journal of Economic Theory*,
1 (June), 48–59.

Smith, K. R. (1970) 'Risk and the optimal utilization of capital', *Review
of Economic Studies*, **37** (April), 253–259.

Smith, V. L. (1957) 'Economic equipment policies: an evaluation',
Management Science, **4** (October), 20–37.

Smith, V. L. (1966) *Investment and Production*. Cambridge, Mass.:
Harvard University Press.

Smith, V. L. (1970) 'Corporate financial theory under uncertainty',
Quarterly Journal of Economics, **84** (August), 451–471.

Smith, V. L. (1972a) 'Default risk, scale and the homemade leverage
theorem', *American Economic Review*, **62** (March), 66–76.

Smith, V. L. (1972b) 'A theory and test of credit rationing: some
generalizations', *American Economic Review*, **62** (June), 477–483.

Solow, R. M. (1967) 'The new industrial state or son of affluence', *The
Public Interest*, **9** (Fall), 100–108.

Spence, M. (1976) 'Entry, investment and oligopolistic pricing', *Discussion Paper No. 466*, Harvard Institute of Economic Research.

Stapleton, R. C. (1972) 'Taxes, the cost of capital and the theory of
investment', *Economic Journal*, **82** (December), 1273–1292.

Steigum, E. (1977) 'Flow of funds and the speed of capital stock adjustment', Norwegian School of Economics (mimeo).

Stevens, G. V. G. (1974) 'On the impact of uncertainty on the value and
investment of the neoclassical firm', *American Economic Review*, **64**
(June), 319–336.

Stigler, G. (1939) 'Production and distribution in the short run', *Journal
of Political Economy*, **47** (June), 305–327.

Stiglitz, J. E. (1969) 'A re-examination of the Modigliani–Miller theorem',
American Economic Review, **59** (December), 784–793.

Stiglitz, J. E. (1972a) 'Some aspects of the pure theory of corporate
finance: bankruptcies and take-overs', *Bell Journal of Economics and
Management Science*, **3** (Autumn), 458–483.

Stiglitz, J. E. (1972b) 'Value maximization and alternative objectives of
the firm', Stanford University (mimeo).

Stiglitz, J. E. (1973) 'Taxation, corporate financial policy and the cost of
capital', *Journal of Public Economics*, **2** (February), 1–34.

Stiglitz, J. E. (1974) 'On the irrelevance of corporate financial policy',
American Economic Review, **64** (December), 851–866.

Taubman, P. and Rasche, R. H. (1969) 'Economic and tax depreciation
of office buildings', *National Tax Journal*, **22** (September), 334–346.

Taubman, P. and Wilkinson, M. (1970) 'User cost, capital utilization and investment theory', *International Economic Review*, **11** (June), 209–215.

Terborgh, G. (1949) *Dynamic Equipment Policy*. New York: McGraw-Hill Inc.

Thalberg, B. (1960) 'The market for investment goods: an analysis where time of delivery enters explicitly', *Review of Economic Studies*, **27** (February), 99–108.

Theil, H. (1954) *Linear Aggregation of Economic Relations*. Amsterdam: North-Holland Publishing Co.

Tinbergen, J. (1938) *Statistical Testing of Business Cycle Theories*, Vol. I. Geneva: League of Nations.

Tobin, J. (1969) 'Comment on Borch and Feldstein', *Review of Economic Studies*, **36** (January), 13–14.

Treadway, A. B. (1969) 'On rational entrepreneurial behaviour and the demand for investment', *Review of Economic Studies*, **36** (April), 227–239.

Treadway, A. B. (1970) 'Adjustment costs and variable inputs in the theory of the firm', *Journal of Economic Theory*, **2** (December), 329–347.

Treadway, A. (1971) 'On the multivariate flexible accelerator', *Econometrica*, **39** (September), 845–856.

US Department of Commerce (1971) 'Fixed non-residential business capital in the United States, 1925–1970', *Supplement to the Survey of Current Business*.

Whalley, J. (1974) 'Taxation and corporate financial policies in general', equilibrium models: some evidence from recent UK experience. London School of Economics (mimeo).

Whittington, G. (1972) 'The profitability of retained earnings', *Review of Economics and Statistics*, **52** (November), 345–355.

Winfrey, R. (1935) *Statistical Analyses of Industrial Property Retirements*, Bulletin 125 (December), Iowa Engineering Experiment Station.

Winston, G. C. and McCoy, T. O. (1974) 'Investment and the optimal idleness of capital', *Review of Economic Studies*, **41** (July), 416–428.

Witte, J. G. (1963) 'The microfoundations of the social investment function', *Journal of Political Economy*, **1** (October), 441–456.

Wood, A. (1975) *A Theory of Profits*. Cambridge: Cambridge University Press.

Wykoff, F. (1970) 'Capital depreciation in the post-war period: automobiles', *Review of Economics and Statistics*, **52** (May), 168–172.

INDEX